AF700010

Prof. Ackerman

It was a privilege meeting you.

Best wishes

Willie van Heerden

Unisa
South Africa
1992-09-09

PLUTOCRATS AND PAUPERS

Wealth and poverty in the Old Testament

H.L. Bosman, I.G.P. Gous, I.J.J. Spangenberg (eds.)

J.L. van Schaik

Published by J.L. van Schaik (Pty) Ltd,
1064 Arcadia Street, Hatfield, Pretoria
All rights reserved
Copyright © 1991 Authors

No part of this book may be reproduced or transmitted in any form or by any means, electronic or mechanical, including photocopying, recording or by any information storage and retrieval system, without permission in writing from the publisher

First edition 1991

ISBN 0 627 01778 9

Cover design by Barrett Joubert
Typeset in 9½ on 11 pt Century Old Style by ORBiT CC, Pretoria
Printed and bound by Creda Press, Cape Town

Foreword

The book in your hands is the outcome of a number of South African Old Testament scholars' decision to write a work on the theme of wealth and poverty in the Old Testament. In this way we want to participate in the discussion of this problem in our country. By way of example we take the narrative of Naboth's vineyard (1 Ki 21) and on this text we base and develop our theme. We trust that our readers will not find this monotonous, but that they will be continually surprised by fresh facts that come to light.

The book comprises five sections, the first of which is orientational. It deals briefly with the problem of poverty, the meaning of religion and the way people make sense of a text.

The second section covers the various ways in which the Old Testament has been read and interpreted in changing circumstances. The way this material is presented may strike the reader as strange. We proceed from the present to the past, that is from the twentieth century and current exegetical methods back to the first century and the interpretive methods that were customary in those days. The focus is on the role of the readers and their circumstances in the hermeneutic process.

The third section fills in the background to certain issues: Israelite history, Palestinian geography, the sociocultural situation of the people, the social changes they experienced, their religious development, etc. This should make readers of this book better informed Bible readers.

Against this background, the fourth section offers three perspectives on the phenomena of wealth and poverty in Israelite society during the premonarchic period, the monarchy, the exile and post-exilic era.

The fifth section reviews the substance of the book and relates its theme – that of wealth and poverty – to our own society.

We trust that this book will not merely be informative but will move you to join in the reflection on God, on our understanding of the Bible and on a sensitive and topical issue of our day: wealth and poverty.

H L Bosman
I G P Gous
I J J Spanenberg

Note: *Biblical quotations were taken from the Revised Standard Version which is an American translation. This accounts for the American spelling. Quotations from the Apocrypha were taken from the Revised English Bible.*

Contents

A

Orientation

1

Wealth and poverty in South Africa

FERDINAND DEIST

1.1 This book is about Old Testament perspectives on wealth and poverty. The reason for choosing this theme is that to South Africans the contrast between First World affluence and Third World poverty is not an academic question but is part of our economic reality. As theologians, as biblical scholars, as ministers of religion, as lay Christians, this is *our* problem. And as Christians we have a duty to consider it *biblically*. In this book, therefore, as one contribution to the debate on wealth and poverty, we want to raise two issues:

- ways of interpreting the Old Testament in order to consider wealth and poverty in biblical terms, and
- some Old Testament perspectives on the problem of poverty and wealth.

1.2 To give some indication of what it is all about, this chapter gives a few examples of the contrast between First World wealth and the poverty of the Third World, and between rich and poor in South Africa. We do not propose to paint the whole picture. Those interested in a more detailed analysis can consult the thirty volumes of *The second Carnegie inquiry into poverty and development in Southern Africa* (1984). All we shall do is cite a few examples to illustrate what this book is about.

A. LIVING STANDARD AND QUALITY OF LIFE

1.3 "Wealth" and "poverty" are primarily economic concepts. That is, they have to do with what people possess, and thus with their standard of living; but they also have to do with their quality of life. By "standard of living" we mean the *comfort* in which people live and the facilities at their disposal, for instance: Do they own a house, a bed, a stove, a refrigerator, a radio? Can their children be sure of getting a good education? What access do they have to medical services?

1.4 But standard of living does not give one a direct indication of people's quality of life. By "quality of life" we mean how people *experience* their circumstances: Do they find their lives meaningful or meaningless, dreary or interesting? Do they see any hope of improving their lot, or do they see none? Sometimes the rich experience their lives as meaningful, while the poor experience life as meaningless. But it can also be the other way round: rich people may experience life as meaningless while the poor find it meaningful. Although standard of living and quality of life do not correlate directly and *meaning*ful living depends on more than just possessions, a high standard of living does contribute significantly to people's experience of meaning in life.

B. LIVING STANDARDS IN THE FIRST WORLD AND THE THIRD WORLD

1.5 When one compares the circumstances of Africans with those of people in Europe, one finds that Africans are much poorer than Europeans and consequently have a much lower standard of living. To illustrate this contrast we shall compare one of the richest countries in the world – West Germany – with one of the poorest, Mozambique. In order to indicate the relative position of South Africa we also provide statistics for this country as a whole.

1.6 Three cautionary comments are called for. Firstly, our comparisons between countries are based on *averages*. A wealthy country like West Germany also has poor people and an impoverished one like Mozambique has some rich inhabitants. Secondly, the comparisons below are based mainly on the 1988 publication of *The Economist*, *The world in figures*, which contains statistics for 1985. Thirdly, these statistics are merely intended to give some idea of the *relative* poverty of Africa's inhabitants: we want to depict the poverty of Africans measured against the wealth of the Germans, rather than to give an accurate picture of the *exact current* living standard of Germans, Mozambicans or, for that matter, South Africans. The statistics quoted are taken from various sources dating from the eighties. Although the actual situations of the countries under consideration are probably very different today, African countries are still poverty-stricken *in comparison with European countries*. All we want to do is to sketch this "comparative" poverty, and in so doing demonstrate why we – writing this book in Africa, and more specifically in South Africa – should concern ourselves with the theme of poverty and wealth.

1. A comparison between Germany, South Africa and Mozambique

1.7 In Germany people earn on average eight times as much as people in South Africa and 75 times as much as those in Mozambique. It follows that Germans can live in far greater comfort than either South Africans or Mozambicans. It also appears that Germans by and large use 60 times as much energy and 55 times as much electricity as Mozambicans, indicating that the Germans have more mod cons (using electricity and other forms of energy) than the people of Mozambique. This is borne out by the fact that Germany has 62 times as many (energy consuming) private vehicles as Mozambique. In addition one out of every two Germans owns an (electrically powered) radio and one out of every three has a television set, compared to respectively one out of 50 and one out of 5 000 Mozambicans.

1.8 We could add to this list of indicators of wealth:

- Germany has 80 times more road communication per square kilometre of land surface than Mozambique and 13 times more than South Africa. Consequently Germans can travel a great deal more easily than either South Africans or Mozambicans.
- One out of every 39 South Africans and one out of every 280 Mozambicans read

a daily newspaper, as opposed to one out of every three Germans. Thus Germans on the whole are better informed about national and world affairs than the populations of South Africa and Mozambique. Moreover, 400 out of every thousand Germans possess radios as opposed to 282 South Africans and 21 out of every thousand Mozambicans.

- Germany has 621 telephones for every thousand people; South Africa has 138 and Mozambique 4 per thousand inhabitants. One could therefore say that Germans communicate more easily with one another than people in our part of the world.
- In Germany there is one doctor per 431 inhabitants. South Africa has one per 1 900 and Mozambique one for every 39 000 human beings. Germany offers one hospital bed for every 89 patients; South Africa has one for every 152 and Mozambique one for every 950. Thus Germans have far better medical services than people on our subcontinent, which explains why German men may expect to live to the age of 70 and German women to the age of 77, whereas Mozambican men and women respectively have a life expectancy of 48 and 51.

1.9 It is evident that in regard to standard of living the people of Mozambique are much worse off than the Germans, and that South Africans, while on the whole considerably better off than Mozambicans, still fare much worse than Germans.

1.10 What prospects do the populations of these countries have of a brighter future? In 1985 the German population was declining at a rate of 0,2% annually, while the populations of South Africa and Mozambique were increasing by 2,5% and 2,9% respectively each year. On top of this the German economy was growing at a rate of 1,3% per annum, while the Mozambican economy was deteriorating by 1,7% per annum at that time. This implies that every year Germany had more to distribute among fewer and fewer people. Although the South African economy at that stage was growing by 2% annually, the population was increasing by 2,5%, so that South Africa too had less and less every year to divide among its growing population.

1.11 If one assumes that people need better schooling and postschool education to earn more in order to improve their standard of living, then the prospects in our part of the world are again gloomier than in Germany. Whereas a mere 17% of the German population are below the age of 15, 33% of South Africans and 40% of Mozambicans are below that age. Thus our part of the world has far more children in need of education, while we also have much less of the wherewithal to pay for it. This explains

- why Germany has only 14 pupils per teacher, compared to 28 in South Africa
- and 53 in Mozambique, and 100% of German children below the age of 15 are literate, as opposed to a mere 27% of Mozambican children of that age group.

1.12 Because we have so many children and such limited means in our part of the world, many of them receive no schooling and are obliged to become manual labourers. This is illustrated by the fact that only 15% of the German population work on farms (which are almost completely mechanised), whereas 84% of the Mozambican population are farm labourers doing manual work.

1.13 So far we have been speaking about South Africa as a whole. But within this country there are major discrepancies between the various segments of the population. We shall confine ourselves to the white and black populations, with reference to data from *South African statistics* (1988), which reflect the position in 1985.

2. A comparison between different population segments in South Africa

1.14 If one considers the distribution of occupations between whites and blacks, one finds that the types of work requiring least training are predominantly performed by blacks, whereas whites preponderate in occupations requiring training:

Occupation	% **Whites**	**Blacks**
Non-classifiable work	4,3	82,5
Farmer/fisherman/hunter/farm labourer	6,2	78,3
Unskilled	1,1	76,6
Service worker	10,4	76,3
Mine/quarry worker/operator	7,7	74,1
Transport/communication	15,2	70,4
Clerk/sales person	53,0	27,3
Professional/technical	60,0	27,0
Tradesperson/apprentice	61,5	16,4
Manager/executive/administrator	87,5	4,2

1.15 This state of affairs is partly attributable to the fact that in 1985 almost three-quarters of the South Africans who had attended school only up to standard five were black, whereas almost three-quarters of those who had a matric certificate were white and therefore qualified for better jobs. This in turn means that whites earn on average seven to eight times as much as blacks.

1.16 If one considers, moreover, that the average black household has to cater for two and a half times as many children below the age of 15 as white households, it is clear that black children do not have much of a chance of improving their living standard. Their parents simply do not have the means to provide for them properly or to give them a good education. Although the majority of black children are attending school today (in 1991), the quality of their education is not on a par with that offered in white schools.

1.17 Black children are taught in much larger classes than other South African children – the average is 41 pupils per teacher compared to 20 per teacher in white schools. If one examines specific areas the picture is even more distressing. Thus, according to the *The second Carnegie inquiry into poverty and development in Southern Africa* (1984, Vol 10, p 15), there were 52 pupils per teacher in Lebowa primary schools and 37 per teacher in high schools.

1.18 A further consideration is that teachers in black schools are less well qualified than those in white schools. In the early eighties only 15% of black teachers had a matric certificate and a meagre 2% had degrees. By contrast only 3% of white teachers had less than matric plus a teaching diploma.

1.19 This thumbnail sketch tells nothing about health services and private ownership (e.g. of land and other fixed property). But it does give one some impression of the situation of self-perpetuating poverty in which biblical scholars in our part of the world have to interpret the Bible. In this country the discrepancy between rich and poor, between privilege and deprivation, is a major economic, political and moral problem. This is the situation in which we have to interpret the Bible in order to open up a religious perspective.

1.20 What is a "religious perspective" and what is the function of religion in society? Before we can start interpreting the Bible for our situation we should first consider this question.

2

Why do people believe?

IG GOUS

A. INTRODUCTION

2.1 Religion and faith are extremely complex phenomena, which means that they cannot possibly be exhaustively discussed or described in this chapter. We confine ourselves, therefore, to a single question which is pertinent to the subject of this book – that of what faith does in people's lives.

2.2 Scholars differ on why people believe, on what faith contributes to life and what life contributes to faith. Will people's faith determine their behaviour towards one another in the new South Africa, or will the new South Africa and other circumstances determine their way of believing? Although there is no consensus on the proper answers to these questions, many people in this country are believers. Consequently it is worthwhile examining why they believe and what the mechanics of faith are. We cannot hope for final or complete answers, but the mere attempt may help us to understand the Bible, ourselves and those who disagree with us a little better. Maybe we will find more points of agreement than we expected.

B. THE MECHANICS OF FAITH

2.3 All human behaviour is aimed at need satisfaction. This applies to faith as well. Believing satisfies many needs – needs that differ from person to person and from one stage of a person's life to the next. Thus it may help someone to work through some loss or bereavement, to achieve a personal or a political goal, or to establish a pattern of behaviour. Fundamentally, however, it satisfies a universal human need: the need for meaning in life. Animals are born with a built-in "road map". Their instincts ensure that their behaviour will be meaningful and functional – that they and their species will survive. People enter this world without any orientating mechanism of this kind. They have to be shown their place in life and in the world, and they have to learn what that place is. Only when one knows how one fits into the scheme of things, what one's place and task in life are – in other words, which cog am I in the machine and what are the other cogs and the whole machine like? – only then will life seem worthwhile. Such a system of meaning in life is known as a world view. The way one understands the meaning of one's life thus depends on one's view of life as a whole and of one's own role in it.

2.4 To many people *religion* represents their system of meaning or orientating principle. We shall therefore take a look at the mechanics of religion, that is, at how religion creates meaning in life. Just remember, that is not all there is to religion and faith. Nevertheless it is an important aspect on which we shall concentrate for the sake of finding a perspective on the Bible and on ourselves.

2.5 Firstly, religion is a *system of symbols*. People "translate" their thoughts, experiences, desires and beliefs into symbols. The symbol might be an object like a crucifix, an altar, a church building, even a congregation. Or it could be an action like the eucharist or the baptismal rite. Thus the symbol embodies an idea or set of ideas whose meaning is known to the group who use it. On the whole it facilitates and simplifies communication. But it can also complicate communication, particularly when different groups use the same symbol in different ways. Baptism is a good example. In the Reformed faith it usually represents God's agreement with humans to care and assume responsibility for them, whereas among charismatics it is very often a public confession of having admitted God to one's life. In all events, to understand a religion or a specific expression of it one has to know its symbols and what they stand for. From such symbols and their interrelationship one can infer not only what people believe about their world and reality, but also what they would like that world and reality to be like.

2.6 Secondly, *religion creates a certain disposition or attitude towards life*. People see reality in terms of their symbolic system. It affects the way in which they experience events and how they respond to them. Thus their world view determines what they regard as desirable or undesirable, good or bad, right or wrong; also how they will feel and act when confronted with a particular situation or choice. It is a matter of the values that govern a person's reactions and decisions.

2.7 Thirdly, *religion directs a person's life*. On the basis of the place one occupies or is assigned in the world, one pursues certain goals and works at certain projects. Some religious people believe it is their duty to serve others irrespective of their own needs. Others regard honest hard work for their own sake as a virtue. We call people's attitude and orientation towards life their *ethos*.

2.8 Fourthly, *religion imposes order on the world* around one. Because human beings are not born with a built-in road map, they draw their own. When they come up against an uncharted area of life, or when their map fails to give them adequate directions, they experience anxiety. Order, predictability and the ability to interpret experience are prerequisite for meaningful living. There are mainly three kinds of experience that people perceive as uncharted and anxiety-provoking: inexplicable experiences, experiences of suffering and the experience of an undeserved fate.

2.9 Because people accept that the world is an orderly place, they expect things to be understandable and explicable. When something extraordinary occurs, they have conventional explanations for it. Take the way people react to unusual natural phenomena. Some see it as a sign from God, others offer a scientific explanation. But if their explanations fail to satisfy, they begin to question – not just their methods of explanation, but the very order of reality.

2.10 Suffering is such a departure from normality. It impairs the quality of life. In times of hardship we all tend to ask, "Why?" Some scholars maintain that religion helps people to avoid or to allay suffering. It is probably more accurate to say that faith makes suffering more bearable. This is because it helps to explain suffering, to articulate the accompanying emotions and to suggest a course of action. Thus one can carry on believing that life is worthwhile.

2.11 On the whole we expect that things will go well for us provided we lead decent lives. Some regard good fortune as a reward for keeping to the straight and narrow, others see it simply as sound judgement. But people frequently experience suffering as undeserved: they suffer even though they live unexceptionable lives. This makes them question the assumption that reality is orderly and predictable. Why is a virtuous life rewarded with punishment? It also casts doubt on the religious person's moral judgement. The blow of fate, experienced as punishment, shows that people are unable to discriminate between right and wrong. In addition it makes people feel insecure and helpless. Religion seeks to provide answers to such problems. It affirms the assumption that life is meaningful and explicable.

2.12 Thus faith offers a particular *world view* – one of universal order which enables believers to find meaning on their way through life.

2.13 Finally, *religion affirms meaning in spite of life's pressures*. This is because religious gatherings give believers a particular view of reality. At these gatherings a road map of life is inculcated in them and they are given directions how to follow it. At such gatherings world view and ethos fuse and become one. Thus a religious gathering is both a reflection of life and a model for living. That means that one can infer from it what a certain group of people rates as important and worthwhile and what ideal they strive for.

C. FAITH AND CONTEXT

2.14 The interpretation of religion described above can help us in a number of ways. First, it makes us realise that faith relates to contemporary events. Religion has to do with people's questions and experiences. We need to know, therefore, how and what they believe. In addition it makes us realise that religion affects current affairs, and vice versa. All believers should be conscious of this, otherwise they will misunderstand themselves and their fellow believers. Many differences and even heated conflicts between Christians all over the world and in South Africa are attributable to disregard of this reciprocal relation. Thus one finds people who feel that they and they alone act and judge correctly. If we want to understand the Bible properly, we have to consider the existential questions of a particular age, the influence of religion on these and also the influence of these questions on people and their religious practice. That is why we start with a contemporary issue: wealth and poverty in South Africa.

3

The exegete's tools

FERDINAND DEIST

3.1 In the previous chapter it was postulated that the primary function of religion is to help people to find meaning in the circumstances of their lives. If wealth and poverty rob people's lives of all quality, then the task of religion would be to give rich and poor alike a frame of reference in which they can live *meaningfully*. More specifically: as Christians we owe it to one another to ponder the meaning of life in our particular context and to help people improve the quality of their lives.

3.2 The Bible, which we Christians use as a point of orientation, is in the first place a religious book. That is why we who occupy ourselves with the Bible are concerned with religion and are commissioned to interpret the Bible in a way that will help ourselves and others to find meaning in whatever circumstances we find ourselves. How does one set about this task? What does one need to be able to interpret the Bible to find that meaning?

3.3 Acts 8 tells about an African who, while travelling from Jerusalem to Ethiopia, was reading Isaiah 53. He was joined by Philip, who asked him: "Do you understand what you are reading?" "How can I, unless some one *guides me?*" the Ethiopian answered. Philip helped him to understand what he was reading and the Ethiopian was able to proceed on his journey *rejoicing*, having discovered *meaning* in what he had read.

3.4 The biblical scholar's task is to help people understand the Bible – understand it in a way that will deepen the meaning of their lives. This book is designed to introduce prospective biblical scholars to certain skills and the kind of knowledge they need to become biblical exegetes.

A. THE KNOWLEDGE A BIBLICAL SCHOLAR NEEDS

1. Knowledge about the perspective on life of one's community

3.5 One cannot interpret the Bible in general terms. Religious people live in specific circumstances and they have specific needs and pertinent questions. They want to hear the Bible's message for *their* situation. Thus biblical exegetes should in the first place be in touch with the situation in which they are interpreting the Bible, and consequently with the existential questions that plague their fellow believers. That is why we started this book with an outline of the *situation* of wealth and poverty.

3.6 One might feel that one has some sort of gut-level knowledge of what people think and how they experience their lives. But one's own perception of a situation is a far cry from the way in which *other people* perceive and experience it. One's perspective – the angle from which one views a situation – *shapes* that situation in a particular way. A simple example will illustrate the point.

3.7 If one shines a light vertically from above on a torch battery, it will cast a *circular* shadow. If the same light is shone from the side, the resultant shadow will be *oblong*. The circular shadow and the oblong shadow are images of the same object, yet they differ because the *light shone from a different angle*. By the same token one and the same life looks different if viewed from different "angles" (e.g. those of wealth and poverty). The vital point here is that *nobody* can ever see the situation "as it really is". Everyone interprets life from the angle of his or her own circumstances and questions its meaning in that perspective. But the problem does not end there.

2. Knowledge about the perspective from which the Bible is read

3.8 Just as one may labour under the delusion that one has gut-level knowledge of the situation in one's society, so one may be deluded into thinking that one knows at gut-level what the Bible has to say about some issue or other. But interpreting the Bible is no different to interpreting life: the perspective in which one sees the Bible has a great deal to do with the meaning one attaches to a particular passage. Again an example will help to make the point. Compare the following three versions of Genesis 1:2:

Authorised Version

And the earth was without form, and void; and darkness was upon the face of the deep. And the *Spirit of God* moved upon the face of the waters.

New English Bible

... the earth was without form and void, with darkness over the face of the abyss, and a *mighty wind* that swept over the surface of the waters.

New World Translation

Now the earth proved to be formless and waste and there was darkness upon the surface of [the] watery deep; and *God's active force* was moving to and fro over the surface of the waters.

The translators of the *Authorised Version* proceeded from the premise that

- God is triune (Father, Son and Holy Spirit), and
- it was the Spirit of God (the Holy Spirit) that was moving across the primeval waters.

The translators of the New World Translation

- reject the doctrine of the Trinity, and
- interpret the biblical words rendered in the Authorised Version with "Holy Spirit" simply as "active force".

The translators of the New English Bible work on the assumption that

- Genesis 1 dates from an age when the Israelites, like all people in the ancient Near East, speculated about the origins of the earth, and
- a church doctrine like that of the Trinity cannot necessarily be inferred from such an ancient (mythological) text. (An alternative rendering appears in a footnote, however: "and the *Spirit of God hovering*", implying that the doctrine of the Trinity is not rejected.)

Thus the presuppositions with which each of these three translators read (and interpreted) Genesis 1:2 led each of them to attach a different meaning to the words of this text.

3.9 The mind of a Bible reader, then, is not like a photographic plate on which the alphabetic characters of the biblical text leave an imprint. The prior knowledge or presuppositions on which readers base their interpretation of a text helps to determine what they will take to be its meaning. The exegete plays a definite role in the interpretation of the Bible, and every biblical expositor should be keenly aware of this. If not, one may be inclined to treat one's own interpretation of the Bible as self-evident, and therefore as the only correct one, whereas in reality it is only self-evident if viewed in that particular *perspective*.

What determines a Bible reader's perspective?

3.10 A number of things help to determine the perspective in which each of us reads the Bible. We mention a few factors by way of illustration.

3.11 First, one's church tradition acts as glasses through which one "looks" at biblical texts. Some churches or church groups tend to spiritualise the Bible and to treat religion as a strictly private matter for the inner chamber, whereas others regard religion as a specifically public affair with a mission to influence and change the social order. Some church groups identify separate doctrines in individual biblical sayings, whereas others interpret the Bible as a coherent narrative. Some churches take each biblical tale literally as history, whereas others read them more as folklore or stories. Thus one could go on describing the lens tint of each church's reading glasses. The next two chapters provide concrete illustrations of two such perspectives: Itumeleng Mosala writes about the biblical view of wealth and poverty from the angle of a poor black South African and William Domeris explains the perspective in which affluent people regard the same biblical message. Because ordinary Bible readers are even less inclined than biblical scholars to interpret the Bible independently of their particular religious tradition, their traditional prior knowledge exercises an even greater unconscious influence on their interpretation. But biblical *scholars* should be alert to the possibility that their own tradition may colour their reading of the Bible.

3.12 The fact that one's tradition's or denomination's exposition of the Bible in a sense skews one's perception of its meaning does not necessarily mean that one is *mis*interpreting. It does mean, however, that the truth about God and the meaning of life is complex and multifaceted, and that one's own interpretation, deriving from a particular perspective, represents at most one possible interpretation of a biblical text. Once one realises this, one is more inclined to listen to and consider other possible interpretations. Thus willingness to listen to alternative interpretations is one of the skills a biblical scholar has to learn.

3.13 But ecclesiastic tradition is not the only determinant of the meaning one will discover in a biblical text. One's personal experience also helps create the perspective in which one interprets the Bible, for one's peculiar biography more or less determines what questions one will ask of it. Thus someone who has never really experienced hardship may suddenly discover a whole lot of new questions when calamity strikes and may then read the Bible with fresh eyes. Previously such a person may have read the Bible in order to refute some theory such as that of evolution. But when disaster strikes people's lives they look for *comfort* or they wrestle with the question of *divine justice* and they turn to the Bible for an answer. Similarly one's economic, political and educational experience influences one's perspective on the Bible and gives rise to specific questions. Thus biblical scholars should have knowledge that enables them to judge other exegetes' interpretations in terms of their particular questions.

3. Knowledge of the perspectives and situations of biblical authors

3.14 Although believing Christians accept that it is God who speaks through the Bible, biblical scholars must always be aware that these are texts written by *people* – people, moreover, who, like us, sought to discover God's will from within certain physical and historical situations and religious traditions.

3.15 From chapter 17 of this book onwards we deal with some of the religious traditions or perspectives in which the biblical authors participated. Thus we refer to a prophetic perspective, a wisdom perspective and a legal perspective. If biblical scholars are not conscious that a textual passage was written in the perspective of a particular religious tradition and in a particular historical situation, they may easily misinterpret it and draw false inferences from it.

3.16 One's perception of who God is likewise affects the perspective in which one sees life and the way one answers questions about its meaning. Chapter 16 deals with changes over the ages in people's conceptions of who and what God is.

3.17 The physical environment in which people live and the (political and economic) history they experience also help to shape their perspective on life and the kind of questions they ask. Accordingly chapters 13 and 14 are about the geographical and historical space in which the biblical texts originated, in order to help us understand the authors and their stories better.

4. Knowledge of the methods of earlier biblical scholars

3.18 We are not the first to try and expound the Bible. Biblical exegesis dates back more than 2 500 years and as biblical scholars we should know that history. The fascinating thing is that exegetes over the ages directed different questions to the Bible and therefore used different sets of tools or exegetical techniques to discover the Bible's meaning for their age and situation. We today are privileged to be able to choose from their methods those which help to expound the Bible in a way that meets the needs of our time. More than that, we can see where past generations have misused their tools or used them for the wrong purpose. Thus we can learn from their mistakes.

5. Is everything relative?

3.19 What we have said so far may seem to have shaken the foundations of the biblical message. If the biblical authors wrote in their own perspectives, and we can only understand their perspectives in terms of our own, how can we be *sure* that it is really *God's* voice that we hear in the Bible? The question is valid and merits consideration.

3.20 Firstly, our argument so far indicates quite clearly that biblical interpretation for a specific situation (e.g. the South African one) is not a task for one person. *Because* our perspective limits our insight we need the insight of other exegetes who interpret the Bible in different perspectives. If we interpret the Bible exclusively *in the isolation of our own tradition and group* we run a very real risk of finding simply what we would like to find and of using the Bible merely to justify our own perspective yet again. If we seek to know God's will, we need one another and for that we need great tolerance.

3.21 Secondly, the fact that biblical passages were written in specific perspectives indicates that one may never isolate some parts of the Bible from the rest. To discover God's will one must listen to the full biblical choir. We tend to read only those parts of the Bible that support our own views and to regard these as expressing God's will. But the Bible invariably offers *various perspectives* on an issue and should therefore be heeded in toto.

3.22 Thirdly, our discourse up to now maintains that biblical exegesis is a *human enterprise*. Our biblical interpretation is provisional and our understanding of what the Bible says imperfect. Exegesis is not a mechanical device that can "make God speak to us". At most it paves the way for people to learn the will of God. Thus our exegesis cannot strip bare the "word of God". That word is not a thing, but an *event*. God's word happens while we are wrestling with the Bible and with one another. It happens when people, in confrontation with the Bible, are convinced of the truth by the Spirit of God and their lives are changed by the experience.

3.23 Fourthly, things are not really as relative as all that. There are ways in which we can to some extent test our interpretation of the Bible. We can adduce *arguments* to substantiate the particular way in which we expound a biblical passage. These arguments relate to our exegetical methods, to which we now turn our attention.

B. THE SKILLS NEEDED BY BIBLICAL SCHOLARS

3.24 To be able to expound a text like the Bible and conduct a logical argument about it, biblical scholars need another skill not mentioned so far, and that is the ability to identify linguistic and literary phenomena in the Bible. These are discussed under separate headings.

1. Proficiency in the languages (Hebrew and Aramaic) in which the Old Testament was written

3.25 If a text originally written in Zulu is translated into French, the French version never renders exactly what the Zulu original said. That is self-evident.

3.26 Because most people read the Old Testament in their mother tongues, they tend to take it for granted that they understand what has been written. One often hears people say, "I'm telling you, that's exactly what the Bible says". However, the Old Testament – which is what this book is about – was originally written partly in Hebrew, partly in Aramaic and was only translated into the various modern languages much later. Every time it is translated, something of the original text is lost. If a sentence in the original text has different possible meanings, the translator chooses one and writes that down. The reader of the translated version never knows whether the original sentence might have had a second possible meaning. Besides, many shades of meaning in the original text are lost in the translation process. Obviously, then, one stands a better chance of understanding the Old Testament if one is able to read Hebrew and Aramaic.

3.27 However, the ability to decipher a language like Hebrew does not mean that you will understand what you read. That was the problem experienced by the Ethiopian who was reading Isaiah 53 when Philip joined him (Ac 8:26–40): although he could read *Hebrew*, he did not understand what he was reading. To understand properly a reader needs a certain *linguistic proficiency*, which we shall illustrate with reference to examples.

2. The ability to establish connections between words

3.28 When one sits reading a book on one's own it is very easy to establish the wrong connection between words and thus misconstrue the meaning of a text. The following excerpt from a verse by an anonymous poet illustrates the point:

Here lies my wife Dot
in heaven she is not
in hell that I know well

3.29 The *connections* between words in a text have a close bearing on the meaning the sentences evoke in the reader's mind. A Bible reader must therefore be able to establish the right connections between the words and sentences of a text.

3. The ability to understand idiomatic nuances

3.30 A Bible reader must be able to discern delicate nuances in the language of a text. Even in everyday speech some sentences are ambiguous. When Bill tells Paul, "That was very clever of you!" he may mean two quite different things: he may be complimenting Paul, or he may be insulting him if "clever" was said in a snide tone of voice. In the latter case, Bill's words should be interpreted ironically rather than literally. In the same way a Bible reader must know whether a biblical expression should be taken literally or figuratively. Take Psalm 51:5: "Behold I was brought forth in iniquity and in sin did my mother conceive me". Should it be taken literally or should it be read as a hyperbole (exaggeration)? One could only tell the answer to this question if one knows

- that there is such a thing as a hyperbole, and
- what a hyperbole looks like in Hebrew and how it may be identified.

Thus one needs to know the figures of speech of the language in which a text is written in order to grasp its meaning. But that is not all.

4. The ability to identify the genre of a text

3.31 Just as a sentence may mean different things, so larger linguistic units can have different meanings too. It makes quite a difference whether one reads the story of Adam and Eve in paradise as history or as a parable. If it is history, the text reports the actual vicissitudes of the very first *human couple* on earth. If it is a parable, it recounts the change of fortunes of *all* human beings. Either way one will attach a different value to the narrative and interpret it differently.

3.32 Thirdly, then, proper understanding of a text requires that one knows what *kind* of text one is reading so that one may interpret it according to appropriate expectations and with the right approach Poems are expounded differently from factual reports, and reports are interpreted differently from parables. It takes some expertise to be able to do all these things.

3.33 Although these examples in no way exhaust the many aspects of linguistic proficiency, they give some idea of how important it is for a Bible reader – even when reading a translation – to be versed in the different ways in which a text may use language. Chapter 6 deals with these abilities in more detail, and chapters 7 and 8 contain related information.

5. The ability to integrate knowledge

3.34 Merely having a command of the language of the Bible does not mean, however, that a reader will always interpret it correctly. We have pointed out that there are other factors – such as the perspective of the biblical author, his religious tradition and situation – which affect the meaning of a text, not to mention the work done by past generations of exegetes. Thus a biblical scholar must acquire the ability to integrate all this knowledge into the exposition of the text.

C. SUMMARY

3.35 Without true tolerance and without sound arguments biblical interpretation will lead to total relativism. Then every little group of Christians will simply cherish their own version of the truth in the fond belief that they have found the whole truth. The situation is quite different if we are

- informed about the exact problems confronting us and the kind of existential questions they evoke in people's minds,
- aware that our personal perspectives may colour the meaning of a biblical text and that therefore we need one another when we interpret the Bible,
- conscious that the biblical authors themselves had different perspectives and wrote in different situations and that we should therefore consult the entire Bible with due regard to the context of each part,
- proficient in the languages and literature of the Bible,
- conversant with the methods of past generations of exegetes and their reasons for working thus.

Given all these things, we should be able to adduce sound arguments for our own interpretation of a biblical passage. We should also be able to engage in meaningful dialogue with one another, so that together we can look for God's will regarding the problems of our society.

3.36 The "rules" for sound biblical exegesis laid down here merely indicate that we espouse a particular *method* of scriptural interpretation. But the authors of this book are not the first to devise such a method. In chapters 6 to 12 we consider some of the methods that have been used in the past to expound the Bible. And the method recommended in this book draws liberally on virtually all the recognised methods of the past.

B

interpretations of wealth and poverty

4

Ownership or non-ownership of land forms the basis of wealth and poverty: A Black Theological perspective

ITUMELENG MOSALA

A. INTRODUCTION

4.1 To read the Bible in a black perspective one must situate oneself squarely and consciously within black history and culture. In order to be genuinely liberating, however, such a reading should be also critical. By this I mean that the reader's aim should be to critically appropriate both black history and culture, and the texts of Scripture. This implies that not all of black history and culture, nor all of the biblical texts, can be assumed to be liberating for oppressed and exploited black people.

4.2 It is important in this chapter, therefore, to identify pertinent aspects of black history and culture when tracing the theme of wealth and poverty in the Bible from a black perspective. In my view any such attempt must tackle the following three issues: land, economics and culture. These are the issues around which the problems of wealth and poverty cohere. An analysis of wealth and poverty in the Bible must thus determine in what way these factors define the position of the people of ancient Israel in their society. It must also enquire into the societal position black people have occupied in the different phases of their history. The question of people's place in society – whether in ancient Israel or in black Africa – immediately raises the issues of land and economics.

B. LAND AND ECONOMICS

4.3 In the entire socioeconomic history of ancient Israel land was a fundamental means of production. This being the case, ownership or non-ownership of land formed the basis of the wealth or poverty of the ancient Israelites.

4.4 In his monumental work which redefines the origins of early Israel, Norman Gottwald (1983) has contributed significantly to our understanding of the role of land in the enrichment or impoverishment of social classes in that society. The exodus movement was based on the struggle for land ownership and control and the right to cultivate the land. In the period of the Amarna letters bitter struggles were fought by peasant producers inside Palestine to retain ownership and control of their land. The reason was that the meagre agricultural surplus which the peasant classes were generating was being siphoned off by the *comprador* Palestinian ruling class. This local oppressor class consisted of the leaders of the city states. Their task was to squeeze the societally produced economic surplus out of the direct producers in order to pay for the perpetuation of their own class. The oppressor class was also intent on maintaining the Egyptian colonial administrative and military personnel garrisoned in each of the city states of Palestine. This class furthermore exacted the tribute which each colonial city state was obliged to pay to the colonial power. This control over the economic surplus produced by the peasant classes inevitably led to all manner of alienation and conflict. The first type of alienation was, of course, estrangement of the products of the labour of the oppressed and exploited peasants. These Palestinian lower classes were furthermore alienated from the source of their wealth, namely the labour which they expended on the land.

4.5 The alienation of land took two different forms. In some instances peasants fell into debt slavery, because they had used their plots of land as security to obtain loans to enable them to undertake the next season's production. They would then fall into debt slavery because the next season's production was not adequate to create the necessary surplus to service the loan, pay tribute, subsist with one's family and finance the next season's productive activities. In other cases land was alienated through flagrant dispossession. The wealthy classes were able to exercise their power over the peasant producers in such a way that they were able to expand their estates into large latifundia. On these latifundia gangs of alienated labour – that is, workers who no longer had any control over their labour – were employed. Others existed on the fringes of this system as rural proletariat.

4.6 The period immediately preceding the exodus was characterised by large waves of unrest and insurrection throughout what had until then been known as the Egyptian empire. This territory included the city states of Palestine. The official correspondence between the chiefs of the city states and the Egyptian empire, known as the Amarna letters, point to the social and economic origins of this unrest and insurrection in the political economy of Palestine, as described above.

4.7 One important group of socio-cultural and political resisters who feature prominently in the Amarna letters is called the *apiru*. A common characteristic of the *apiru* is their displacement within the Palestinian society of that time. Some of them were driven into some form of social banditry, others became mercenaries in the frequent military conflicts among the city states of Palestine. Still others engaged in deliberate revolutionary action against the state feudalism of the Palestinian city states. Their common socioeconomic displacement was fundamentally attributable to their landlessness.

4.8 Thus the exodus signifies, among other things, the conflict between the wealthy and the poor classes of society. This conflict was based on a struggle over land. It could be argued that the rest of the history of the biblical communities – from the Davidic and Solomonic monarchies to the Babylonian exile and the subsequent New Testament times under Roman rule – was likewise a history of struggle over land. Wealth and poverty in the biblical experience are functions of ownership or nonownership of land.

4.9 Nowhere else in the Bible is the conflict between the wealthy and the poor demonstrated as vividly as in the narrative of Naboth's vineyard. Here again the cardinal bone of contention was land. In fact, it is remarkable how 1 Kings 21 reflects almost all the issues that inspire Black Theology's thinking on wealth and poverty. I refer here specifically to Black Theology in South Africa. As a theory of the weapon of faith of the oppressed and exploited black masses in South Africa, Black Theology would identify with the fundamental issues of 1 Kings 21. These are:

4.10 (1) *The vineyard* – later referred to, significantly, as *nahalah* (inheritance, *lefa, boshwa, ilifa*). Land is the key to every biblical reference to vineyards or *nahalahs.* For blacks in South Africa no other issue qualifies better than land to represent *nahalah, lefa la bo-Ntata rona, boshwa jwa bo-Rrarona, ilifa loBao,* inheritance from the ancestors. The significance of vineyards as economic power bases defining the freedom or unfreedom of the people of the Bible appears clearly in Micah 4:3–4: "They will beat their swords into plowshares, their spears into pruning knives ... Each man [sic] shall sit under his vine, under his fig tree; and no one will be terrorised, for the mouth of Yahweh of hosts has spoken". In my *Biblical hermeneutics and Black Theology in South Africa* I have dared to suggest that this is the only really socialist part of the Bible, and also the most representative of the aspirations and struggles of the majority of the people of God in all the phases of biblical history.

4.11 (2) *Fair price* (v 2) – symbolising the power relations underlying the market. The issues of wealth and poverty in South Africa today are closely connected with the role assigned to the economic market. Those who have power and possess wealth believe that the market forces of the economic system of "free enterprise" should be left to determine the creation and distribution of wealth. The powerless majority of black people in South Africa have no faith in the market. They argue that the market is an instrument of competition among those who already own wealth. It is an instrument for further dispossession of the oppressed and exploited black people. Thus the notion of "a fair price", as enunciated by the ruling classes of biblical times (Ahab, etc.) no less than by the economic bosses of our times, is a hoax.

4.12 (3) *Political power* (vv 6 and 7) – represented in the text by the king's ability to remove people forcibly from their land and the role of the officials and leading citizens of Jezreel in the deliberate miscarriage of justice. One parallel in contemporary black experience would be the actions of some community councillors and homeland leaders, for instance the way community councillors use their powers to evict people from their houses in order to provide houses for their supporters.

4.13 (4) *Violence* – a feature which a Black Theological reading of this narrative could not miss. In many ways violence always accompanies the struggle between the wealthy and the poor, both in the Bible and in contemporary societies. Historically, black people in particular have been on the receiving end of this violence. Three types of violence are discernible in the text. Firstly, there is the violence of the state or institutional violence, demonstrated in the king's act of expropriating Naboth's land. Secondly, there is the violence of the political functionaries of the state which eventuates in the death of Naboth. Thirdly, there is the violence necessarily embodied in the state as an instrument of class rule. This text was obviously written in the light of events which had already taken place. The violence referred to in 1 Kings 21:23–24 actually happens later, as described in 1 Kings 22:33–37 and 2 Kings 9:30–37. A Black Theological reading, grounded in the experiences of the black community, would inevitably link the unprecedented violence against and in the black community during the 1980s and 1990s to the violence in this text. The basis of such a link is that this community, like its counterpart in the northern monarchy of king Ahab, is characterised by immense poverty leading to all manner of violence in it, against it and by it.

4.14 (5) *The role of ideology* is a point of particular interest to a Black Theological interpreter of the Bible. It functions at two levels. Firstly, there is the way in which ideology functions in the events of the story to justify particular actors and actions. This is illustrated by the use of state ideology when Jezebel asks of king Ahab: "Are you the king or aren't you?" (v 7), or when she says in the letter she wrote to the officials and leading citizens of Jezreel: "Proclaim a day of fasting, call the people together, and give Naboth the place of honour. Get a couple of scoundrels to accuse him to his face of cursing God and the king ..." (vv 9–10). Secondly, ideology functions at the level of the text itself. A Black Theological reading recognises that ideology does not only function in the historical situation described in the text, but that the text itself has its own ideological intentions. On which side, for example, are our sympathies enlisted? The author (or authors) of this story invokes God not just to subject the actions of the powerful classes to moral critique, but to introduce into the discourse of the text another struggle – that between the state and the prophets. The latter group is represented by Elijah. The question of the political economy during the rise and history of the prophetic movement and its message is one that requires separate treatment. Suffice it to note that here, as in every other passage where prophets crop up, the dispossessed cease to speak for themselves. Their voice is replaced by that of the prophet. In this text Naboth's own voice is limited to his protest: "I inherited this vineyard from my ancestors ... the Lord forbid that I should let you have it!" (v 3). Be that as it may, in the ideological intentions of the text there are the God of Naboth, who is about to be impoverished through expropriation of his land, and the God of Elijah, representing the middle class interests of the Deuteronomic writer who has a score to settle with the northern monarchy of "king Jeroboam son of Nebat" (vv 20ff). Questions of wealth and poverty are articulated by different ideological intentions in the Bible, even within the same text. Thus a Black Theological reading of the Bible is at the same time an ideological reading, as indeed are all readings of the Bible. The only real question is: in the interests of which social class, race, culture, and gender is the reading conducted?

C. CULTURE

4.15 The struggle to free oneself from poverty caused by landlessness is an act of culture. This is so because the wealth of the powerful classes, both in the Bible and in black history, was also a product of cultural domination. As Amilcar Cabral (1980:142–143) points out:

4.16 Study of the history of liberation struggles shows that they have generally been preceded by an upsurge of cultural manifestations, which progressively hardened into an attempt, successfully or not, to assert the cultural personality of the dominated people by an act of denial of the culture of the oppressor. Whatever the conditions of subjection of a people to foreign domination and the influence of economic, political and social factors in the exercise of this domination, it is generally within the cultural factor that we find the cultural germ of challenge which leads to the structuring and development of the liberation movement.

4.17 Since time immemorial Biblical scholars have argued that in the biblical communities there was no division of labour between actors operating in the spiritual and the material spheres of life. Consequently the cultural resistance of the oppressed communities of the Bible inevitably took a religious form. Culture in the Bible, as indeed in black communities, is spiritual in character, being in effect the mode in which the material life of the people manifests itself.

4.18 It is thus not surprising that to the extent that a society is socioeconomically homogeneous it has one culture, although not necessarily an evenly developed one. Where, however, there are divisions due to the possession of wealth or the lack of it, we have to speak of a culture of the wealthy and a culture of the poor. In the Bible it manifests itself in the differences in the ethos of the various covenants. For example, the covenant with Moses on Mount Sinai led to a perspective that can be traced throughout the Bible, one which represents a movement of protest and struggle on the part of the poor and disinherited. The God of this perspective tends to intervene decisively against any form of oppression and exploitation. The covenant with David, on the other hand, represents a movement in the Bible whose emphasis is on law and order, on the consolidation of the established and secure classes of society. This perspective "articulates its theological vision in terms of a God who faithfully abides and sustains on behalf of the ordering" (Brueggemann, in Gottwald 1983:308f.).

4.19 In the biblical history of the struggle against poverty and oppression the people of Israel consistently appealed to the cultural/spiritual traditions of resistance. Sometimes, however, these traditions existed in a form that indicated that they had been co-opted by the wealthy and powerful classes to legitimise their power and wealth. The Davidic covenant of 2 Samuel 7 is a case in point.

4.20 It is on these grounds that Black Theology insists on a critical historical and biblical hermeneutics of liberation. No culture of the Bible is automatically liberating. No culture of black society is automatically liberating. The task of the biblical cultural worker involved in the struggle for freedom from poverty is to liberate the Bible so that the Bible can liberate us. Cabral (1980:143) is right when he writes:

4.21 A people who free themselves from foreign domination will not be culturally free unless, without underestimating the importance of positive contributions from the oppressor's culture and other cultures, they return to the upwards paths of their own culture ... We see therefore that, if imperialist domination has the vital need to practise cultural oppression, national liberation is necessarily an *act of culture*.

5

God cares for his chosen ones: A prosperity reading

WILLIAM DOMERIS

A. INTRODUCTION

5.1 This chapter represents a journey into the past, although the reader will be quick to spot links with present theological debates taking place in this country about groups as varied as Rhema and the Zionist churches. I have set out to answer the question concerning the biblical roots of what some people refer to as the "prosperity cult". I prefer to speak of a "prosperity reading", since churches like Rhema have recently distanced themselves from the prosperity cult. I found that a number of churches transplanted from the USA do not so much constitute cults as that they exhibit a common style of reading the scriptures which deal with wealth and poverty. I seek neither to justify nor to criticise such a reading, but rather to show how such groups use the Bible to support their basic beliefs. Moreover, I will indicate why this reading has such a strong appeal in the South African religious milieu.

5.2 Imagine that you are present in the congregation of a great church like Rhema, or one of the other so-called "New Testament" churches. The offering has just been taken, but instead of beginning his sermon, the preacher pauses and says, "I feel that there are people here who have not been obedient to the prompting of God. When we took up the offering, you did not give the amount which God had put in your heart. Instead you kept back some, because you were afraid that your needs would not be met. I believe that God is saying that you must trust him and give what he has laid in your heart to give". So the offering is taken again, and it might even be taken a third time before the service ends. The people respond warmly and give generously. Sometimes the amount might be announced during the service. In such a community, giving is an essential part of worship. People give sacrificially rather than just shedding their loose change!

5.3 For some of us, brought up in one of the traditional churches, this style of offering smacks the sensationalism. In fact, other churches have been quick to point fingers and to speak of a "prosperity cult". But for the people who attend a church like Rhema or a similar church with North American connections, such an emphasis on "giving" is considered quite natural. Indeed, the neglect of tithing would appear to them to be a great sin.

5.4 Several of the 2 000 groups among the African Zionist Churches (ZCC) place particular emphasis on tithing. The offering is not a hurried affair, but forms the central element of their worship. It is a time of intense emotions with much singing and clapping, as one by one the people bring forward their offerings. Some might come back several times as they feel prompted by the Spirit. The whole affair reminds one more of an auction sale than a service of worship, yet one cannot deny its deep spiritual reality for the people involved. What then are the roots of such a celebration?

5.5 The central tenet of a "prosperity or welfare reading" holds that *God cares* for his "chosen" or "elect" and is prepared to "open the windows of heaven" and inundate them with blessings should they show themselves to be his true followers. The second tenet has been described as the *Protestant ethic,* which advocates hard work as the key to success, both in the material and the spiritual sphere. Without denying the validity of the Pauline belief in justification by faith alone, the Protestant ethic holds that hardworking obedience to God will bring rewards both in this life and in the life to come. Work itself is ordained by God as a worthy pursuit for humankind.

5.6 In exploring the biblical roots of this view and of what the Germans have called a *Wohlfahrt* reading, we come across a number of key concepts, the first of which is that of reward and blessing. I shall present these concepts from the standpoint of the members of a prosperity cult and thus as a welfare reading, but I begin with a discussion of 1 Kings 21, the story of Naboth's vineyard.

B. NABOTH'S VINEYARD

5.7 The story of Naboth's vineyard is well known and is usually used to illustrate the sin of Jezebel and Ahab. However, there is another side to it which I would like to discuss, namely the perspective of Naboth. When he refuses to sell the vineyard to Ahab, he does so for several reasons. In the first place, the vineyard is not his to sell. He is simply the steward of the farm on behalf of his family. He has been entrusted with the vineyard by God, and it is his duty to work it and to harvest the fruits of his labour. Secondly, the vineyard is the avenue by which God can bless him and his family. As a righteous steward he is to follow the task set for him by God, so that by obeying God and offering to him the due tithes, Naboth ensures that in return God will shower blessings upon him. Such blessings are inconceivable outside the context of the family vineyard and its fertility. So Naboth clings to his land, for it is the inheritance of his children and represents his God-given duty to work this particular slice of the promised land. Herein lies his hope that God will bring prosperity on his house in return for his labour.

5.8 Ahab, by contrast, wishes to gain blessings for which he has not laboured and to which he has no right. His theft of Naboth's land therefore entails more than the taking of a piece of land – it entails the theft of potential prosperity and blessing which should have accrued to Naboth and his family. In his blind selfishness, Ahab reduces the vineyard to a potential vegetable patch and Naboth's family to the level of working animals. He fails to see their special place within the community of God's covenant. So he would strip them of their land and locate them somewhere else, on foreign soil which holds no promise of prosperity – for it is not the piece of land which God has entrusted to them.

5.9 In South African history we often read of people being forced from the land of their ancestors. Officialdom, like Ahab, fails to realise the significance of the relationship between a group of people and their family land. They do not see the invisible bond which ties that group to that piece of the country, nor do they understand its significance in terms of the prosperity of the people. To move from that land is both to destroy the future security of the children and their unborn children, and to turn one's back upon the ancestral spirits who bequeathed that land to those families. In both cases the end result is the same – poverty and rootlessness!

C. UNDERSTANDING MATERIAL BLESSINGS

5.10 The Hebrew term *barak* (bless) has a variety of meanings ranging from "worship or praise" to "invoking benefits" upon someone (Meyers 1979:523). The latter meaning is of particular interest for this study. When God is said to bless a particular person it means that he grants that individual physical and spiritual grace which manifests itself in "long life, affluence, and power" and fertility (Meyers 1979:523).

5.11 The early Hebrew writers summed up the situation of blessing as one of idyllic rural life: "So Judah and Israel lived in safety, every man *under his vine and his fig tree,* from Dan even to Beersheba, all the days of Solomon" (1 Ki 4:25). From the fact that there is scant reference to life after death in the Hebrew Bible (Old Testament), one may infer that the minds of the writers were largely closed to that option. Blessings therefore had relevance only in so far as they affected one's earthly existence, or that of one's family. So the ideal is one of growing old gradually, relaxing beneath the trees planted in one's youth, surrounded by numerous grandchildren. One has a vision of the South African counterpart relaxing on his veranda with a cup of coffee, or beneath a thorn tree in the kraal drinking deeply of mother's best-brewed beer.

5.12 Wealth is also associated with blessing associated with good fortune because of the fertility of the soil. Such affluence was probably less obvious than that which we are accustomed to see in TV sagas like *Dallas* and *Dynasty.* Israel – particularly the central highlands, where many of the major settlements were found – was not a very fertile region. Resembling the Transvaal Highveld in vegetation, and the Cape in climate, this region often experienced droughts, hot dry summers and wet winters. For the Israelite farmer life was hard and farming offered a precarious existence (cf. Gn 3:17–19). The religious festivals associated with the first harvest (the festival of Weeks), and the late harvest (the festival of Booths), reinforced the people's deep dependence upon the blessings of God in the form of adequate rain at the right time. So affluence was really no more than having sufficient to provide a secure life for one's family. Nevertheless there were a few very wealthy people, as both the Bible and archaeology show. They tended, however, to be exceptions and it does not seem that the average farmer aspired to such levels of wealth.

5.13 Power and status feature much more prominently in the Hebrew Bible than wealth (see Malina 1981:82–85). Status is the rank which your community assigns to you. You can lose your status and, with some difficulty, have it restored to you. The higher your status, the greater your power within the community. So one seeks status rather than wealth, and power rather than just possessions. Blessing therefore includes status and power, as we see in the lists of blessings at the conclusion of Genesis and Deuteronomy (e.g. Gn 49:3, 8 and Dt 33:13–17).

D. REWARD AND PUNISHMENT

5.14 The idea of reward for faithfulness to God is nowhere more obvious than in the prose sections of the book of Job (especially chapters 1 and 2). Scholars suggest that Job is set against the backdrop of a type of new year festival, at which time the people believed that God and the angels decided the fates of all the people during the coming year. The occasion for the gathering of the angels or "sons of God" in Job 1 and 2 fits into such a pattern. They gather to decide how to punish or reward the people on the basis of their track record during the previous year.

5.15 God meets the accuser (satan) and speaks of the righteousness of Job. The satan in return challenges God, suggesting that the reason for Job's faithfulness is the consistency with which God rewards him (Jb 1:10). He has no reason to be unfaithful in the face of the manifold blessings, in the form of children and material possessions which God has poured out upon him. God accepts the challenge and twice gives for the satan permission to act against Job (Jb 1:12; 2:6), although in the normal course of events his righteousness would justify reward and not punishment. Job proves faithful in the face of all manner of terrible calamities and God at last rewards him and restores to him the fullness of wealth (Jb 42:12–17).

5.16 The writer of Job does not consider the option of reward and punishment after death found in later Judaism (Dn 12:1–3). On the whole the people of his day lived close to nature, which meant that God's blessings were expected to be spelled out in terms of their day to day existence. The reward of Job is therefore described as an increase in status (Jb 42:11, 15) and in wealth – (donkeys, camels, sheep and children) – rather than as what we would call "spiritual blessings" like peace of mind, joy or contentment. This is typical of the Hebrew Bible and explains why even today God may manifest his blessings in the form of material possessions for those who love and serve him.

E. CONDITIONS FOR BLESSING

5.17 Jesus speaks of God blessing good and bad alike (Mt 5:45). So too the book of Job speaks of the treasure houses of heaven where the frost and snow, the winds and rain are kept in abundance (Jb 38). The prophet Malachi (Ml 3:10), writes however that if the people bring their tithes, God will open the "floodgates of heaven" (NIV) and pour out his blessings. So, clearly, while some blessings are for all humanity, God does reserve special blessings for his elect.

5.18 In the struggle between Elijah and the prophets of the Tyrian Baal on Mount Carmel (1 Ki 18) the story centres on the question of fertility and, most importantly, the sending of the rain. The country is in the grip of a drought and both Elijah's God and Baal claim to be the God who speaks with thunder and lightning. So Elijah and the Baalite prophets wait with bated breath for the winning flash of lightning which will declare their God the victor. Finally the God of Elijah answers, and shortly thereafter the rain comes. In triumph Elijah clutches the hem of his garments and sprints through the rain in front of king Ahab's chariot.

5.19 Apart from general blessings like rain which God sends on all flesh, other specific blessings accrue to people in return for their good deeds. The most important of these for the Old Testament is obedience to the law of Moses. As in many ancient Near Eastern covenants and treaties, a list of blessings and curses was attached to the covenant made at Sinai. The book of Deuteronomy includes God's stipulations and the string of blessings and curses which will come upon those who obey or disobey (see Dt 27, 28). In other words, if we are obedient to the law of God, we will be rewarded in a material way. Hence we often read of God's blessings which he pours out on the righteous (e.g. Ps 1). Zionist Christians speak of a similar "outpouring" in return for their faithful service and work for their church

5.20 The Hebrew word for the condition of sinlessness in the sight of the law is *tzedekah* or righteousness. The word conveys the meaning of being found not guilty on the day of God's judgment. The Bible consistently emphasises the God of righteousness, who rewards the righteous and punishes the doers of evil. Since the rewards are invariably understood in terms of material benefits, it was often assumed that the wealthy and powerful were those blessed by God. Naturally such people could become corrupted by their wealth, as happened during the time of Amos, and the prophet was obliged to point out their sin. Indeed, Amos went so far as to suggest that the real "righteous" in his time were the poor and oppressed. But, as in the case of Job, wealth was usually seen to be the tangible sign of God's blessing. The same thinking is found among Christians today, where steel magnates and other industrial leaders attribute their wealth and power to their dedication to tithing and obedience to God.

5.21 The book of Proverbs and the later book of Ecclesiasticus (part of the Apocrypha) continually warn people of the dangers of laziness and bad planning. Poverty is seen to be the direct consequence of either slothfulness or poor planning (Pr 6:6–11). By contrast, security from want accrues to the wise and careful (Pr 27:23–27). For those people who are under the will of God, it stands to reason that some material blessings will come as a reward for their hard work. Just as God does not intend that his chosen ones should suffer harm, so it is not part of his plan that poverty should rob them of the full and abundant life which is their due. What some people have dubbed the "prosperity cult" is, in its simplest form, the recognition of the loving nature of God and the natural rewards which must flow from dedication to and untiring effort for the kingdom.

5.22 The prophet Malachi prophesies in the post-exilic period, some time after Nehemiah and Ezra had worked at rebuilding both the physical and spiritual aspects of Judean life. His focus is the cultus of the temple, and he knows that without the tithes of the people, that same temple cannot operate. So he urges the people to bring their full tithes and offerings (Ml 3:10). In exchange, God will grant them the blessings for which they long, namely fertility for their fields, absence of diseases and rain for their crops (Ml 3:11–12). The same principle operates today in the view of those Christians who espouse a prosperity reading. If we want to see the signs of God's blessings all around us, we need to bring him the offerings which are his due – both our tithes and the sacrifices of our lives. Once we have put our all on the altar, we can expect God to open up the windows of heaven and inundate us with his blessings. The storerooms of heaven are crammed with such blessings, and all that God is waiting for is our readiness to dedicate ourselves and our offerings to him. Forgiveness of sin, inner or spiritual healing, physical healing, the fruits and gifts of the Spirit are all there for the asking. Yet we fail to claim these priceless treasures. Consistently this hope features in the teaching of the Zionist congregations and the American-based "New Testament" churches like Rhema.

F. GOD'S ABUNDANT PROVISION

5.23 The Hebrew Bible is full of instances which underline God's care and provision. The exodus tradition is the prime example, as God makes provision for the care of his people during their lengthy sojourn in the wilderness. He guides them with a pillar of fire by night and a cloud by day. He gives them manna to eat, and provides quail and water from a rock. He leads them through the Red (Reed) Sea, protects them from snakes and their enemies, to guide them at last to the promised land. Here is a model for all God's people to contemplate!

5.24 A similar picture emerges from the writings of Isaiah, who speaks of the joy of the redeemed (Is 35): streams in the desert, flowers in a wilderness, and old people leaping and running in the presence of God. Such is the vision that later gave rise to the desire of the Jews to return to their homeland. There can be few greater pictures of the loving nature of God. But one cannot leave the passage without noting that the path on which the redeemed walked was called "the way of holiness", for without faith one cannot please God (Heb 11:6). This point is not ignored by those who subscribe to a prosperity reading.

5.25 As God provided for the needs of the people of that time, so he provides for our needs today. God is the everloving father, who pours out his love on his own. He knows our hearts, he discerns both good and evil. Yet in spite of our natural sinfulness, he forgives and forgets. Then he begins to bless us, and as we respond to those blessings, he blesses us again and again. In fact he gives to us "the desires of our hearts!" (Ps 37:4).

5.26 The Psalmist announces that if we commit our paths to the Lord, he will give us the desires of our hearts. Here is a promise that obviously held great meaning for the early Israelites and today is cited as a key text by particular groups of modern Christians, especially the New Testament churches planted in South Africa from the USA. Most of these Christians hold the view that God promises, in return for our faithfulness to him, to give us not just our needs in terms of food and clothing, but much more than that – the desires of our hearts. The more extreme form of the prosperity reading might argue that one should pray not just for a car, but for a luxury car, on the understanding that God wants the very best for his people!

5.27 The desires of our hearts may mean those desires put there by God, such as a desire to be faithful to him, to be truthful and generally to live our lives in accordance with his will. In other words, the process of committing our paths to God ensures that our desires are in line with this spiritual state. But such circular thinking is not typical of the Hebrew mindset. The simpler form is preferable, namely that God rewards in a material way those who dedicate themselves to his service. There are good grounds for expecting such blessings from God, and even for requesting such blessings from him. The deeper our dedication and the greater our faith, the more abundant the blessings.

5.28 The desire for wealth and security is not dissonant with the will of God, so argues the prosperity reading. He desires the best for his people, in terms of their standard of living, their possessions and their families. We are encouraged to bring the desires of our hearts to him, not to hide them away as if there was something wrong with desiring such good things. The fruit of our labour is a just reward for our hard work in the service of the King. Why should we shy away from the very things with which God wishes to bless us – wealth and prosperity? If the desire for a thing – a car or a house – is found in our hearts, and if we are right with God, then surely God has placed that desire there.

G. LABOUR: BLESSING OR CURSE?

5.29 When Adam began to toil in the world beyond the garden of Eden, he found that the elements, once so favourable, had become harsh and unfriendly. He won his bread by the sweat of his brow. This does not mean that the Bible presents work or labour as a curse in itself. No, it is rather the natural condition of humankind, both men and women, to toil side by side. Work is ordained by God as the vehicle for service here on earth, a gift from God (Ec 3:9–13). But the prosperity reading suggests further that we need to accept the status that God has given us and to work hard to improve our lot here on earth. Work in all its forms is a blessing from God, and our place in the great plan of God is found at the workbench which he has chosen for us. If we show ourselves to be worthy work people, as Noah, Moses, Joshua and others did, then we shall enjoy the fruits of our labour here on earth, and even more in heaven.

H. THE APPEAL OF THE PROSPERITY READING

5.30 The basic philosophy underlying the doctrine of work expressed here is that of capitalism or free enterprise. This system holds that it is the right of individuals to benefit from their own initiative. Poverty is a consequence of failing to take full advantage of the system. If one really works hard, then one can lift oneself out of poverty into the ranks of the wealthy. Here is one of the great appeals of a prosperity reading, for one receives in this life, and not just in life hereafter, the tangible benefits of being a Christian. Poverty is seen to be outside God's will for the average Christian! Instead of pinning all one's hopes on the next world, one experiences "abundant life" here and now. Thus, in a capitalist country like South Africa, Christianity and the capitalist economic situation are able to go hand in hand. Conversely, those who oppose the system see socialism as fitting in with their forms of liberation theology.

5.31 In the South African context, a prosperity reading has several appealing features. In the first place, in terms of capitalist philosophy, it seems logical that effort should be rewarded. Why should God not give generously to those who work sacrificially on his behalf? Surely the testimony of the Bible speaks of God's provision for his loved ones. Such a message has great appeal not just to the workers (who make up the bulk of the ZCC) but also to the middle and upper class Christians who attend Rhema and its sister churches. It is very comforting to know that one's financial future is in good hands, especially in a time of great political and social instability, and that God will reward one for one's efforts.

5.32 More important, however, for those who are wealthy or desire wealth, is the notion that God does not discourage the actual possession of good things. In the face of the social gospel, which emphasises giving to the poor and decries the oppression of the poor by the wealthy, the prosperity reading helps ordinary people to come to terms with living as well-fed Christians in an age of hunger. Such a reading goes a long way towards lifting the terrible burden of guilt which the social gospel has placed on the shoulders not just of the rich, but of the average salaried Christian. At long last, one need no longer be embarrassed by the fact that one lives in a nice house or drives a luxury motor vehicle. In a country like South Africa, where there are unprecedented opportunities for wealth, Christians need a haven where the sermons will not always demand that they forfeit the fruits of a market economy. For members of the ZCC, the prosperity reading holds a great hope for the future, when the riches of the whites will be distributed among the now deprived blacks.

5.33 The strength of the prosperity reading lies in its integration of worship and sacrifice. To place *sacrificial giving* at the heart of one's worship implies more than the conversion of one's soul – it is the conversion of one's pocket! It is a wholesome integration of the business side of life with its spiritual side.

I. CONCLUSION

5.34 I have tried here, firstly, to sketch the basic framework which functions when one reads the scriptures from the vantage point of an average well-to-do member of the "New Testament" churches. Secure in the knowledge of their own wealth and position, they interpret the Bible accordingly. Secondly I have hinted at ways in which the less affluent ZCC might look forward to material blessings in the coming age. Many of these prosperity readings have presuppositions which are buried in Scripture, but clearly one can also build them into fantasy castles. It is up to the readers to decide for themselves about the validity of such a reading.

6

How is the biblical text structured? Immanent exegesis

JIMMIE LOADER

A. INTRODUCTION: WHAT IS "IMMANENT EXEGESIS"?

6.1 This chapter deals with what is known as an "immanent" way of doing *exegesis* or, which is much the same thing, an "immanent" way of reading a text.

6.2 An exegesis or exposition of a text is really just our account of how we read and understand that text. The word "immanent" means "inherent", so that when we speak of an "immanent" reading it means that we consider only that which is given in or intrinsic to the text. We pay no attention to things outside the actual text, such as what the author had in mind (that would be an intentional reading) or the things the words refer to (that would be a referential reading). Neither do we relate it to other texts (which one could call an intertextual reading). The text is read as an independent entity, approached as a system of *related* elements. The elements in the network of the text refer to one another, resulting in a particular *interrelationship*. One could call this the structure of the text and when we study it we see how the text fits together. To use an architectural analogy, an "immanent" approach is concerned with the relation between foundations, walls and roof – not with what the architect had in mind with the building, its role in the local community or how it tones in with other buildings in the vicinity.

6.3 The word "immanent" is placed in quotation marks because it is not possible to sever every connection between a text and things "extraneous" to it. For the text uses words which derive from *language*; it is placed in a world which, however fictitious it may be, incorporates gardens, palaces, kings, queens, villains, court cases and the like – all of them concepts that are *known* in the world outside the text. Every reader of the story of Naboth's vineyard is familiar with its concepts from sources other than the text. In addition the *readers* of a text approach it with all manner of presuppositions, talents and deficiencies, all of which play some role in their minds quite independently of the text. Besides, an "immanent" reading may cause readers to discern a message in a text, which they may then apply to their *real-life* situations. Thus a person could conclude that the text of 1 Kings 21 means that God is averse to rich people abusing their power to enrich themselves still further. This conclusion would be meaningless unless stated in relation to the extratextual world.

6.4 We therefore use the word "immanent" in a special sense to refer to a study of a text which focuses on its structure.

6.5 There is more than one "immanent" way of reading a text. Indeed, there is a whole battery of methods which differ considerably from one another. In this chapter we illustrate only one such method, but do bear in mind that there are many others. The best way to become acquainted with them is to ask oneself where these "immanent" methods originated.

B. WHERE DID THIS KIND OF EXEGESIS ORIGINATE?

6.6 In nineteenth century Europe, as will be seen in the next chapter, the prevailing approach to the reading of the Old Testament was to concentrate on the *origin* of the texts. This was the result of a world view according to which everything was considered to be continually developing or evolving. Thus the accent was on the origins and subsequent development of all objects of study, including the Old Testament. This historical approach was highly analytical and sought to *un*ravel the very fibres of the Old Testament.

6.7 By the turn of the century this approach had begun to change. First certain philosophers started advocating the study of actual phenomena rather than their causes or effects. According to this view anything that one studies – be it a tree, a painting or a text – should be examined as a self-contained, existing entity. Exponents of this (phenomenological) approach treated artworks as independent entities to be *understood* in their own right rather than *explained* in terms of their history of origin.

6.8 In *linguistics* the Swiss scholar Ferdinand de Saussure insisted that in order to be meaningful, a thing had to be structured. This notion had a considerable impact, also on the reading of texts. The school known as the *Russian formalists*, which included such scholars as Vladimir Propp, took this approach further and focused on certain fixed patterns in narrative structure. In the Anglo-Saxon world these developments gave rise to *New Criticism* – an approach which insisted on minute analysis ("close reading") of all textual phenomena such as structural and sound patterns, imagery and the like, but with due regard to the work as a whole. An allied trend in the German speaking world was known as *Werkinterpretation*, which emphasised the form and structure of the text. Finally there was *French structuralism*, a product of all these influences combined plus that of the anthropologist Claude Lévi-Strauss. This approach assumed various forms, the most famous being A J Greimas' method for the analysis of narrative texts. Here the aim is not to study the observable style of texts or their meaning, but rather to probe beneath the surface to the deep level where the typical processes and characters common to all stories become visible.

6.9 These developments had an impact on the reading and exposition of the Old Testament, for most of the approaches were applied to the reading of biblical texts as well. The ideas of New Criticism and *Werkinterpretation* were reflected in innumerable stylistic studies, as was the French interest in the subsurface forces in Old Testament texts. In South Africa the structuralist approach to biblical texts was popular during the seventies, when attempts were made to demonstrate the structure and interrelationships of the text as we have it today. This approach continues to be influential and the example in this chapter is related to it. We shall call it the "method of the seventies".

6.10 Please remember, there is no such things as *the* "immanent" method. We have indicated that there are many such methods which differ quite radically from one another, the common factor being that all of them proceed in an "immanent" manner. What is true of methods from other folds applies equally to those from the "immanent" fold: there is no one "correct" method. A method exists to serve a particular *purpose*. It depends on the purpose whether the method is appropriate or, as we put it, effective. If a method suits one's purpose, the sole requirement is that it should be used according to the rules.

C. WHAT IS THE STRUCTURE OF 1 KINGS 21?

6.11 The structure of a text is, first of all, a matter of how its various sections are linked together or divided from one another. Among the techniques used to make such a *division* are the following:

6.12 1. The method of the seventies starts by *dividing a text into sentences*. This is not strictly necessary, since any text is already divided into sentences, but the idea is to arrange these sentences in linguistic units. Thus 1 Kings 21:2 consists of a single sentence, whereas verse 13 comprises five. In some instances one has to be careful, for all the sentences in a passage of direct speech in fact constitute one sentence, as in verses 20b–24 where all the sentences are covered by the verb "Elijah answered".

6.13 2. Next one looks for clues indicating how these elements or sentences are interrelated. What connects them and what separates them? If a number of sentences represent the direct speech of two speakers addressing one another, these elements constitute a unit known as a *dialogue*. Our chapter contains several such units or sections: verses 2–3 (Ahab and Naboth); verses 5–7 (Jezebel and Ahab); and verses 20–24 (Ahab and Elijah). When new actors come on the scene this marks the beginning of a new section. Once again our chapter contains an example: verses 17–19 introduce the Lord and Elijah after a section in which they did not feature (see below). In the same way one looks for things that connect different sayings, such as conjunctions, or which set them apart, such as introductory formulae.

6.14 3. Another important phenomenon is *word patterns*.

6.15 In the Hebrew text Ahab's name is not mentioned from verse 4 to verse 14 of our chapter; he is still referred to pronominally in verse 4, but from verse 5 onwards not at all, and he only makes a comeback in verse 15. This focuses the attention on Jezebel, whose name occurs several times in the central portion of the chapter. This formal phenomenon has significant implications for the meaning of the story and substantiates the argument of some exegetes who maintain that Jezebel, not Ahab, is the villain of the piece.

6.16 A cruciform pattern (chiasm) is a cohesive word pattern. When Ahab talks to Naboth (v 2), he first offers him another vineyard as a substitute and then a cash price. When he tells Jezebel about it (v 6), he inverts the sequence, mentioning the cash price first and then the other vineyard. The sequence is therefore: exchange – cash – cash – exchange. In this way the two dialogues are linked together across the intervening text so that they, with their associated interpolations, present a clearly structured section of the chapter:

• A 2–3	*dialogue* about sale (Ahab and Naboth)
B 4	Ahab's *reaction* to the dialogue
A 5–7	*dialogue* prompted by Ahab's reaction (Jezebel and Ahab)
B 8–10	Jezebel's *reaction* to the dialogue

6.17 (c) If one compares the word pattern in Jezebel's instructions to the city dignitaries (vv 9–10, hence part of the conclusion in the table above) and the pattern of the execution of these orders (vv 12–13), one observes that the two series are identical in both detail and sequence: fasting – seat of honour – two scoundrels – opposite him – charge – cursing – take out – stone to death. Apart from expressing Jezebel's complete control over the elders and nobles and the perfect success of her scheme, this serves to connect the second main section (vv 11–18) with the first (vv 2–10), for the end of the one and the beginning of the other match in every detail.

6.18 (d) Let us consider this second section:

• A 11–13	*execution* of Jezebel's orders – inter alia "stone him to death"
B 14	*message* to Jezebel – inter alia "stoned to death"
B 15	*message* of Jezebel – "stoned", "Naboth dead", "take possession"
A 16	*execution* of Jezebel's orders – "Naboth dead", "take possession"

6.19 Here too there is a word pattern (of which only a skeleton is given above). It is a cruciform pattern: the beginning and end correspond, as do the two middle parts. If we take into account what we have noted in paragraph 6.17(c), we can establish that the second main section is firmly integrated with the first. In addition everything revolves around Jezebel, so that we can see from the very shape of the tables that she is the key figure. To crown it all there is a touch of humour in the relationships of the A-sections: the city fathers obey the queen who acts on her husband's behalf, using his official seal (see v 8); yet he too obeys her orders (v 16) even though she is dependent on the authority of his seal. Again we see which character has the power.

6.20 4. *Sound patterns* too are important. In verse 7 Jezebel says: "Do you now govern Israel?" The Hebrew literally has "you now" and these two words are exact homophones although their spelling differs (*'attâ* *'attâ*). Going purely by ear, the expression may sound like both "now now" and "you you", which is not only conspicuous but also suggests derision. The same verse contains another play on sound – "I will give you", which in Hebrew reads *'ani 'ettên*. The second word means "I will give", the first is the pronoun "I". With the pronoun preceding the verb, the "I" in effect appears twice, giving it great emphasis. This is the same device as was used in the derisive expression with which she started addressing Ahab: "You now, you govern Israel!" Thus she contrasts her own dynamic personality ("I, I shall give") with the passive king of Israel ("you, you tin-pot king"). Thus it is another stylistic device to make Jezebel the central character.

6.21 5. *New subjects* indicate a new section. The third main section starts in verses 17–19, for this is where some new characters take the stage. But if we compare the Lord's instructions to Elijah with their execution (from v 20), we observe a number of structural hiatuses. Elijah is told to announce that the dogs will lick Ahab's blood in the same place where they licked Naboth's (hence in Jezreel, not in Samaria). Without delving into other texts (after the fashion of historical criticism) which tell how the dogs licked Ahab's blood in some other city and searching for an explanation, we can say, simply on the strength of what is "in" our text (i.e. immanent), that there is something amiss. Elijah indeed pronounces a judgment on Ahab, but the elements are very different from those of his instructions. Besides, there is a hiatus between verse 19 and verse 20, for there is no introductory formula to bring Elijah into Ahab's presence – he simply appears from nowhere.

6.22 6. In verses 20–29 we have difficulty discerning the same subtle patterns that we observed earlier in the chapter. Verse 27 links up with verses 20–24, for "[and when he heard] this" could only refer to Elijah's words which are reported there. This means that verses 25–26 are unassociated with the others. Structurally one can only point out that it is a parenthesis – one must leave it to historical criticism to find an explanation for it (is it a Deuteronomic insertion, and why would it have been inserted here?).

6.23 7. Right at the beginning of the chapter (v 1) we find two sentences. The first establishes a connection between our chapter and the preceding events. What "these words" (in the Hebrew text) refers to is problematic and relates to the history of origin of the text (see the next chapter to learn how historical criticism deals with such problems). The second sentence is the introduction to the present chapter, separating the previous narrative from this one by transposing us to a new location.

6.24 Although many other features have to be considered before one can trace the structure of the chapter properly, we have seen enough to allow us to give an overview of it:

- 1a *connecting formula* with what precedes
  1b *introductory placing* of the ensuing events

- A 2–3 *dialogue* about sale (Ahab and Naboth)
  B 4 Ahab's *reaction* to dialogue
  A 5–7 *dialogue* prompted by Ahab's reaction (Jezebel and Ahab)
  B 8–10 Jezebel's *reaction* to dialogue

- A 11–13 *execution* of Jezebel's orders
  B 14 *message* to Jezebel
  B 15 *message* from Jezebel
  A 16 *execution* of Jezebel's orders

- 17–19 *Divine oracle* against Ahab
  20–24 *dialogue* about divine oracle (Ahab and Elijah)
  25–26 *parenthesis* (idols do not feature in chapter)
  27 Ahab's *remorse* following oracle
  28–29 *Divine oracle* on Ahab's remorse

6.25 This division of the chapter actually traces its structure as it appears to the *reader*. This is not a trivial academic exercise, for it creates a framework for further analysis of the content and meaning. Such a disciplined framework makes for *controlled* exegesis. It does not mean that one has to interpret everything mathematically according to formalist rules and thus automatically arrive at the "correct" meaning of the text, ruling out any creative exegesis.

6.26 "Discipline" and "control" merely mean that the exegete maps the most accurate route possible for reading the details of the text. Thus the reader accounts for the way in which the techniques of a particular *strategy* were applied. By noting these one gains access to all sorts of information and one observes phenomena which one might otherwise easily have overlooked. Just as it is advisable for travellers to use a map to keep their bearings in the country they traverse, so readers are well advised to pay close attention to the details of a text. And just as a map cannot take the place of an actual journey across a landscape, nor determine the traveller's *impression* of the scene, so an exegetical map can never replace the readers' further discovery of the text or their *impressions* of it. Hence such an "immanent" reading of a text is (or ought to be!) simply a meticulous reading, noting every detail of it – what New Criticism calls *close reading*.

D. WHAT ABOUT CONTENT?

6.27 Let us look at a few things we might observe while tracing our map. Some of them could turn out to be helpful in answering the sort of questions raised by historical criticism; or they may illuminate the text in a way that affords fresh insight into certain aspects of it; or we may discover an idea in the text to help us arrive at a religious viewpoint for our own times. We shall not attempt to be exhaustive; we merely note a few points.

6.28 1. In verse 1b Ahab is referred to as "king of Samaria". Why such a peculiar title if he was king of the whole country of Israel anyway and not just of that one city? Although this title appears in one other text (with reference to Ahab's son Ahaziah in 2 Ki 1:3), it is extremely unusual. Disregarding any possible historical-critical explanations, it is remarkable that the introductory sentence juxtaposes Ahab's connection with Samaria with Naboth's connection with Jezreel. The point is unmistakable, for Naboth is linked with Jezreel on two occasions, the second time in an ambiguous phrase. The Hebrew could read either: "Naboth the Jezreelite had a vineyard that was in Jezreel ...", or: "Naboth the Jezreelite who was in Jezreel had a vineyard". Either way the suggestion is that Naboth had a stronger claim to land in Jezreel than Ahab: after all, Naboth is from Jezreel and Ahab from Samaria – what claim has Ahab to a vineyard in Jezreel? However great the power that historians assign an Israelite king, the introductory sentence's "immanent" contrast between the man from Jezreel and the man from Samaria anticipates the impending injustice.

6.29 This impression is confirmed by God's words when he speaks to Elijah (v 18). He refers to Ahab as "king of Israel, who is in Samaria", adding that he may be found in "the vineyard *of Naboth,* where he has gone [the Hebrew literally means "whither he has descended"] to take possession". Thus Ahab is not in his proper place.

6.30 The impression is reaffirmed when, at the end of the first main section (in v 8), Jezreel is referred to as "his [Naboth's] city". This could simply mean that he lived there, and even though there is no question of Jezreel actually being his city in the same way that Samaria was Ahab's, in an "immanent" sense it helps to point out the contrast underlying the injustice: Naboth belongs in Jezreel and Ahab in Samaria – at any rate as far as their properties are concerned. *All these "immanent" pointers may be read as a subtle protest against the excessive land ownership of wealthy potentates at the expense of the citizenry.*

6.31 2. The main sections of the chapter set the scene for conflict. In the first we have Ahab opposed to Naboth. But Ahab is also the antithesis of Jezebel – her dynamic attitude in opposition to his sullen passivity. By the same token Jezebel is the literary antithesis of Naboth, even though she never meets him, for she takes Ahab's place in the conflict.

6.32 In the second main section the leading citizens of Jezreel are counterpoised to their fellow leader on the orders of the queen (see below). The two scoundrels whom Jezebel has sent for are similarly in opposition to Naboth.

6.33 In the third main section Ahab and Elijah are in opposition. Elijah appears on the scene unexpectedly – there is no mention of his departure for Jezreel. This hiatus (omission) creates a shock effect to match the shock expressed by Ahab when he realises that Elijah has found him. It is a further sign that he does not belong there, this time an unintentional admission from his own lips, reminiscent of a good detective story.

6.34 The polarisation of the characters in the various main sections fits in with the theme of the chapter as a whole an innocent party versus a guilty one. This applies even in the case of Ahab/Jezebel, for although Ahab is not innocent, the real Lady Macbeth is Jezebel. *These polarities may be read as contributing to the basic theme: conflict between oppressive potentates and their lackeys on the one hand and the powerless on the other.*

6.35 3. Jezebel's brazen guilt is underscored. Without turning a hair she orders "scoundrels", thugs, to be used to institute a bogus lawsuit against a prominent citizen. She also does not scruple to issue written instructions, telling people to commit perjury. The leading citizens of Jezreel obey her, knowing that they are having the heinous murder committed on the queen's orders, not the king's. This is evident in verse 14, where their reply to Jezebel refers to the details of how meticulously they have executed her orders (vv 11–13), which in turn refers to the detailed instructions in the first main section (vv 8–10). Although Jezebel wrote *in the king's name* under his official seal (v 8), and although we are not told how the recipients knew that the orders actually emanated from the iron lady behind the throne, we read that the city fathers' report was sent directly to *Jezebel* (v 14). The hiatus (how did they see through the official royal document?) suggests some sort of secrecy. While there is nothing to stop historical criticism from suspecting that this is an incongruity or inconsistency in the text, an "immanent" reading would permit one to interpret this as *criticism of a bad monarch who countenances corruption among the ruling classes and benefits personally by the wrong done to the powerless.*

6.36 4. Naboth speaks only once (v 3). Swearing by God, he refuses to sell the heritage of his ancestors to the king, even though he was offered better farming land or a handsome price for it (cf. the king's embarrassment about the land because of its location, v 2). Historical criticism considers background information which may cast light on Naboth's motives, but an "immanent" reading discerns only a religious motive (which concurs with the findings of some historians). The oath by Yahweh indicates that Naboth sees it as a religious matter not to dispose of the family land that has belonged to them for many generations. Starting with the opening dialogue, then, the story has an important dimension – to wit, a religious one. The third main section confirms this in no uncertain terms. There God himself condemns the injustice and, through his prophet, announces a commensurate punishment – a case of poetic justice. Although historical criticism finds this punishment problematic (the dogs did not lick Ahab's blood in the same place as Naboth's), an "immanent" reading of our text could see the religious element as *indicating that socioeconomic wrongs are also religious wrongs and are punished by God.*

6.37 5. Ahab's remorse and the consequent mitigation of his punishment is reported in the final section of the chapter (vv 27–29). This may be associated – as historical critics maintain – with the fact that the punishment announced by Elijah (vv 21–24), which differs from the oracle God had instructed in verse 19, was never fulfilled. But our "immanent" reading reveals *a tendency to mitigate the punishment of penitent oppressors, especially ones who were not directly responsible for the oppression, even though they were prepared to enrich themselves through the injustice.*

6.38 6. The religious element is further underscored by the parenthesis (vv 25–26). This is an incongruity in the text, however, since Ahab's idolatry does not feature in this chapter. The other incongruity need not concern us here: the parenthesis compares Ahab with Jeroboam, which is applicable only to their idolatry; in respect of the theme of this chapter (the injustice of a royal potentate towards his subjects) the two kings differed completely, since Jeroboam ruled the northern kingdom for the very reason that he sided with those who were oppressed by a callous monarch (1 Ki 12). But such studies we leave to historical criticism.

6.39 If we read the various italicised passages above, we find that our "immanent" exercise on 1 Kings 21 has produced a fair amount of material which we, the readers, can fruitfully apply to particular situations. Thus it could be made to address the contemporary South African situation. The expression "*made* to address" leaves ample scope for the religious and political views of readers, and for their creative interpretation of the text. Our interpretation of the text is far from complete. The "immanent" method is only a starting point. All we have done was to read the text (we trust thoroughly), map our reading and note the possibilities that this opens up. Now we can embark on the adventure of the actual journey!

E. STRENGTHS AND WEAKNESSES OF "IMMANENT" EXEGESIS

6.40 In the course of the preceding discussion certain pros and cons of "immanent" exegesis were pointed out. Actually one should rather speak of the pros and cons of certain ways in which it may be *applied.*

6.41 Like any other method, this one entails *certain risks* – ones to which our South African experience testifies.

- The first is that such an exegesis may be conducted *in a partisan way*. Many scholars who use some form of "immanent" exegesis fall into this trap and become blinkered. The result (in many instances) is that virtually every analysis of a biblical text resembles a marionette – with many strings attached!
- Secondly, the use of this method may be accompanied by a belief that there is a *"true" meaning concealed in the text* which merely has to be discovered through mathematically precise structural analysis.

6.42 Subject to certain conditions, however, there are *definite advantages* attached to this method.

- The first is that it is conducive to careful reading (cf. "close reading") of the text. The exegete learns to be alert to every detail, to connectors and separators, patterns and relationships, constructions, figures of speech and the use of sounds.
- To do this the reader obviously needs to have a good command of the language in which the text is written. At the same time such a reading of the text actually develops one's *linguistic proficiency*.
- This method also cultivates the reader's ability to spot *both detail and broad relationships*. We have concentrated on a single chapter, but one could read a whole book in the same way. Thus one develops a sensitivity both for the individual trees in all their dendrological detail and for the forest as a whole.
- Used in the way we have suggested, this method constitutes a "first reading" – an *exploratory exercise* which, far from precluding the use of other methods, may even provide a foundation for their subsequent application. Thus an "immanent" reading may yield data that may well be useful for historical criticism (cf. the structural problems in vv 20–29 which are open to historical-critical study). To cite another example, liberation theologians could do a lot with the data yielded by our reading of this chapter if they are applied within the framework and for the purposes of their method.
- The possibilities are endless.

7

Where do the biblical texts come from? Historical-critical exegesis

FERDINAND DEIST

A. INTRODUCTION: WHAT IS HISTORICAL CRITICISM?

7.1 In the previous chapter you were introduced to exegetical methods that try to establish how biblical texts are structured. This approach only emerged when, for various reasons, exegetes began to abandon the historical-critical method of scriptural exposition, in which the key question is: where do the biblical texts come from? This chapter deals with the type of questions that occupy historical-critical exegetes and the way they set about interpreting the Bible.

7.2 The historical-critical method, which originated in the nineteenth century, is still widely used today. The main aim is to expound the biblical text *in terms of its own historical background* – hence the term "historical". The rest of this chapter deals with the exact implications of this term.

7.3 To illustrate this approach we shall consider Gray's exposition (1970) of the story of Naboth in 1 Kings 21. First we briefly note the procedures of historical-critical exegesis. Then we look into the question of why this method developed. Finally we try to assess the pros and cons of this method of scriptural exposition.

B. PROCEDURES OF HISTORICAL-CRITICAL EXEGESIS

1. Historical clarification of words and concepts in a text

7.4 The words and phrases in bold typeface in the first few verses of 1 Kings 21 are the kind that historical-critical exegetes usually comment on. The excerpts from Gray's commentary on Kings (1970) reproduced below gives an impression of their way of expounding such words and concepts.

> [1]And it happened after these things that Naboth of **Jezreel** had a certain vineyard which was in Jezreel adjoining **the palace** of Ahab the **king of Samaria.**

This is the first occurrence of [the Hebrew word] hekal in Kings in the sense of "palace". It is derived from the Sumerian e-gallu ("the great house"). The designation of Ahab as ... "King of Samaria" ... probably reflects the crown possession of Samaria as the basis of the power of the house of Omri. It may reflect the consciousness that the house of Omri was not truly representative of the people of Israel.

[The city of] Jezreel, Arab Zer'cin, at the foot of the north-west spur of the Gilboa ridge, gave its name to the great central plain (Greek, the valley of Esdraelon), stretching from the [Mediterranean] sea to the Jordan. Commanding access from the east to the ... plain, it was occupied by Ahab, no doubt as a base of operations against Damascus ... It could also have served as a winter resort for the king (18:45).

> 2And Ahab spoke to Naboth, saying, Give me your vineyard that I may have it as a vegetable-garden, for it adjoins my house, and let me give you in its place a better vineyard or, if you think fit, I will give you silver as the price for it.
> 3But Naboth said to Ahab, **God forbid** that I should give you the heritage of my fathers.

The exclamation halila-li [God forbid] expresses the conception that the course of action deplored was profane (halal), or wrong, in the eyes of God. The attitude of Naboth regarding his ancestral land reflects the solidarity of the family among the Palestinian peasants. Moreover the status of Naboth as a freeman, and probably a gibbor hajil ("man of substance"), was bound up with his possession of his ancestral land. To have accepted Ahab's offer, fair as it seemed, would have prejudiced his own status and that of his family, relegating them to the status of royal dependants.

> 4So Ahab went to his house sullen and aggrieved on account of the word which Naboth of Jezreel had spoken to him saying, I will not give you the heritage of my fathers. And he lay down on **his couch** and covered his face, and did not eat food.

mittato need not mean "bed", but rather "couch", such as was used for feasting.

> 5Then his wife Jezebel came to him and she said to him, Why so that your temper is sullen and you eat no food?
> 6And he spoke to her, Because I spoke to Naboth of Jezreel and said to him, Give me your vineyard for money, or, if you wish, I shall give you another vineyard in its place. And he said, I will not give you my vineyard.
> 7And Jezebel his wife said to him, Now is it you who exercises royal authority over Israel? Rise up, eat food and set your mind at ease. I shall give you the vineyard of Naboth of Jezreel.
> 8**So she wrote a letter in the name of Ahab and sealed it with his seal, and she sent the letter to the elders and to the freemen who were in his city**, the neighbours of Naboth.
> 11And **the men of his city, the elders and the freemen**, did as Jezebel had sent to them, as it was written in the letter she sent to them.

The fiction of communal law [which Jezebel tries to create] is noteworthy. Jezebel's reliance on the local elders and freeborn men of Jezreel suggests that Ahab was personally influential. This indicates perhaps that the persons concerned had been long accustomed to follow the lead of the family of Ahab. This situation is readily intelligible if Ahab's family was from Jezreel, the modern Arab analogy suggesting that the influence of a powerful local family ... is more or permanently dominant. This is the first specific mention of the freeborn (horim) as a class. In Jeremiah 27:20; 39:6 the freemen, or nobles, of Judah (hore yehûda) are mentioned as among the chief victims of the Babylonian conquerors.

7.5 These few excerpts illustrate the kind of historical questions posed by historical-critical exegetes when reading a text – questions concerning *geographical, linguistic* and *social* references. What was a "palace"? Why was Ahab called "king of Samaria" and not "king of Israel"? Where was Jezreel located? What was its status in the kingdom of Israel? What was the social position of Naboth and the other characters in the story, and how did Naboth see the situation at issue?

7.6 In much the same vein this commentary goes on to discuss Naboth's position in society, why Jezebel was in a position to proclaim a fast (v 9), the nature of capital crimes in Israel (crimes for which society could impose a death sentence – v 10), Naboth's seat of honour at the head of the banqueting table (v 12), what it signified to curse God and the king (v 13) (i.e. the nature of the charge against Naboth), and so on.

7.7 To historical-critical exegetes, then, the biblical text *reflects* a particular historical event and they try to interpret textual references *in terms of the historical background to the text.*

7.8 Thus far we have considered how historical-critical exegesis attempts to clarify the text from a historical point of view. But that is not all there is to it.

2. The "critical" element in historical-critical exegesis

7.9 The "critical" element in historical-critical exegesis has two components. Most Bible readers take it more or less for granted that a narrative text such as 1 Kings 21

- was written by a single author in a single session, and
- is a precise rendering of what happened at that time.

The historical-critical exegete, however, probes the text with a delicate scalpel, analysing it to determine whether these assumptions are valid (*critical* means primarily "analytical"). The following passages from the text and the accompanying excerpts from Gray's commentary illustrate this procedure.

2.1 Is the present text in fact the original one?

7.10 The example below shows how historical-critical exegetes set about answering this question. The words in bold typeface illustrate the *kind* of information in a text that prompts the historical-critical exegete's critical questions, while the excerpts from Gray's commentary illustrate *how* the exegete asks and answers these questions.

> [21]And it happened **after these things** that Naboth of Jezreel had a certain vineyard which was in Jezreel adjoining the palace of Ahab the king of Samaria.

In this chapter we revert to an incident in which Elijah is a protagonist, at least in its final phase, and it is natural to regard it as part of the Elijah narrative of chs. 17–19. In fact, G [the Septuagint, Greek translation of the Old Testament] places it after ch 19. In this case the objective historical matter from the account of the Syrian wars is conveniently grouped together, and the position of ch 21 in ... [the Hebrew text] is doubtless suggested by the oracle anticipating the death of Ahab [21:21], which is narrated in ch 22. Chapter 21 differs from chs. 17–19, however, in that it presents the matter much more objectively than in the rest of the Elijah narrative.

7.11 Certain points in this commentary are noteworthy. *Firstly*, the words in verse 1: "after these things", immediately prompt the exegetical question: "Which things? To what do these words allude?" And the conclusion is that they allude, not to the verses immediately preceding them, but to 1 Kings 17–19. *Secondly*, the exegete calls supporting evidence in the form of the Greek version of the Old Testament, where chapter 21 indeed appears immediately after chapter 19. *Thirdly*, he tries to account for this: the Greek version groups events relating to the Syrian wars together, whereas the Hebrew text places the oracle predicting Ahab's death and the report of his death together.

7.12 Thus historical-*critical* exegetes do not *take it for granted* that the text they read is the one recorded by the original author long ago. When they encounter things that lead them to suspect that this is not the same text that was originally recorded, they try as best they can to restore the narrative to its *most original form*. In the present instance, Gray concludes that originally 1 Kings 21 had appeared immediately after 1 Kings 19.

> [19]And you shall speak to him [i.e. Ahab] saying, Thus says Yahweh, Have you done murder and moreover taken possession? And you shall speak to him saying: Thus says Yahweh, **In the very place where the dogs have licked the blood of Naboth, the dogs will lick your blood, even yours.**

The fact that Elijah's prophecy about the dogs licking Ahab's blood is cited in 2 Kings 9:25 as a prophecy of the fall of the house of Ahab has caused some exegetes to surmise that the entire prophecy in the Naboth narrative (v 19) was a fabrication of a later author and that Elijah initially played no role in the Naboth story. In two details this (the prophecy in 2 Kings 9:25) differs from the oracle in 21:19, namely the mention of Naboth's sons (in 2 Ki 9:25, but not in 21:19) and the reference to the dogs licking Ahab's blood (mentioned in 21:19 but not in 2 Ki 9:25). This strongly suggests the originality of the oracle in 21:19, since, had the account of the Naboth incident in ch 21 been secondary to 2 Kings 9, the discrepancy would have been avoided. As it is, the discrepancy between the oracle in 21:19 and its fulfilment in 2 Kings 9:25 and 1 Kings 22:38 indicates an original tradition of the ipsissima dicta (actual words) of Elijah at 21:19.

7.13 Here, although dealing with the actual story, the exegete nonetheless tries to establish whether the text as it stands is the *original version* of that story. Consider in this regard the question whether verse 19 reflects the *ipsissima dicta* of the prophet.

7.14 We can reconstruct his argument as follows:

- The story of Naboth ends logically at verse 19a, since this is where judgment is pronounced on Ahab.
- Verse 19b introduces a new divine oracle (cf. the expression, which is repeated a second time, "And you shall speak to him saying").
- Verse 20 introduces a new episode (cf. "And Ahab said unto Elijah"). It seems, therefore, as if the story had originally ended at verse 19a and that the rest (the new divine oracle and the new episode) was added subsequently.

- This addition to 1 Kings 21:19a could have been made apropos of 2 Kings 9:24–26.
- If so, the person who amplified the text of 1 Kings 21 from 2 Kings 9 would have been at pains to ensure that the oracle in 1 Kings 21:19b tallied with its fulfilment in 2 Kings 9:24–26 in every detail.
- However, the two texts differ on certain crucial points. Since this makes it unlikely that verse 19b was inserted apropos of 2 Kings 9, we must assume that the oracle in 21:19b is Elijah's actual words.

> 20And Ahab said unto Elijah, **Have you caught up with me, O mine**
> **enemy?** And he said, I have caught up with you. Because you have sold
> yourself to do evil in the sight of Yahweh,
> 21lo I shall bring harm upon you and **I shall make a riddance of you, for I**
> **shall cut off him belonging to Ahab that pisses against the wall, to**
> **the very last in Israel.**
> 22**And I shall make your house as the house of Jeroboam the son of**
> **Nebat and as the house of Baasha the son of Ahijah, on account of**
> **the provocation which you have caused and the sin in which you**
> **have involved Israel.**
> 23**And concerning Jezebel also Yahweh spoke saying, The dogs will**
> **eat Jezebel all around Jezreel.**
> 24Him belonging to Ahab who dies in the city will the dogs eat, and him
> belonging to him who dies in the country will the birds of the heavens eat.
> 25(But there was none such as Ahab, who sold himself to do evil in the sight
> of Yahweh, incited by Jezebel his wife.
> 26And he committed great abomination in following idols, according to all that
> the Amorites did, whom Yahweh had dispossessed before the Israelites.)
> 27**And it happened that, when Ahab heard these words, he tore his**
> **clothes and put sackcloth on his body and fasted, and lay in**
> **sackcloth and went about quietly.**
> 28**And the word of Yahweh came to Elijah the Tishbite saying,**
> 29**"Have you seen how Ahab is subdued before me? Because he is**
> **subdued before me, I shall not bring about ill in his days; in his**
> **son's days shall I bring the harm upon his house."**

The content of Elijah's denunciation and oracle of doom ... is probably limited to verse 19. The rest of the passage (vv. 20–29) consists of a number of secondary statements from various sources. [The way Ahab greets Elijah in verse 20 is strongly reminiscent of 18:17–18, and creates the impression of a Deuteronomic amplification.] First there is the Deuteronomic condemnation of Ahab in vv. 25f. Then one notices the repetition of the phraseology of the doom of the houses of Jeroboam and Baasha (vv. 21b, 24, cf. 14:7–11; 16:1–4) to which v. 22 should be added ...
The oracle on Jezebel in v. 23, which breaks the sequence of vv. 22–24, is probably a fragment of a different tradition concerning Elijah ... [cf. 2 Ki 9:36]. The final passage on Ahab's submission ... (vv. 27–29) should be seen as another late insertion.
In our opinion, vv. 20–22, 24, vv. 27–29 and v. 23 are all late attempts to explain the fact that the proclamation that the dogs would lick the blood of Ahab in the very place where they licked the blood of Naboth was not literally fulfilled. One explanation was that

this was in consequence of Ahab's contrition (vv. 27–29); another (vv. 21f., 24) emphasized the extinction of Ahab's house in the death of Jehoram (2 Ki 9:24–26) and the rest of Ahab's family (2 Ki 10:1–11) ... Not yet satisfied, another redactor noted that in what concerned the dogs in the oracle there was an instance of prophecy and fulfilment in the case of Jezebel's death at Jezreel, the scene of Naboth's death (v. 23, cf. 2 Ki 9:36).

7.15 According to Gray, the original account of Elijah and Ahab ends at verse 19. The rest of the chapter was added piecemeal afterwards, giving three explanations why the judgment that Elijah pronounced on Ahab was not fulfilled:

- Ahab repented (vv 27–29);
- the disaster in fact befell Ahab's descendants (vv 21–22, 24); and
- Elijah's words were literally fulfilled at Jezebel's death (v 23).

Thereafter a redactor revised the scene of the meeting between Ahab and Elijah to accord with the account of their earlier encounter in chapter 18 (v 20) and then added the comment on Ahab in verses 25–26.

7.16 Whether or not Gray's arguments hold water does not concern us here. We have made our point: historical-critical exegetes want to satisfy themselves as best they can *about the exact origin of every bit of the text they are reading.* They want to know who was the author of every portion of the text and when it was written. As soon as a passage disrupts the course of the narrative or shows signs of being a later insertion, they start surmising that it might be the work of a different author.

2.2 Questions about the accuracy of the information contained in a text

7.17 The historical-critical method does not merely concern itself with text reconstruction. It also examines the *historical value* of the information contained in a text. We cite one illustration from Gray's commentary.

> 7 And Jezebel his wife said to him, Now is it you who exercises royal authority over Israel? Rise up, eat food and set your mind at ease. I shall give you the vineyard of Naboth of Jezreel.'
> 8 So she wrote a letter in the name of Ahab and sealed it with his seal, and she sent the letter to the elders and to the freemen who were in his city, the neighbours of Naboth.
> 9 And she wrote in the letters saying, Proclaim a fast and give Naboth the seat at the head of the people ...
> 15 And it came to pass, when Jezebel heard that Naboth was stoned and was dead, that she said to Ahab, Rise up and take possession of the vineyard of Naboth of Jezreel, which he refused to give you for money, for Naboth is not alive, but dead.

Fohrer assumes that the centrality of Jezebel does not quite correspond to historical fact, but rather reflects the intense hatred of prophetic circles which transmitted the tradition. For her to contrive the judicial murder of Naboth within the letter of Hebrew law, she [an alien in Israel] would have been, Fohrer declares, "a world's wonder of learning and resource". She may nevertheless have been advised by a subservient Israelite, though undoubtedly the decree for the fast [v 9] would have been issued by Ahab himself. To this extent, then, we can agree with Fohrer that the predominant role of Jezebel reflects the prophetic version of the tradition. This is not to say, however, that Jezebel was not the motive force behind the injustice. We should retain the passage as the prophetic version of a significant tradition of Elijah and Ahab which retains, though not literally in every detail, a true reflection of the consequences of the policy of the house of Omri to effect a synthesis of Israelite and Canaanite tradition ...

7.18 Two questions are at issue here:

- Could things actually have happened as the text recounts them?
- What kind of literature does one find in the text?

7.19 Could Jezebel really have done what the text says she did? A princess from Phoenicia, she was unfamiliar with Israelite customs. How could she have known that the Israelites proclaimed a fast at certain times (e.g. during droughts)? How did she know precisely what legal procedure to follow so that Naboth could be murdered without arousing suspicion? Could a king's wife in fact act so autonomously in those days? Is this history, or some other kind of literature?

7.20 Fohrer maintains that what we have here is a story, written in prophetic circles, whose authors were intent on describing Jezebel's guile (rather than historical details) – that in fact she never did perpetrate the things attributed to her. Gray concedes that we are dealing with a *prophetic narrative* (rather than history), but is more confident about its basic historical accuracy.

3. Historical-critical exegesis

7.21 To sum up, historical-critical exegesis is primarily concerned with how *accurately a text refers* to the reality it describes. Hence the commentary on place names, customs and other textual details. This kind of commentary reflects the exegete's interest in the *historical* circumstances reported in the text, the assumption being that the better we understand that background, the better we may understand both the text and the words of God contained in it.

7.22 But the historical-critical exegetes' scalpel cuts deeper than just to the background to the text. They want to be sure that we are dealing with the *original text* and the *original words*, for instance Elijah's actual words and the original text in which they were recorded. Secondly, they want to understand why later generations made certain additions to the text, and what purpose and meaning these had; for, these exegetes maintain, the insertions indicate how later generations interpreted and used the original text.

7.23 Historical-critical exegetes furthermore want to know whether or not they should read the text as a "true" account of events. If a story like the one in 1 Kings 21 is a prophetic narrative, it probably does not record every detail of the actual historical events, but gives a prophetic *perception* of these events. In that case the exegete must first try and determine the authentic events and words, and then examine the prophetic (or other) perception reflected by the text.

C. WHAT IS THE ORIGIN OF THIS KIND OF EXEGESIS?

1. Background: church dogma and scientific historiography

7.24 Before the advent of historical-critical exegesis theologians regarded the Bible more or less as a book of unsystematised *dogmas*. It was also considered to be of divine rather than human origin. Consequently the framework of biblical interpretation was not so much the historical circumstances and time of origin of the Bible, but the dogma of the church Thus at that time the Bible was used mainly to affirm the doctrines of the church

7.25 Roughly from the Reformation onwards there was a growing insistence that the Bible should be interpreted in terms of *its own background*. However, if one needed to be acquainted with the historical background to a text in order to interpret it correctly, one had to be conversant both with history generally and with the particular history of the biblical texts.

7.26 By the nineteenth century exegetes were so impressed by the need for *historical* scriptural exegesis that they turned to historians to learn how to interpret ancient documents. They discovered that historians evaluate their documents critically. Thus, if one was studying the ninth century before Christ, one had to

- ensure that one's documents date to *that age*;
- evaluate and treat all later documents or glosses to ancient documents differently from the original ones;
- realise that a heroic epic recounts history differently from an archival document, and therefore classify one's documents according to literary genre;
- try to reconstruct the actual events as best one can by considering various arguments; and then
- "feel" the original situation in order to understand what actually happened.

7.27 The historical-critical exegesis which adopted this procedure is a thoroughly *scientific historical* exegetical method and should be used and evaluated accordingly.

2. Why the emphasis on historical exegesis?

7.28 In contrast to earlier exegetes who sought to expound the Bible in terms of church doctrine, historical-critical interpreters had two aims:

- They wanted to uphold the Reformation principle that Scripture *alone* – and not church tradition – should form the basis of our faith. To this end they sought to expound the Bible (to start with, at any rate) without regard to church doctrine, in order to let the text speak *for itself* and in order to understand the *original* words of God in their *original* historical context.

- They were convinced that God revealed himself to *human beings* and in *history*. In view of this, one needed to have the best possible reconstruction of history and the best possible understanding of the human recipients of divine revelation. For, they argued, if contemporary readers could understand the people and the history of those days properly and could "feel" the original situation, they would have access to the original, and hence authentic, revelation of God.

D. STRENGTHS AND WEAKNESSES OF HISTORICAL-CRITICAL EXEGESIS

1. Questionable features of the method

7.29 We can sum up the basic drawbacks of this method as follows:

- The historical-critical emphasis on the historic uniqueness of biblical accounts may open a gulf between the biblical text and the Bible reader. If a text like 1 Kings 19 recounts a ***unique*** historical incident enacted in a ***unique*** cultural environment millennia ago, there is little hope of reopening communication between such a text and a modern reader. Thus God's revelation is, so to speak, locked up in a unique historical period.

- The historical-critical emphasis on the analytical aspect of scriptural exposition may hamper readers' insight into the *relationship* between scriptural passages. That was why exegetes eventually came to pay more attention to the coherence or structure of biblical texts, as you learned in the previous chapter.

- The historical-critical emphasis on "objective" study of biblical documents and the role of cold logic in this process can have various adverse effects:
  - It may sever the subjective bond of faith between the reader and the biblical text.
  - The "sceptical" attitude demanded by the method may make it difficult to surrender oneself wholly to the text.
  - It may create the impression that through sheer intellectual effort a Bible reader can arrive at "unmistakable, objective truth".
  - This in turn may lead to the misconception that dogmatic and political convictions and the reader's socioeconomic circumstances have no real influence or effect on textual interpretation. The illusion of objectivity can obscure the input of human experience in the process of understanding, resulting in irrelevant exegesis.

2. Positive features of the method

7.30 Historical-critical exegesis can contribute greatly to our understanding of the Bible. The benefits may be summed up as follows:

- The emphasis on the meaning of a text *in its own age* largely frees exegesis from the dogmatic framework in which the Bible used to be interpreted, thus allowing it once again to speak for itself. This challenged the church to reflect anew on its doctrine, also – perhaps more particularly – its doctrine concerning Scripture. In the face of all the new information at its disposal, the church had to explain what was meant by such concepts as the "reliability" and "authority" of Scripture, "revelation" and "inspiration". It also had to consider what was the role of human reason in biblical interpretation, and what role the Holy Spirit played. Thus historical criticism made a major contribution to theological thinking generally.

- It affords insight into the various types of literature found in the Bible. The Bible is not just history from beginning to end. It is a book in which various literary genres were used to describe and sing the greatness of God and his concern with human beings. Each of these literary genres has to be expounded appropriately.

- It affords insight into biblical times and particularly into the growth process that the biblical texts underwent – as our illustrations indicate. The Bible did not simply drop from the sky. It is the product of centuries of human striving and divine revelation, so that the text we have today reflects the religious history of many ages. Historical-critical exegesis can help us to disclose that history which lies hidden behind the structure of the present text.

7.31 In the text we have taken as our example it appears that believers were perplexed by a problem: why was Ahab, who had abused his power at the expense of an innocent subject, not punished according to the prophet's oracle? After all, the oracle was a judgment from *God*. Does it mean that God is unjust? Does he not carry out what he says he will do?

7.32 As history progressed, different generations gave their answers to the question. The first generation pointed out that Ahab eventually repented and was not punished for that reason. A second generation pointed out that Jezebel, the real instigator, was in fact punished for her wickedness. And a third generation pointed out that Ahab's descendants, who followed him in his unjust ways, were also punished. Thus the text tells us: God sees injustice and oppression and he acts against them – as in the case of Jezebel and Ahab's descendants – *unless*, like Ahab, the oppressor repents.

8

What does God's word refer to? Historical-grammatical exegesis

EBEN SCHEFFLER

A. WHAT IS HISTORICAL-GRAMMATICAL EXEGESIS?

8.1 In this book we are in a sense tunnelling back into the history of exegesis from our vantage point in the present. The previous chapter introduced you to historical-critical exegesis. Although historical-grammatical exegesis is treated in this, a subsequent chapter, it should be noted that in actual fact it is the precursor of historical criticism. Historical-grammatical exegesis is an offshoot of the sixteenth century Reformation and, despite the rise of historical criticism, which it triggered, it still has its adherents today. While it has a lot in common with historical criticism, there are many differences. Consequently a comparison with historical criticism would deepen our understanding of this kind of exegesis.

8.2 The historical-grammatical method is sometimes called the *grammatical-historical*, the *historical-philological*, and even the *historical-literal* method. Taken together, these names give one some idea of what the method is about. The following are some of its salient features:

8.3 (i) Historical-grammatical exegesis seeks to interpret the text *historically*, accepting it at face value as referring to *actual* events in history. Unless a text contains definite signs that it should be interpreted differently (e.g. as fable, cf. Jdg 9:8–20), it is taken to represent the genre of historiography.

8.4 (ii) Because the entire biblical text is regarded as historiography, *literary form* or *genre* receives little attention. Thus, contrary to historical-criticism (e.g. Würthwein 1984:248), historical grammarians would not classify the story of Naboth's vineyard as a *novelette* of which the author of the text was a co-creator, since they would take it to represent an actual incident in the life of king Ahab.

8.5 (iii) It follows that the text has to be expounded in terms of its contemporary *background*. Any information that may help to clarify the text is considered important. Consequently historical grammarians are keenly interested in the geography and archaeology of Palestine.

8.6 (iv) A historical interpretation implies that the text is seen as a *unit*, written at a particular time by a single author; it does not have the long history of origin that historical criticism attributes to it. Where there are flagrant discrepancies or contradictions in a text (e.g. concerning the place where Ahab died), historical grammarians do not discern various 'sources' from which the text originated; they would rather try to harmonise the facts. The famous Reformer John Calvin, who favoured this kind of exegesis, specifically referred to his commentaries on the Pentateuch and the Gospels as *harmonies*. Although these exegetes were much concerned with history, their historical method was designed to uphold the historicity of the text rather than to question it.

8.7 (v) Historical-grammatical exegesis is strongly opposed to *allegorical interpretation* that seeks to expose a so-called deeper spiritual meaning, thus assigning the elements of the narrative purely symbolic value (e.g. Ahab as sinful man; Jezebel as temptress or Satan; Naboth as the righteous man or the good Christian). The Reformer Martin Luther referred to such a treatment of the text as monkey tricks (*Affenspiel*). Despite their vehement reaction against allegorical interpretation, historical grammarians could not rout it out completely. But historical criticism took over and retained the historical grammarians' aversion to allegory.

8.8 (vi) The second component of the designation of this method – grammatical or philological – also relates to the historical aspect: because a text is a faithful rendering of actual events, it is imperative that one is fully conversant with the language and grammar in order to understand the text and come closer to the events recorded in it.

8.9 Exponents of this method therefore insist that the text has to be interpreted from the original languages (Hebrew and Aramaic in the case of the Old Testament). Their practical exegesis was much concerned with words, their meanings and grammatical context in a sentence. The emphasis was on words as determinants of the meaning of a sentence; the sentence was not the basic point of departure (as it is in text-immanent analysis, see ch 6). Consequently the focus was very much on the 'original' meanings of words (etymology).

8.10 (vii) What is less directly discernible in the term 'historical-grammatical' is the fact that *dogmatic premises* or *religious presuppositions* play a major role in this kind of exegesis. This stems from the assumption that the Bible, being the *word of God*, is inspired and therefore authoritative.

8.11 (viii) These religious presuppositions not only account for the heavy emphasis on the *historicity* of the text already referred to above; methodologically, they also result in *Scripture being compared with Scripture*. When faced with an obscure passage, historical grammarians will refer to another passage which, in their view, clarifies the problem. They may even cite the New Testament to help expound Old Testament passages. Thus the accent is on the unity, not only of individual sections of the text (e.g. 1 Ki 21:1–29), but of the Bible as a whole.

8.12 (ix) It follows that, although historical grammarians inquire into the meaning of a text in terms of its own times, they do not assume such a tremendous gulf between its original meaning and what it means to us today. The text is expounded as if it had a *universal meaning* which, being God's word, is true for all times and all situations. As was seen in the previous chapter, historical criticism found this point of view problematic.

8.13 We shall now look more deeply into historical-grammatical exegesis by examining how these exegetes go about their task. To this end we scrutinise a commentary on Kings. We then try to clarify the method further by considering its origins. Finally we try and determine the pros and cons of this method of biblical exposition.

B. THE METHOD OF HISTORICAL-GRAMMATICAL EXEGESIS: AN EXAMPLE

8.14 It is intriguing that the Reformers Luther and Calvin left no commentaries on the two books of Kings. Luther, who could be quite scathing about certain biblical books, actually stated his reasons for this omission. He said that the books of Kings were only concerned with the succession of Jewish kings and that anyone who preached from these books would have to proclaim violence! Possibly the story of Naboth's vineyard helped him to arrive at this opinion. In all events, he clearly read the books of Kings without giving them 'Christian status' by way of allegorising or probing for deeper symbolic meanings. But Luther was alone in his criticism of the books of Kings. Later historical grammarians insisted on the inspired character of every biblical book, including 1 Kings.

8.15 Although it is hard to tell how early historical grammarians would have expounded 1 Kings 21, we have noted that the method is still in use today. Indeed, until the rise of historical criticism in the nineteenth century, it was the most widely used exegetical method. For a closer look at the method in practice we now turn to a nineteenth century commentary on Kings – that of C.F. Keil ([1868] 1950:223–226). We shall cite excerpts from the text and then point out how the method was used. Because the commentary largely follows the text of 1 Kings, we shall not reproduce the English version of chapter 21 as was done in the previous chapter. It may be a good idea, however, to keep the RSV handy. The English equivalents of Hebrew words (which, in the nature of the method, crop up frequently in the commentary) appear in parenthesis.

1. Summary of 1 Kings 21

8.16 Chapter 21: Ahab's robbery and murder of Naboth

> *After these events Ahab was seized with such a desire for a vineyard which was situated near his palace at Jezreel, that when Naboth, the owner of the vineyard, refused to part with his paternal inheritance, he became thoroughly dejected, until his wife Jezebel paved the way for the forcible seizure of the desired possession by the shameful execution of Naboth (v. 1–15). But when Ahab was preparing to take possession of the vineyard, Elijah came to meet him with the announcement, that both he and his wife would be visited by the Lord with a bloody death for this murder and robbery, and that his idolatry would be punished with the extermination of all his house (v. 16–26). Ahab was so affected by this, that he humbled himself before God; whereupon the Lord told Elijah, that the threatened judgment should not burst upon his house till after Ahab's death (v. 27–29).*

8.17 The very heading of Keil's commentary indicates that he concurs with the text's judgment of Ahab's actions. A more neutral heading would have been, 'Naboth killed on Jezebel's orders'. But historical grammarians never dissociate themselves from value-judgments in the text. If the text calls the execution of Naboth murder, the historical-grammarian accepts this and even uses it as a heading in his 'scientific' commentary.

8.18 Note also that Keil's exposition starts with a summary of the entire chapter. According to this summary the events described follow in logical sequence and the chapter constitutes a definite unit. In the previous chapter we saw that historical critics disagree as to whether or not chapter 21 should follow directly after chapter 19. Historical grammarians do not consider this possibility. Consequently Keil's commentary on this section starts with 'After these events' – that is, the events described in chapter 20, which Keil in fact commented on in that sequence. Verses 17–19 in particular – which historical critics regard as late insertions – are treated as integral to chapter 21. It is evident that historical-grammatical exegesis accepts the text at face value.

2. 1 Kings 21:1–2

8.19 *Ahab wanted to obtain possession of the vineyard of Naboth, which was in Jezreel (... ['aser, which] refers to ... [kerem, vineyard]), near the palace of the king, either in exchange for another vineyard or for money, that he might make a vegetable garden of it. From the fact that Ahab is called king of Samaria we may infer that Jezreel, the present Zerin (see at Jos. 19:18), was only a summer residence of the king.*

8.20 The references to the Hebrew words *'aser* and *kerem* reveal the *linguistic* concern of historical-grammatical exegesis. To Keil it is important that the pronoun 'which' should refer to 'vineyard', since the text would only make historical sense if Naboth's vineyard was actually situated in Jezreel. The word could, however, also be rendered as 'who', in which case it would relate to Naboth himself. Literally, according to the specific sequence of the words, the Hebrew reads: '*There was a vineyard for Naboth the Jezreelite which/who was in Jezreel adjoining the palace of Ahab king of Samaria.*' Thus it is possible that Naboth's vineyard was in Samaria, a possibility which Keil excludes. The Greek version (the Septuagint) omits the words 'which was in Jezreel', and the Greek translation may have been made from an earlier Hebrew text than the one we have today. Since historical-grammatical exegesis concentrates on the *Hebrew* text as being the original, the possibility that these words may have been inserted later is not considered.

8.21 Keil's comments on Jezreel also reveal his concern with the *historical background* to the text. He provides the modern Arabic name for Jezreel, as well as a reference to another commentary of his (on Joshua) where the reader can learn more about Jezreel. Finally he mentions that Ahab had a summer palace in Jezreel. This information does not derive from the text, but represents a historical inference made by the exegete in order to render the story factually consistent. Not that the inference is necessarily wrong (although it could equally well have been a winter palace). The point is that historical-grammatical exegesis requires the information in the text to be historically correct and internally consistent, and that is why such matters are commented upon.

3. 1 Kings 21:3

8.22 *Naboth refused to part with the vineyard, because it was the inheritance of his fathers, that is to say, on religious grounds (... [hâlîlâ lî meyhwh, the Lord forbid]), because the sale of a paternal inheritance was forbidden in the law (Lv. 25:23–28; Nm. 36:7 sqq.). He was therefore not merely at liberty as a personal right to refuse the king's proposal, but bound by the commandment of God.*

8.23 Once again Keil refers to the *Hebrew source text* to substantiate his argument that Naboth's reasons for refusing to sell his vineyard were religious ones. In the previous chapter we saw that Gray (1970) explains Naboth's attitude as 'the solidarity of the family among the Palestinian peasants' and 'Naboth's status as a *freeman*'. This explanation does not, of course, exclude a religious motive, but it should be noted that Keil seeks to account for Naboth's action primarily on *religious* grounds. By so doing Keil wants to remove any suspicion in the reader's mind that Naboth may have been selfish (after all, Ahab had offered a fair price, and he was the king to boot). This may relate to Keil's perception of the Bible as the word of God: it would be incongruous to have a 'virtuous' character like Naboth act unreasonably while an 'evil' character like Ahab behaves reasonably. Consequently arguments are adduced to give Naboth's conduct a religious motivation, for in that case he must be *right*. Accordingly Keil does not merely cite the expression 'The Lord forbid' from the Hebrew text, but refers to other biblical passages which would justify Naboth's behaviour. Here we have a typical feature of historical-grammatical exegesis: *the comparison of Scripture with Scripture.*

4. 1 Kings 21:4

8.24 *Instead of respecting this tender feeling of shrinking from the transgression of the law and desisting from his coveting, Ahab went home, i.e. to Samaria (cf. v. 8), sullen and morose (... [sar wezâref, bitter and angry] as in ch 20:43), lay down upon his bed, turned his face (viz. to the wall; cf. 2 Ki 20:2) ... and did not eat. This childish mode of giving expression to his displeasure at Naboth's refusal to comply with his wish, shows very clearly that Ahab was a man sold under sin (v. 20), who only wanted the requisite energy to display the wickedness of his heart in action.*

8.25 The commentary on verse 4 clearly illustrates how the *Hebrew source text* is used, in conjunction with *other scriptural passages*, to clarify the text under discussion. The text is also clarified *historically* by specifying that Ahab went home '*to Samaria*'. The commentator's *religious presuppositions* are again clearly in evidence in this section. Naboth's refusal is described as 'tender feeling of shrinking from the transgression of the law', as opposed to Ahab's anger, which is seen as a sinful expression of 'the wickedness of his heart'. The commentator does not consider the possibility that at least at this stage Ahab was still respecting Naboth's rights. Instead Elijah's words in verse 20 (that Ahab had sold himself in order to do what is wrong in the eyes of the Lord) are invoked here, at the beginning of the story, to interpret his actions. It makes one wonder whether Keil's characterisation of Ahab as 'a man sold under sin' is not expressive of some sort of covert allegorisation. Naboth, on the other hand, is the perfect upright man, with his 'tender feeling of shrinking from the transgression of the law'.

5. 1 Kings 21:5–7

8.26 *When Jezebel learned the cause of Ahab's ill-humour, she said to him, 'Thou, dost thou now exercise royal authority over Israel?' ... ('attâh, you) is placed first for the sake of emphasis, and the sentence is to be taken as an ironical question, as it has been by the LXX. 'I (if thou hast not courage enought to act) will procure thee the vineyard of Naboth the Jezreelite'.*

8.27 This comment highlights the *linguistic* concern of the exegete. Not only is the Hebrew text cited, but attention is drawn to the position of a word in a sentence, and we are told that the sentence has to be interpreted *ironically* (i.e. as implying the opposite of what it says). In the process Ahab is again depicted unflatteringly, reflecting the exegete's *religious presuppositions.*

6. 1 Kings 21:8–10

8.28 *The shameless woman then wrote a letter in the name of Ahab, sealed it below with the royal seal, which probably bore the king's signature and was stamped upon the writing instead of signing the name, as is done at the present day among Arabs, Turks, and Persians ... to give it the character of a royal command (cf. Es 18:13, Dn 16:17), and sent this letter ... to the elders and nobles of his town (i.e. the members of the magistracy, Dt 16:18), who lived near Naboth, and therefore had an opportunity to watch his way of life, and appeared to be the most suitable persons to institute the charge that was to be brought against him. The letter ran thus: 'Proclaim a fast ...' Jezebel ordered the fasting for a sign, as though some public crime or heavy load of guilt rested upon the city, for which it was necessary that it should humble itself before God (1 Sm 17:6). The intention was, that at the very outset the appearance of justice should be given to the legal process about to be instituted in the eyes of all the citizens, and the stamp of veracity impressed upon the crime of which Naboth was to be accused ... To preserve the appearance of justice, two witnesses were appointed, according to the law in Dt 17:6, 7, 19:15, Nm 35:30; but worthless men, as at the trial of Jesus (Mat 26:60) ... (berek 'elohîm), to bless God, i.e. to bid Him farewell, to dismiss Him, as in Job 2:9, [is] equivalent to blaspheming God. God and king are mentioned together, like God and prince in Ex 12:27, to make it possible to accuse Naboth of transgressing this law, and to put him to death as a blasphemer of God, according to Dt 13:11 and 17:5, where the punishment of stoning is awarded to idolatry as a practical denial of God. Blaspheming the king is not to be taken as a second crime to be added to the blasphemy of God; but blaspheming the king, as the visible representative of God, was eo ipso (in itself) also blaspheming God.*

8.29 The commentator explains the use of the royal seal, the background information serving as *historical clarification* of the text. Not only does he cite the modern use of seals in order to explain the usage of those days, but he also refers to Esther 8:13 and Daniel 6:17 – all this without once considering that the use of seals may have changed from Ahab's days to those of Esther and Daniel (not to mention our own!). *Thus Scripture is invoked to expound Scripture.* In similar fashion the elders and notables are equated with the judges and officers mentioned in Deuteronomy 16:18. The reference to the fast followed by the people's confession at Mizpah (1 Sm 7:6) implies that the Jezreelites too had a great sin to confess; and the appointment of *two* witnesses is clarified in terms of Mosaic law. Most anachronistic of all is the reference to the *false witnesses* in Matthew 26:60, which is tantamount to comparing Naboth's trial with that of Christ. Not only is it a correlation of texts separated by many centuries, but the covertly allegorical interpretation of Naboth as the perfect upright man (analogous to Jesus) is probably most pronounced at this point. Job 2:9, Exodus 22:27 and Deuteronomy 13:11 and 17:5 are used equally uncritically to expound this text from 1 Kings 21.

8.30 With regard to the cursing of the king, Keil is at pains to make the point that Naboth's crime was of a *religious* nature (again arguing his case by comparing Scripture with Scripture). Again this emphasis on the religious dimension is expressive of the *religious framework* in which Keil interprets the text: the false accusation against Naboth is all the more scandalous when he – the perfect upright pious man – is charged with, of all crimes, blasphemy.

7. 1 Kings 21:11–13

8.31 *The elders of Jezreel executed this command without delay; a striking proof both of deep moral corruption and of slavish fear of the tyranny of the ruthless queen.*

8.32 The expressions 'deep moral corruption', 'slavish fear' and 'ruthless queen' (which do not appear in the text) once more reveal the exegete's *religious presuppositions.*

8. 1 Kings 21:14–15

8.33 *When the report of Naboth's execution was brought to her, she called upon Ahab to take possession of his vineyard (... [res = ras, take possession of], Dt 2:24). As Naboth's sons were put to death at the same time, according to 2 Kings 9:26, the king was able to confiscate his property; not, indeed, on any rule laid down in Mosaic law, but according to a principle involved in the very idea of high treason. Since, for example, in the case of blasphemy the property of the criminal was forfeited to the Lord as cherrem (Dt 113:16), the property of traitors was regarded as forfeited to the king.*

8.34 The *Hebrew source text* features once again (*res, herêm*); *Scripture is compared with Scripture* (Dt 2:24; 2 Ki 9:26; Dt 13:16); and the text is made *historically consistent* (e.g. information about the death of the two sons is incorporated from 2 Ki 9:26). An interesting feature is that, when it comes to the confiscation, Keil is less ready to assume a close link between the king and God than in the commentary on verses 8–10 above. To be sure, Ahab is entitled to the vineyard, but according to Keil this 'right' has no legal basis and is therefore, properly speaking, 'wrong'. The exegete's *religious presupposition* is again in evidence: as the arch-villain of the piece, Ahab is forever in the wrong.

9. 1 Kings 21:16–19

8.35 *But when Ahab went down to Jezreel to take possession of the vineyard of Naboth, Elijah came to meet him by the command of God, with the word of the Lord, 'Hast thou murdered and also taken possession?' The question served to sharpen his conscience, since Ahab was obliged to admit the fact. ...* (*asêr besomerôn, who is in Samaria) means 'who lives at Samaria', for when Elijah came to meet him, Ahab was in Jezreel. Elijah then said to him still further: 'Thus saith the Lord: In the place where the dogs have licked the blood of Naboth, will they also lick thine, yea, thy blood.' ... This threat was only so far fulfilled upon Ahab, from the compassion of God, and in consequence of his humbling himself under the divine judgment (v. 27–29), that dogs licked his blood at Samaria when the carriage was washed in which he had died (ch 22:38); but it was literally fulfilled in the case of his son Joram, whose corpse was cast into Naboth's piece of ground (2 Ki 9:25, 26).*

8.36 In his commentary on verses 16–19 Keil again quotes the *Hebrew*. His point is that Ahab merely *lived* in Samaria and that he was not there when he took possession of Naboth's vineyard. The commentator is determined to render the information in the text consistent. By quoting the Hebrew he seeks to clear up any misconception the reader may have (e.g. that Naboth's vineyard actually adjoined Ahab's palace in Samaria).

8.37 After quoting Elijah's prophecy, Keil is at once obliged to comment on the fact that this very oracle remained unfulfilled. Ahab's blood was not licked on Naboth's land (1 Ki 22:38), so that according to the text of the book of Kings it was only partially fulfilled. Historical criticism tends to make much of such discrepancies, whereas historical grammarians are more inclined to try and salvage the *historicity* of the reported events. A comparison of the way these two exegetical methods treat the final verses of 1 Kings 21 clearly illustrates how they differ in respect of what should be considered 'historical'. Historical criticism often looks for a solution by discerning other 'sources' behind the text, whereas historical-grammatical exegesis strives to play down the discrepancies and harmonise the text. Since Jehoram (Ahab's son) was in fact thrown on Naboth's land (2 Ki 9:25–26), Keil considers the oracle to have been literally fulfilled in his case.

10. 1 Kings 21:20–24

8.38 *Ahab answered, 'Hast thou found me (met with me), O mine enemy?' (not, hast thou ever found me thine enemy? – Vulgate Luther) i.e. dost thou come to meet me again, mine enemy? He calls Elijah his enemy, to take the sting from the prophet's threat as an utterance caused by personal enmity ... [hitmakker la'asôt hâr'a], to sell one's self to do evil, i.e. to give one's self to evil so as to have no will of one's own, to make one's self the slave of evil (cf. v. 25, 2 Ki 17:17). The consequences of this is ... (peprasthai hupo tèn hamartian, to be sold under sin; Rom 7:14), sin exercising unlimited power over the man who gives himself up to it as a slave.*

8.39 Keil criticises both the Vulgate (the Latin version of the Bible) and Luther's translation in order to make his point that Ahab is trying to denigrate Elijah's prophecy. But there is no actual textual evidence to warrant Keil's interpretation that Ahab regarded Elijah's prophecy against him as an expression of personal enmity. It would almost seem as if Keil has identified with the text's portrayal of Ahab as the villain of the piece, to the extent that he reads evil intentions into his words and actions even where there are none. This is because of the historical grammarian's conception of the text as the *word of God* which must be believed. Historical critics would be more neutral towards value-judgments in the text and would identify them explicitly as reflecting the perspective of the redactor, author or narrator.

8.40 In his commentary on the text Keil shows that he used not just the *Hebrew* and *Latin* versions, but also the Greek New Testament. The portrayal of Ahab as the arch-villain reaches a climax when Keil cites Romans 7:14 to pinpoint the key characteristic of sin. In the process *Scripture is again compared with Scripture*, overlooking the centuries separating the respective passages. Because historical grammarians regard the Bible as God's word and therefore as a unit, they are able to move easily from one biblical book to another. From their point of view Paul's perspective on sin is *universal* and hence equally applicable to Ahab. The perception of Ahab as the prototypical sinner again smacks of allegorical exposition. Although historical grammarians were vehemently opposed to the allegorical tradition, it was their matrix and they had difficulty extricating themselves from it.

11. 1 Kings 21:25–26

8.41 *Verses 25 and 26 contain a reflection on the part of the historian concerning Ahab's ungodly conduct, whereby he brought such an ignominious end upon himself and his house.*

8.42 The previous chapter gave the historical-critical interpretation of verses 25–26 as deriving from what is known as the Deuteronomic redactor. According to this view, verses 25–26 did not form part of the original chapter but were inserted later. Keil, on the other hand, considers them to be the historian's epilogue. 'The historian' clearly refers to the putative historian who wrote not merely the whole of this chapter, but the entire book. No sources or late insertions are identified as in historical criticism. The term 'historian' moreover indicates that the text should be treated as *history*. To Keil the chapter represents a unit and the oracles pronounced in it correspond with 'historical fact'.

12. 1 Kings 21:27–29

8.43 *This terrible threat made such an impression upon Ahab, that he felt deep remorse, and for a time at least was sincerely penitent. Rending the clothes, putting on the mourning garment of hair (... [saq]), and fasting, are frequently mentioned as external signs of humiliation before God or of deep mourning on account of sin ... (yehallêk 'at), he walked about lightly (slowly), like one in deep trouble. This repentance was neither hypocritical, nor purely external; but it was sincere even if it was not lasting and produced no real conversion. For the Lord Himself acknowledged it to be humiliation before Him (v. 29), and said to Elijah, that because of it He would not bring the threatened calamity upon Ahab's house in his own lifetime, but only in the days of his son ... If it had been a genuine conversion, Ahab would have tried to make some form of restitution for the wrong he had committed [last sentence translated from German original].*

8.44 Keil gives a *historical explanation* of mourning customs in ancient Israel. On these grounds, as well as Ahab's walking about lightly/slowly (note the use of the *Hebrew* version) and the Lord's reaction, he concludes that Ahab's remorse was genuine. Nevertheless, Keil points out that it 'produced no real conversion', since Ahab had not made restitution. Here Keil is clearly allowing his own *dogmatic presuppositions* about repentance (e.g. in the sense that Zaccheus had to make restitution, Lk

19:8) to colour his interpretation of the text. Possibly it is also in order to maintain his view of Ahab as the arch-sinner.

8.45 Bearing in mind the insights of historical criticism, which came after historical-grammatical exegesis, it is interesting to compare their respective interpretations of verses 27–29 (see ch 7). According to historical-grammatical exegesis the *historical information* in the text is *correct:* Ahab truly repented; his repentance accords well with the events described in the remainder of the chapter (and in the books of Kings as a whole). Thus the text constitutes a *unit*.

8.46 Historical criticism, on the other hand, does not regard the chapter as a unit but sees verses 27–29 as an insertion by a *later redactor* who was trying to explain why Elijah's oracle against Ahab was not literally fulfilled. Thus the *genuineness* of Ahab's repentance is also at issue, since it is not mentioned in the older part of the text. If Ahab had truly repented, why only partial clemency? Even if his remorse was only partial, would the harsh judgment in verse 25 still have applied to him? Unlike historical grammarians, historical critics do not accept the text at face value but in fact *question* its 'historical assumptions'.

8.47 This discussion of Keil's commentary indicates that it displays the main features of historical-grammatical exegesis to a greater or lesser extent. To sum up, then: historical-grammatical exegesis typically (i) accepts the *historicity* of the narrated events at face value; (ii) does not reflect very deeply on the *literary form* of the text; (iii) expounds the text in terms of the *historical context* of that age; (iv) accepts the *unity* of the text; (v) rejects *allegory* while still retaining covert vestiges of it; (vi) focuses on *philological* and stylistic features, especially the *source language*, of the text; (vii) works with certain *religious presuppositions*; (viii) compares *Scripture with Scripture* ; and (ix) assumes that the text *communicates directly* with modern readers.

C. WHERE DID THIS KIND OF EXEGESIS ORIGINATE?

8.48 During the first five centuries of the Christian era two opposing exegetical schools emerged in Alexandria and Antioch The Alexandrian school (which included the church father Origen) was influenced by Plato's philosophy and propounded *allegorical* exegesis. The Antiochian school (which included Diodore, Theodore and Chrysostom) was influenced by Aristotelian philosophy and favoured a *historical* and *typological* approach (e.g., Old Testament events and characters were interpreted as 'types' prefiguring Christ). It would seem, then, that historical-grammatical exegesis originated from the Antiochian school. Because of certain decisions made by the Council of Constantinople (A.D. 553), the Alexandrian school became the dominant one, however, and during the Middle Ages the church moreover dictated how the Bible should be expounded.

8.49 Exegesis in the Middle Ages (see ch 9) was characterised by the *fourfold meaning of Scripture* (literal, allegorical, moral or tropological and anagogic). From the time of Cassian (c. 435) onwards students of exegesis had to memorise the following rhyme:

8.50 *littera gesta docet* (the literal tells what happened)

quid credas allegoria	(the allegorical tells you what to believe)
moralis quid agas	(the moral, what to do)
quo tendas anagogia	(the anagogic, what to strive for)

8.51 Each text contained all four of these 'meanings' and the reader had to trace all of them in every passage. While this type of exegesis still maintained a certain balance between literal and figurative interpretation, the allegorical component eventually became dominant, with the result that the historical dimension was relegated to the background. In addition allegory was used in such a way that it increasingly interpreted the message of the text according to the church's expectations (see ch. 9).

8.52 With the European Renaissance and the rise of humanism in the fifteenth century interest in the civilisations of ancient Rome and Greek revived and the classical languages were studied once more. *"Ad fontes"* (back to the sources) became the maxim. Everything, including the authority of the church, was subjected to the critical scrutiny of human reason. The influence of the Renaissance was also felt in the ecclesiastic sphere where it contributed greatly to the Reformation, which called into question the authority of the Roman Catholic Church

8.53 The Reformation radically influenced the method of biblical interpretation and most of the features of historical-grammatical exegesis can be traced to this impact. The Reformers shared the humanist interest in *history*, so that the emphasis was once more on *historical exegesis*. There was a vehement reaction against *allegorical* exegesis, since this was one of the ways in which the church controlled people's ideas about the Bible.

8.54 The pope's and the church's prerogative to decide what constituted correct biblical interpretation was called into question. Church tradition was no longer the criterion: the Bible itself became the supreme norm. The Reformation had three axioms: *sola scriptura, sola fide* and *sola gratia* (by Scripture alone, by faith alone and by grace alone). These tenets were applied to biblical exposition as well. Having become the supreme norm, the Bible was the criterion for its own exegesis – hence the principle that Scripture had to be expounded by Scripture (*sacra scriptura sui ipsius interpres est*, holy Scripture is its own expositor). Problematic passages had to be interpreted with references to less obscure ones. The principle of by faith alone, in turn, gave rise to the axiom of *omnes intellectus ac expositio scripturae sit analogia fidei* (all understanding and interpretation of Scripture should accord with the faith). As was apparent in the discussion of Keil's commentary, the religious presuppositions of the historical grammarians consciously affected their exegesis.

8.55 In regard to the *philological* or *grammatical* component of their method, too, the Reformers were children of their age. As we have seen, the humanists set great store by the study of classical languages and Desiderius Erasmus (a humanist who remained in the Catholic fold) insisted that the Bible had to be studied in its *original languages*. Calvin and Luther agreed with him, and Luther personally translated the Bible into German. The aim was not to stop at the Hebrew or Greek texts, but to make these accessible to lay readers. This also accounts for the emphasis on the universal meaning of the ancient text for the present day. Among Jewish exegetes, too, there was a resurgence of interest in the Hebrew Old Testament and many historical grammarians were taught Hebrew at these schools. The Jewish scholars also favoured a historical approach to Old Testament exegesis and they influenced the historical grammarians in this respect.

8.56 Historical-grammatical exegesis was the precursor of historical-critical exegesis as regards both the historical and the philological aspects. During the Enlightenment in the seventeenth century, however, human reason was the point of departure and the historical component was reappraised. Faith and Scripture were no longer the criteria for testing the results of scriptural exegesis. The texts were read more critically in terms of their origins, literary form and function in their own age (*Sitz im Leben*, real-life situation).

8.57 A feature of historical criticism was that the text was no longer accepted at face value. This provoked fierce reaction from historical grammarians, who insisted on the 'literal' interpretation of the text as describing actual history. From this arose what is known as *historical-literal* exegesis, popular mainly among fundamentalists with their accent on the infallibility of the Bible. It should be noted that, despite considerable correspondence between the premises of historical-grammatical and historical-literal exegesis, there is a marked difference in focus. The Reformers readily acknowledged 'errors' in the Bible – Luther was extremely critical of biblical books which, in his view, did not proclaim Christ properly (e.g. the books of the Kings!). In addition the Reformers saw 'historical' as referring to the manifest meaning of a text in its historical context, whereas the whole point of historical-literal exegesis is that the events described in the text happened exactly like that (e.g. the serpent in Gn 3 actually spoke). Other elements of their method (e.g. the insistence on original languages and the use of archaeological data) mostly had to serve this purpose.

8.58 Thus historical-grammatical exegesis was the progenitor of two other methods: historical-literal and historical-critical exegesis. All three of these approaches are still used by modern exegetes in their attempt to understand the Bible. Below is a diagram depicting the historical development of historical-grammatical exegesis.

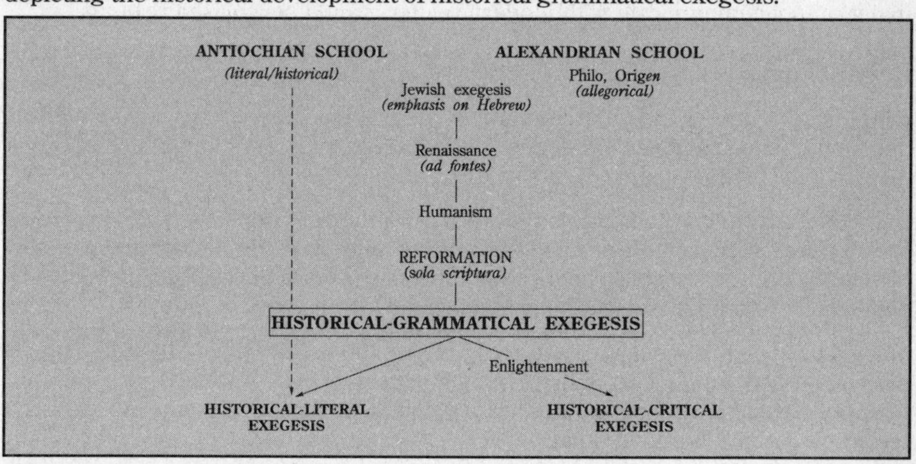

Development of the historical-grammatical method

D. STRENGTHS AND WEAKNESSES OF HISTORICAL-GRAMMATICAL EXEGESIS

1. Strengths

8.59 The historical grammarians' opposition to *allegorising* is a positive feature. Although the claim that allegory deals with allegedly 'deeper spiritual' levels of a text may sound laudable, such an approach can lead exegetes to link anything they consider important to the text. Thus the text becomes no more than a vehicle for their subjective notions (however devout) and *exposition* proper goes by the board.

8.60 The accent on the *historical* aspect of exegesis should also be regarded as a positive feature, with certain reservations. It includes reading the text within its original historical context and clarifying it by means of background information.

8.61 The greatest contribution of historical-grammatical exegesis was undoubtedly its emphasis on the *original languages* and the *philological* and *stylistic* detail of a text. This has the advantage that exegesis can be verified to a considerable extent – after all, translations are susceptible to all manner of subjective interpretation. It also paved the way for the Bible to be translated into many languages and ensured that all translations could be tested against the source language.

8.62 Because historical grammarians believed the Bible to be God's word, they had tremendous reverence and love for the text and studied it with great devotion. Their method of expounding *Scripture in terms of Scripture* meant that they were extremely erudite in respect of all the biblical texts.

8.63 Despite the hermeneutic problems associated with reading the text with a view to its *universal meaning,* such a reading must be rated positively as being in accord with the intentions of the biblical authors. Although the first biblical authors wrote their books primarily with a view to their original audiences, they were simultaneously trying to communicate universal religious truths which (to their minds, at any rate) would speak to all generations. Thus to read the text on the presupposition that it cannot communicate with modern readers would be a biased reading.

2. Weaknesses

8.64 Despite the historical grammarians' aversion to *allegorising,* certain *traits* of this kind of exposition remain noticeable in their work. It could be a result of their need to have the text communicate at any cost.

8.65 The accent on the Bible as the word of God meant that *historical problems* in the text were often disregarded and that its historicity was accepted at face value simply because of the exegete's conception of what the word of God is. This has to be deprecated, which historical criticism in fact did.

8.66 The sometimes exaggerated emphasis on the universality of the message results in *forced* readings, that is, discerning things in the text of which there is no real textual evidence. The many ages of history that have elapsed since the text was written are not always borne in mind.

8.67 Related to this is the major role played by *dogmatic premises* in the exposition of the text, which in fact implies that a nonbeliever is unable to understand or interpret it. (The question of how these nonbelievers were ever to become believers did not seem to trouble the historical grammarians unduly.)

8.68 Despite the erudition that resulted from the principle of *Scripture being its own expositor*, there are grave hazards attached to such an approach Historical grammarians were not always too discriminating about the times of origin of the various biblical books. As a rule the books were assumed to have originated in the period when the events recorded in them took place, with the result that different parts of the Bible were correlated *anachronistically* – notably the way the New Testament was used to expound Old Testament texts.

8.69 Finally, in terms of the overall theme of this book, it should be pointed out that the historical grammarians, too, were children of *their* age. Religious presuppositions peculiar to their times usually determined the message they found in a text (e.g. the notions of humanity as sinful and of what true conversion implied). In Keil's commentary, for instance, we saw that the problem of wealth and poverty (or oppressors and oppressed) did not feature at all. This was probably because these exegetes were members of the European middle class, and in their society real poverty – the kind that causes people to starve to death – was rare.

9

The Bible speaks in four ways: Bible interpretations during the Middle Ages

CHRISTINA LANDMAN

A. INTRODUCTION

9.1 During the Middle Ages those who were literate spent a great deal of their time reading texts. Most of these people were monks and clerics. Because the contents of documents that have been preserved from the Middle Ages are largely religious, one tends to think of medieval people as being very religious. In reality all one can infer from this is that the literate people of those times were clergy and that, particularly in the early Middle Ages, they set great store by the Bible.

B. A MEDIEVAL VIEW OF WEALTH IN SOCIETY

9.2 A monk living in a monastery had no possessions; neither was he much concerned about wealth and poverty. As long as people, including the king, gave their order land and gold so that the inmates of the monastery could carry on studying the Bible, and as long as people did not grow so wealthy that they could no longer be bothered with the church, the monks did not hold any strong views on wealth and poverty, nor did they write much on the subject. Late medieval commentaries by monks on such scriptural passages as the episode of Nathan and David or the story of Naboth's vineyard relate these events to moral conduct and do not interpret them as a judgment for or against wealth. Those both within the church and outside it who isolated themselves specifically to live a life of poverty either did not write anything or their writings were not preserved.

9.3 From the eleventh and the twelfth century onwards the popes began to free the church from royal domination. Monarchs were naturally not prepared to supply the church's material needs unless they had some say in church affairs. There were also many monks who, unlike the popes, felt that kings had been appointed over the church by God and that the church may – indeed, must – receive land and money from them. In the writings of these monks the theme of wealth crops up frequently, because the wealth of the monasteries was being endangered by the reform policy of the papacy. To substantiate their arguments for ecclesiastic wealth the monks naturally made use of biblical texts. One of these monks was Hugh of Fleury (d. 1120).

9.4 Being a monk, Hugh knew whole tracts of the Bible off by heart, for he was reading or praying passages from it every two hours throughout the day, which was actually one long liturgy. Being a monk, he lived in a monastic culture in which he was presented with a standardised religious life. The standard was laid down in the monastic rule.

9.5 Hugh of Fleury lived in the twelfth century, in an abbey – that is a large monastery – under the Benedictine rule. According to this rule his day started at two in the morning with prayer and Scripture readings, which offices were repeated with variations seven times in the course of the day. This did not mean that Hugh merely read the Bible; he also dwelt on the text imaginatively during the four hours of daily Bible study to which his rule enjoined him. The Old Testament fascinated him particularly, as is evident in his *Tractatus de regia potestate et sacerdotali dignitate* (Treatise on royal power and priestly dignity). In this work Hugh explains his conception of what society ought to be like and what role wealth ought to play in it.

9.6 The following is a paraphrase of the substance of the *Treatise*.

Society, in a nutshell, should be like heaven, Hugh maintains. Heaven has only one head – God the Father. By the same token there should be only one head on earth – the king, who should rule over the church By making just Adam alone, a solitary human being, God indicated that two people cannot rule the earth simultaneously. Later on Moses, as king, was to rule over Aaron, the high priest.

Hugh assigned the following duties to the king. Firstly, the sovereign must preserve society as it is by passing laws, thus preventing it from disintegrating as Israel did before it had a king (Jdg 17:6). The people should obey their king unconditionally; if God gives them a wicked monarch, it is because they deserve it, as may be inferred from Hosea 13:11 and Job 34:30. Secondly, the king has to appoint the clergy to holy orders. He has to see to it that these clergy want for absolutely nothing. Thirdly, the king must assist the poor, as Job claimed to have done (Job 29:15–16). Fourthly, one of the king's cardinal duties was to adorn the sees in his realm with splendid churches, as the monarchs of antiquity had done.

In order to maintain the church's position in society as it had been through the ages – that is, according to Hugh, since Old Testament times – the king had to have the following attributes: He had to value the wise council of the clergy above gold and silver. After all, Joseph's council was worth more to Pharaoh than any amount of money would have been. The king himself should shun luxury and live unpretentiously; yet he must be royal and liberal towards the church A king who disrupts the social order for the sake of gain will, like Nebuchadnezzar, come to a shameful, poverty-stricken end.

The bishop too should see to it that society observes moderation and must not upset the status quo. He must persuade the rich not to trust in their precarious wealth, but to give readily to the church so that they may become rich in good deeds. Once the bishop has thus persuaded society to be moderate and generous, he should reward the people by dispensing religion bounteously, filling them with banquets of the word of God.

A bad bishop is one who acquires his see by means of money, who thinks that he can teach God's law without being devout himself. The Holy Spirit alone can make a man a bishop, and the Spirit does so free of charge. What a bishop is, he is by virtue of God's free gift. A fool, says Job – and he is referring to foolish bishops – is one who lives solely for enjoyment and wealth.

A bishop may excommunicate a king who does not observe the laws of society. However, the bishop must remember that Elijah did not personally punish Jezebel for her excesses, but waited for God to do so. In any case the bishop should receive the king back into the church after due repentance, as Nathan acquitted David after he had publicly confessed his sin. A king must accept that the bishop will address him as his inferior. After all, Balaam had his misconceptions corrected by the dumb beast that he usually rode (Nm 22:23–33).

Hugh holds that one can trace the history of the church, and especially the way in which the crown has endowed the church with riches, from the days of Moses. As king, Moses served the church by building a tabernacle in the wilderness. He also disciplined society by subjecting it to God's commandments. After him Joshua led the people across the Jordan into the promised land where they could once more lead an ordinary life. Saul was a good monarch to begin with, expanding God's kingdom by warfare. But he became bad when he claimed personal credit for these successes; as a result God was angry with Saul. David too was a good king who, apart from one or two misdemeanours, submitted to the laws of society. His son Solomon excelled particularly when he built the Lord his God a temple from imperishable wood and precious stones – an image of holy mother church Solomon also composed a song in which, in a bridal hymn, he celebrated Christ's mystical union with the church Only when Solomon grew conceited about all his treasures and glory did God become angry with him and incited Jeroboam against him.

Thus, says Hugh, the history of the Old Testament bears witness to the way in which illustrious monarchs, inspired by God, enriched the church according to their means. Not even the holy prophets, Hugh believes, served the church as well with the gold of their wisdom as the kings who adorned it with buildings. Hugh adds a note explaining that he calls the synagogue the church because it is a shadow of the present church – a shadow which eventually fled before the dazzling light of the gospel.

9.7 Hugh concludes his treatise with the following message to the king, the bishops and the rest of society: God hates everyone who does not live according to the present order which God has planned since the beginning of time. The Psalter in particular testifies that God compels those who break away, however exalted they may be, to return to a simple life.

C. PRESUPPOSITIONS OF SUCH A WAY OF USING THE OLD TESTAMENT

9.8 When Hugh maintains that the earth should be like heaven he is bringing society a twofold message. Earthly society, like the heavenly one, should not change. It must adhere to the social precepts laid down in the Old Testament. Secondly, all members of society are equal. They do not have the same status – even heaven has a hierarchy – but they occupy the same position before God and God's law. This law requires everyone to be average, especially in respect of wealth; that is, the king and other wealthy people should enrich the church and share their money with the poor so as to create a balance in society.

9.9 But why should Hugh, a monk, want such a society, with the king ruling over the church and the church, enriched by the king, dependent on him for that very reason? And how does he use the Old Testament to corroborate his theory?

9.10 We are assuming that any author writes a text with three kinds of presuppositions: conscious, semiconscious and unconscious ones.

1. Unconscious presuppositions

9.11 To find out what heaven is like, Hugh read the Bible. To link heaven and earth together, he used an ideology. An ideology is a world view to which people subscribe, unaware that it dominates their thinking. One characteristic of an ideology is that it does not operate from heaven to earth as Hugh professes, but the other way round. This implies that when Hugh read in the Bible what heaven was like, he was in fact reading how he would have liked earth to be. When he required society to remain unchanging and moderate, with enough money for the church and sufficient spiritual riches in the church, he found these precepts in the Bible, especially in the history recounted in the Old Testament.

9.12 Unconsciously Hugh's ideology fed on two sources. His spontaneous propensity to think symbolically was worked out for him many centuries earlier by Augustine and Pseudo-Dionysius.

9.13 In Hugh's day monks believed that everything on earth symbolised something in heaven. This type of monastic emphasis had evolved from a long tradition of symbolic thinking. Plato was perhaps the first person who held that everything on earth essentially partook of an ideal type which belonged to a different reality. The people whose lives are reflected in the Old Testament were evidently too earthy for such other-worldly ideas. But Hugh believed that earth does and must point to heaven, and that the Old Testament tells about earth as a reflection of heaven. He believed that Adam as the head of humankind represented earthly kingship in the image of the heavenly king. And he believed that the Old Testament, particularly the book of Job, admonished people who were arrogant because they were rich

9.14 How did it happen that Hugh unconsciously assimilated this perception of society and this use of the Old Testament into his theological thinking? He looked at society through the eyes of Pseudo-Dionysius. Of course, the name this man chose for himself was simply Dionysius, but to give authority to his writings he pretended to be Dionysius the Areopagite who, according to Acts 17:34, was converted by Paul in Athens and was said to have later become bishop of that city. Long after Hugh's

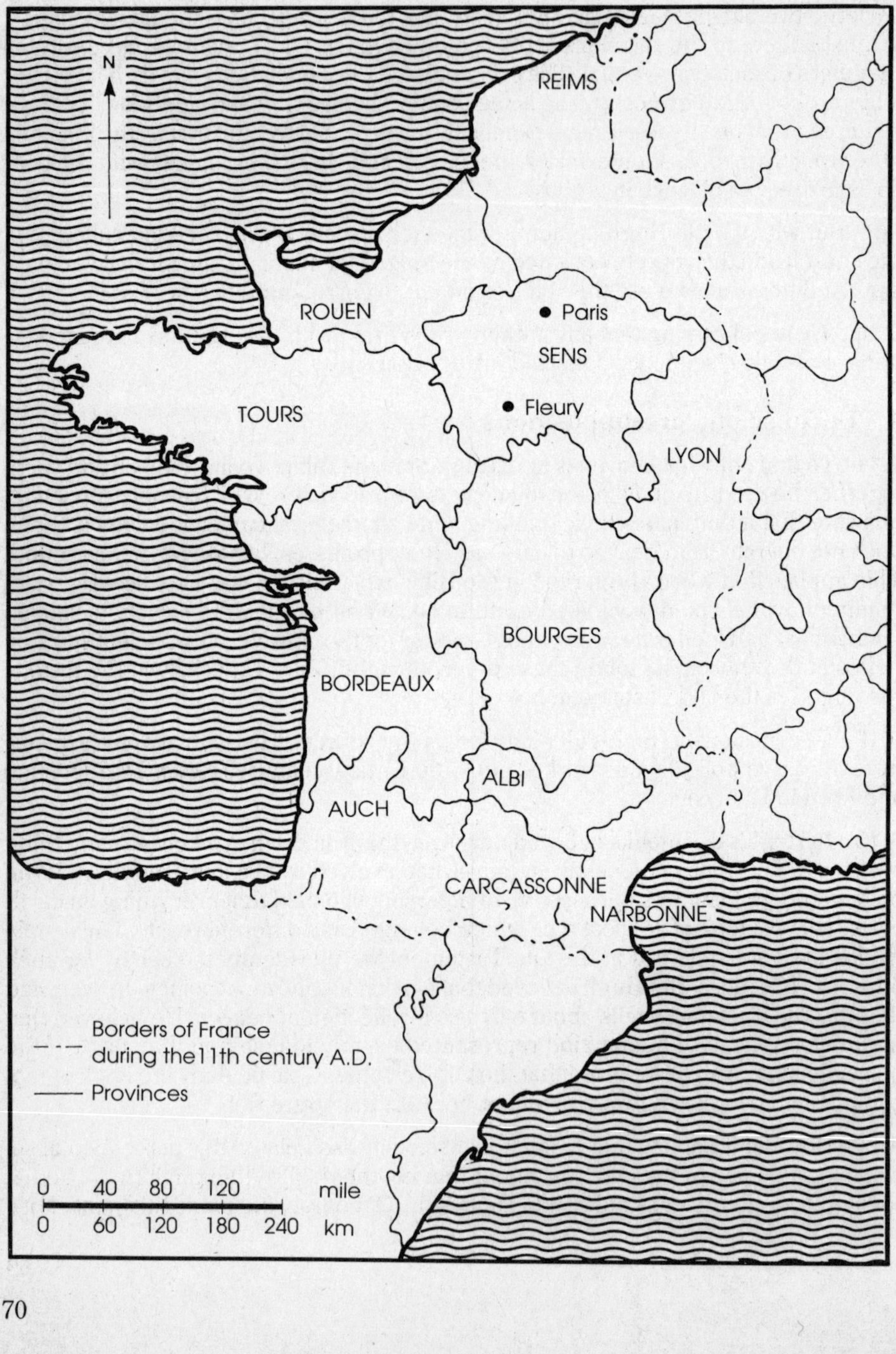

day it was established that this Dionysius was actually a Syrian writer from the early sixth century A.D. His writings – which describe in great detail how earth was an image of and therefore referred symbolically to heaven – greatly influenced medieval writers like Hugh. Dionysius' account of heaven and earth unconsciously justified Hugh in dictating the following precept to earth: just as there is no concern about money in heaven, so the church on earth should not be concerned about money. Hugh then amplified his precept: in order to be unconcerned about money, the church should observe an earthly hierarchy headed by the king, as a likeness of the hierarchy in heaven.

9.15 The legacy that the twelfth century monastic theologians received from Pseudo-Dionysius accorded with exegetical principles inherited from Augustine. According to Augustine the contents of the Bible reflected God's will – or, in Pseudo-Dionysian terms, the ideal "heavenly" state – so indisputably that exegetes can make every word in the Bible signify anything and point any way, as long as the resultant exegesis conformed to the church's rule of faith.

9.16 This is the system that made it possible for Hugh to idealise Elijah's conduct towards Ahab and Jezebel. In Hugh's view Elijah set an example for all ages by waiting for God to execute punishment on king Ahab and his wife Jezebel for their greed rather than confronting and punishing them himself. Hugh commends Elijah as an extremely holy man who fled from Ahab's tyranny and Jezebel's excesses, rather than elevate himself above the king. This man of the church (in Hugh's terms) preferred to distance himself from a king who arrogated more than moderate powers and a queen who desired more than moderate wealth rather than do them injury. Hugh manifestly deviated greatly from the content of the intertext. According to the biblical text (1 Ki 19–21) Elijah had fled when Jezebel wanted to kill him, long before the Naboth episode. Elijah personally delivered the message of their impending death to Ahab and Jezebel – a task he did not flee from. Hugh was making use of the Augustinian freedom to interpret events in accordance with the church's doctrine concerning society, and with the Pseudo-Dionysian notion that what the Bible says is a symbol instated by heaven.

2. Semiconscious presuppositions

9.17 Authors' semiconscious presuppositions are usually determined by their circumstances. The rites and values to which they subscribe in daily life compel them to adopt certain positions in regard to the topic they write about. In Hugh's case the monastic culture of the abbey where he lived led him to assume certain things about the way wealth should be divided between king and abbey.

9.18 A cardinal feature of the monastic culture to which Hugh semiconsciously submitted was its extreme conservatism. Hugh was vaguely aware – and his work makes us, his readers, acutely conscious of it – that he was opposed to all change. He was a status quo theologian.

9.19 What was his status quo? The abbey of Fleury where he lived was in France, 120 kilometres south of Paris in the ecclesiastic province of Sens, a royal diocese. The king gave the church certain land and buildings, as well as military protection. In return the church was well disposed to the crown and admonished its members to recognise the king's authority. Other abbeys, in return for royal endowment, had to allow the king a say in the election of their abbots (the title of the head of an abbey). However, over the years Fleury had retained the right to elect its own abbots without royal sanction.

9.20 From Hugh's *Treatise* one gathers that this situation especially the agreement between his abbey and the king concerning the division of wealth between them suited him down to the ground. Apparently it suited the entire province in which he lived, for during this time Sens, through its archbishop, strongly condemned the church reforms launched by pontiffs ever since the previous century with a view to lessening the church's dependence on the crown. These pontiffs wanted the church to take charge of its own wealth so that they would not be royal property.

9.21 Hugh disliked reform. Things had to stay as they were, or rather, as they had always been. And Hugh's proof that what was had always been so was the Bible, more particularly the Old Testament. To use the Bible to justify one's conservatism was very much part of the conservative monastic culture. Thus monastic theologians objected strongly to the schoolmen's use of nonbiblical sources such as Aristotle as a basis for their scholastic theology. In the monasteries only the Bible and the early church fathers were read and, as we have noted, these readings were part of their daily liturgy.

9.22 To justify the retention of the status quo Hugh made the history of the Israelite kings the rule for the kings of his day; and he used the relationship between Joseph and Pharaoh to prescribe the measure in which the clergy had to be enriched by the king.

9.23 In Hugh's view the history of the early Israelite kings demonstrated how kings had always looked after the church King Moses built a tabernacle in the wilderness (Ex 35, 36); king Joshua (Jos 10:13) and king Saul (1 Sm 11) protected God's people against their foes. King Solomon built a temple (1 Ki 6) where the rites instituted by his father David could be performed. It is evident how selectively the Old Testament was used as intertext to work out this theme. To be consistent Hugh had to make Moses a king; he had to select mainly the good qualities from the Old Testament portrayals of the early kings in order to turn them into actors in salvation history – the salvation history of the Christian church It is also noteworthy that Hugh steered clear of all biblical material that advocated the avoidance of wealth since he would have been obliged to opt for the monastic culture – that is, the wealth of the Benedictines – against these biblical values.

9.24 Hugh also believed that Joseph had served Pharaoh better with his counsel than if he had accumulated a hoard of money for him. Accordingly Hugh took it as read that the king should rate the counsel of the clergy more highly than gold. To arrive at this precept he had to adapt the intertext considerably, since the text (Gn 41) clearly indicates that Joseph's schemes greatly enriched Pharaoh. But Hugh made a different inference from this Old Testament story: to him the example of Joseph's inestimable service to Pharaoh indicated that kings can hardly reward the clergy highly enough for their counsel.

3. Conscious presuppositions

9.25 In his use of the Bible, and especially his preference for the Old Testament, Hugh could exercise a conscious choice between several exegetical methods.

9.26 He could interpret the biblical text *literally.* Thus he could take a text like Job 29:15, "I was eyes to the blind, and feet to the lame", to refer literally to helping the blind and the lame. The scholastic theologians liked to take biblical texts literally. But it is unlikely that Hugh would have inclined towards such an interpretation, partly because of the monastic theologians' emphasis on the symbolic character of earthly reality and partly because at this time Jewish scholars were condemning them for their spiritual reading of the Old Testament. To this criticism the monastic theologians responded by denying the literal contents of the Old Testament even more adamantly. Being a monastic theologian, Hugh would most likely have opted for one of three spiritual readings of the Bible.

9.27 The most spiritual reading of the Bible in Hugh's tradition was the *anagogic* one. Perhaps one should rather speak of an anagogic use of the Bible than of an anagogic reading, since Hugh and his peers did not read the Bible first and then use it to clarify a specific situation or doctrine; they first read the situation or doctrine the way they wanted it to read and then used the Bible to support this reading. To use the Bible anagogically is to use it in order to explain God. If Hugh were to have read Job 29:15 anagogically, he might have related it to God's omnipotence to put an end to natural afflictions.

9.28 Hugh could also have interpreted Job 29:15 *allegorically*. This would imply bringing the biblical text to bear on the rule of faith. In that case he would have related the blind and the lame mentioned in the text to heretics and atheists, while the church and the orthodox faith, the alternative to these, would be the eyes and the feet.

9.29 The lowest spiritual plane at which a biblical text could be interpreted was the *tropological* level. Texts were read tropologically to dictate to people how they should behave and what morals they should observe. This was how Hugh used Job 29:15 to dictate to the king how he should act towards society, and more specifically towards the church He was not really concerned about actual blind and crippled people in society. His concern, in the context that this verse is used in his *Treatise,* was that the king should enrich the church, and to make it serve this purpose he read it tropologically. He was not necessarily trying to portray the king as sighted and sound of limb in contrast to a blind and crippled church This was not how this tradition's exegetical mentality operated. These medieval exegetes did not consider it necessary to analyse each and every subsection of a verse tropologically (or allegorically, or anagogically). Something in a particular verse caught a theologian's fancy, whereupon he used it as a peg on which to hang whatever topic engaged him. It was the notion of helping in Job 29:15 that tempted Hugh to use it to illustrate the king's financial obligations to the church

9.30 Accordingly, when Hugh correlates the beautiful biblical texts that insist on protection for widows, orphans and the poor with Job 29:15, he gives the king this actually quite modern injunction:

> It is the duty of the legitimate king to guide the people in justice and equity and to defend holy mother church with all his might. He must be a mentor to minors, a protector of widows and a help to the poor so that, together with the blessed Job, he may tell the Lord: "I was eyes to the blind, and feet to the lame ... and I searched out the cause of him whom I did not know".

9.31 However, as a child of his times Hugh did not regard ordinary people primarily as human beings in need of upliftment but rather as God's people who have to be provided with church buildings. This is evident when he adds immediately:

> "The hallmark of a great king and leader is to adorn the sees of his realm with splendid buildings, to expand those sees with his works and willingly to preserve them in the culture of the faith".

D. CONCLUSION

9.32 The period that we call the Middle Ages lasted over a thousand years, covering more than half the history of Christianity. In this chapter we have indicated how a theologian from this lengthy era, espousing one of the numerous theological traditions of those times, read the Old Testament. *Unconsciously* he allowed his ideology to influence his reading of Old Testament texts. *Semiconsciously* he let his culture influence his use of Old Testament material. And he *consciously* selected from the exegetical insights offered by his age and his tradition the interpretive method which his theme seemed to require.

10

The owner of private property is a child of Cain: A typological reading of the Old Testament

JASPER BURDEN

A. A TYPOLOGICAL SERMON FROM AFRICA

10.1 Typological preaching is particularly popular in Africa. In his *The Christian ministry in Africa* the famous missiologist Bengt Sundkler (1961:101–102) tells about a dramatic Easter sermon he once heard from a black minister, Michael Mzobe, at a mission station in Natal. Some 500 Zulu men and women had gathered for the greatest church festival in Africa, the Paschal celebration. The celebration reached its climax on Sunday morning, the day of the resurrection. The entire congregation marched in procession to the cemetery singing an Easter hymn:

> *Kusasa lapha laphuma,*
> *UMagdalena wahamba ...*
> (With the first light of morning
> Magdalene went out ...)

As the sun rose, the procession halted in front of a cross set among the graves. It bore the inscription: "I am the resurrection and the life." Michael Mzobe took his text from the Old Testament, Ezekiel 37, known as the "chapter of the resurrection". He proceeded thus:

> In the beginning God created heaven and earth, the sea, the animals and man. He made man in his own image. But Adam sinned. Through the fall of Adam, death and adversity came into the world. When he died, he was taken up to Paradise (to heaven), for he was after all Adam. There he was given a place of honour. He alone sat on the balcony of heaven, and from this vantage point he could watch the history of mankind unfolding.
>
> He watched as his eldest son, Cain, murdered his own brother Abel and, on his heavenly balcony, called out in sorrow and shame: "*Icala lami, icala lami elikhulu*!" (My guilt, my great guilt!) Then came the Flood and – in Paradise! – again he cried out: "*Icala lami, icala lami elikhulu*!"
>
> Even David, the anointed king, sinned because of Adam. Generation upon generation is born on earth to sin and die because of Adam's fall.

Zulus, imagine the great burden of sorrow in the heart of Adam, our great ancestor! Misery and sorrow – and all on account of his sin!

But Zulus, men and women, imagine too the incredible joy, the indescribable gladness that filled Adam's heart on that day of the first Resurrection when Heaven's Hero walked up the path from the temple of heaven to the throne of the Almighty with his crown of thorns transfigured into a shining crown of victory! There he declared that from that day onwards, Satan, sin and death had been vanquished. For on this day He, the second Adam, was victorious. And the first Adam found peace.

10.2 How did Michael Mzobe use the Bible in this sermon? He used it typologically, because he did two very important things:

- He took people (like Adam, Cain, David) as *examples* of our sinfulness and Christ's suffering – and he did so without even mentioning Christ by name. Thus he made Adam, Cain and David "*types*" of Christ.
- In this way Mzobe gave certain events from the past *spiritual significance*: Christ died and rose again, thus bringing salvation from the sins of Adam, Cain and David, and from ours.

10.3 Michael Mzobe was not the first preacher to use *typology* in his sermons. Typological exegesis has come a long road – a road we shall now briefly follow.

B. TYPOLOGY IN THE OLD TESTAMENT

10.4 As we have seen in Mzobe's sermon, *typology* is the reintroduction of people and events (even things, as will be seen below) from the past in a new context.

10.5 The *Old Testament* authors already used this device. The story of Genesis 1–11 culminates in the Abraham episode in chapter 12, but in fact it is merely a preamble to the great narrative which runs from Genesis through to Kings, of which David is the real climax. One could argue that Abraham is a (proto)type of David, as is evident in the genealogies in Chronicles. These start with Adam (1 Chr 1:1) in a broad, cosmic vista (1 Chr 1:1–54); after that the focus narrows, first to the twelve sons of Jacob (1 Chr 2:1–2), then to the tribe of Judah (1 Chr 2:3–55) and finally to David alone (1 Chr 3:3). This use of Adam as a "type" of David had special significance for the faith of Israel: Adam, David and Israel existed in order to further the salvation of humankind. Thus a type is an example from the past which eventually acquires new meaning. After all, the history of Israel was not recorded to satisfy the curiosity of later historians, but to testify to God's dealings with his people. God's history with them functioned as a confession of faith, as may be seen in Deuteronomy 6:4–13 and 26:1–11.

10.6 Particularly in times of crisis – such as the exile and the coming of Christ – Israel recalled and resuscitated the good things in its history. Isaiah saw the future release from Babylonian exile as a second exodus (Is 51:9–10), and Jeremiah (31:31–34) spoke of a new covenant. What is remarkable is that in the prophetic writings a type acquires *prophetic or futuristic meaning*. Malachi (4:5–6), for instance, anticipated Elijah's future return, and the New Testament authors in fact saw John the Baptist as this Elijah (Mt 11:14). For this reason many scholars believe that the outstanding feature of a type is that it refers prophetically to the future.

C. TYPOLOGY IN THE NEW TESTAMENT

10.7 The word "typology" derives from the Greek *typos*, which may be translated as reproduction, copy, stamp, imprint, likeness, prototype, model. In the New Testament the word is used four times to indicate a correspondence between:

- Adam and Christ (Rm 5:14);
- the exodus and Christian living (1 Cor 10:6);
- the Old Testament priesthood and Christ's (Heb 9:24); and
- Noah's ark and baptism (1 Pt 3:21).

10.8 *New Testament preachers* used the word in their sermons and writings to explain to their audiences how to understand Christ and the new faith. Because the Old Testament was the first Christians' only Bible and because they were so familiar with it, these preachers took examples from it in order to communicate their message about Christ. From the references given above it appears that they used persons (Adam, a priest), events (the exodus) and things (the ark) as *types*.

10.9 We could explain the New Testament authors' and preachers' conception of a type as follows: If you were to take a photograph of your father or mother and compare it with one of yourself, you will probably see many resemblances but also certain differences. You might even be the spit image of one of your parents. The first Christians, believing Christ to be not merely the fulfilment of the Old Testament but also the herald of a far better era, sought to demonstrate both the *correspondences* and the *differences* between him and the Old Testament examples by means of typologies. Romans 5:14 is a good illustration:

> Yet death reigned from Adam to Moses, even over those whose sins were not like the transgression of Adam, who was a type of the one who was to come. There is a *correspondence* between Adam (type, example, photo image) and him (i.e. Christ) who was to come, but in regard to the gift of grace they are *different* ...

10.10 Here Adam is the Old Testament *image* (or *type*) and Christ the New Testament *counter-image* (or *antitype*). There are correspondences, but there are differences too. The correspondence lies in the fact that, because of Adam's transgression, he, Christ and all human beings have to die; the difference is that, through God's gift (i.e. Christ), "[life] abounded for many" (Rm 5:15). In regard to death Adam and Christ are alike, but in regard to the gift of life they differ, Christ far surpassing Adam. He brought something better, more lasting – eternal life.

10.11 The New Testament preachers actually believed the Old Testament examples to be no more than "predictions" of Christ. They were, so to speak, simply "copies and shadows" (Heb 8:5) – photographs – of what Christ would bring. In Hebrews 9:9 the author says explicitly about the Old Testament examples that they are "symbolic for the present age". This explains why the New Testament depicts Christ as the *new* Adam (Rm 5:15), the *new* Moses (Mt 5:1f.; Jn 6:14), the *new* temple

(Jn 2:19–21) and the giver of the *new* covenant (Lk 22:20; 1 Cor. 11:25; Heb 9:15). He came to make everything better (Heb 8:6) and is not a mere copy (Heb 8:5) or photograph, but the real thing. Everything, including the Old Testament, has to be interpreted in terms of Christ.

10.12 Some further examples from the New Testament serve to illustrate the use of typology. The following Old Testament characters are types of Christ: Moses (Heb 3:1–6)), David (Heb 1:20; 2:25–28), Solomon (Mt 12:39–42), Adam (Rm 5:14), Melchizedek (Heb 7) and Jonah (Mt 12:39). Key events in Israelite history have typological meaning. Thus the passage through the Reed Sea is a type of baptism (1 Cor 10:2); the manna and water in the wilderness are types of the eucharist (1 Cor 10:3f.); the flood too is a type of baptism (1 Pt 2:2f.). According to the Johannine Gospel the serpent in the wilderness (Jn 3:14) and the manna (Jn 6:48–58) are types of Christ. Apart from these historical types, the ceremonial types – especially in Hebrews – include all the sacred places (tabernacle, temple), persons (high priest, priesthood), actions (sacrifice) and times (sabbath, Day of Penitance, Easter, Pentecost and the Feast of Tabernacles).

D. TYPOLOGY AS THE EXEGETICAL METHOD OF THE ANTIOCHAN SCHOOL

1. Antioch: location and background

10.13 Antioch, in Syria, is the modern Turkish town Antakiya on the Syrian border. It was the most famous of the sixteen cities that bore this name and was founded by Seleucus I Nicator on the Orontes river round 300 B.C. It had its own harbour, Seleucia Pireia. Under the Romans it became the capital of the province of Syria and the third largest city of the empire, renowned for its culture and wealth, its beautiful temples and other buildings. The Seleucids granted Jewish immigrants full citizenship. When Pompey conquered the city in 64 B.C. it became a free city. The Antiochans were notorious political activists and rebelled against Rome on several occasions. Nearby was Daphne, known for its forests and its shrine to Apollo where drinking orgies often occurred.

10.14 Antioch is closely associated with the beginnings of Christianity. Nicolaus, one of the seven deacons, haled from that city (Ac 6:5), and after the martyrdom of Stephen many Christian fugitives from Jerusalem travelled the 483 kilometres to Antioch to seek refuge. After the conversion of large numbers of gentiles the church in Jerusalem dispatched Barnabas, who invoked the aid of Paul, to Antioch (Ac 11:22f.). The designation “Christian” was used here for the first time (Ac 11:26). Because many of its members were affluent, this young church in pagan parts was able to send alms to the older but impoverished church in Jerusalem when famine struck (Ac 11:27–30). Because of its wealth it could also send out the first missionaries, Barnabas and Paul (Ac 13:1–3). When the church in Jerusalem exerted pressure on the young church in pagandom to observe Jewish customs, they sent Paul and Barnabas to Jerusalem where the matter was settled at the “first synod” (Ac 15). Galatians 2:11–14 also mentions a dispute between Paul and Peter in Antioch about the relationship between Jewish and gentile converts.

10.15 Antioch was struck by numerous disasters, including an earthquake on 21 July 365; famine from 382 to 384; an insurrection – one of many – in 387; and an earthquake on 29 May 526 which all but destroyed the city.

10.16 The map below shows the location of Antioch in relation to Jerusalem and Alexandria in Egypt.

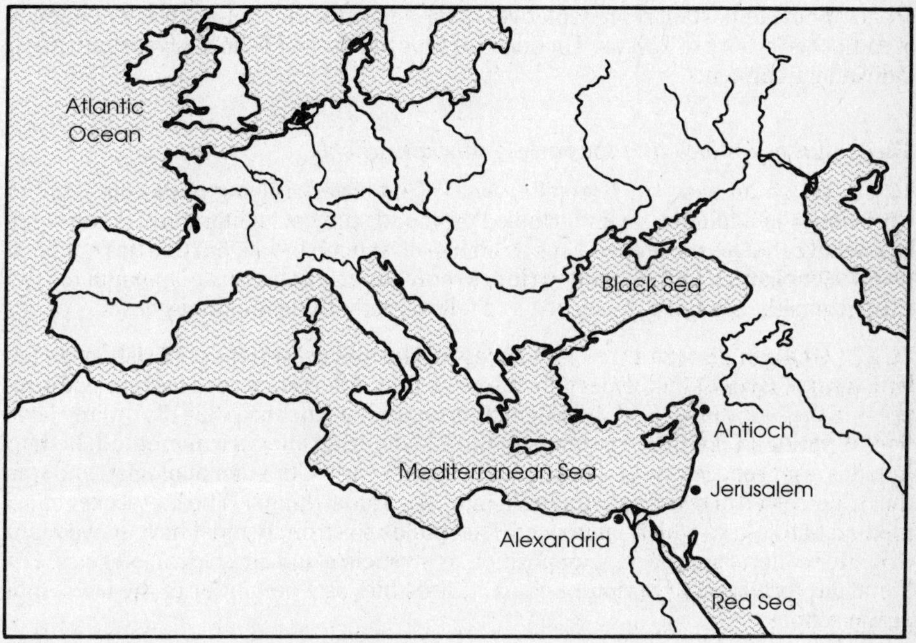

The location of Antioch, Jerusalem and Alexandria

2. Exegetical method of the Antiochan school

10.17 So far we have been citing examples of Old and New Testament typology, used to further the *proclamation*, the *kerygma* or *message* of a biblical passage. Here types were used as figures of speech, in the sense that the word in question (e.g. Adam, ark, exodus) was interpreted figuratively, not literally, as an example or analogy of something else. The Antiochan school was the first to use typology as an exegetical method with specific rules, as a counterweight to the allegorical method of the Alexandrian school (see next chapter).

10.18 When describing the method of the Antiochan exegetes one needs to distinguish between an early and a later school. The first Antiochan school dates to the late second century, and the second to the latter half of the fourth century. There were two emphases in Antiochan exegesis: the literal, and especially the historical, meaning of the Old Testament; and typological interpretation.

10.19 Although discussions of the Antiochan school usually stress the influence of

Jewish literal interpretation, this does not mean that they did not develop their own style of literal interpretation. Their method differed from the allegorical one of the Alexandrian school because they were convinced that the narrative parts of the Old Testament should be interpreted primarily at the *historical* level. When it came to the prophets and the psalms, which were usually considered to be messianic, the Antiochans allowed for a "fuller" meaning besides the historical one (see below).

10.20 Some important representatives of the Antiochan school, such as Theophilus of Antioch, Diodore of Tarsus, Theodore of Mopsuestia and John Chrysostom, merit individual treatment.

Theophilus of Antioch and the early Antiochan school

10.21 Of Syrian descent, Theopilus was well educated. Having been converted to Christianity in adult life, he undertook a profound study of its literature. Some scholars believe that he succeeded Eros as bishop of Antioch in 169, but this has not been firmly established. Of his many writings, only the *to autolygos*, an apologia for the Christian faith, has been preserved and tells us something about his views.

10.22 One can discern three influences in Theophilus' work – a Christian, a Hellenistic (i.e. Greek) and especially a Jewish one. After emperor Hadrian had suppressed the Palestinian Jewish insurrection under Bar Kochba (132–135), many Jews fled to Antioch Like the exponents of the Alexandrian allegorical method, bishop Ignatius – a predecessor of Theophilus – was an early Christian apologist who was much interested in mysticism (belief in hidden spiritual things). The literal exegetical method of the Jews which influenced Theophilus so strongly must have moved him to opt for a literal approach, in opposition to mysticism and allegorical exegesis. His literal interpretation of Scripture characterises him as a precursor of the later Antiochan school.

Diodore of Tarsus

10.23 Diodore (d. 392) is generally considered to have founded the later Antiochan school more than 200 years after Theophilus had started the early one. He became bishop of Tarsus and Cilicia in 378. His fiercest opponent was Apollinaris, bishop of Laodycia (361–377), who taught at the Antiochan school in 373, counting even the church father Jerome among his pupils. Apollinaris started the Arian heresy, according to which Christ was human in body but not in spirit. Diodore's best-known work was a commentary on the psalms, in which it is clearly evident how Antiochan exegesis managed to be historical and christological at the same time. David is considered to have been the author of the psalms, but because of his prophetic gift some of the psalms refer historically to the age of later kings and prophets, to the exile and even to the time of the Maccabees. Diodore's exposition of Psalms 2 and 22 represents the two extremes of Antiochan exegesis. Psalm 2 is interpreted *christologically*: this psalm is about the Lord (Jesus), telling how the Jews handed him over to Herod and Pilate, and how he will save those who believe in him and destroy the unbelievers. Psalm 22, on the other hand, is interpreted *historically*: notwithstanding Jesus' citation from this psalm while he was on the cross (see Mt 27:46), Diodore maintains that it has nothing to do with Jesus since his passion is not the same as the suffering described in the psalm – the latter refers to the return of the exiles from Babylonia.

10.24 Diodore also wrote a treatise on biblical exegesis and greatly influenced two of his pupils, Theodore of Mopsuestia (350–428) and John Chrysostom (354–407).

Theodore of Mopsuestia

10.25 Theodore – like his contemporary John Chrysostom – was a student of Libanius, an influential teacher and talented writer of Antioch He entered the monastery run by Diodore and Carterius and was consecrated to the priesthood by bishop Flavian of Antioch in 383. He lived in this city until he was appointed bishop of Mopsuestia in Cilicia. He was the natural successor to Diodore and continued teaching his theology about the human and divine nature of Christ in opposition to Arianism. Like John Chrysostom, he strongly emphasised what was termed the "original meaning" of Scripture.

10.26 In addition to this historical approach, he also set great store by the literal meaning of the words of the Bible and explicitly rejected the allegorical method with its accent on the spiritual meaning of Scripture. The question that arose was: when should a passage be interpreted historically, and when should it be expounded typologically as well? That is, when does a text have additional "future" meaning? Theodore's answer to this was as follows: when the language of a passage is so hyperbolical (i.e. exaggerated) that the message conveyed cannot possibly be actualised in its own time, then the text has additional meaning. Thus Zechariah 4:9 speaks of Zerubbabel in such hyperbolical terms that the words could not possibly refer to him alone but had to have some additional meaning. Theodore wrote:

> Here we have a passage which is not to be understood as if one moment it referred to Zerubbabel and the next moment to Christ. The passage primarily applies to Zerubbabel. But it speaks of him in language so hyperbolical that the prophecy could not be wholly fulfilled in him. The final fulfilment is only to be found in Christ.

John Chrysostom

10.27 John was a preacher of renown, a gift which earned him the nickname of Chrysostom ("golden mouth"). Born in 354, he was ordained deacon in 381 and priest in 386. The son of a prematurely deceased civil servant, he was acquainted with prominent Antiochans like Libanius. During his lifetime conditions deteriorated in every sphere of Antiochan life. A depressed economy was further weakened by drought in 382 to 384 and an uprising in 387. Corruption in the public service and the judiciary led to revolution. While Libanius was flagellating the Roman government with his pen, John tried to strengthen Christians with his sermons. After the iconoclasm of A.D. 387, his 21 homilies appeared under the title *On the statues.* His views on wealth and poverty will be considered in due course.

E. TYPOLOGY AND ALLEGORY

10.28 The use of typology as a method can be traced to Philo (c. 20 B.C. – A.D. 50), the Jewish philosopher who persuaded the Alexandrian Jews to accept the allegorical method. He was the first scholar to use the word *typos* in biblical exegesis. He drew on the theory of the great Greek philosopher Plato to expound the deeper meaning of biblical history. Philo saw the conceptions of God as archetypes imprinted on the human minds of biblical characters such as Adam, Abraham and David as types (copies), thus moving them to actualise the concepts of God in their historical life world. Because Philo believed that this heavenly stamp was imprinted on earth from above, his use of this exegetical method is usually called "vertical typology" (see ch 9). In this approach typological interpretation shares the notion of a deeper meaning with the allegorical method. Examples of the two methods show a certain measure of overlapping. At a later stage the church father Agustine (d. 430) went so far as to combine the allegorical method of the Alexandrian school and the literal-cum-historical method (including typology) of the Antiochan school.

10.29 Nowadays, however, we make a distinction between the allegorical and typological methods, as is evident in the synoptic table below.

Typology	**Allegory**
Concentrates mainly on interpretation of events, persons, things	Concentrates mainly on interpretation of words
Takes the original situation seriously	Ignores the original situation
Based on literal meaning	Based on supposed "deeper" meaning of words

10.30 Typological and allegorical exegesis have one major weakness in common, in that neither does justice to the historical facts of the Old Testament. Typology, to be sure, acknowledges the authenticity of the historical events and characters described in the Old Testament and in this way it formed the basis of subsequent historical methods. In addition it possibly does not spiritualise the text quite so directly as the allegorical method. But because the Old Testament is viewed from a New Testament perspective, its historical context is rarely if ever given its due. Like the allegorical method, the typological one can be applied without restraint, regardless of historical context or genre. As a result it can give rise to the most fantastic mental gymnastics.

F. TYPOLOGY, POVERTY AND WEALTH

10.31 There is a fascinating typological application of Cain that touches on the issue of wealth and poverty. In an early Christian novel known as the Pseudo-Clementines, the name of the first fratricide, Cain, is given an intriguing etymology: it is said to have a dual meaning, deriving from the two Hebrew words for possessions and jealousy. From this the author concludes that the possession of goods is sinful for all people. The association of Cain's name with possessions is based on an ancient Graeco-Judaic tradition, referred to by both Philo, the Jewish philosopher, and Josephus, the Jewish historian. Josephus stresses that in his wickedness Cain cared only about the acquisition of possessions and that he was the first person to till the soil (cf. Josephus' *Antiquitates* 1:52; and Philo, *De sacrificiis Abelis et Caini* 1:2). This implies that Cain was the first landowner and the first to violate nature. In other words, he was the type of all owners of private property. This notion that private property is the root of contention among human beings is a persistent theme in the social preaching of the early church fathers. They held that the struggle for personal property destroyed the original good cosmic order in which everybody shared God's gifts in nature equally. The great Antiochan preacher, John Chrysostom, thinking of the farmers, bakers and other Antiochans, stated explicitly:

> Mark the wise dispensation of God! That he might put mankind to shame, he has made certain things common, as the sun, air, earth, and water ... whose benefits are dispensed equally to all as brethren ... observe, that concerning things that are common there is no contention, but all is peaceable. But when one attempts to possess himself of anything, to make it his own, then contention is introduced, as if nature herself were indignant, that when God brings us together in every way, we are eager to divide and separate ourselves by appropriating things, and by using those cold words "mine and thine". Then there is contention and uneasiness. But where this is not, no strife or contention is bred. This state therefore is rather our inheritance, and more agreeable to nature.

G. THE USE OF TYPOLOGY TODAY

10.32 The obvious questions that come to mind are: can we Christians identify with the faith of the Old Testament? If so, how should the Old Testament be expounded to permit us to feel at home with its faith?

10.33 We have seen how the early Christians in Jerusalem, Alexandria, Antioch and Rome managed to accomplish this. We find the evidence in the New Testament and the history of the early church We have also seen something of their views on wealth and poverty. But can we still interpret the Bible in their way today? Can we still make use of literal, allegorical and typological exegesis? How should the poor – and, of course, the rich as well – strengthen and deepen their faith by means of the Bible? Must we discard all modern exegetical methods and revert to the exegeses of yore? The answer is both yes and no.

10.34 Gerhard von Rad, a German Old Testament scholar at the beginning of this century, proposed that typological exegesis could still be applied today. He maintained that the same God who declared himself to us in Christ left his footprints on the history of the people of Israel. However greatly the thought world of the Old Testament differs from that of the New, we see the Christ events foreshadowed in the Old Testament. And this is the only analogy or example that makes it possible for us moderns to interpret the Old Testament theologically.

10.35 Von Rad summarised the use of typological exegesis as follows:

- Typological exegesis relinquishes the Old Testament people's historical understanding of their faith, going beyond it by seeing the Old Testament as a preparation for what was yet to come.
- It draws on the entire Old Testament, so that the number of Old Testament types is limitless since everything and everybody foreshadows Christ.
- Typological exegesis is limited to the *credenda* or articles of faith and does not in-

clude parallels in the historical, cultural or archaeological details of the two Testaments.

- It acknowledges the provisional, imperfect nature of salvation under the old dispensation, recognising that the promises of land, eternal peace, long life and the like will be fulfilled in the perfect salvation effected through the entire Christ events.
- A typological and a historical-critical interpretation of the Old Testament are not mutually exclusive as some scholars appear to think. On the contrary, they include each other, since both use analogy as an interpretive method. After all, according to Von Rad "historical" exegesis is best conducted in terms of the Christian faith, as witnessed by Paul's exposition of the splendour of the new dispensation in Christ that far exceeds that of the old (2 Cor 3:7–11).
- Typological exegesis gives vitality and meaning to the arid tales told by Old Testament authors without any clarificatory commentary, thus giving them theological meaning.
- Typological exegesis does not impose any didactic constraints on the text but leaves scope for the freedom of the Holy Spirit.
- In a typological sense one can speak of the Old Testament witness to Christ since our knowledge of him would be incomplete without that testimony.

10.36 To sum up: we can proclaim and expound Christ in the light of persons, events and things in the Old Testament which then serve as analogies to him, but we should guard against pursuing minute analogies in our exegesis. The Easter sermon of Michael Mzombe cited at the beginning of the chapter is a good example of the meaningful use of typology in preaching in our African context.

H. CONCLUSION

10.37 We find three dominant exegetical methods in three different places: literal exegesis in Jerusalem, allegorical in Alexandria and typological in Antioch Why these differences? They relate to differences in place, time, culture, language, philosophy and circumstances. Nowadays we speak of contextual differences. After all, context is still a major determinant of exegetical method today. Thus some rationalist Westerners prefer historical-critical methods, some liberation theologians incline to materialistic methods, and so on. But every exegete should take into account that different premises will affect their exegetical results, and that exegetes should allow scope for and learn from one another.

11

God also loves the rich: An allegorical reading of the Old Testament

JURIE LE ROUX

A. INTRODUCTION

11.1 All along we have been stressing the importance of the reader's context. As this context changes, so does the reading of a text. Context therefore has a profound impact on the reading and understanding of texts. It alters the readers' eyes and ears so that they hear and see different facets of the text. Nobody can escape his context. To illustrate this, we shall take a look at Clement of Alexandria. He was responsible for a totally new perception of wealth and poverty. This was not surprising, since he lived in a society that made him see Scripture in a new way. Like many others, Clement was overwhelmed by the wealth and culture of Alexandria. But wealthy people often felt uneasy in the company of Christians and church people, many of whom believed that the rich could never enter heaven. After all, Scripture contains numerous sayings to the effect that it is easier for a camel to squeeze through the eye of a needle than for a rich man to pass through the gates of heaven. Clement, who was himself wealthy and educated, knew the minds of the rich He thought it was very important that the rich should not be lost to the church and for that reason he interpreted Scripture differently. This made it possible for the rich and the learned to find their way into the church by slow degrees. In so doing Clement had to fly in the face of prevailing views on wealth and poverty. His views will be expounded more fully below. First we examine ideas about wealth and poverty in his day; then we focus on the metropolis of Alexandria because it had such an influence on Clement; we also deal with his exegetical method; and finally we take a look at these "new" perceptions of wealth and poverty.

B. POVERTY IS IN, WEALTH IS OUT

11.2 During the first two centuries the position of the rich was not at all clear. One gets the impression that the poor were so much in the limelight that the wealthy must have felt excluded. Initially Christianity drew its followers mainly from the lower strata of the population. According to Paul there were few erudite, influential or important people among the first believers. By worldly standards the people whom God called were lowly and insignificant (1 Cor 1:26–29). This does not mean that the early Christian community had no wealthy members; but they were a minority. In all likelihood their presence was often an embarrassment. Thus the author of James's letter points out that the rich should not receive preferential treatment at the expense of the poor, since God had chosen the poor to be rich in faith. Besides, the rich were oppressors: "Is it not the rich who oppress you, is it not they who drag you into court?" (Ja 2:6). Paul complained about the way the rich behaved at the *agapé* feast. Some of them had a meal at home beforehand or brought their own food and ate it separately so that the poor did not get enough; some even arrived inebriated (1 Cor 11:21).

11.3 This negative attitude towards the rich was to persist for a long time. There were earnest discussions about private property and the position of the wealthy and the educated within the church Some of the leading theologians of the early church were extremely negative on this issue. They held that Scripture generally disapproved of wealth and therefore the few rich people in their ranks could not occupy top positions or count on special treatment merely on account of their wealth. Thus in the early third century the church of Rome elected Callistus, born of a family of slaves, as its bishop in preference to the educated and affluent Hippolytu and this despite the fact that it was a wealthy congregation. This choice reflects the early church's approbation of the poor and its suspicious attitude towards the rich

11.4 This perception is also apparent in pagan attacks on Christianity. In the latter half of the second century there was an intellectual campaign against the Christians. The pagan intelligentsia felt a compelling need to oppose Christianity. One eminent representative of this intellectual movement was Celsus, who wrote a major work against Christianity in A.D. 178. Although the tone of this book was haughty, it nonetheless displayed considerable knowledge of both Christians and the Bible. Celsus strongly disapproved of Christians. In the first place, because Christianity attracted mainly people from the lower income groups, it followed that they were *poor.* According to him, the church was composed of slaves, manual workers, children and women. In his opinion this was to be expected, since Jesus, the founder of the church, had been a carpenter and a member of the lower classes. Secondly, said Celsus, Christians were *stupid*. Their intelligence was limited and they were unable to understand their own teachings or discuss them sensibly. It was unacceptable that Christians should regard "stupidity" as an important characteristic. No wonder that Christianity consisted of dimwits and was a religion for the unintelligent. Finally, Christians were *uncultured*. They warned people against Greek culture and dissuaded them from pursuing worldly and scientific knowledge. As a result they had to forego all the marvellous, enriching and edifying things in Greek culture which greatly impoverished them. Seventy years later, Origen, Clement's successor and an eminent representative of the catechetical school in Alexandria, wrote a response to Celsus. Despite his exaggerations, Celsus had painted a significant picture of the church in the second century. In the eyes of the world the church was a bunch of paupers and dimwits, among whom wealthy, cultured people did not really belong.

11.5 After A.D. 200, however, the wealthy and the educated joined the church in large numbers and found a spiritual home in it. This change did not happen spontaneously; the theological spadework was done by the previous generation, and one of the principal contributors was Clement of Alexandria. As will be seen below, it was no mean task.

C. THE OVERWHELMING EXPERIENCE OF ALEXANDRIA

11.6 Everything of any note happened in the great metropolis of Alexandria. It was round about the year 180 that Clement settled in this city. Born in Athens of a wealthy family round 150, he had been taught the Greek language and Greek literature and philosophy since early childhood and was familiar with the ways and customs of the affluent. As was the custom of the rich in those days, Clement left home to travel the world in order to gain knowledge. In this quest for wisdom he wandered from one mentor to another. In the course of his wanderings Clement was converted to Christianity. It could be that he heard about the famous catechetical school of Alexandria in this period and decided to go there. At all events, when he arrived in Alexandria in 180 he must have found a great deal that appealed to him. There was wealth, with which he was familiar, and intellectual stimulation which he craved. In a nutshell: the Alexandrian experience was to influence his theology profoundly.

11.7 In the first place the beauty of the city must have impressed him. This metropolis of antiquity was founded by Alexander the Great in 331 B.C. Situated on a narrow strip of land between the Mediterranean and Lake Mareotis, this splendid city was built with wide streets and promenades, busy harbours to accommodate the maritime traffic, a famous lighthouse, numerous theatres, a museum, a famous library and many public gardens. Alexandria was a rich merchant city of the ancient world and many of its inhabitants shared in its wealth.

11.8 Alexandria was also a major cultural centre, the hub of Hellenistic culture and philosophy. Nobody who lived there could avoid the powerful thrust of Greek culture and thought. In addition to Greeks, the population contained a large Jewish component who occupied two of the five residential areas of the city, as well as a large number of Egyptians. Each community set great store by erudition. Each expressed its own philosophy within the same cultural atmosphere. Various approaches emerged, which led to the establishment of at least three "universities" or schools. One can hardly overestimate the intellectual force and stimulation that emanated from these three schools, to which we now turn our attention.

1. The school of Hellenistic culture

11.9 This school gathered at the famous museum and library. Their achievements were remarkable. At first they concentrated exclusively on textual and philological projects. By means of textual research and a profound study of Greek grammar they produced standard works on classical and contemporary Greek. The Greek philosophers, particularly Plato, were also studied. In due course the school broadened its scientific interests and turned its attention to mathematics, astronomy, geography, botany, anatomy and physiology as well.

2. The Jewish school

11.10 Although the Jews were a separate community, they could not escape the powerful influence of Hellenism, either culturally or economically. Eventually they no longer spoke Hebrew but Greek. Their school studied the Old Testament and other sacred scriptures, and many books were written. Their aim was partly to defend the Jewish cause against outside criticism and partly to commend their religion and life style to gentiles. The school is renowned for two reasons. One was a translation project that took two decades to complete. Because fewer and fewer Jews still spoke Hebrew they started to translate the Old Testament into Greek. This mammoth work was called the Septuagint. The Jewish school also became famous through the work of a brilliant scholar, whose name was Philo. He wanted to demonstrate that Moses' works outshone Greek literature in every respect, and that Old Testament wisdom was more than a match for Greek philosophy. To this end Philo made use of the allegorical method, and it was this method that was to influence Clement and Origen.

3. The Christian catechetical school

11.11 The Alexandrian catechetical school was famous throughout the Christian community. Its origins are uncertain, but it had its heyday in the time of Pantaenus (d. 200), Clement (d. 215) and Origen (185, 186–254). There were fixed curricula; the student body comprised people from different cultural and religious backgrounds; no tuition fees were charged, but wealthy patrons donated large sums of money. The main occupation was Bible study. Naturally this school also imbibed Hellenistic science. Its principal method was that of allegory.

D. A GRAVE PASTORAL PROBLEM

11.12 This, then, was the remarkable city in which Clement settled in A.D. 180. It was totally different from all other cities and its influence was such that it was bound to give birth to a different kind of theology. That is what happened in Clement's work. We do not know precisely what he did immediately after his arrival in Alexandria. Probably he first made contact with the church, where he became acquainted with Pantaenus, head of the catechetical school. Possibly Pantaenus did not have a vacancy for him right away, so that Clement might have started his own school for the time being. Only later did he succeed Pantaenus as head of the catechetical school. At all events, this was where he came into contact with wealthy and educated Greeks, Jews and others. He was overwhelmed by the cultural atmosphere of the city and enjoyed its wealth. He thrived in this context of affluence and erudition. In view of his background and education this was to be expected, but it was also to present him with tremendous theological problems. Up to that time the church was strongly opposed to wealth and totally rejected the science of those days. Gradually two points crystallised for Clement. One was that the rich had to be won over to the church It could not continue indefinitely to exclude the rich from its ranks and, by implication, from the kingdom. That would be to alienate the rich from the church for ever. Secondly, Clement also had strong feelings about Hellenistic culture and philosophical traditions. To reject these out of hand would be to impoverish the church But how was he to realise his ideals? In practice it boiled down to reading the Bible in a new way.

E. THE ALLEGORICAL UNDERSTANDING OF REALITY AND SCRIPTURE

11.13 Clement had a useful instrument at his disposal in the allegorical method. It was to help him greatly in achieving his goal. It is amazing that Clement was able to change the early church's approach to poverty and to some extent curb the biased movement in favour of the poor, all by means of his exegetical method. He managed to negotiate a place in the congregation for the rich and to put education and culture in a new light. All this he achieved by means of the allegorical method. Of course, those awkward texts that include the poor and offend the rich still existed; allegory merely helped Clement to circumvent them. He was not the originator of this method, but was greatly influenced by Philo, formerly a resident of Alexandria. Philo had observed how the Greek philosophers managed to interpret the negative elements in Greek literature in such a way that a meaningful message emerged. He wanted to apply this approach to his study of the Pentateuch Its message had to be discerned not in the outward text, one had to probe more deeply. Clement adopted this method, and his student and eventual successor Origen elaborated it systematically and magnificently, applying it to the entire Bible.

11.14 The allegorical method of exegesis is not just a method; it is primarily a world view. That is to say, the method is based on a particular way of understanding and expounding reality. In this regard Plato's thinking was quite significant. In his search for genuine goodness he arrived at the notion of a different, invisible reality of pure, perfect, eternal ideas. In this world we can only perceive the feeble, ephemeral, perishable shadows or forms of this other, perfect reality. These ideas of Plato's greatly influenced people's understanding of reality. Increasingly they held that the visible world was not real but merely pointed to a perfect reality beyond. On the one hand there was the external world – obviously an inescapable part of reality but in the final analysis not very important, for it merely veiled something more profound. On the other hand there was invisible reality – abiding, eternal, the actual meaning of all reality; only the initiate can fathom this deeper spiritual meaning. In terms of this Platonic interpretation one always operated in two worlds, one of which was more important than the other. In addition external reality was deprecated and the invisible was considered to be the true reality.

11.15 It is important to realise that this dichotomous description of reality was incorporated into the allegorical method. This method in effect embodied the Platonic world view. The visible words and sentences, the literal meaning of a text did not really matter. According to the allegorical approach the biblical authors embedded the real meaning of a text below the visible surface, and it was up to the exegete to disclose it. Consequently allegorical exegesis is intent on finding the true message concealed in the external words and sentences. Inevitably this emphasis on the "invisible" spiritual meaning led to the refutation of the literal meaning, literary context and historical circumstances of texts.

11.16 As we have said, Clement and Origen assimilated Philo's allegorical method into their own exegetical apparatus. Clement still relied heavily on Philo, but Origen developed and expanded it in his own way. He claimed that the Bible could be expounded in three ways: somatically or literally, morally, and pneumatically or allegorically. This third way, which disclosed the true spiritual meaning, was the goal and terminus of all exegetical work. It did not exclude the somatic or literal meaning of the text in any way. In fact, nobody in the early church cast more light on the physical form of the Bible than did Origen. His *Hexapla,* for instance, was monumental. It juxtaposed and contrasted the Hebrew text of the Old Testament with the various Greek versions. He devoted more than thirty years to this enormous task, taking infinite pains over philology, translations, historical comments, geographical references and the like. But that was not sufficient. A purely literal study of the Old Testament could never disclose its real message. Of course the work on the externals of the text was important, but these were only the medium through which the Holy Spirit communicated. One continually had to probe for the underlying meaning.

11.17 We conclude this section on allegory with an example from Origen's work. It deals with the parable of the good Samaritan. Naturally one can only focus on the physical text and its literal meaning – determine the right text, make a careful translation, trace all historical references, and so on. At this first level one can glean important and fascinating information to enhance one's understanding of the parable. And for many simple believers such a literal exposition can mean a great deal. But more is needed; one has to probe the underlying meaning as well. The true spiritual message of every word has to be studied. The major elements of the parable may then be expounded as follows: the man who is attacked by robbers is Adam; Jerusalem represents heaven and Jericho the world; the robbers are the enemies of humankind, namely Satan and his henchmen; the priest refers to the law and the Levite to the prophets; Christ is portrayed by the good Samaritan; the beast of burden who carries the injured man is the body of Christ; the inn is the church; the two coins symbolise the Father and the Son; and the Samaritan's promise that he will return refers to the second coming of Christ.

F. MATERIAL RICHES ARE HARMLESS

11.18 Thus Clement of Alexandria lived and worked in a context in which reality as the Bible were interpreted allegorically. He internalised this approach It is remarkable how consistent he was in his allegorical interpretation of reality and Scripture. He perceived the world in terms of the visible and the invisible. In the same way Scripture was expounded in terms of external and inner meaning. The outward and visible is consistently denigrated, being merely the husk enclosing something more profound. Everything boiled down to the invisible, the internal: this constituted the meaning of life and the real message of Scripture. By dint of this allegorical understanding and the resultant dichotomy between text and reality Clement found a new perspective on the problems of wealth and poverty.

11.19 True to his allegorical approach, his point of departure was the visible. Unlike many other theologians of the early church, he did not reject material wealth and luxury out of hand. After all, externals do not represent the essence of Christian life. This enables Clement quite simply to say that God does not exclude people from the kingdom purely because of their riches. Riches per se are harmless. What on earth is wrong with accumulating great wealth through care and hard work before one's conversion? Neither can one blame people for being born, through no fault of their own, into an affluent family. On the origin of wealth, then, Clement differs considerably from a theologian like Irenaeus (A.D. 140–190), who regarded the very possession of wealth as a consequence of sinful actions. Those who had riches could have acquired them only through the unrighteous Mammon – either through personal avarice or through the unfair actions of a parent, relative or friend. Clement's sharp distinction between external and inward reality permits him to be more temperate on the subject of material wealth.

G. MATERIAL POVERTY MEANS LITTLE

11.20 Clement's allegorical interpretation led him to condemn material poverty. In his view visible poverty is not to be commended. To go without money or wealth is not in itself laudable or wonderful. If it were, then the hordes of beggars who go about the streets daily would have been God's elect – which they are not.

11.21 It is nothing new, moreover, for rich people to give up their money for the sake of some cause. Many have done so long before the rise of Christianity. Outwardly it appeared laudable, but inwardly they hankered after money. Hence, although outwardly poor and apparently obedient to the commandment, many were "rich" in the desire for the money they had given away. To Clement this was further proof that poverty is not primarily material in nature.

11.22 Lack of material, visible riches also prevents believers from alleviating the need of others. Without money the hungry cannot be fed, the thirst of the thirsty remains unquenched, the naked cannot be clad and the homeless cannot be sheltered. Clement points out that Scripture commends the spending of money for the good of others. What is the point of the commandment to help one's neighbour if everybody has to be materially poor?

H. EXTERNALS ARE NEUTRAL

11.23 Riches should on no account simply be disposed of. External things cannot do that much harm. Money in itself is neither good nor bad; it all depends on the person using it. Clement illustrates the point by citing a musical instrument which, if not played properly, produces discords. One cannot blame the instrument for this; the fault lies with the player. Sweet harmonious music is a result of skillful use of the instrument. The same applies to wealth. It is simply an instrument and a great deal depends on the "player". If handled improperly, all manner of evil will result. Elsewhere he uses the image of a snake: only an adept knows how to grab it by its tail so that it cannot coil itself around the arm and bite the person. Someone who grabs a snake foolishly without reflection can incur calamity. Clement maintains that the same is true of money. If one gets caught in its clutches the consequences are destructive. Rich people's hold of their money (the snake) should be such that they are always in control of it.

I. POVERTY SHOULD BE SPIRITUAL

11.24 Any injunction in Scripture to abjure riches should not be interpreted crudely and insensitively, that is to say, literally. These sayings were not meant to be interpreted literally or materially. To substantiate this postulate scripturally Clement cites a number of Old Testament texts at random. It is impossible to explain it systematically, for the references are fragmented and disparate, scattered throughout his writings. In one of his books the focus is very much on the book of Proverbs, of which the following are quoted:

> My son, if you receive my words and treasure up my commandments with you, making your ear attentive to wisdom and inclining you heart to understanding ... (Pr 2:1–2). Does not wisdom call, does not understanding raise her voice? ... "To you, O men, I call and my cry is to the sons of men. O simple ones, learn prudence ..." (Pr 8:1,4–5). Happy is the man who finds wisdom, and the man who gets understanding, for the gain from it is better than gain from silver and its profit better than gold. She is more precious than jewels, and nothing you desire can compare with her (Pr 3:13–15).

11.25 Possibly we should first comment briefly on Old Testament wisdom. According to this view Yahweh created an order in which everybody had a place. Everyone had to know his or her place in the overall scheme and to this end all people have to behave in a particular way. The book of Proverbs provides guidelines on how people can live wisely. Thus wisdom was partly a matter of proper conduct. In the passages quoted above young Israelites are admonished to take wisdom – that is, correct conduct – seriously. Such conduct led to prosperity and therefore it was important to find the right way. Indeed, Clement used the entire book of Proverbs to show the wealthy people of Alexandria the proper way to live. However, he uses the texts entirely out of context. Of course he was unfamiliar with the perspective of Israelite wisdom and it did not function in his writings. To him wisdom is pre-eminently inward. In other words, true wisdom is none other than spiritual poverty. This spiritual state had to be pursued unremittingly, for it was worth more than silver, gold or jewels.

11.26 Thus the focus is shifted entirely from externals to inner reality. Scripture commends spiritual rather than material poverty. After all, it explicitly proclaims blessing on the poor in spirit and on those who hunger and thirst after God's righteousness. Those who interpret the injunction to poverty literally and seeks to embody it outwardly misunderstands it altogether. Such people are wretched and God-forsaken. Thus Clement spiritualised poverty. The inner world is the centre of Christian life. Salvation depends not on outward but on inner things. It is the soul, not the material body, that is destined to live and bear spiritual fruit. This is the source of virtues like faith, hope, love, fellowship, knowledge, humility and the like.

11.27 The soul is also the place where one fierce battle after another is waged. Clement maintains that there are two kinds of persecution (note, yet another dichotomy) – one inward, the other outward. Wicked people sometimes launch attacks on innocent believers, which naturally causes great pain. But the inner struggle is far worse. All sorts of desires can drive the believer to distraction. What makes this battle so tough and unrelenting is that it is waged inwardly and incessantly. Christians carry their enemy within them and can never escape him. Fire can inflict great injury, but it is as nothing compared with the devouring inner fire of desire. War can cause death, but it lasts a limited time while the inner struggle rages throughout one's life.

11.28 The struggle in one's soul is mainly about money. People always hanker inwardly after abundant material gifts. The pure soul is one which is poor in all manner of desires for riches. Poverty is not a matter of visible deeds but refers to something greater, more divine and more perfect. It means banishing all passions relating to wealth from the heart. Only when these old desires are banished can we become true disciples of God. Impure souls are rich in all manner of lusts and desires. Instead of carrying the Spirit in their hearts, such people cherish their worldly goods. They are caught up in diseased thoughts centring on money alone; they are attached to it with their whole being; their all-absorbing preoccupation with their wealth causes excessive desire for it; they are constantly devising ways of acquiring yet more riches. Clement characterises this kind of person with reference to Genesis 3:19, which says that man is dust and will return to dust. Although the text is applicable to all human beings, Clement applies it only to those who are unable to rid themselves of worldly and material passions. Those who are unable to become poor in their "rich" desires will perish like dust. This internalisation of poverty is typical of allegory. True poverty is invisible and inward. In other words, poverty that is not primarily spiritual is inauthentic.

J. TRUE WEALTH IS SPIRITUAL

11.29 In terms of the above there is nothing wrong with wealth. Since externals did not really matter, one could enjoy one's riches. But these are not real wealth, which is likewise spiritual. Fundamentally it is something to be experienced inwardly. The same thing is required of the rich as from everybody else: to become poor in spirit. This means obeying God's commandments, keeping one's gaze fixed on him, being lowly of heart, poor and free from desire for money, to act with self-control and have good relations with other people. This is to experience true riches. Thus true riches too are transposed to one's inward life.

K. HELPING THE NEEDY

11.30 The only part of wealth and poverty that should be outwardly observable is help to the needy. There is a grave obligation on people of means to share it with others. An important text in this regard is Proverbs 10:4b, "... but the hand of the diligent makes rich". In the book of Proverbs and the wisdom literature generally wealth features prominently. It indicated that a person was right-minded and lived according to the will of Yahweh. Wealth was a result of good work. To Clement this text does not depict wealth as a product of diligence, but as signifying that the hand of the rich should be ready to help the poor. Again the text is spiritualised out of context, so that it says something other than its literal meaning.

L. CHRISTIANS AND CULTURE

11.31 Clement's allegorical interpretation of reality also made it possible to harness Greek culture in the service of the church Mere externals like culture and science could not do much harm, after all. Consequently it was quite unnecessary to forego the positive elements of Hellenism. In his scientific work Clement rigorously adhered to Hellenistic scientific ideals. In addition to scriptural grounds, he wanted to adduce philosophical evidence in support of his case. This did not strike him as problematic. A deeper insight into Greek philosophy and the Old Testament prophets assured him that both pointed to Christ in their different ways. In fact, outwardly Christianity was akin to other religions but if one probed more deeply one realised its superiority. Clement was thus opposed to all those who mistrusted science and Greek philosophy. To him they were like children who are afraid of something illusory. External scientific work and the search for knowledge does not necessarily injure the soul. Thus Clement believed that Christians were cultured beings who could unreservedly enjoy the benefits of Hellenistic culture and science. Any form of physical or scientific asceticism had to be eschewed. Earthly pleasures were gifts from God who created them for the believer's enjoyment.

M. CONCLUSION

11.32 Previously we have stressed the importance of context and understanding. Clement was overwhelmed by the intellectual and cultural context of Alexandria. Discussion with scholars and rich people opened up new horizons for him. He thought it important that the church should open its doors to such people. Concepts like wealth, erudition, culture and science should not be dismissed out of hand. His problem was that the church's accepted views of wealth, poverty, culture and science ruled out this possibility. In order to posit a new point of view, Clement had to read Scripture differently. A literal or a historical interpretation posed problems. In his Alexandrian context an allegorical understanding of reality and Scripture was very helpful. It led him to the conclusion that material wealth and poverty had no real worth. It was entirely a matter of inward poverty or wealth. Those who are poor in spirit are truly poor, but at the same time truly rich This allegorical interpretation of reality and Scripture made it possible to have the rich and the learned feel at home in the church and opened the doors to Hellenistic culture.

11.33 In the course of church history Clement's work was judged in different ways. Some scholars felt that he had capitulated. He had conceded too much and adapted the gospel too drastically in order to accommodate the rich and the educated. In the long run Hellenistic culture and science had weakened the church Fortunately this was not the only evaluation. Over the centuries many theologians who wrestled with the problem of faith and reason, faith and science, church and culture have looked gratefully to Clement for clearing a way for them.

11.34 Clement of Alexandria's struggle with Scripture and his world is relevant to us in South Africa. It is not just something that happened long ago; it has meaning for this country today.

- Our study of Clement has reaffirmed the importance of the reader's context. Everyone is born in a particular social, political, ecclesiastic and theological context, and can never escape it. It greatly influences the way in which a person understands reality and Scripture. One's wealth or poverty in earthly goods drastically affects one's understanding of Scripture.
- Studying Clement of Alexandria necessarily broadens the mind. In this country the church and theologians tend to be narrow-minded, accepting only one understanding of Scripture and one set of values as right and true. Anyone who does

not toe this line is summarily expelled from such circles. Clement's life work sensitises us to views and values other than our own.

- Clement opens one's eyes anew to the spiritual meaning of poverty and wealth. In South Africa "rich" and "poor" refers to specific, antithetical groups. Often the terms are politically loaded. Clement of Alexandria reminds us of the spiritual value of wealth and poverty: the poor may be spiritually rich and the rich spiritually poor.
- An allegorical understanding of Scripture presents us with a major challenge. The excesses of this method can never be emulated or condoned. It is also impossible to apply this method in exactly the way the Alexandrian school did. What is significant is the emphasis on spiritual meaning. Its adherents' tireless search for a spiritual message should fire the enthusiasm of all exegetes. No scientific study of the Old Testament is complete unless it establishes the spiritual meaning.

12

Good news for the poor: How does the New Testament use the Old?

EBEN SCHEFFLER

A. INTRODUCTION

12.1 Many people will be inclined to think that the Bible, being the word of God and "a lamp to our feet and a light to our path" (Ps 119:115), should also be a guide to the "right" exegetical method. The renowned Swiss theologian Karl Barth, for one, maintained that anyone who claimed to be able to interpret the Old Testament better than the New Testament does must prove his or her case. And in chapter 8 we saw that historical-grammatical exegetes believed that Scripture should be expounded in terms of Scripture. Consequently, when Christians look for a way to interpret the Old Testament, the obvious solution would be to turn to the Bible itself. And since the Old Testament was already in existence by the time the New Testament came to be written, we are in the fortunate position that we can simply look how the New Testament authors read the Old Testament, also as regards the theme of wealth and poverty.

12.2 This is what we shall be doing in this chapter, but we shall find that it is not as simple a solution as we may have thought. Although the New Testament authors read and interpreted the Old Testament, it is a moot point whether one can call this exegesis in the modern scientific sense of the word. We shall therefore first examine how certain "exegetical" methods current in those days were applied in the New Testament. Then we look at a particular example of the New Testament's use of the Old specifically to illustrate the theme of poverty, namely the use of Isaiah 61 in Luke 4:16–30. We then consider the New Testament's (and especially Luke's) use of the Old in a broader context. Finally we briefly evaluate the "New Testament method".

B. "EXEGETICAL METHODS" IN THE NEW TESTAMENT

12.3 In the heading the term "exegetical methods" appears in quotation marks. This is meant to indicate that we are speaking of an exegesis of the Old Testament which was made long before people had begun to reflect on exegesis and methods as explicitly as we do today (e.g. in this book). It would be a mistake, however, to conclude that the New Testament authors did not consider method at all or that they were totally unaware of using certain interpretive techniques in their reading of the Old Testament. Nonetheless they would never have taken a particular biblical chapter, demarcating pericopes according to given procedures and then formally analysing the structure of these units. Neither did they inquire into the origin and function of such demarcated passages as historical-critical exegetes do nowadays. When we refer to "exegetical methods" in the New Testament, then, it should be remembered that these were rather *interpretive techniques* that were current at that time. We now consider some of the more important of these techniques.

1. Allegory

12.4 It was noted in chapter 9 that the allegorical method was widely used right up to the Middle Ages. It was already in use in the New Testament, although not as a component of what medieval exegetes called *fourfold sense of Scripture*. According to the allegorical method a text should not be interpreted at face value; instead one must consciously search for a deeper or hidden meaning in the words. The allegorical method should not be confused with allegory as a literary genre, in which the author deliberately uses allegory to make the text communicate (e.g. John Bunyan in his *Pilgrim's progress*, or the allegory on old age in Ec 12:1–6). Such texts are usually incomprehensible unless one spots the allegory. The allegorical *method*, on the other hand, is a means of expounding a text which makes perfectly good sense already (e.g. if taken literally) in terms of a "spiritual" meaning assumed to be hidden in the words.

12.5 In Galatians 4:21–31 Paul interprets the story of Abraham, his two sons and their respective mothers, Hagar and Sarah. Because Hagar was a slave, Paul describes her son as "according to the flesh", whereas the son of Sarah, a free woman (i.e. not a slave), is said to have been born "through the promise" (Gl 4:23). Paul then continues:

> Now this is an allegory: these women are two covenants. One is from Mount Sinai [i.e. the law], bearing children for slavery; she is Hagar ... But the Jerusalem above [represented by Sarah, the gospel] is free, and she is our mother (Gl 4:24, 26).

12.6 Paul is clearly looking for a deeper spiritual meaning in this story from Genesis (see especially Gn 16:15; 21:2,9). This "deeper meaning" relates to the message Paul was seeking to convey to the church in Galatia, namely that Christians are not bound by the law. The law (like Hagar) was part of the old covenant; Christians are born like Isaac from Sarah (the new covenant) and thus are free from the law. The fact that Paul expounds this text specifically thus is significant, since the story in Genesis contains no apparent reference to either the law or freedom from the law.

12.7 Allegory was an acceptable exegetical method in Judaism in New Testament times. It was used by the Jewish philosopher Philo to expound Mosaic law in terms of Greek philosophy in order to demonstrate that Moses was far ahead of the Greeks in terms of their own thinking. In Judaism Moses' law was the primary "deeper spiritual meaning" exposed by allegorical exegetes; the New Testament counterpart was the Christ events. (Other New Testament examples of allegory may be found in Mk 4:10–20; 1 Cor 5:6–8; 9:8–10; Heb 9:6–12.)

2. Typology

12.8 Typology is so closely related to allegory that one could ask if there is any real difference between the two methods. In the case of typology the actual meaning of a text is not supposed to be hidden in the words; it is rather a matter of events repeating themselves in history. As a rule Old Testament characters and events are interpreted as "types" of New Testament characters and events. Thus Old Testament characters are often interpreted as "types" of the Christ. Joseph, treacherously sold into slavery by his brothers (Gn 37), is a "type" of Jesus betrayed by Judas; and Moses, who saves Israel from the slave house in Egypt, is a "type" of Christ saving Christians from the slavery of sin (Heb 3; 8:5–9). In Hebrews 4 the Old Testament sabbath is seen as a "type" of the eternal sabbath rest (i.e. heaven) which is to come (see especially Heb 4:4, 9–11); and in Hebrews 7 the priesthood of Melchizedek (Gn 14:18; Ps 110:4) is interpreted as a "type" of Christ's eternal priesthood.

12.9 Possibly the main difference between typology and allegory is that in the former the exegete does not disregard the original event. The apparent meaning of the original text is not denied – indeed, it has to be fathomed properly in order to clarify the idea that the New Testament author is trying to express.

12.10 From the examples cited above it is evident that the New Testament author of the Letter to the Hebrews is particularly fond of interpreting the Old Testament typologically. This could be because the letter was addressed to Jews, steeped in the Old Testament, to whom the author of Hebrews wanted to proclaim the merits of Christ. In this letter typology is not used to clarify the theme of wealth and poverty.

3. Pesher exegesis of Qumran

12.11 In 1947 archaeologists excavated a settlement of Jews (known as the Essenes) at Qumran near the Dead Sea. These people had broken away from the temple in Jerusalem in the second century B.C. and embarked on an ascetic life in reaction against the "official" cult. The community had its own scriptures, many of which were manuscripts of the Bible and commentaries on biblical books.

12.12 In their commentaries they made use of an interpretive technique which became known as *pesher exegesis* (*pesher* means interpretation). It differed from the allegorical method mainly in that it had a fixed form. The Qumran exegetes proceeded as follows. A certain Old Testament text was cited, followed by the word *pesher*. Then there was an exposition of the text as though it referred directly and specifically to the Qumran community. The following commentary on Habakkuk 2:15 is an example (taken from the community's commentary on this book):

> *Woe to him who makes his neighbours drink of the cup of his wrath, and makes them drunk to gaze on their shame!*
> Interpretation *(pesher)*: This refers to the wicked priest who persecutes the teacher of Righteousness (the head of the Qumran community).

12.13 The Qumran exegete clearly paid no attention to the historical context of Habakkuk. To his mind the only context at issue was that of his own community, so that the present situation of the reader provides the sole key to the meaning of the text.

12.14 In Romans 10:6–7 Paul uses the same *pesher* method to expound Deuteronomy 30:12–13:

"Who will ascend into heaven?" (*that is* [*pesher,* interpretation], to bring Christ down) or *"Who will descend into the abyss?" (that is,* [*pesher,* interpretation], to bring Christ up from the dead).

12.15 Paul is citing the Old Testament in typical Qumran fashion, interpreting it as though it referred to his own argument concerning righteousness and faith in Christ. This is particularly evident in his exegesis of Deuteronomy 30:14 in Romans 10:8–10:

The word is near you, on your lips and in your heart (that is [*pesher,* interpretation], the word of faith which we preach); because if you confess with your lips that Jesus is Lord ... you will be saved.

12.16 Interestingly, Paul omits the final words of Deuteronomy 30:14, "so that you can do it", replacing them with his *pesher*. The original context of Deuteronomy, dealing with the law which is neither in heaven nor over the sea, is not taken into account. Like allegory and typology, then, *pesher* exegesis – used mainly by the Qumran community, but also further afield – appears to have been a contemporary technique used by New Testament authors to proclaim Christ in Old Testament terms.

4. Rabbinical exegesis: *a minori ad maius* (generalisation)

12.17 In the Judaism of New Testament times rabbinical scholars (teachers of Jewish law) formulated fixed exegetical rules for expounding texts. One such rule was that of rabbi Hillel, according to which inferences were made *a minori ad maius* (from the smaller to the greater). This entailed generalising from a single instance in a text that is expounded to other or more significant instances.

12.18 In Matthew 12:1–8, Jesus refers to 1 Samuel 21:1–6, in which David and his entourage entered the temple and ate holy bread, and to Numbers 28:9, which tells how the priests had to prepare the sacrifices in the temple on the Sabbath. The point he makes is that, if such activities on the sabbath were permissible for David and his men and for the priests, how much more so (*a minori ad maius*) for Jesus and his disciples, for "something greater than the temple is here" (Mt 12:6).

12.19 When using this method the focus includes the present context of the exegete, while the original context of the cited text is presupposed. The parallel between Jesus' and David's followers was that both groups were hungry. In the cited instance Jesus features not just as the one who makes the law redundant; in the present situation he makes the law redundant because of the *hunger* (poverty?) of his disciples. To him people's material need counts for more than laws which have purely external religious value. Immediately after this argument *a minori ad maius* Jesus reaffirms the message, again quoting from the Old Testament: "I desire mercy, and not sacrifice" (Hs 6:6).

12.20 Our example of the use of this rabbinical exegetic rule shows that the New Testament also interpreted the Old Testament with reference to the theme of wealth and poverty, or material human need. (See also Dt 25:4 in 1 Cor 9:9–10; other examples of the method are the use of Lv 16 in Heb 9:13–14; Ex 24:12 in 2 Cor 3:7–8.)

5. Promise and fulfilment

12.21 According to this interpretive technique a contemporary event is reported (e.g. the birth of Jesus), and then we are told that it took place in fulfilment of some Old Testament promise or prophecy. This technique is used particularly in Matthew's Gospel. The virgin birth (Mt 1:22–23) is regarded as the fulfilment of Isaiah 7:14; the nativity in Bethlehem (Mt 2:5–6) as the fulfilment of Micah 5:1; the flight to Egypt (Mt 2:14–15) as the fulfilment of Hosea 11:1; and the casting of lots over Jesus' clothes (Jn 19:254) as the fulfilment of Psalm 22:19. Luke's Gospel likewise regards the coming of Christ as the fulfilment of Old Testament promises (Lk 1:54–55, 68–75; 4:18–21).

12.22 This method too has a great deal in common with the ones discussed above, in that the exegesis is determined by the contemporary context of the New Testament author. Not that the original Old Testament context is consciously violated: it is the author's honest opinion that the things written in the Old Testament predict contemporary events (particularly sensational ones). Ignorance about the actual Old Testament context further contributes to the way in which the author's own context overshadows the original one.

6. Creative reinterpretation

12.23 According to this technique an Old Testament text is used to compose a completely new account. It is not so much an exposition of the Old Testament text as the creation of a new one in which the Old Testament text plays a major role. Luke's Gospel in particular makes use of this method. The parable of the good Samaritan (Lk 10:30–36) was based on 2 Chronicles 28:8–15, which tells of Samaria's merciful treatment of Judah. The episode of the widow of Nain (Lk 7:11–17) originated from the report on the widow of Zarephath in 1 Kings 17:8–24; the grateful Samaritan (Lk 17:11–19) was written by analogy with 2 Kings 5; and the Emmaus episode was based on Jeremiah 14:8–9.

12.24 When using this method the author's own context features so prominently that a new text is in fact created. The Old Testament text is obscured to the extent that one cannot even be certain that the new text is in fact based on it in all instances. As a result it is a moot point whether we can call this an exegetical method at all. It is, however, one way in which the New Testament made *use* of the Old and it is mentioned here because the creativity it displays is very similar to the kind of creativity encountered in the other exegetical methods.

7. Conclusion

12.25 Although the interpretive techniques or methods discussed above vary greatly, there are certain similarities. The cardinal one to bear in mind is surely that the New Testament authors were primarily intent on communicating a particular idea they had in mind. The methods they used in no way represent formal scriptural exegesis which seeks to interpret the text systematically and without bias. Not that such exegesis is completely unknown in our day. Scripture was used in support of certain views, much as present-day theologians or preachers may bolster their arguments by continually citing corroborative biblical texts. They might briefly expound the cited texts, but without dwelling in any depth on the context; and when the context is indicated, it with the information from the cited biblical text serves only to reinforce the argument. In the next section we shall see how this is done with regard to the theme of poverty and wealth.

C. HOW IS ISAIAH 61 USED IN LUKE 4:16–30?

12.26 The Gospel according to Luke is indisputably the New Testament book which devotes most attention to wealth and poverty. In his double volume (Luke-Acts) Luke draws liberally on the Old Testament, with Isaiah featuring particularly prominently. It seems appropriate, therefore, to examine one example from this Gospel more closely. To illustrate Luke's method clearly, we juxtapose the texts of Luke 4:16–21 and Isaiah 61 and then consider the way Luke used this Isaiahan passage.

12.27

Luke 4:16–21	**Isaiah 61:1–4**
And he came to Nazareth, where he had been brought up; and he went to the synagogue, as his custom was, on the sabbath day. And he stood up to read; and there was given to him the book of the prophet Isaiah. He opened the book and found the place where it was written,	
"The Spirit of the Lord is upon me, because he has anointed me to preach good news to the poor.	The Spirit of the Lord God is upon me, because the Lord has anointed me to bring good tidings to the afflicted;
He has sent me	he has sent me to bind up the brokenhearted,
to proclaim release of the captives	to proclaim liberty to the captives,
and recovering of sight to the blind, to set at liberty those who are oppressed, and the opening of the prison to those who are bound;	
to proclaim the acceptable year of the Lord".	to proclaim the year of the Lord's favor, and the day of vengeance of our God;
And he closed the book, and gave it back to the attendant, and sat down; and the eyes of all in the synagogue were fixed on him. And he began to say to them, "Today this scripture has been fulfilled in your hearing".	to comfort all who mourn; to grant to those who mourn in Zion – to give them a garland instead of ashes, the oil of gladness instead of mourning, the mantle of praise instead of a faint spirit; that they may be called oaks of righteousness, the planting of the Lord, that he may be glorified.
	They shall build up the ancient ruins, they shall raise up the former devastations; they shall repair the ruined cities, the devastations of many generations.

12.28 If we compare the two texts, there are a number of points that call for attention if we are to understand properly how Luke used Isaiah 61.

12.29 The first is *Luke's specific use of the Greek translation, the Septuagint.* Luke 4:18–19a is a quotation from Isaiah 61:1–2a. However, in the versions appearing in the two columns above several discrepancies are discernible. This is because the translation of Isaiah 61:1–4 is from the Hebrew text, whereas Luke had used the Septuagint, which was in fact the early Christians' Bible. The Greek version is the same as Luke's text, except that he omitted the phrase, "to comfort all who mourn" and inserted Isaiah 58:6d, "to let the oppressed go free". The fact that Luke used the Greek translation current in his day indicates that he was primarily concerned with the relevance of the text to his own context rather than with "scientifically" studying the "original text".

12.30 The second point is *the original historical context of Isaiah 61.* In order to get a clear picture of Luke's use of this text we have to know what Isaiah's text meant in its original context. The text probably dates to the time of the Jews' return to Palestine after the exile (fifth century B.C.). Isaiah 61:3–4 tells how the Lord was about to alter the fate of "those who mourn in Zion" – which could refer to either the exiles or the lower classes of the population who had stayed behind in Palestine during the exile. There is much ado about vengeance on the enemy (possibly the Babylonians) and the reconstruction of cities (as happened e.g. under Nehemiah). To grasp Luke's interpretation of this text we must remember that the original text referred to a situation which was by then almost five centuries ago and which he then applied anew to New Testament times by way of a particular interpretive technique.

12.31 The third point is that *the text is interpreted in terms of a scheme of promise and fulfilment.* In Luke 4:21 Jesus, having read the passage from Isaiah, says, "Today this scripture has been fulfilled in your hearing". This comment of Jesus' indicates that Luke was reading the Isaiahan text as a *promise*. What we have said above about the original context of this text did not enter into his thinking at all, for in his view Isaiah's words were meant as a prophecy of a later event – the day Jesus read from this scroll in Nazareth. The present context was manifestly more important to Luke than the original one.

12.32 The fourth point is *Luke's messianic or christological interpretation of the text.* In our discussion of the various New Testament exegetical techniques we pointed out that the Christ events usually formed the substance of New Testament interpretations of the Old Testament. This is largely true of Luke 4:18–19 as well. When Jesus claimed that the scripture had been fulfilled that day, he was referring to and therefore applying it to himself. In other words, he was the one *anointed* by the Spirit to evangelise the poor and free the afflicted. On the one hand, then, the text makes the point that Jesus was the Messiah (Hebrew for "anointed"; "Christ" in Greek). At the same time it indicates clearly what is meant by "Messiah" in this context: the term refers particularly to Jesus' compassion, both in word and in deed, for the poor and the suffering (see also Lk 7:22).

12.33 In the fifth place there is *Luke's selective use of the text.* Apart from the fact that, as we have seen, he had used the Septuagint in preference to the Hebrew scriptures, we have noted that he omitted one phrase and inserted another from Isaiah 58:6d. He did so in pursuance of his purpose in quoting this text. Consequently he also calculatingly ended the quotation with a reference to the "acceptable year of the Lord" (Is 1:2a). Luke had to stop the quotation at this point since the rest of Isaiah's text deals with a day of retribution for the enemy and comfort intended exclusively for the people of Zion (the post-exilic Jews). But as we know from the rest of Luke's Gospel (see Lk 3:6; 13:29), he considered the salvation brought by Christ to be destined for all people and all nations, and this is in fact what the rest of the Nazareth episode communicates (Lk 4:25–27). Thus Luke transforms the particularist or exclusivist perspective of Isaiah's text into an inclusive, universalist one. Jesus is the Messiah who allays suffering – not only for the Jews but for everybody; and Scripture is cited in a way that underscores this message.

12.34 The sixth point is *the way the text is applied in the New Testament context.* The converse of Luke's relative disregard of the original context of Isaiah is that the New Testament context plays a dominant role. This context is twofold, comprising the situation of Jesus himself and that of the author, Luke. With regard to *Jesus' context*, the quotation from Isaiah clearly marks an occasion during his earthly ministry when he read from a scroll in the synagogue at Nazareth and applied the text to himself. It is to this end that Luke supplies the information contained in verses 16 and 17. In the rest of the passage we see, moreover, how Jesus' action nearly led to his death (Lk 4:28–29). As for *Luke's context*, this was mainly what he had in mind for the community in which he was living at the time when he was recording these events. In section D we consider this aspect.

12.35 The seventh point is the *literal conception of the word "poor"*. The text of Isaiah 61:1 reproduced above, which is based on the Hebrew text, speaks of "the afflicted", whereas Luke 4:18 merely refers to "the poor". By using the Greek text (which also has "poor"), Luke is placing great emphasis on material poverty. The Greek word for "poor", *ptochos*, literally means destitute or "begging poor" and is never generalised or spiritualised in the New Testament. From the rest of the quotation it is evident that Jesus also had in mind other forms of affliction (albeit ones closely associated with economic poverty). The heavy emphasis on physical poverty (see also Lk 7:22) not only accords with the trend in the rest of Luke's Gospel (cf. paras 12. 37–38 below), but underscores the fact that God regards the human being (body and soul) as a unified entity and that Christ came for the sake of the entire person, not just to meet people's purely religious needs.

12.36 *To sum up*: Luke uses a contemporary interpretive technique (the scheme of promise and fulfilment) to expound Isaiah 61. As is his wont, he uses the Septuagint and quotes selectively from the text, in a way that communicates his own train of thought to his readers. Its substance concerns Jesus the Messiah who shows compassion for the poor and the oppressed.

D. WHERE DO THE "NEW TESTAMENT" METHODS COME FROM?

12.37 Of all the New Testament books, Luke's devotes most attention to poverty –

so much so that he has on occasion been called the "evangelist of the poor". It should be noted that in Luke poverty is not spiritualised (as may be said of Mt 5:3), but refers to material bread-and-butter want. According to Luke, Jesus was himself poor (Lk 2:7; 2:22–24 [cf. Lev 12:8]; 8:3; 9:58) and the fact that he was proclaiming the good news to the poor (Lk 6:20–21) is cited to John the Baptist as proof of his messiahship (Lk 7:22). When one gives a banquet the poor should also be invited (Lk 14:13,21). One should be prepared to sell one's possessions and give the proceeds to the poor (Lk 3:11; 11:41; 12:33; 18:22) in order to have a treasure in heaven, unlike the rich fool (Lk 12:13–21). Consequently the behaviour of Zaccheus (Lk 19:8–9) and the poor widow (Lk 21:3) is commendable, as is that of the early Christians who owned everything communally (Ac 2:44–47; 4:32–35).

12.38 The parable of Lazarus and the rich man communicates Luke's attitude towards poverty most movingly. This parable describes dramatically how those in material need should be cared for. Lazarus' miserable lot and the rich man's callousness are depicted so vividly that the reader unconsciously identifies with the former and finds the rich man's attitude incomprehensible. The gravity of the issue is underscored by the view that people's eternal destiny is influenced by it. This makes it all the more inexplicable when readers have to acknowledge in the end that, although they identify with Lazarus, they nonetheless behave like the rich man.

12.39 In terms of our overall theme of wealth and poverty in the Old Testament, it is interesting to note that Luke's parable about Lazarus and the rich man is most probably based on the Old Testament. At the end of the parable Abraham refers the imploring rich man to Moses and the prophets (Lk 16:31), implying that if he had heeded the Old Testament he would not have ended up in the eternal flames. The Old Testament passage Luke had in mind here – and which may have given rise to the composition on this parable, using the technique of *creative reinterpretation* – is Deuteronomy 15:4–11:

> But there will be no poor among you ... if only you will obey the voice of the Lord your God, being careful to do all this commandment which I command you this day ... If there is among you a poor man ... in any of your towns within your land ... you shall not harden your heart or shut your hand against your poor brother ... [lest] he cry to the Lord against you, and it be sin in you. You shall give to him freely, and your heart shall not be grudging when you give to him; because for this the Lord your God will bless you in all your work and all that you undertake. For the poor will never cease out of the land; therefore I command you, You shall open wide your hand to your brother, to the needy and to the poor, in the land.

12.40 These examples from Luke's Gospel demonstrate sufficiently clearly that poverty was very much in the mind of this evangelist. To communicate his views in this regard he drew freely on Old Testament traditions. He proceeded in the typical fashion of all New Testament authors, possibly adding to their repertoire his technique of creative reinterpretation. But what was there in Luke's situation that compelled him to adopt this attitude towards poverty and to resort to the Old Testament to state his case?

12.41 We know that Luke was a Greek and that the Christian community to which he addressed himself lived in Asia Minor (possibly in Antioch). This community was undergoing suffering and temptation. By now it was some sixty years after Christ's crucifixion and the second coming (their final redemption) had still not materialised. The church was being persecuted by emperor Domitian, which probably meant not only that their lives were in jeopardy but also that their property was being confiscated. In these dismal circumstances some of the faithful relaxed their vigilance, while middle-class Christians began to live increasingly for worldly pleasure, despising and exploiting the poor (see Lk 8:14; 12:45). It could have been that less well-to-do Christians hated the rich and wanted to oust them from their fellowship as the Jews had done to the tax collectors of old. Luke wanted to remedy this situation with his account of Jesus of Nazareth and consequently stressed care of the needy and an austere life-style, as well as the importance of accepting all social groups (e.g. tax collectors and wealthy people). To communicate this message Luke, besides using the two sources at his disposal (Mark and the so-called Q source), drew freely on the Old Testament (in addition to Is 61:1 and Dt 15:4–11, see also 1 Ki 17 and 2 Ki 5 in Lk 4:25–27). The quotation from Isaiah appears right at the beginning of Jesus' public career and in fact serves to characterise his entire ministry. So important is this issue to Luke that he includes in his Gospel several other narratives created on the basis of Old Testament stories (see paras 12:23–24 above for further examples).

12.42 Although less prominently than in Luke's Gospel, poverty also features in *the rest of the New Testament* (Mt 5:3; 11:1; 19:16–21; 26:6–11; Mk 10:17–22; 12:41–44; 14:1–9; Jn 12:1–8; 13–29; Ac 6:1–6; Rm 15:25; 1 Cor 1:28; 16:1; 2 Cor 8:4; Eph 4:28; 2 Th 3:7–10; 1 Tim 6:17–19; Ja 1:27; 2:14–27; 1 Jn 3:17). Jesus himself was poor and his disciples comparatively so. Moreover, Christianity spread mainly among the lower classes of society, although there were wealthy Christians who were usually called on to assist the poor. Paul, on the other hand, exhorted Christians to try to be self-sufficient as he was – in other words, they had to do something to improve their own lot (2 Th 3:7–10). But James is par excellence the one who, in almost revolutionary terms, attacks wealthy Christians who look down on their poor brethren (Ja 2:1–17).

12.43 Thus poverty was part of the early Christians' situation and we have seen that in all the New Testament interpretive techniques the authors' own situation was an important factor. In order to cultivate a charitable attitude towards the poor, these early Christians turned to their Bible, the Old Testament. In their exegesis the emphasis was on actual material poverty – it was only in later church history (when Christianity began to penetrate to the upper social classes) that the concept was "spiritualised". It is interesting to note that allegory was never used for this purpose in the beginning.

E. ADVANTAGES AND DISADVANTAGES OF THE "NEW TESTAMENT METHODS"

1. Advantages of the New Testament methods

12.44 The final point made in the previous paragraph should be noted here as an advantage. *The New Testament never uses allegory to evade the problematics of poverty.*

This is all the more commendable since allegory was in fact a method used by New Testament authors.

12.45 The second advantage is related to the first one. The New Testament shows fine *judgement* in its application of the available interpretive techniques. If a method does not produce the desired results it is not imposed willy-nilly. The New Testament authors knew very well what they wanted to communicate (the Christ events) and in a sense they read the Old Testament critically from this perspective.

12.46 Their critical approach to the Old Testament meant that the New Testament authors – notwithstanding the fact that the Old Testament was their Bible – tended to *avoid "negative traditions"*. Because charity to the poor and love of one's enemies were key tenets of Jesus' ethics, Old Testament traditions that glorify wealth (e.g. king Solomon's, 1 Ki 3:10–14) and commend war (e.g. 1 Sm 15:3l; Ps 137:9) were shunned. In Luke's use of Isaiah 61 we saw that he avoided both its particularism or exclusiveness and its promise of wealth (Is 61:2, 6).

12.47 Although critical of the Old Testament in terms of their perspective on the Christ events, the New Testament authors were not hypercritical. They did not blow up the Christ events to the extent of dismissing the Old Testament altogether. *Positive Old Testament traditions were accepted.* The converse of their avoidance of Old Testament particularism, for instance, was the use of traditions that supported universalism (e.g. the references to the widow of Zeraphath and Naaman the Syrian, Lk 4:25–27). The same applies to Old Testament traditions that are well disposed towards the poor. In addition the Old Testament inspired Luke so much that he created new stories on the basis of Old Testament ones that communicated compatible themes (creative reinterpretation).

12.48 Finally one should rate positively the New Testament authors' attempt to read the Old Testament with a view to its *relevance* to everyday life (despite the problems this caused). These authors did not sit in an ivory tower studying the Old Testament just to amuse themselves and further their academic ambitions. It was applied to the daily lives of Christians which were often characterised by extreme deprivation (including poverty).

2. Disadvantages of the New Testament methods

12.49 The New Testament authors were children of their age and used methods that were prevalent then, particularly in Judaism. But Christian exegesis produced different results from that of the Jews. Whereas Christianity usually interpreted the Old Testament in terms of a focus on the Christ events, Judaism, using the same methods, interpreted it as focusing on the law. This was possible because of the nature of these techniques: they could be used to prove *any point* on the basis of the Old Testament.

12.50 The defects of *allegory* have been pointed out already. The search for profundities in the text usually meant that its manifest meaning went by the board.

12.51 Most of these exegetical techniques ignore the *historical context* of the Old Testament text, either because of ignorance or deliberately (as in Luke's use of Is 61).

As a result their interpretation of the Old Testament is not primarily an *exposition* of the text but an importation of their own ideas into it.

12.52 The converse of this is that the Old Testament text was overshadowed by the *New Testament context*. The Old Testament was read as if it was addressing the New Testament period directly and was applicable mainly to the Christ events. Despite the resultant relevance to daily living, this meant that the Old Testament writers were not given a proper hearing.

C

Old Testament Background to Wealth and Poverty

13

The historical scene in which the Old Testament was enacted

FERDINAND DEIST

13.1 History – which is what this chapter is about – is not simply a chronology of the succession of kings to thrones, of battles won or lost. History is also, perhaps more especially, about the vicissitudes of ordinary people's lives. The historical setting in which the Old Testament originated can only be properly understood against the background of the physical environment and the economic, social and political circumstances of ordinary people in those days.

13.2 For the purpose of our description we distinguish the following periods in the history of Israel:

- the premonarchic period, that is until the establishment of the kingdom of David and Solomon
- the monarchic period, that is
  - the period of the Davidic and Solomonic empire, and
  - the period from the division of the Davidic and Solomonic empire into a northern and a southern kingdom until the fall of the two kingdoms
- the period of the Babylonian exile
- the period from the return of the exiles up to New Testament times, that is the age of Persian, Greek and Roman overlordship.

This analysis can be depicted graphically as follows:

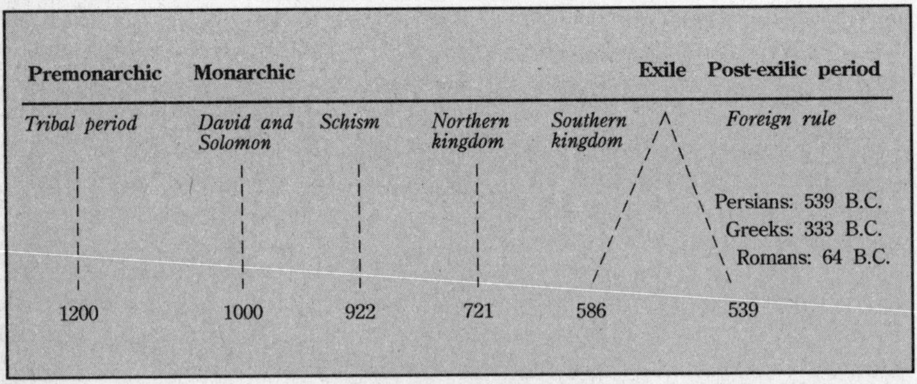

Time-scale of major events in the history of Israel

A. THE PREMONARCHIC PERIOD

13.3 Palestine was one of the tiny, impoverished countries of the Fertile Crescent; a country of extremes in structure and climate and with little arable land. The people lived mainly in small, self-sufficient villages and hamlets and, because of the dearth of resources and technology, they relied heavily on one another for their subsistence. There were a few large towns and cities where tradespeople and merchants lived and where local governments were sometimes situated. The country had experienced considerable population growth from 1200 B.C. onwards, which presented a challenge to the people's technical ingenuity.

13.4 The inhabitants of Palestine derived mainly from *two ethnic sources* – Canaanite and Israelite. The Canaanites were predominantly tradespeople and merchants in the northern territory (Ephraim), living mainly in the larger urban centres. The Israelites were mostly farmers living in country villages and hamlets. Culturally the two groups had a reasonable amount in common, although they differed greatly in the religious, economic and political spheres.

13.5 Whereas Canaanite *religion* was polytheistic, the Israelite religious tradition would not countenance or permit a pantheon. *Economically* too they differed: the Canaanite tradespeople sold their services, traded and had an elementary form of monetary economy, whereas the Israelite peasants bartered their produce for whatever else they needed and had a largely subsistence economy. *Politically* most Canaanites were subjects of city state monarchs, while the Israelites had a system of clan and tribal government.

13.6 The fact that we draw these distinctions between the Canaanites and the Israelites does not imply that the latter were a homogeneous group. Some of the tribes had already had a long history in Palestine by the time our story begins, round 1200 B.C.; others migrated into the territory from abroad (e.g. from Egypt) round about that time, as recounted in the narratives of Exodus and Joshua. A process of assimilation followed. Thus the group from Egypt was assimilated quite rapidly into the ranks of the original inhabitants of Shechem; for we have no account anywhere that Shechem was ever taken, yet it soon became a leading Israelite city (see Jos 24). In other instances assimilation took longer. We read in 1 Samuel 14:21 that even in the days of Saul, some 200 years after the entry into Palestine, a distinction was still made between Israelites and Hebrews.

13.7 Thus, although Israel was distinct from, for example, the Moabite, Canaanite and Philistine inhabitants of Palestine, it did not have a single origin and was not ethnically homogeneous. Consequently one can hardly call it a nation in the technical sense. Not until the reign of David (1000 B.C.) were the people joined in a precarious political, religious and cultural union.

13.8 The basic structure of the Israelite communities was the economically self-sufficient extended family, while several related families together formed a clan; clans in turn might co-operate in a tribal context for economic or security reasons. The physical environment, subsistence economy and social structure made individuals highly interdependent, so that the community could only function as long as the social and economic structures were maintained and everybody did their duty. It follows that there would be explicit rules to ensure that the values and customs of the communities were observed. Children were instructed in these values, customs and usages from infancy. The values of clans and tribes were articulated in numerous adages which we can read today in the book of Proverbs (especially Pr 10–16). These were passed down from one generation to the next and were designed to teach people to act wisely in every sphere of life so as not to impair the fibre of communal life. Consider the following:

> A slack hand causes poverty, but the hand of the diligent makes rich (Pr 10:4).
> A man who is kind benefits himself, but a cruel man hurts himself (Pr 11:17).
> The soul of the sluggard craves and gets nothing, while the soul of the diligent is richly supplied (Pr 13:4).
> Better is little with fear of the Lord than great treasure and trouble with it (Pr 15:16).

13.9 It was equally necessary to introduce measures to punish those who transgressed the cultural agreements, and who thereby endangered the solidarity and survival of these communities. Many of the *laws* that we find in the Old Testament reflect such measures. Thus *Exodus 21–23* regulates the rights of slaves, blood feud and what action to take when children are disrespectful towards their parents, when people fight, when someone steals, and so on. Consider, for example:

> "Whoever strikes his father or his mother shall be put to death.
> "Whoever steals a man, whether he sells him or is found in possession of him, shall be put to death.
> "Whoever curses his father or his mother shall be put to death" (Ex 21:15–17).

Although there were differences in status between freemen (Israelites), slaves and "strangers" (non-Israelites), among the Israelites themselves the law did not discriminate between the mighty and the lowly, the affluent and the less affluent, or between old and young. Since these ancient laws contain no stipulations to regulate relations between rich and poor, one assumes that there were no extremes of wealth and poverty and that everybody was more or less equally poor or well-to-do. The legal rules under discussion were probably uncodified and formed part of customary law, which was transmitted orally and was therefore familiar to all.

13.10 The histories of the various Israelite clans and tribes (see Jos 4:6, 21; also Gn 12–35; Jos 14:6–15; 15:13–19; 17:14–18; Jdg 6–8; 10:6–12:15) were also passed down the generations by word of mouth. Whenever families merged into clans and clans into tribes, the stories of these groups would have fused into larger wholes. These extensive narratives were then recounted to the guests on festive occasions (see Dt 16:16) by dignitaries (usually priests).

13.11 Israel, like everybody else in those days, viewed the whole of life and every action in a religious perspective; in fact, their entire life was in a sense enacted in a sacral space. As a result they not only narrated their history in a religious perspective and gave their rules of conduct and laws a religious motivation; they also had innumerable religious precepts to keep the community in harmony with the religious order and many rules on how to rectify contraventions of the divine order. Some of these are to be found among the ritual laws in *Exodus, Numbers* and *Leviticus*.

13.12 In premonarchic times, then, Israel comprised a variety of well-organised clans and tribes. Virtually everybody engaged in subsistence farming; everyone shared the same basic view of life and lived in relative isolation from the Canaanite element and international influences. Although certain clans were more eminent than others, most people in the community owned roughly the same property and had equal access to the law.

13.13 Politically and especially militarily, however, they were poorly organised. Consequently they were unable to make immediate decisions and defend themselves against powerful hostile invaders (cf. 1 Sm 11:6–7). It was this weakness that eventually compelled them to establish a state with a central government and permanent army. And once this happened the entire community changed drastically.

B. THE MONARCHIC PERIOD

1. The period of the united kingdom

13.14 As long as there was no serious military threat, the book of Judges tells us, the various Israelite clans and tribes were able to withstand sporadic attacks by other groups. But the persistent raids of the Philistines compelled them to unite and raise a permanent army (cf. 1 Sm 4:1–22; 7:2–11; 13:16–14:46; 2 Sm 23:9–17). David was the one who finally pulled it off, unifying the tribes into a single political structure and raising an army which decisively routed the Philistines (2 Sm 21:15–22).

13.15 The establishment of the Davidic empire had profound implications. The mere fact that there was a permanent army to be catered for and a royal court to be maintained meant that taxes had to be levied, which meant that officials had to be appointed. In addition the royal palace required the services of numerous other officials such as scribes ("recorders") and bookkeepers. A section such as 2 Samuel 7 to 1 Kings 4 was probably based on the notes of the scribes at the royal court. International political and trade relations were established and officials had to be trained to perform in the international arena.

13.16 The country was therefore no longer administered by local authorities (the patriarchs of the clans and tribes) but by a central government, run not by elders but by *officials* (bureaucrats). Thus a rudimentary clan democracy was superseded by an ever more sophisticated bureaucracy. In this regard 1 Kings 4:1–28 is illuminating, indicating as it does how every facet of society became *bureaucratised* as public servants took control:

Verse	Official	Sphere
2	Azariah	Religion
4	Zadok, Abiathar	Religion
3	Elihoreph, Ahijah	Royal court
3	Ahilud	Finance
4	Benaiah	Security
5	Azariah	National administration
6	Ahishar	International relations
6	Adoniram	Labour
7–19	Various parties	Economic affairs

13.17 Whereas formerly *government* and *justice* were administered "at the gates" (i.e. in the public eye) (Dt 16:18; 17:5, 8; 21:15; 25:7), the officials now functioned mainly behind the scenes, out of the public eye. Whereas clan governments were elected from the populace (cf. Ex 18:21–23) and were therefore directly accountable to the clan members for their actions, the officials were *appointed* by the king and were responsible directly to him. Whereas the old system had been based largely on mutual respect, officialdom now occupied a position of *power* vis-à-vis the citizenry.

13.18 Ancient tribal protocol, such as that a person petitioning a headman was expected to bring a gift as a token of respect, now acquired a very different meaning: a gift to an official was tantamount to *bribery*, designed to earn favour for the donor.

13.19 The state, which was now responsible for the safety of its citizens, had to expand the army, modernise it (e.g. by purchasing war chariots and horses – cf. Jos 17:16 with 1 Ki 4:26; 10:26, 28) and fortifying the cities. To survive in the international world of that age commercial links had to be developed and more had to be produced locally to pay for imports (cf. 1 Ki 10:22, 29). At the same time the opulence of the royal court cost more and more (cf. 1 Ki 4:22–23; 10:14–21) and citizens were commandeered to render services to the crown without recompense (cf. the mention of the supervisor of *forced labour* in 1 Ki 4:6).

13.20 All these public projects and the concomitant bureaucracy had to be financed from *taxes* (cf. 1 Ki 4:27–28), and to collect these yet more officials had to be appointed (1 Ki 4:7–19). The peasants on their smallholdings could no longer produce just enough for their own subsistence. They had to produce surpluses in order to pay their taxes. Formerly they had bartered their produce to procure their requirements; now *money* – referred to as "silver and gold" in the Old Testament – played an increasingly important role. Farmers had to sell their produce in order to buy what they needed. Formerly their herds were their "bank"; now they needed to have savings or obtain a loan when they wanted to purchase something. Thus moneylenders featured more and more prominently. As taxation to finance state expenditure became heavier, the farmers grew poorer, while the moneylenders (as suppliers of credit) and officials (because of their position of power) obtained a greater hold on them. Thus the creation of a state led to the emergence of *rich and poor classes* in a community that had once been fairly egalitarian economically.

13.21 To top it all, the state "centralised" the religious life of the people. Formerly the tribes used to celebrate their feasts and worship at local sanctuaries such as Shechem, Shiloh, Gilgal, Bethel and Beersheba. Now the central temple (of Solomon) increasingly took over the function of these small sanctuaries. What had once been local feasts (such as the Paschal celebration) now became pilgrim festivals for which people had to travel to Jerusalem. As circumstances changed new religious rules were laid down to regulate the sacrifices and feasts. Large portions of books like Leviticus (cf. Lv 1–8) reflect this development in Israelite religion.

13.22 Because the people continued to view life in a religious perspective, it follows that in the *literature* of this period the events recounted above were described from a religious angle. Thus *psalms* like Psalm 2 and Psalm 110 extol the monarchy and

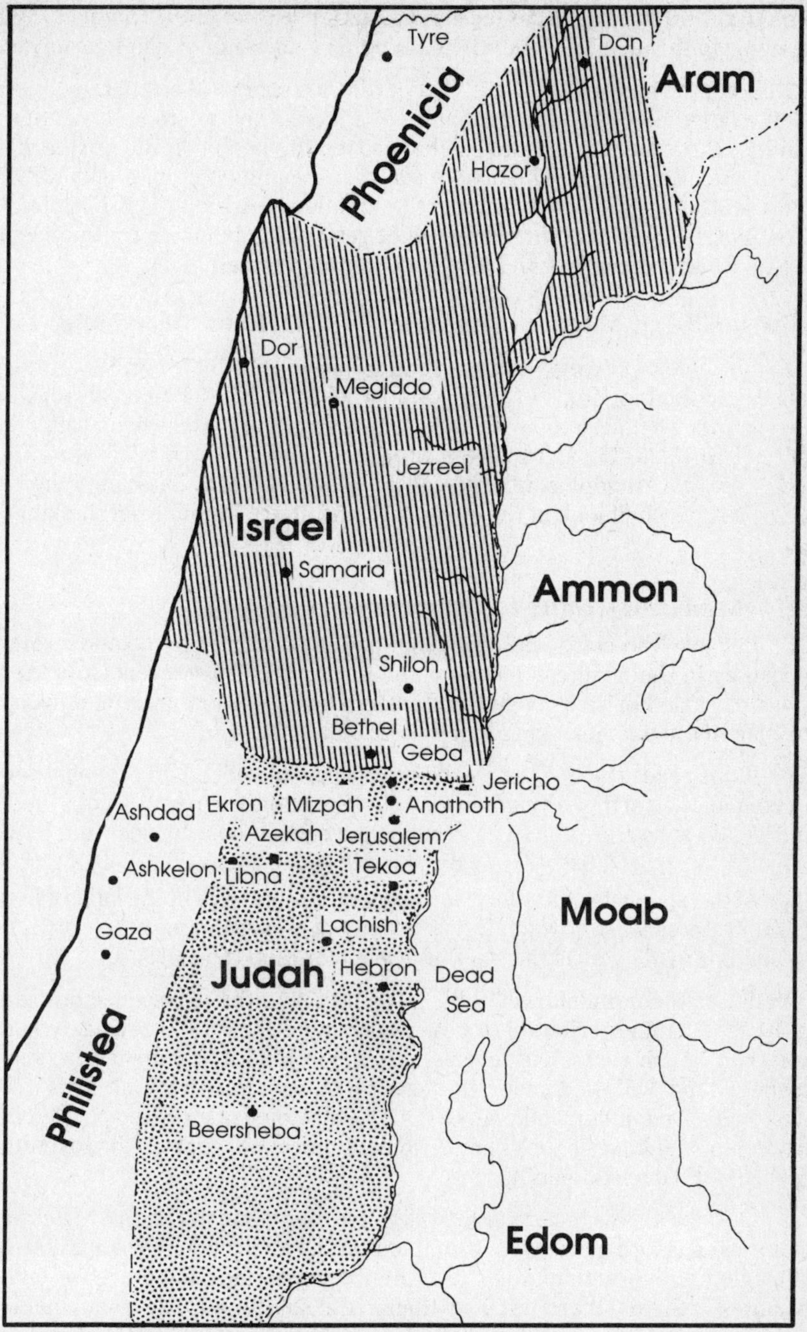

Map of Palestine showing the two kingdoms

Psalms 46 and 48 the capital city, all in religious terms. Similarly, 2 Samuel 7 recounts how people in that age interpreted the hereditary kingship in religious terms.

13.23 From the above it is evident that hardly any sphere of ordinary people's lives was left unaffected by the establishment of a monarchy in Israel. It was this social revolution, and especially the taxes, that caused the people in the northern region to rise against Rehoboam. The upshot was that the unified empire of David and Solomon eventually split in two to form the kingdoms of Judah and Ephraim/Israel (1 Ki 12:1–24). These two kingdoms will be referred to below as the southern kingdom (Judah) and the northern kingdom (Ephraim/Israel).

2. The northern kingdom (Ephraim/Israel/House of Joseph)

13.24 The book of Kings that we read today is an edited version of the court chronicles of the kingdoms of Judah and Israel (cf. 1 Ki 14:19–20, 29; 15:7, 23, 31). In the story as we have it today the two sets of annals are interwoven with cross-references (1 Ki 15:25, 33). Because the situations in which the biblical literature originated in the two kingdoms differed considerably, we need to separate the two narratives. First we shall look at the story of the northern kingdom or the kingdom of Israel.

2.1 A basically conservative community under the law of Moses

13.25 Because the clans and tribes that had been part of the exodus from Egypt lived mainly in the northern territory, the memory of those events and the values that had prevailed in the ancient tribal system featured more prominently in the religious life of the northern kingdom than in that of the south.

13.26 If one reads the book of *Deuteronomy*, part of which had probably served as the "Bible" of the northern kingdom, one observes how frequently it cites the sojourn in and deliverance from Egypt as grounds for certain observances and legal rules (cf. Dt 1:30; 4:34; 5:15; 6:21–22; 10:19; 11:3, 10; 15:15; 24:22; 28:27, 60; 29:16; 34:11):

> Love the sojourner therefore; for you were sojourners in the land of Egypt ... Your fathers went down to Egypt seventy persons; and now the Lord your God has made you as the stars of heaven for multitude (Dt 10:19, 22).

The traditional "communal will" which was based on the experience of the exodus from Egypt was their criterion of how God wanted them to live. God, who lived in heaven and not on earth, had revealed his will to Moses and the patriarchs. Those who obeyed that will lived under his blessing, but anyone who flouted his will in any sphere of life lived under God's curse (Dt 27–28). Consequently the people could not sanction just any kind of social or economic innovation, such as the institution of a typical Near Eastern monarchy.

13.27 Because of this historical and religious orientation the people of the northern kingdom were more conservative, both culturally and religiously, than those of the south. Their conservatism was strengthened by the fact that there were far more Canaanites in the northern territory than in the south. Because traditional Israelite values were under heavier pressure in the northern kingdom a sort of ethnic exclusiveness developed: the people saw themselves as God's chosen race who must on no account integrate with the Canaanites. Because God had chosen them from among all nations, the nation was holy and its holiness had to be manifest in their life. Consequently Mosaic law was applicable only to Israelites and not to the other inhabitants of the country (cf. Dt 14:21; 15:1–3; 23:17–20):

> You shall not eat anything that dies of itself; you may give it to the alien who is within your towns, that he may eat it, or you may sell it to a foreigner; for you are a people holy to the Lord your God (Dt 14:21).

13.28 Accordingly one of the greatest dangers feared by the people in the northern kingdom was cultural and religious alienation. The ethnocentrism reflected in many of their laws (cf. Dt 15:3; 23:1–4, 19–20) and the frequent legal and prophetic warnings against religious alienation testify to the reality of this threat (cf. Dt 11:16–21; 13; 16:21–22; 18:9–14; 23:17–18; Hosea):

> You shall not plant any tree as an Asherah (a Canaanite goddess) beside the altar of the Lord your God which you shall make. And you shall not set up a pillar, which the Lord your God hates (Dt 16:21–22).

It is because of this situation that prophets of the northern kingdom were far quicker to protest against the social and economic abuses of the monarchy than the southern prophets. Whereas the first prophets of the southern kingdom, such as Isaiah and Micah, only started prophesying round 740 B.C., men like Elijah and Elisha in the northern kingdom began to protest against the religious and social decay of monarchic Israel almost a century earlier, round 860 B.C. Consider, for instance, Elijah's words to Ahab following the latter's confiscation of Naboth's vineyard (1 Ki 21:19):

> "Have you killed and also taken possession? ... In the place where dogs licked up the blood of Naboth, shall dogs lick up your own blood".

13.29 Because of their conservatism the Israelites of the northern kingdom, after the division of the Davidic and Solomonic empire, were continually striving for a nationally orientated administrative and judicial system. It was not so much the monarchy per se that they opposed, but they wanted to ensure that the king would not be another despot like Solomon. The king had to satisfy certain standards, such as those set in Deuteronomy 17:14–20:

> ... you may not out a foreigner over you (as king) ... Only he must not multiply his horses for himself, or cause the people to go back to Egypt ... And he shall not multiply wives for himself ... nor shall he greatly multiply for himself silver and gold. And when he sits on the throne of his kingdom, he shall write for himself in a book a copy of this law ... and it shall be with him, and he shall read it all the days of his life ...

To them a king was someone who had to administer divine law, which they believed to be embodied in the law of Moses, received by him from God himself during the exodus.

13.30 This means that the people reserved the right to depose a king if he ruled unjustly in terms of Mosaic legal norms. One result of this was that twenty kings reigned in the two centuries between the division of the empire (922 B.C.) and the fall of the kingdom of Israel (721 B.C.), compared to twenty kings in Judah in over

300 years from the time of the schism until the fall of the southern kingdom (586 B.C.). In addition numerous kings were overthrown in coups in the northern kingdom, whereas in the southern kingdom there were only three coups in three centuries (2 Ki 11; 12:19–20; 14:19). At one stage there were four coups in Israel in a single year, the last of which culminated in a three-year civil war (1 Ki 16:8–23).

13.31 Thus the people of the northern kingdom tried, even under royal administration, to uphold as best they could the values of the old tribal system with its more or less egalitarian economic, social and legal structures (cf. Dt 15:1–11; 16:19–20; 19:15–21; 20:1–8):

> If there is among you a poor man, one of your brethren, in any of your towns ... you shall not harden your heart or shut your hand against your poor brother, but you shall open your hand to him, and lend him sufficient for his need (Dt 15:7–8).

That is why one finds that Deuteronomy displays such manifest sympathy with simple, poor folk in the community:

> No man shall take a mill or an upper millstone in pledge; for he would be taking a life in pledge ... You shall not oppress a hired servant who is poor and needy ... you shall give him his hire on the day he earns it, before the sun goes down (for he is poor, and sets his heart upon it); lest he cry against you to the Lord, and it be sin in you (Dt 24:6, 14–15).

To a great extent they were successful in maintaining social justice until they, like the old tribal system, were compelled to change because of military problems.

2.2 Revolution after the reigns of Ahab and Omri

13.32 Constant Philistine, Moabite and Aramean attacks and Assyrian expansionist pressure, together with friction between Israel and Judah, eventually compelled Israel to adopt a different political and economic course that dramatically changed life in the northern kingdom.

13.33 The story of Aramean harassment and the hostility between Israel and Judah is recounted in 1 Kings 15:16–24. Israel now needed a permanent army and a strong government that would not be toppled every few years or months. After several coups (cf. 1 Ki 15:27–30; 16:9–22) Omri ascended the throne of Israel. He immediately proceeded to organise a royal seat of government (1 Ki 16:23–24). After his death he was succeeded by his son Ahab (1 Ki 16:29).

13.34 Ahab managed to get rid of the Philistine, Moabite and Aramean pressure, to make peace with Judah and to repel the Assyrians. He instituted Samaria as the first proper capital of Israel, fortified strategic towns such as Megiddo and Hazor and built up a powerful army. The timber required for his building operations had to be imported from Phoenicia and food paid in exchange; and Phoenician craftsmen had to be contracted, since Israel did not have the necessary technical skills. Manual labour was probably supplied free by Israelite forced labour.

13.35 To feed the officials and the army, fill the storerooms in the fortified cities and pay Phoenicia for imported goods and services, two measures were urgently necessary. One was to levy taxes and the other to increase food production (wheat, oil and wine). The peasantry were the only people who could supply food, since the officials and soldiers were obviously not food producers. As a result the tax burden on the peasants grew heavier.

13.36 By that time their land holdings had become very small as a result of centuries of subdivision on inheritance, so that they were barely able to provide for their own families. Because they were under pressure to produce more, they could no longer practise crop rotation or leave fields to lie fallow as they had done in the past. Consequently the available soil became exhausted. Since not all land was suitable for agriculture, uneconomic projects were occasionally launched; but new land had to be found and new terraces built. Thus the hillsides were gradually deforested and erosion set in, so that the chances of making a living from the soil became increasingly slender.

13.37 The farmers needed more implements which they either had to buy for cash or exchange for produce. In addition it took years for a newly planted vineyard or olive grove to bear fruit. If on top of that, as happened during Ahab's reign, there was a protracted drought lasting several years (1 Ki 17:1), the prospects for farmers were poor. Nevertheless taxes had to be paid if the state was to survive.

13.38 Thus the farming community gradually became impoverished, whereas the (predominantly non-Israelite) merchants and tradespeople, who were paid by government and were not dependent on the land, prospered. Some of the Israelite farmers had to borrow money to keep going, which meant that part of their crops went to pay the money lenders. When money lenders felt the pinch because of their extravagant living they simply increased the percentage that the farmers had to give them, leaving the latter with even less to live on. As time went by some farmers had to leave their land in the care of their families and go out in search of manual labour. As landowners they used to have a certain social status; now they were manual workers and hired servants at the bottom of the social ladder, with little legal protection.

13.39 Apparently the government of the day also embarked on food production on crown land. It might even be that the state eventually bought up peasant holdings in order to consolidate them into larger tracts. The episode in 1 Kings 21, in which Naboth's land was expropriated, could have been part of this process. Be that as it may, 1 Kings 21 certainly shows the extent to which the peasant community was at the mercy of the crown and officialdom. It also shows how corrupt some eminent Israelites had become – so much so that they were willing to collaborate with Jezebel to expropriate Naboth's land (1 Ki 21:8–14).

13.40 Thus the state could guarantee the security of its citizens, and those who were money lenders, merchants, officials or in some other kind of paid employment prospered; but Israelite peasants were in dire straits. It is against this background that one should see the ministries of Elijah and Elisha during the reigns of Ahab and his descendants. The outcome of Ahab's reforms was a bloody revolution against his government (2 Ki 9–10).

13.41 The rebel general Jehu immediately set about reviving traditional Israelite institutions. It could be that parts of the Deuteronomic laws which reflect traditional tribal values were in fact recorded during this period as a guide book in order to reinstate those values. We do not know to what extent Jehu's social reforms succeeded. We know, however, that both economically and militarily the state declined rapidly and that Aramean and Assyrian pressure increased. While famine (cf. 2 Ki 6:24–31; 8:1) and suffering ravaged the country, Israel forfeited its independence during Jehu's reign and became a tributary to Assyria.

13.42 This situation continued unchanged for some fifty years until Jeroboam II ascended the throne in 786 B.C. (2 Ki 14:23–29). On this occasion the historians note:

> For the Lord saw that the affliction of Israel was very bitter, for ... there was none to help Israel ... so he saved them by the hand of Jeroboam the son of Joash (2 Ki 14:26–27).

Jeroboam's policy of economic rehabilitation and his military strategy were much the same as Ahab's; so were the consequences for the populace. The military and economic rehabilitation of the state cost money and once again the peasants were taxed to foot the bill. Again the peasantry were impoverished to the advantage of the urban tradespeople and money lenders. As we may gather from the remonstrations of prophets like Hosea and Amos, the traditional judicial system collapsed because it was not geared to this type of economic administration. Thus we read:

> ... they [the people of Israel] deal falsely, the thief breaks in, and the bandits raid without. But they do not consider that I remember all their evil works (Hs 7:1–2).
>
> They hate him who reproves in the gate, and they abhor him who speaks the truth. Therefore because you trample upon the poor and take from him exactions of wheat, you have built houses of hewn stone, but you shall not dwell in them; you have planted pleasant vineyards, but you shall not drink their wine (Am 5:10–11).

13.43 In 746 B.C. when Jeroboam's son Zechariah succeeded him, the northern kingdom was once more in decline. The next 25 years saw one coup after another and no fewer than six successive governments (2 Ki 15:8–31; 17:1–6), whereafter the Assyrians invaded the country and its capital, carried off the cream of the population to exile in different countries and resettled aliens from other countries in Israel (2 Ki 17:6, 24):

> In the ninth year of Hoshea the king of Assyria captured Samaria, and he carried the Israelites away to Assyria, and he placed them in Halah, and on the Habor, the river of Gozan, and in the cities of the Medes ... And the king of Assyria brought people from Babylon, Cuthah, Avva, Hamath and Sepharvaim, and placed them in the cities of Samaria instead of the people of Israel ...

Of the erstwhile twelve tribes of Israel and the united realm of David and Solomon there remained only the southern kingdom, Judah.

3. The southern kingdom (Judah)

13.44 As we have seen, the people of the northern kingdom were strongly orientated to the law of Moses and the traditional values of the first Israelite settlers from Egypt. The people of the southern kingdom, the Judaeans, had different points of reference, which we should briefly consider. They were:

- the *kingship* of David and the divine promise to David that his dynasty would rule for ever (2 Sm 7);
- the *city* of Jerusalem which they regarded as God's dwelling place (1 Ki 6:1–38; 8:12–21) because it was the site of the temple of the Lord; and
- the holy *land* which God had given to their forebears.

The Davidic monarchy was *a Judaean* institution from the outset, having been initiated by the patriarchs of Judah in Hebron (2 Sm 2:4). Only later did the people of Ephraim request David to become their king as well (2 Sm 5:1–5). And when the contract they entered into with David to be their "shepherd" (2 Sm 5:2) was contravened by Solomon and breached by Rehoboam (1 Ki 12:1–15), the people of the northern territory abandoned it and went their own way:

> And when all Israel saw that the king [Rehoboam] did not hearken to them [i.e. their request for lower taxes], the people answered the king: "What portion have we in David? We have no inheritance in the son of Jesse. To your tents, O Israel! ..." (1 Ki 12:16).

From that time onwards, except for an interlude when Ahab concluded a treaty with the southern kingdom, there was often overt warfare between the two Israelite territories (see 1 Ki 15:6, 16). Unlike the people in the northern kingdom, those in the south found the notion of a monarchy quite normal.

13.45 Jerusalem was also seen as God's abode. The people in the northern kingdom believed that God lived in heaven, declared his will from there and that at most his "name" "lived" in the temple (Dt 12:11; 14:23; 16:2). The people of Judah, on the other hand, held that God had personally moved into the temple in Jerusalem (cf. Ps 11:4; 18:7; 68:29–30; 84; Hab 2:20), so that the city itself was considered to be holy and unimpeachable:

> Within her citadels God has shown himself a sure defense.
> For lo, the kings assembled,
> they came on together.
> As soon as they saw it, they were astounded,
> they were in panic, they took to flight ...
> As we have heard, so have we seen
> in the city of the Lord of hosts,
> in the city of our God
> which God establishes for ever.
> We have thought on thy steadfast love, O God,
> in the midst of thy temple (Ps 48:3–9).

They believed that as long as a Davidic king occupied the throne and the temple stood in Jerusalem, Judah would be safe.

13.46 Because God lived there, it was the country – and not, as in the north, the people – that was holy. Consequently the stipulations of the law were applicable to all its inhabitants, whether they were native Israelites or not (cf. Ex 12:19; Lv 18:26; Nm 9:14). Those who defiled the land would be "vomited out" by the land (Lv 18:25, 28; 20:22).

13.47 Although Judah was less isolated geographically than Israel and consequently did not cross swords with enemy forces as often (cf. however 1 Ki 14:25–28), the southern court was far more cosmopolitan than any court of the northern kingdom. David first concluded a treaty with Hiram of Phoenicia (2 Sm 5:10–11), which Solomon renewed (1 Ki 5:1–10). David moreover subjugated all the surrounding nations to Judah and made them pay tribute to Jerusalem (cf. 1 Ki 4:21), while Solomon had widespread international contacts and sealed numerous treaties with marriages (1 Ki 11).

13.48 As indicated in paragraph 13.16 above, there were various officials at the royal court, each in charge of an administrative department. Since Judah took some time to become an international power, Jerusalem occasionally relied on foreign expertise to train its public servants. Relics of this training by "the wise" (philosophers) may be found in the instructions to public servants in Proverbs 22:17–23:35, which show a close resemblance to similar Egyptian proverbs. Consider, for example:

Wisdom of Amen-em-opet	**Proverbs 22–23**
Incline thine ears, hear what is said ...	Incline your ear, and hear the words of the wise ...
to put them in thy heart is beneficial ...	For it will be pleasant if you keep them with you ...
Guard thyself against robbing the wretched and against being puissant over the man of broken arm ...	Do not rob the poor ... or crush the afflicted ...
Remove not the landmark at the boundaries of the arable land ...	Remove not the ancient landmark which your fathers have set.

13.49 Since the temple in Jerusalem – the only legally sanctioned sanctuary in Judah – and the palace formed a single architectural structure, and the priests were moreover appointed and dismissed by the king, there was reasonably firm control over the ordinary people's (religious) thinking: God, so they were taught to believe, had promised the throne to David and his house, and therefore it had to continue in perpetuity. To be sure, their religious practice was not pure Yahwism (cf. 1 Ki 14:21–24; 15:3) and several kings had to institute major religious reforms (cf. 1 Ki 15:11–14; 2 Ki 12:4–16) to purge the Judaean cultus of foreign religious elements. Nonetheless they conceived of God, the king, the temple and the country as roughly synonymous (cf. Ps 2, 46, 48, 110). Consider the following statement about the king:

> He who sits in the heavens laughs [at hostile nations];
> the Lord has them in derision ...
> "I have set my king on Zion, my holy hill ..." (Ps 2:4–6).

13.50 It would seem that by and large the royal house tried to rule the people of Judah as justly and equitably as they could. Solomon, for instance, financed his extravagances and building projects from two sources: the tribute exacted from small nations that had been subjugated to Judah, and taxes and forced labour from the northern kingdom. Thus the Judaeans themselves had little to complain about.

13.51 The upshot was that the populace accepted that the political and social order, as well as the economic system, under the king of Jerusalem was God's will for them and that it had to remain like that for ever. Their obedience to God was expressed partly in their attitude that things had to stay "as they had always been". This was how the young were brought up. Consider, for example:

> Inspired decisions are on the lips of a king;
> his mouth does not sin in judgment ...
> A king's wrath is a messenger of death,
> and a wise man will appease it.
> In the light of a king's face there is life;
> and his favor is like the clouds that bring the spring rain (Pr 16:10–15).

That is why the people of Judah patted themselves on the back complacently when the northern kingdom came to a fall. To their way of thinking the people of the northern kingdom had deserted God when they seceded from David and Jerusalem. Therefore God had rejected them. But because the Judaeans had remained faithful to the Davidic house, and hence to God, the Lord had protected them:

> He rejected the tent of Joseph,
> He did not choose the tribe of Ephraim;
> but he chose the tribe of Judah,
> Mount Zion which he loves.
> He built his sanctuary like the high heavens,
> like the earth which he has founded for ever (Ps 78:67–69).

For a long time, then, the southern kingdom felt no need for a critical prophetic voice.

13.52 In due course things changed. Initially the "people of the land" (2 Ki 11:14; 21:24; 23:30) – who formed a significant component of the Judaean government – were rural heads of clans and tribes. As time went by they became wealthier and drew closer to the central government in Jerusalem. They no longer represented the interests of the ordinary farmers, and eventually the situation came to resemble that of Israel: peasants and ordinary folk became the victims of the rich and the illustrious.

13.53 As the northern kingdom began to totter, the number of fugitives to Judah increased. Their reports of their experiences in the northern territory, and especially their religious perspective on life, did not leave the Judaeans untouched. Echoing the spirit of the laws in Deuteronomy, a Deuteronomically minded movement arose in Judah – that is, a growing number of people accepted the law of Moses as a criterion alongside the Davidic tradition. Today scholars call this the *Deuteronomic* movement because it concurred closely with concepts found in Deuteronomy.

13.54 It is remarkable that the ministries of Isaiah and Micah, the first prophets of the southern kingdom, should have coincided with the rise of the Deuteronomic movement and that they should have protested against economic and social abuses in Judah (cf. Is 1:10–31; 3:9–12; Mi 2:1–9).

13.55 The prophets of Judah inveighed against the same kind of transgressions that had occurred earlier in the northern kingdom: the law is violated, the rich oppress the poor and the mighty exploit the lowly:

> How the faithful city has become a harlot,
> she that was full of justice!
> Righteousness lodged in her,
> but now murderers ...
> Your princes are rebels
> and companions of thieves.
> Everyone loves a bribe
> and runs after gifts.
> They do not defend the fatherless,
> and the widow's cause
> does not come to them (Is 1:21–23).

Judging by the prophets' words, there was no real difference between the socio-economic history of Israel and that of Judah.

13.56 But the high and the mighty in the southern kingdom paid no attention to the prophets or to the Deuteronomic movement. Indeed, the priests and the elite were inclined to treat the prophets with derision and sought to silence them. The southern prophets moreover did not manage to gather a large following, as Elijah had once done in Israel. This indicates that the Judaean tradition of faith in God's unconditional promise to the royal house of David and in the temple had a firm grip on the Judaeans.

13.57 Despite the reforms attempted by kings like Hezekiah (715–686 B.C) and Josiah (640–609 B.C.), and even though Josiah's reforms were explicitly Deuteronomic (2 Ki 22:3–27), the basic faith of the people of Judah remained unchanged. They believed that nothing could happen to them while the temple of the Lord remained standing in Jerusalem. Even a prophet like Jeremiah could not shake this conviction:

> Do not trust in these deceptive words: "This is the temple of the Lord, the temple of the Lord, the temple of the Lord ... [Rather] amend your ways and your doings (Jr 7:4–5; cf. also Ezk 8:23).

13.58 After Josiah's death in a battle against the Egyptian forces (2 Ki 23:28–30), his attempts at a Deuteronomic reform lapsed into oblivion and the cause of the poor and simple suffered, especially under Jehoiakim (cf. Jr 36).

13.59 The end of the kingdom of Judah was no different from that of Israel (cf. Ezk 23): In 597 B.C. the Babylonian forces under Nebuchadnezzar invaded Judah and overran the countryside, leaving only Jerusalem unconquered. Ten years later, in 586 B.C., Jerusalem too surrendered to Nebuchadnezzar (2 Ki 25; Jr 52; Ezk 33:21–22). The king was captured and, together with the top people in the city, was carried off to Babylon in exile; the temple was burnt down and the walls of the city destroyed. Only the middle and lower strata of the population were left behind: "But the captain and the guard left some of the poorest people of the land to be vinedressers and plowmen" (2 Ki 25:12).

C. THE EXILE

13.60 The leading people of the northern kingdom were banished to diverse regions and disappeared from history, so that no-one knows what happened to them (2 Ki 17:23). By contrast the leading Judaeans were taken to specific parts of Babylonia (cf. Ezk 1:1–3), where they led a relatively free life.

13.61 The poor, who had been robbed of their possessions by the rich and the mighty, remained behind in Judah and could repossess their property and resume their lives. Nevertheless, the fall of Jerusalem was a tremendous shock to them, no less than to the exiles. What the prophets Isaiah, Jeremiah and Ezekiel had foretold in fact transpired, although the people had not believed them at the time. It was as if God had negated the history of five hundred years: what was the point of it all?

13.62 In devastated Judah those who remained behind composed and sang laments which have been preserved for us in the book of Lamentations:

> How the Lord in his anger has set the daughter of Zion under a cloud!
> He has cast down from heaven to earth
> the splendor of Israel;
> he has not remembered his footstool
> in the day of his anger (Lm 2:1).

The exiles too sang despairing hymns of lamentation:

> How shall we sing the Lord's song
> in a foreign land?
> If I forget you, O Jerusalem,
> let my right hand wither! (Ps 137:4–5).

13.63 Everybody – both the poor who stayed behind and the gentry who were carried off – seriously considered who God must be if he was capable of leaving his temple, his king and his country in the lurch, as it were. Different groups sought answers in different parts of their religious traditions. Some searched and pondered the *chronicles of history*; others studied God's *law*; yet others listened to the sermons of *the prophets* of their day to find meaning in their existential crisis.

1. The study of history

13.64 One group of the people who stayed behind in *Palestine* studied the court annals of Samaria and Jerusalem, judging them in the light of Deuteronomic notions concerning the will of God. They found that the prophets had been right: because the kings had not ruled the people according to God's will and because they permitted the people to become like Israel's neighbours, catastrophe had befallen them. The record of their thinking may be found today in what is known as the *Deuteronomic history* (Dt–Ki), which consistently condemns the kings of Israel and Judah and in which people are called to repent of their misdeeds and turn to God.

13.65 Another group (probably priests) studied the stories which told of the time before the invasion of Canaan and decided that the people had to revert to the kind of community that had existed before there was a monarchy and a permanent temple, when the priests still taught the people how to live a holy life and the temple was a mobile tent. They edited the stories from Genesis to Numbers in this perspective to work out a programme for the restoration of Israel. We find the fruits of their labour in what is known as the *priestly narratives* of the Pentateuch

2. The study of the law

13.66 In *Babylonia* the priests concluded that the catastrophe had been a result of the impure life that the people had lived. Thus they turned to the law of Moses, studied it and wrote glosses to it so that people could observe it as punctiliously as was humanly possible. They paid special attention to customs that accentuated Israel's distinctiveness, such as sabbath observance, the laws governing purity and circumcision. Some of the *priestly laws* that we find in the Pentateuch today derive from this source. Because the exiles had no temple they could not bring offerings and had to be satisfied with services consisting of expositions of the law and song. As a result numerous *psalms* were composed at this time.

3. Prophetical proclamation

13.67 Prophets such as the one whose words we read in *Isaiah 40–55* tried to hearten the exiles – God had not rejected them, he was merely punishing them:

> Comfort, comfort my people,
> says your God.
> Speak tenderly to Jerusalem,
> and cry to her
> that her warfare is ended,
> that her iniquity is pardoned,
> that she has received from the Lord's hand
> double for all her sins (Is 40:1–2).

But not just Jerusalem and Judah belonged to Yahweh. He had created the whole earth and ruled over all and everyone – even over the nations who had captured their king, destroyed their temple and taken away their land. He ruled over history and would command the sovereigns of the nations to let his people go free (Is 41). He would take them back to Jerusalem and they would rebuild the city (Is 40). Ezekiel too prophesied that God would resuscitate the dead bones of the exile and restore his people (Ezk 37). The temple would be rebuilt and God, who had deserted Jerusalem (Ezk 10:18–22; 11:22–25), would resume his abode there (Ezk 43:1–4); only the temple and the palace would never again be architecturally one (Ezk 43:7–8).

D. THE POST-EXILIC PERIOD

13.68 The exile came to an end, but the problems that had bewildered believers during that time were not resolved. Indeed, in some respects they became more acute. To grasp this at all we need to take a quick look at world events at that time.

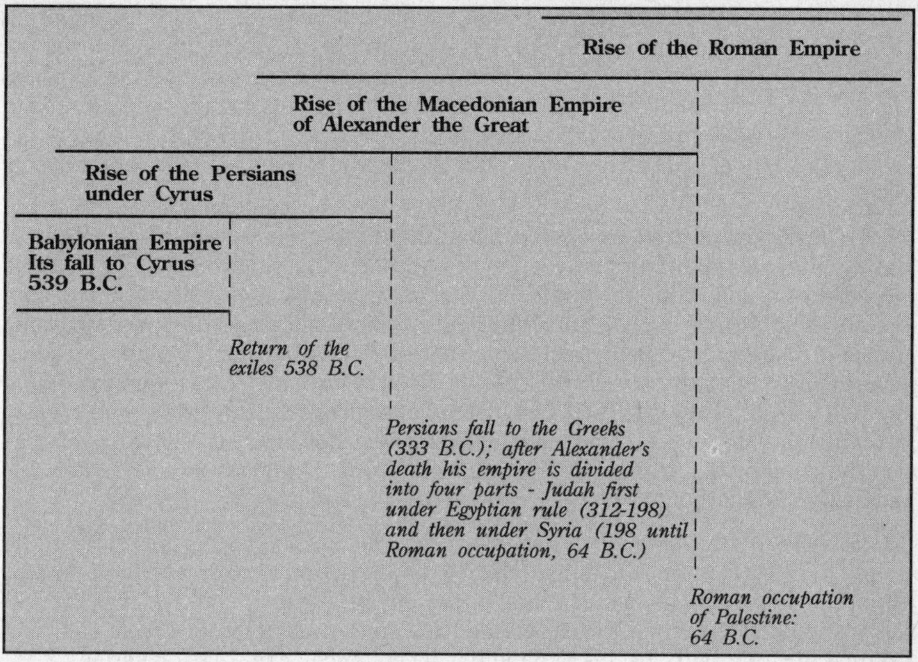

13.69 The most important international events in the period between the Judaeans' Babylonian exile and the New Testament may be depicted graphically as follows:

13.70 In 539 the Persian king Cyrus (cf. Is 45:1) conquered Babylonia. In 538 he proclaimed an edict permitting the exiles to return to Judah (cf. Ezk 1:1–4). A handful in fact returned with Zerubbabel (Ezk 2) and this created fresh problems.

13.71 It stands to reason that the people who had remained in Judah after the fall of Jerusalem, who had reoccupied their land after the departure of the rich and the mighty and had now been in possession of it for half a century, would not lightly let go of it or bow their knees to the erstwhile elite. Ezekiel (11:15) was referring to these people when he wrote: "... (the) exiles ... are those of whom the inhabitants of Jerusalem have said: 'They have gone far from the Lord; to us this land is given for a possession.'" Thus those who had stayed behind saw the returning exiles as ones whom the land had "vomited out" and who for fifty years had lived far from the Lord in an unclean land.

13.72 The returned exiles saw matters differently. For fifty years God had been – according to Ezekiel's vision (Ezk 10–11) – not in Judah but with the exiles in Babylon: "Though I removed them far off among the nations, and though I scattered them among the countries, yet I have been a sanctuary to them ... in the countries where they have gone" (Ezk 11:16). To the returned exiles the fact that those who had stayed behind had not observed the sabbath and had moreover intermarried with other nations was proof that they had set no store by their holiness as the people of God (Neh 13:15–28). Consequently Nehemiah (2:20) said: "... you have no portion or right or memorial in Jerusalem".

13.73 This dissension among the people and the hardships they were still suffering clearly indicated that the deliverance which the prophets had proclaimed during the exile had not yet come. They despaired all over again. In this situation the prophets *Haggai* and *Zechariah* berated the Judaeans and tried to encourage them to rebuild the temple and to reorganise themselves politically (cf. Hg 1–2; Zch 1–8). God would restore the national glory, they said, if the people would but do their bit and worship him.

13.74 Little came of these hopes. True, the temple was rebuilt (Ezk 6:13–18), but the state of salvation that everybody was expecting did not dawn. The people were back in Judah and the temple had been completed, but there was still no king nor any of the glory of yore. In addition their crops failed and they were plagued by plant diseases and locusts. The people were destitute and desperate. Once again a prophet, in the person of *Malachi,* tried to put heart into them, exhorting them to worship God faithfully. But instead of improving, times worsened. In 333 B.C. the Persian Empire, in which people had been permitted freedom of worship, was defeated by the armies of Alexander the Great. The Jews became Greek (actually Macedonian) subjects.

13.75 After Alexander's death his empire was divided among his generals and for a time Judah was under the rule of the Egyptian section (known as the Ptolemaic empire), whereafter it became part of the Syrian (or Seleucid) empire. Under the Seleucids the Jewish temple was desecrated and conservative Jews were actually persecuted for their faith. In this situation believers once again reacted variously. We briefly consider some of the more prominent groups.

1. The nationalist option

13.76 Some Jews hoped that God would resurrect the Davidic state. They expected a political Messiah, one who would restore David's empire. Among these were the Maccabees, about whom we can read in the (apocryphal) *Books of the Maccabees.* These people resisted every form of hellenisation and actually managed to establish an independent Jewish state for a short while (from 134 to 63 B.C.). But in the end they had to yield before the armies of Rome.

2. The "congregational" option

13.77 Others, like the authors of *Chronicles,* accepted that the (Davidic) state of salvation would never again be realised in a political sense. To them the Jewish *religious* community was the goal of Israelite history, and they saw the *congregation* of those days as the state of salvation predicted by the prophets. It was in these circles that the synagogues grew in which doctors of the law (and eventually the Pharisees) read the law and the prophets and expounded the scriptures for a new situation. In these circles the aim was to try and live punctiliously according to Mosaic law, like a holy people of God. This group also began to preach their religion to gentiles and gained scores of gentile proselytes.

3. The adaptation option

13.78 Another group tried to adapt to circumstances following the Greek conquest of the Persians. They sought to understand and reinterpret their faith in terms of hellenistic culture. Scholars in these circles worked diligently at various *Greek translations* of the Old Testament documents, making certain changes to the existing Hebrew texts in order to render their tradition meaningful in a new context. These were the translations which eventually became the "Old Testament" to the Greek-speaking communities when the gospel of Christ was proclaimed among them.

4. The apocalyptic option

13.79 Yet another group accepted that the salvation proclaimed by the prophets was not to be realised in history. Particularly when faithful conservative Jews were persecuted and martyred under the Seleucid administration of Antioch IV Epiphanes, many despaired completely. In their view not only the majority of Jews but the entire world was evil and had to be purged of its wickedness by divine judgment. After that a handful of the faithful would share in God's salvation. They began to study the prophetic writings anew and found that these words were not applicable to the earlier history of Israel, nor to a state of salvation to be established in time. They read the prophets like a kind of secret code to be deciphered only by those with special insight. Thus they found that the seventy years of exile prophesied by Jeremiah in his day (Jr 25:11–14) did not mean that the people would be restored after seventy years, but that 70 was actually a symbolic figure referring to seventy historical eras (Dn 9:1–3, 24–27); the salvation Jeremiah spoke of would only come about at the end of these. Thus they held that the true message of the prophets was an esoteric secret whose true message required special revelation:

> [From] the going forth of the word to restore and build Jerusalem to the coming of an anointed one, a prince, there shall be seven weeks. Then for sixty-two weeks it shall be built again ... but in a troubled time (Dn 9:25; cf. 9:24–27).

Following the Greek word for "to reveal" (apokalypto), this sort of interpretation of history is known as apocalyptic. As time went by various apocalyptic communities arose. We have referred to the book of Daniel, a major part of which was written in such a community. Another was the one at Qumran near the Dead Sea where the books of the prophets were studied avidly, and with which John the Baptist may have been connected.

5. The wisdom option

13.80 A last group turned to religious "philosophy", or wisdom, to discover why people who serve God to the best of their ability should suffer. Some of these people, while critically questioning the answers of traditional theology, nevertheless looked to tradition for an answer. One book to have come out of this reflection was that of *Job*. Others, like the author of *Ecclesiastes*, tried to solve the problem of life's meaning by combining traditional theology with hellenistic philosophy. They arrived at a far more sceptical answer than did the author of Job.

E. SUMMARY

13.81 This chapter affords a bird's eye view of the history of Israel from the arrival in Palestine of the tribes from Egypt to the eve of Jesus' birth. We discussed different perspectives in which believers of those days viewed life and history and how they derived religious meaning from it. We considered the origin of religious perspectives among people who lived in clan and tribal structures, and the way in which their values gradually changed as a result of changing circumstances. We saw how economical and political circumstances necessitated a reappraisal and that different groups responded variously to the same circumstances. An example is the divergent explanations of the meaning and point of the Babylonian exile.

13.82 In our discussion we saw that for various reasons change in the social and political structures of tribal society became unavoidable, and that this change resulted in the phenomenon of economic wealth and poverty, which in turn had an impact on the course of history. We also saw that changing circumstances caused religious people to ponder the meaning of life anew and in different perspectives, such as a wisdom, a legal and a prophetic perspective.

13.83 In the ensuing chapters we shall colour in the background we have been painting further by looking more specifically at

- the physical characteristics of the Holy Land and the cultural environment of the biblical people
- changing social structures in Israel and Judah, and
- changing views of God among Old Testament believers in the course of history.

Once the background has been painted, we shall make a more detailed study of a few Old Testament perspectives on wealth and poverty, specifically the perspectives of the teachers of wisdom, the prophets and the law.

14

Historical-geographical setting of the Old Testament

HANNES OLIVIER

14.1 The aim of this chapter is to cast light on the lifeworld of biblical people. To do this, we first need to describe the *physical* characteristics of the Holy Land – its structure, climate, vegetation and so on. It is generally accepted that the physical characteristics of the Holy Land have not changed much since biblical times and that a reconstruction based on modern geographical information obtained since the beginning of this century would not be far off the mark.

14.2 Secondly, one needs to describe the *cultural* environment of biblical people. This can be reconstructed by modern archaeological research into the way of life of people in a specific area at a given time. It is important to know *what* people in a community produced long ago and *how* they set about it. What technology did they use? What was their annual work cycle? What did they do with their surplus products?

14.3 Finally we consider these people's experiences over the ages on the basis of a reconstruction of ancient Israelite history. The scope of this reconstruction is limited to a socioeconomic perspective on that history.

A. THE PHYSICAL ENVIRONMENT OF BIBLICAL PEOPLE

1. Location

14.4 The biblical narratives are enacted mainly in the territory of the modern state of Israel and, to a lesser extent, Jordan. Geographically this region constitutes an entity which was formerly known by vague designations such as Canaan, Palestine and the Holy Land. It is situated on the narrow (100 km across) southwestern horn of the Fertile Crescent, so named for its agricultural capacity for surplus production. This, the smallest and poorest region in the Crescent, is squashed as it were between the Mediterranean sea and the great Arabian desert, each of which represents a distinct climatic system. Yet it is in fact its strategic location – as an *overland bridge* between Africa and Asia (Minor) with their respective river-based civilisations, and as a *nodal point* between the Mediterranean world and the Middle Eastern world along its eastern shore – that makes this territory a *focus of international events.*

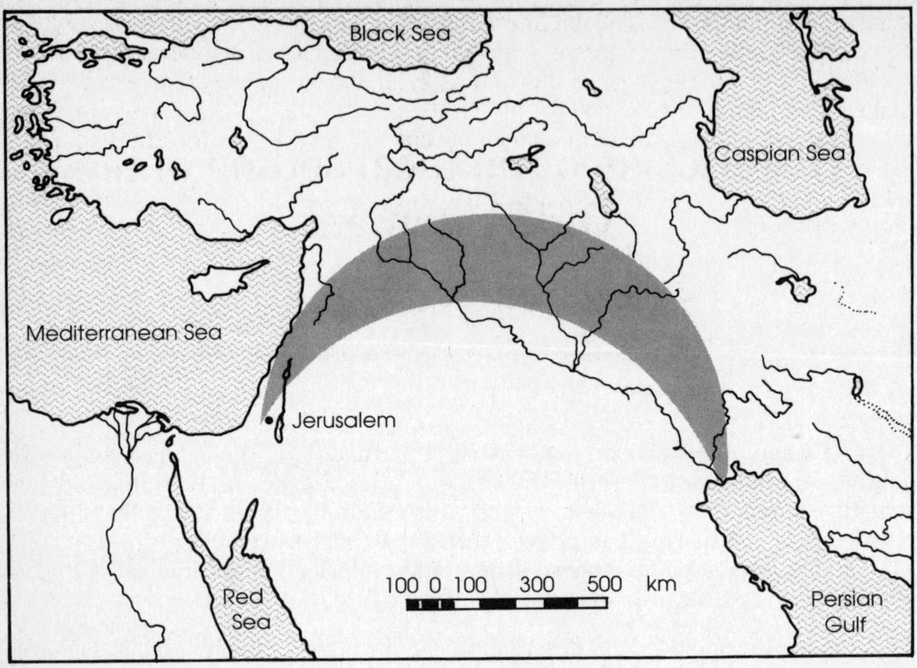

The Fertile Crescent

14.5 Tiny (25 000 km^2), impoverished and in many respects insignificant as it is, this country is nonetheless a whole world in microcosm because of its incredible topographic, climatic and ecological diversity; it is a country full of *contrasts* in terms of structure, rainfall and vegetation. The Holy Land is rather like a kaleidoscope encompassing the environmental conditions of virtually the entire globe within its limited confines: there are pine forests on the snow-clad slopes of Mount Hermon (2 700 m), tropical conditions and swampland in the Upper Jordan area, fertile valleys, arid deserts, oases and much more besides. All these features vitally affect the life style of its inhabitants.

2. Structure

14.6 If one faces directly east from the Mount of Olives one sees, some fifty kilometres away, a level plateau at roughly the same altitude. In between, the earth simply drops away to a depth of some 1 200 metres. Geologists maintain that this early sedimentary plateau – at that time below sea level, possibly even submarine – was transformed by massive geological displacements, curvatures, faults and volcanic eruptions into a variety of topographical areas, each of which in turn affected rainfall, climate, vegetation and soil conditions. From west to east – say from Tel Aviv to Amman (120 km) – the landscape, vegetation, rainfall pattern, temperature and even the life style of the people change continually: first there is the subtropical coastal plain, then a pleasantly undulating hilly landscape (the Shephelah) which rises to the central hilly plateau by way of a steep ascent (the Artuph fault). Thereafter one traverses arid desert up to the rift valley, which lies almost 400 metres below sea level, with its tropical oasis at Jericho. One then mounts gradually to another plateau which closely resembles the central highlands. East of Amman is a harsh desert landscape.

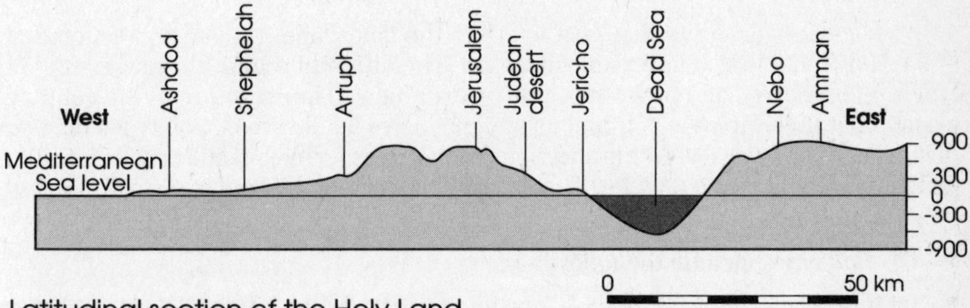

Latitudinal section of the Holy Land

14.7 A latitudinal section of the Holy Land indicates readily distinguishable geographical areas, each of which may be subdivided into regions. Each region in turn has its own distinctive landscape, climate, vegetation and subsistence possibilities. The four narrow regions all run from north to south, the most prominent feature being the Jordan valley (Ghôr).

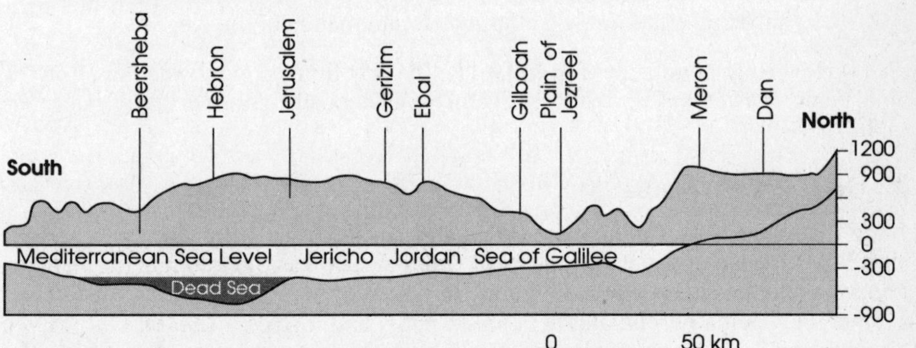

Longitudinal section of the Holy Land

14.8 A longitudinal section of any of these territories does not display such a dramatic topographical variation. The western or Cisjordanian highlands, for instance, are characterised by dense forest and fairly high mountains in the north, Mount Meron (Djebel Djermaq, 1 200 m) being the highest. The landscape then drops fairly rapidly to the warm fertile valleys of lower Galilee, bound in the south by the plain of Jezreel (Esdraelon). Then it rises gradually and becomes increasingly mountainous, reaching its highest peak in the vicinity of Hebron, whereafter it levels off to the basin of Beersheba 500 metres lower down. Across its entire length of 250 kilometres the mountain range is effectively interrupted only by the plain of Jezreel, and to a lesser extent by the valley of Aijalon just north of Jerusalem. Thus it forms a natural boundary between the regions known as Galilee, Ephraim/Samaria and Judah/Judaea. As the rainfall declines from north to south, the vegetation changes from woodland in the north to sparse scrub in the south.

3. Soil types

14.9 The same diversity that characterises the landscape, climate and vegetation of the Holy Land is also noticeable in its soil. The different regions have various soil types, often more than one in the same environment. The structure of the country is such that there are few continuous and extensive fertile areas. Soil types may be divided into four classes: fertile and well drained; less fertile but still arable; infertile soil that can be improved by fertilisation; and totally inarable and stony soil suitable only for pasture.

14.10 Soil types include the following:

- the widely acclaimed terra rossa, a fertile red loam with a reasonable clay percentage which resists erosion;
- alluvial, sandy soil (found mainly in valleys) which, if fertilised, makes good farming land;
- fertile loam with significant quantities of silt found mainly on the plains;
- infertile sand dunes on the coastal strip;
- useless river sand in some parts of the Jordan valley;
- the marshy peat of the upper Jordan valley;
- the various types of limestone soil typical of the central mountain plateau; and
- loess, a hard and inarable type of gravel, found mainly in the Negeb.

14.11 The Holy Land is poor in minerals. In early times copper was mined in the Sinai peninsula and in the vicinity of Elath. Small deposits of iron ore occur near the Jabbok river.

4. Groundwater sources

14.12 Because of its Mediterranean climate, marked by long dry summers, and the structure of the land which causes rapid runoff as soon as the rain hits the virtually impermeable limestone, the Holy Land has no major perennial rivers. A distinction is made between a perennial river (*nahar/nahr*) and a stream (*nahal/wadi*). Even the perennial rivers are small – too small to serve as boundaries. Apart from the Jordan, they all flow either westward towards the Mediterranean or eastward towards the Jordan valley.

14.13 The porous limestone does, however, absorb a fair amount of water which surfaces later in low-lying places as perennial *springs*. The spring of Gihon in Jerusalem is a good example. Wells were also dug. When the water table of a spring dropped, it was excavated deeper and deeper, as in the case of Jacob's well (Sichar, John 4:5) at Shechem. One of the main sources of fresh water in the Holy Land is the

Lake of Galilee (Sea of Chinnereth). This lake has a richly varied bird and fish population, a major supplementary source of food in earlier times. The lyre-shaped lake is at most 21 by 12 kilometres in area and is situated 200 metres below sea level. The

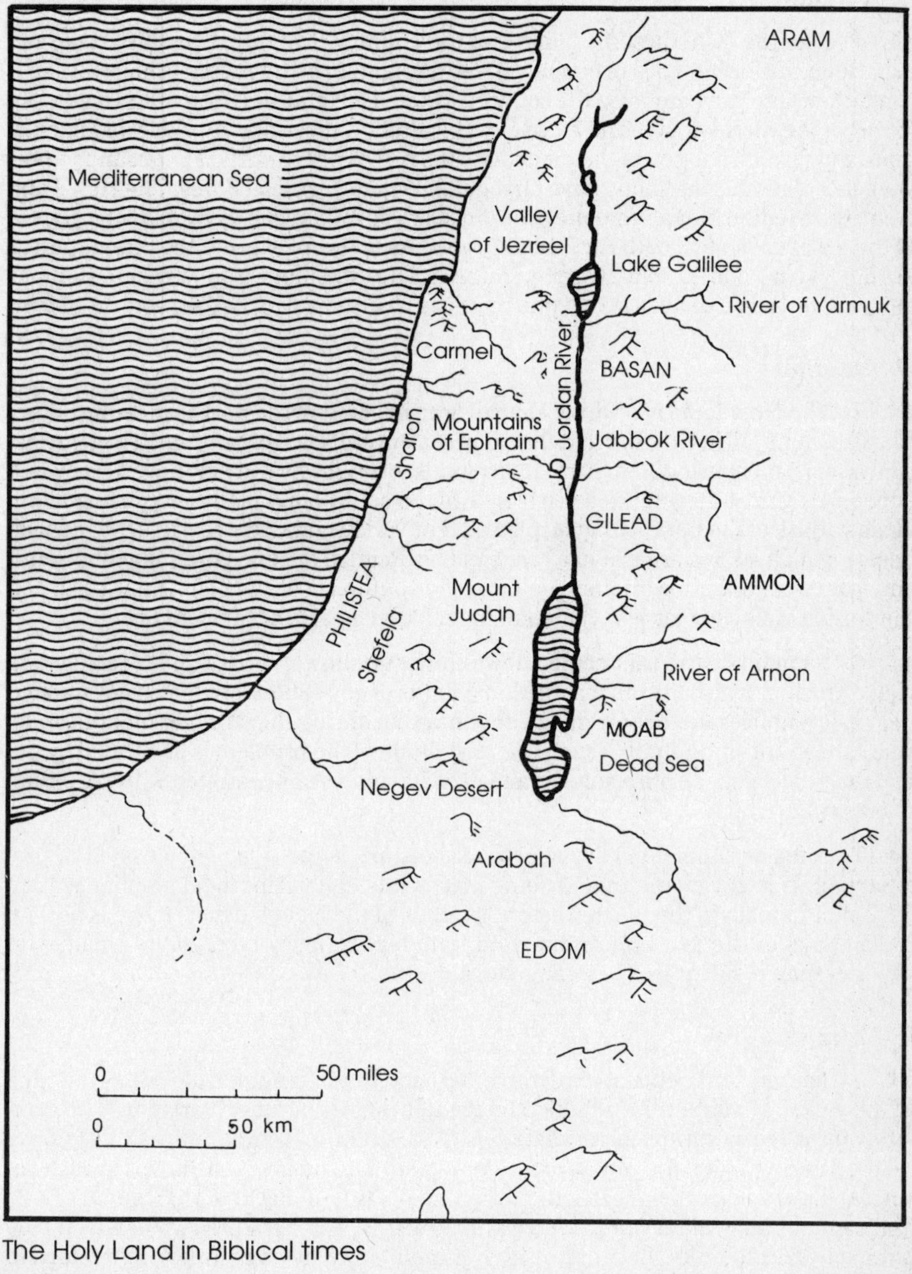

The Holy Land in Biblical times

larger (85 × 15 km) Dead Sea or Salt Sea (400 m below sea level), by contrast, is lifeless.

5. Climate

14.14 Like the structure, the climate of the country is highly diversified. One can experience different types of climate in one day simply by travelling from one region to another. One can gambol in the snow on Mount Hermon and a few hours later gasp for air in the torrid heat of the Dead Sea. In addition there are considerable fluctuations and cyclic changes in the climatic pattern. There are sufficient grounds to believe that climatic conditions have changed little since biblical times. The Holy Land lies in the Mediterranean climatic zone, but it is also influenced by the climatic system of the desert zone of North Africa and Arabia. As in the Western Cape, the summers are hot and dry and the winters rainy and cold. The transitions from winter to summer and vice versa are so abrupt that one might as easily speak of two seasons as of four.

6. Rainfall

14.15 The Holy Land is a winter rainfall area situated in the northern hemisphere. The first rains fall in October and the rainy season ends in April or May. The heaviest falls are in January and February. Rain clouds, brought by the north-westerly wind, condense against the cool western slopes of the central highlands and further along against those of the East Jordanian plateau. For various practical reasons the Judaean desert and Dead Sea area lie in a rain shadow. Rainfall declines from north to south and from west to east, with the result that the southern coastal plain, the Negeb and the Jordan valley get far less rain than the northern parts of the country.

14.16 Sometimes the rain comes down in heavy showers that run off rapidly and cause erosion. It also means that the inhabitants of any settlement that is not situated near a perennial water supply must either migrate during the summer months or devise a means of storing rain water. The magnitude of the problem is illustrated by the fact that Jerusalem's entire annual rainfall of 500 mm is concentrated within a period of 60 days.

14.17 A major supplementary source of moisture is the relatively heavy dew precipitation. It is calculated that in some places it is equivalent to an additional 40 to 50 mm of rainfall. In the north-western reaches of the Negeb desert there is dew up to 250 days of the year. Snow, hail and thunder are fairly rare. Rapid changes of weather may result in frost, causing stock deaths.

7. Temperature

14.18 January and February are the coldest and July and August the hottest months of the year. The higher the altitude, the greater the temperature variation. The average winter temperature in Jerusalem is 8°C. Although temperatures rarely drop below freezing point, the nights are bitterly cold. The further one moves away from the Mediterranean, the greater the difference between day and night (up to 20°C) and summer and winter temperatures (up to 49°C). Temperature is also affected by atmospheric humidity. Because of high humidity the average July temperature of

24°C at Tel Aviv is far less bearable than Jericho's 32°C. On the whole the climate is fairly warm. The central highlands have by far the best weather.

8. Winds

14.19 The west wind from the Mediterranean is always welcome: in winter it brings rain (as does the north-westerly wind) and in summer much needed relief from the afternoon heat. Blowing at about 10 to 15 kilometres per hour, it is strong enough to winnow the chaff during threshing. At the change of the seasons in April and September comes the dreaded east wind (*khamsin/scirocco*), scorching and withering pasture and crops in a matter of hours. Sometimes it is accompanied by periodic droughts that can sorely afflict the region.

9. Vegetation

14.20 The Holy Land has a rich variety of trees, shrubs and flowers. Because of its diversified structure, climate and soil types all three of the so-called protolandscapes – desert, steppe and forest – occur within its narrow confines.

14.21 A desert is an area with an annual rainfall of less than 200 mm and less than half its surface covered with vegetation. This description fits mainly the southern and eastern regions which are only partially covered with scrub. In areas where there are springs or wells it is suitable for sheep and goat farming. The Judaean desert on the eastern slope of the Cisjordanian plateau is such an area: all but devoid of vegetation, it nonetheless offers a little grazing in winter and early spring.

14.22 Steppes (semi-desert) are regions with an annual rainfall of between 300 and 400 mm. They have far more lush shrubs and grass than the desert areas and are eminently suitable for pasture and even for the cultivation of winter cereal crops. They constitute a relatively narrow strip between the desert and the wooded and arable areas.

14.23 Woodlands are regions with an annual rainfall of more than 500 mm. Formerly these parts were covered with dense forest, but the trees have since been felled to clear agricultural land. In addition trees were chopped down to obtain timber for furniture, buildings and implements. In upper Galilee and the Carmel and Adslun area one still finds natural forests. Deforestation, veld fires, overgrazing and periodic droughts have taken their toll. Since Roman times an estimated 2 000 to 4 000 million cubic metres of fertile terra rossa soil has been washed from the Cisjordanian desert and steppe areas, enough to supply 4 000 to 8 000 square kilometres of fertile arable land. In central Syria deforestation was the direct cause of the extinction of elephants by 800 B.C.

14.24 It should be noted that people can hardly settle in densely forested mountainous areas or in the desert, where only a few nomadic tribes migrate from well to well with their herds across a wide area (extensive stock farming). Steppes on the other hand, are suitable for more intensive stock farming as well as a little agriculture – mainly cereals. The early inhabitants of the Holy Land lived on the steppes until they had tamed the dense forests, the soil of which was more fertile.

14.25 An impressive variety of indigenous plant, shrub and tree species occur in the Holy Land. Oaks, cedars, terebinths, conifers, carobs and many others are typical of the forest areas, while tamarisks, poplars, broom and certain thorn trees (e.g. the Christ thorn) occur on the steppes. Here one sees many wild flowers in springtime (anemones, lilies, irises and oleanders) (Can 2:1f.).

14.26 Cultivated plants are mainly cereals (wheat, barley, sorghum) and fruit trees. The latter include olives, vines, figs, pomegranates, mulberries and dates (in order of importance). In early times pomegranates were the only sweet, juicy fruit that could be stored for any length of time and, in an age without Coke, it was much beloved by children. Other fruits such as citrus, prickly pear, apple, pear and banana were not planted until the nineteenth century; neither were blue gums, which are fairly common in the Holy Land today.

10. Fauna

14.27 Because of its situation between Africa and Asia a wide variety of animal species were found in the Holy Land in olden times; there were animals indigenous to Africa, Asia and central and southern Europe. Bears (Ps 80:13; Am 5:19), lions (1 Ki 13:24; Am 3:4), leopards (Jr 13:23), wolves (Is 11:6), foxes (Can 2:15), elephants (only ivory is mentioned in the Bible), crocodiles (Job 40:20–28) and hippopotami (Job 40:10–19) are among the large wild animals referred to in the Bible. The reference by Amos, a sheep farmer, to lions could indicate that they were a common threat to flocks in the Judaean mountains, particularly in the eastern parts. But stock farmers would have been more wary of jackals, wild dogs, lynxes, lammergeyers and snakes that endangered their stock. Cereal farmers would have found mice, rats, rock rabbits and flocks of starlings troublesome, but not owls, eagles and certain types of snakes. Among the worst plagues that struck the Holy Land were the swarms of locusts that devoured all vegetation, depriving humans and animals of their food. Fleas, flies (more than 50 species), ticks, ants, scorpions, moths, lice and worms are all creatures that made life unpleasant. Many types of wild birds such as partridges, quail, wild geese and pigeons were trapped in those times, and small game like rock rabbits, hares and small antelopes were caught in snares. Big game was hunted. Fishing was done with nets, mainly in the Lake of Galilee and rivers. Apparently the people of the Holy Land were somewhat nervous of the open sea (the Mediterranean). Hunting and fishing supplemented their essential protein diet. Few people (even among the rich) could afford to slaughter a sheep or a goat except for special feasts (1 Sm 25:11; 2 Sm 12:1–4).

14.28 The donkey is preeminently the animal used for riding and cartage in the Middle East, while cattle are used for draught purposes. Camels (dromedaries) are desert animals fulfilling all these functions; in addition nomads use their milk to make butter and cheese. There is considerable difference of opinion concerning the time when camels were first domesticated, but it could have been as late as the second millennium B.C. Horses, originally from the southern Russian steppes, were used mainly to pull chariots; they were rarely ridden.

14.29 Smaller livestock consisted mainly of cream-coloured fat-tailed sheep and black goats. In addition to their skins, wool and manure, sheep and goats were an essential source (about 50%) of staples such as milk and dairy products. Small wonder that sheep and goat farming was a major factor in the economy of the Holy Land throughout the ages. Plagues, pests and stock diseases could assume catastrophic dimensions. The custom of migrating with one's livestock to find better pasture, as well as skillful breeding (Gn 30:32), somewhat compensated for the lack of modern veterinary services. One should also remember that in those days farmers did not use chemical pesticides and fertilisers, so that the ecology was sufficiently balanced to keep the natural enemies of plants and animals in check.

11. Summary

14.30 The world in which biblical people lived was characterised by kaleidoscopic contrasts and diversity. The strategic location of the country meant that world history was enacted virtually on its doorstep, whereas its topography ensured that only a few kilometres away from all the drama little communities could lead a tranquil, sequestered existence. The diversity of soil types, climatic conditions and vegetation militated against cultural uniformity and political unity. The country was by no means ideal for agriculture. In order to subsist farmers had to plan, toil and co-operate. The lack of minerals, large continuous fertile plains and adequate water supplies, as well as a harsh and changeable climate means that one can hardly idealise it into a land flowing with milk and honey.

B. CULTURAL ENVIRONMENT OF BIBLICAL PEOPLE

14.31 As soon as people transform their physical environment in order to secure a more stable food supply they create culture. This protracted and complex process is subject to many influences. People react differently to physical conditions; they have their own predilections, ideals and plans. It is not possible to describe here all the various life styles in every individual area and period. We therefore concentrate on the people who lived in the central highlands to the west of the Jordan valley in Iron Ages I and II (1200–586 B.C.). In all probability they constituted the largest percentage of the people then known as Israelites. The material relics that they left behind reflect something of their life style. By recovering as many cultural relics as possible, interpreting them and integrating them into an overall picture one can reconstruct the scenario in which Old Testament people operated. Modern archaeologists, unlike their predecessors, pay attention to absolutely all cultural remains and do not confine themselves to monuments and inscriptions; they study entire areas and regions and not just individual cities; and they research the life styles of people rather than just their achievements and products. They also use socio-anthropological models to test their hypotheses deductively. Archaeological projects are undertaken by a team of scientists, including experts in geomorphology, hydrology, climatology, flora and fauna, osteology, chemistry, architecture, construction, ceramics, epigraphy, philology, anthropology and history. Each specialist field makes a contribution and in the end a holistic picture of all the available data is compiled.

1. The central highlands: physical space of biblical people

14.32 Two areas which in biblical tradition are closely associated with the settlement of the Israelites are Judah and Ephraim. Both are part of the central Cisjordanian highlands (300–1 000 m above sea level), partly divided by the valley of Aijalon. Ephraim is a hilly territory stretching roughly from Shechem (Nablus) to Bethel (Beitin), some 30 kilometres square. Judah extends about 50 kilometres southward from the Aijalon valley and is about 25 kilometres wide. Both regions are characterised by great topographical variation, little arable land (Senonian limestone dominates the landscape) and few perennial water sources. Fairly heavy but inconsistent precipitation occurs in variable cycles during the cold winters. Vegetation is lush on the steep western slopes, but declines to sparse withered scrub in the east, the desert edge. Deep gorges and narrow valleys inhibit mobility. The eastern desert fringe is suitable for pasture and occasionally for the cultivation of winter crops. The various topographical regions are fairly closed ecological and economic units with relatively little mutual contact.

2. Hilltop villages: cultural feature of the *Iron Age I landscape*

14.33 Archaeological surface studies of the central highlands showed that the area became increasingly inhabited and cultivated from the Iron Age I onwards. Villages and hamlets mushroomed on the ruins of ancient cities (e.g. Ai) or on hilltops (e.g. Raddanah). The dramatic increase in the number of hilltop villages from the first to the second Iron Age – almost 600 percent, that is from 23 (1 per 183 km^2) to 114 (1 per 37 km^2), over an area of some 4 200 km^2 – is largely attributable to the discovery of new techniques of water conservation and of developing agricultural land, as well as ways of spreading crop risks in an area where soil, topography, climate and vegetation were anything but propitious for large-scale food production. People were compelled to tame their environment and exploit every scrap of fertile soil to the utmost.

3. Technological developments create new subsistence possibilities

Maximisation of water supplies

14.34 The central highlands have ample rain – as much as 635 mm a year – but 70 per cent of it falls in three months of the year (December to February). Most of the water runs off rapidly and ends up unexploited in low-lying valleys, since the soil is unable to absorb much moisture because of the heavy incidence of limestone. In the absence of a perennial water supply the early settlers had to store rain water, which they did by hewing numerous cisterns in the soft, porous limestone. At virtually every house such a pear-shaped subter-

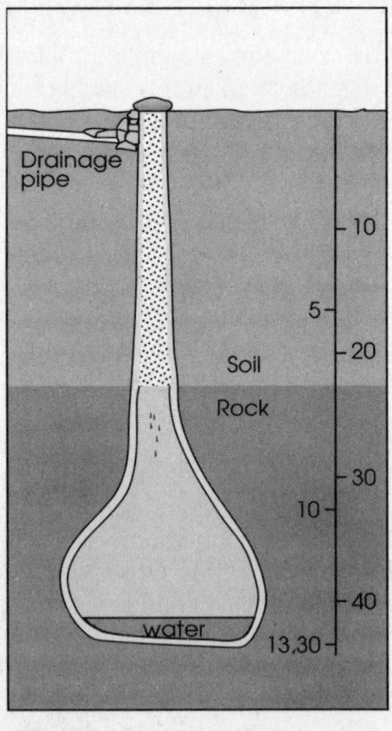

Underground silo at Tell Tannak

ranean cistern was found (some dwellings had up to three), with a capacity of between 5 000 and 25 000 litres. Senonian limestone seals readily when moist, while cracks were plastered over with lime. A lid covered the narrow opening of the cistern to prevent dust, wild animals and sunlight from spoiling the water. As the villages expanded the number of cisterns increased steadily. These cisterns made it possible for people to exist far from perennial water sources, which was the usual situation in the central highlands.

Maximisation of arable land

14.35 The soil and surface of the central highlands are anything but conducive to agriculture. The first settlers had to tame the land. They did so by clearing or setting fire to densely wooded gorges and valleys, since that was where they could find some fertile soil. Logs were removed and the soil tilled with primitive implements. Weirs were built to construct a kind of a very shallow reservoir in which to capture erosion silt when rain water stood in it for a long time. This method insured high crop yields.

14.36 The most dramatic technological breakthrough, however, was the terracing of steep slopes in the hilly region. It was a laborious process requiring a mammoth investment in terms of labour. It compelled the settlers to plan and to co-operate. Limestone was broken and stacked to form a horizontal wall. The space behind the wall was filled up with fertile soil, often transported on the labourers' backs from the bottom of the valley. The walls were constructed so as to retain a maximum of rain water; excess water percolated slowly through the stones of the terrace wall to lower terraces. Thus one terrace after another was built along the contour of the hill.

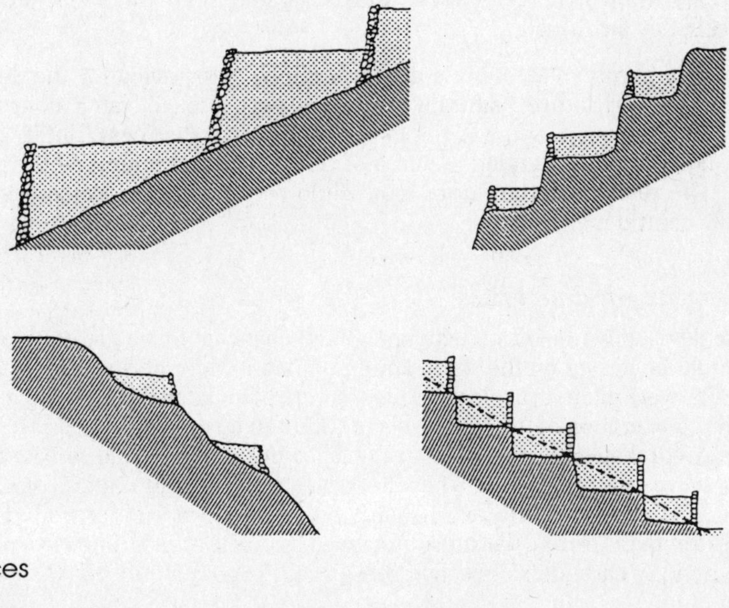

Terraces

14.37 The deep fertile soil behind the terrace walls was excellent for the cultivation of permanent crops, mainly vineyards and olive groves, with the occasional fig or pomegranate tree. Once the root system became established, soil erosion was minimal. The soil retained its fertility through the cultivation of certain pulses, fertilisation and especially the droppings of sheep and goats which were allowed to graze there at certain times. Thorn branches were inserted between the stones of the terrace walls to deter stray animals. Terraces were of varying length and width – some barely a metre wide, some up to 250 metres long. Terracing greatly enhanced the agricultural potential of the region. In some places up to 56 per cent of the land surface was terraced.

14.38 A small piece of terraced land produces constantly as long as the farmer maintains the terrace walls and soil fertility and controls weeds. A family owning such a terraced holding, however small, had a fixed income for centuries. At Khirbet er-Ras and Ein Yalu, some ten kilometres west of Jerusalem, two such terraced farms were discovered that had been under constant cultivation for over two thousand years. The one at Khirbet er-Ras was completely enclosed with a stacked stone wall about one metre thick. Along the western side ran a cobbled pathway that linked it with neighbouring farms. The homestead comprised a typical four-roomed Israelite house (10 m × 13 m). Several pots and hand grinders were found. The remains of another building, a wine press and a nearby cave (the cellar) were sufficient evidence that this had been a wine farm. The most striking feature was the terracing which had been partially restored in hellenistic times and had been under cultivation throughout the centuries – until 1948! The study of the terraces on the adjoining farm, Ein Yalu, is well advanced. The seven terraces vary from ten to twenty metres in width and from 100 to 250 metres in length, depending on the contour of the hill. Water from a spring higher up was led with great ingenuity to a cistern with a capacity of 4 000 cubic metres, from which the terraces were irrigated. A corral of stacked stone formed part of this farmstead.

14.39 One can hardly overestimate the importance of terracing for the development of intensive agriculture. Naturally the slopes were also cultivated along the incline where the risk of erosion was not too great (up to 27 degrees). But it was terracing that both greatly extended the area of arable land and improved the quality of the soil. The result was that more food could be produced more consistently, mainly in the central highlands.

Minimisation of agricultural risks

14.40 The development of new farming techniques meant that a greater variety of products could be grown on the same amount of land. More permanent and more lucrative crops were planted; useless surpluses were eliminated through proper planning and the co-operation of the entire village community; pests, plagues and soil exhaustion were combated by crop rotation and fallowing practices; and care was taken to hoard reserves for lean years. These reserves were kept in underground silos hewn in the soft limestone. Wine, for instance, was stored in jars underground where the constant temperature and darkness enhanced its quality. Wheat and olive oil were likewise stored. By carefully concealing these silos the community could safeguard itself against robbers and enemy raids. In recent times many such silos have been discovered underneath houses in the villages of this area.

4. Town and city: cultural space of biblical people

Village layout

14.41 A hilltop village consisted of a number of houses arranged roughly in a circle. The elliptical courtyard enclosed by the circle of houses varied in size from 45 × 55 to 60 × 85 metres. This courtyard provided a sheltered living area for women and children. For security reasons the back walls of the houses (about a metre thick) had no windows or doors. Access to the silos and water cisterns was also from the courtyard. The houses were built contiguously. Some archaeologists maintain that this type of village layout is the same as that of a nomads' camp. As agriculture became more intensive and a larger, more permanent population settled in the hilltop villages of the central highlands, the layout of the villages began to change. Lower rooms were added on to the outside of the original houses against the slopes. For lack of space there were sometimes two storeys. The outside wall of the lowest room at the back of such a house served as a barricade against attack. Usually the towns were situated so as to derive maximum benefit from the cool west wind. The terraces were in the immediate vicinity of the town. The most distant fields or terraces were about four kilometres from the village. The surrounding area and inarable land served as communal grazing.

14.42 The average village consisted of 20 to 25 houses with 75 to 120 residents. Of the 114 sites in the Ephraim area studied by Finkelstein, 26 were towns (5 000–6 000 m^2), 32 were villages (3 000–4 000 m^2) and 56 were hamlets comprising only a few houses (20–50 residents). The village population of the central highland comprised mainly farmers (at least 80%). Few villages had populations of above 100. Usually they were relatives belonging to one clan consisting of four or five extended families. Thus the area was sparsely populated. Several calculations have put the entire Israelite population by 1 000 B.C. at no more than 55 000.

City layout

14.43 In contrast to the villages, the cities of those days were walled. This was possible because they were quite small – Jerusalem was no bigger than 200 m × 400 m in Davidic times. Each city was fairly strategically situated with a permanent water supply and an extensive hinterland of good agricultural land. The city gates gave access to a circular road along which houses and workshops were built. The storerooms and silos as well as the marketplace were located near the gates. Houses were built back to back and the rear walls of the outer row of houses formed part of the city wall. That is why one reads in Joshua 2:15 that Rahab's house was built *into* the city wall.

14.44 Cities also differed from villages in that various professions and trades were practised, not just farming. Potters, tanners, smiths, soldiers, carpenters, scribes, merchants and officials all plied their trades. In the cities strangers, foreigners and people with different values and (Canaanite) religious beliefs made life more colourful but also more complex. The cities were densely populated (50–75 people per 1 000 m^2). In David's time the population of Jerusalem was about 4 000. The fortified cities on the plains had fewer inhabitants (about 50 per 1 000 m^2), since the palace, arsenal and storage space occupied much of the available space within the city walls. The majority of these cities' inhabitants lived in neighbouring villages, known as the "daughters" of the city.

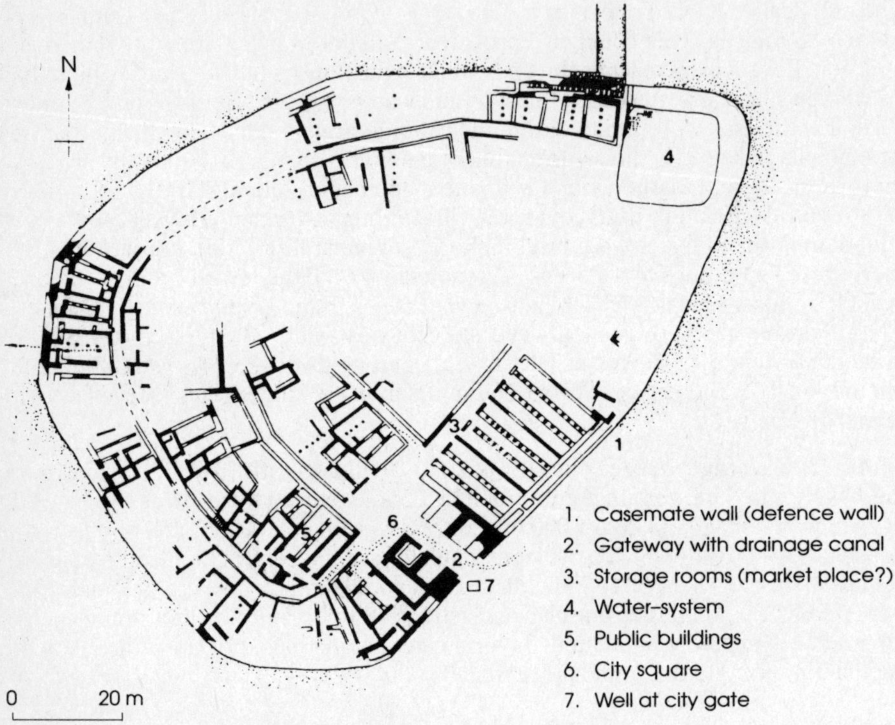

Beersheba

14.45 The main architectural structures in a city were the wall and gates. There were various types of city walls in Iron Ages I and II. At Tell en-Nasbeh (Mizpah) a staggered wall was erected, while casemate walls were built at Hazor, Gezer and Megiddo in Ahab's reign.

14.46 A casemate wall consists of two parallel walls with a space in between that could be filled up in wartime. Otherwise the cells served as storerooms or a fourth room of a house. The city wall of Samaria is an instance of the ashlar building technique, which required enormous amounts of labour because the limestone blocks had to be cut to roughly the same size and then placed in a particular way.

14.47 The sloping area in between the two walls of Lachish e.g. was stamped down solidly and covered with a layer of clay. Such a sloping rampart effectively obstructed enemy onslaughts, especially when water was poured down from the top and the rampart became slippery. Consequently attacks were usually launched at the city gates. Needless to say, these were the strongest structures, preeminently equipped for defence, with several rooms on either side and high towers along the top from which loose stones and boiling tar and oil could be hurled down at the enemy and where archers and spear-throwers could be favourably positioned.

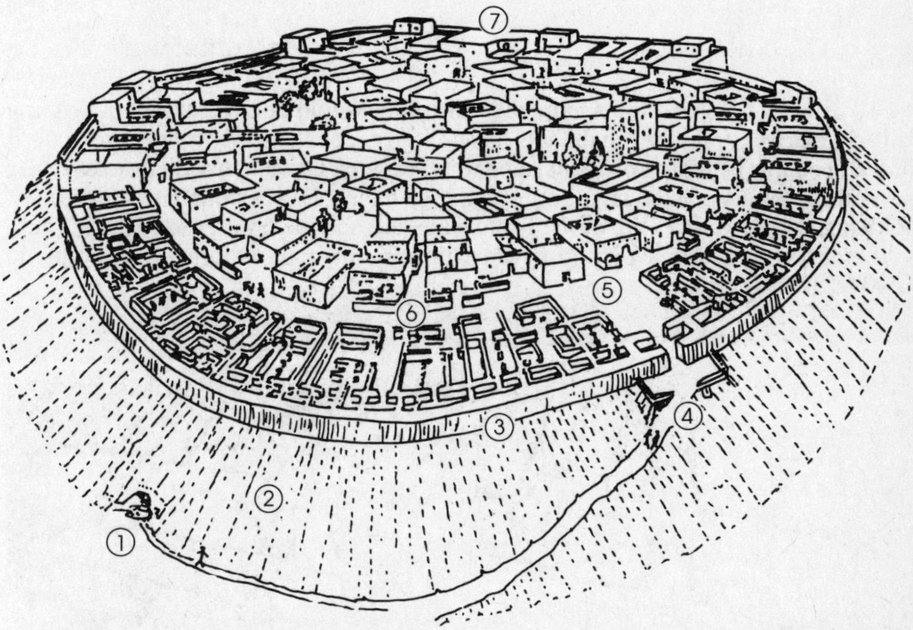

1. Fountain
2. Glacis
3. Wall
4. City gate
5. Public square
6. Circular road
7. Citadel (acropolis) with palace, storerooms and temple

A typical Israelite city in Iron Age

14.48 A city usually had a palace for the king or procurator, situated on the highest spot (acropolis) and sometimes, as at Samaria, isolated from the rest of the city. Apart from administrative buildings and storage places, there was usually a sanctuary or temple. A temple (Hebr. *hêkal*) is actually the palace of a national god, as was Solomon's temple in Jerusalem. But other cities could have a house (*bayit*) for the same god, such as the sanctuary at Arad which was built according to the plan of a typical four-roomed Israelite dwelling.

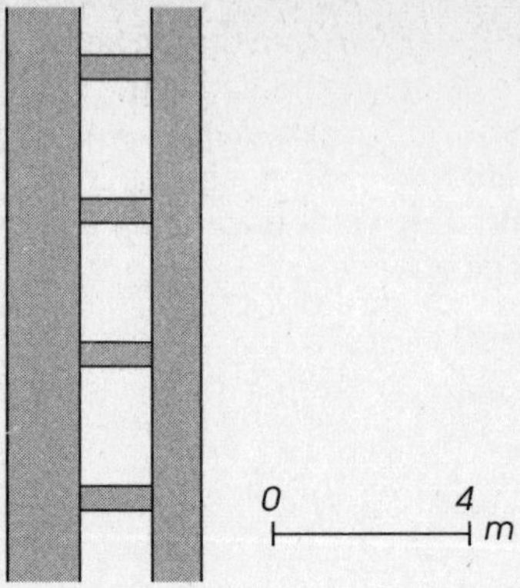

Casemate wall

In and offset wall

14.49 But all the great walls, ramparts and gates would be to no avail if the enemy laid siege to a city and the inhabitants had no water. Consequently every city secured its water supply by means of a concealed water system. Usually this meant excavating several earlier occupation layers and even rock to ensure a permanent water supply. With a good store of cereal, olive oil and wine and adequate water such a city could withstand a siege for a very long time, provided the inhabitants did not panic (2 Ki 6:24f.).

Samaria's wall

Dwellings

14.50 We have mentioned that city dwellings were built close together, side by side and back to back. Each house had only one entrance (door) opening on the circular street or on an alleyway.

14.51 Although the four-roomed house is regarded by some scholars as typically

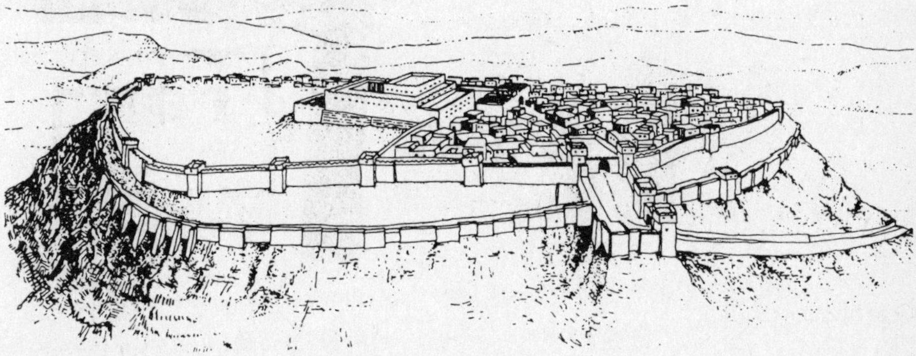

Gates and rampart at Lachish

Israelite, dwellings with the same design have been found elsewhere, for instance in Jordan. It consists of a rectangular courtyard and three rooms all opening into the courtyard – two rooms on either side and a transverse room (the "broad room") along the far side. Thus the house comprised four spaces of roughly the same size. Sometimes one of the side rooms was separated from the courtyard by no more than a few stone pillars. Most houses were built of undressed stone to a height of about one metre above street level, the rest of the wall being built of sun-dried clay bricks (about 400 × 600 × 150 mm) to roof level (about 1,8 m). The floors were paved with stone which, in the bedrooms, was covered with a layer of stamped down clay. The roof was

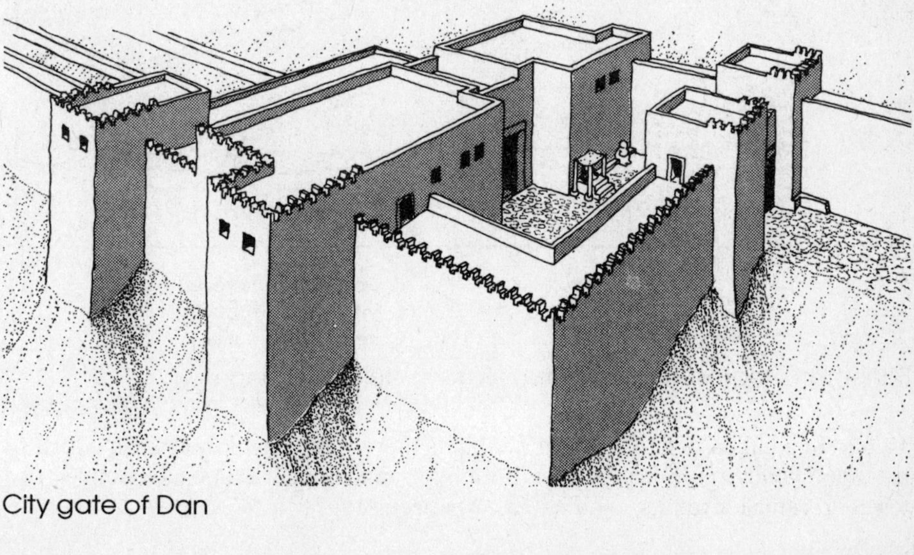

City gate of Dan

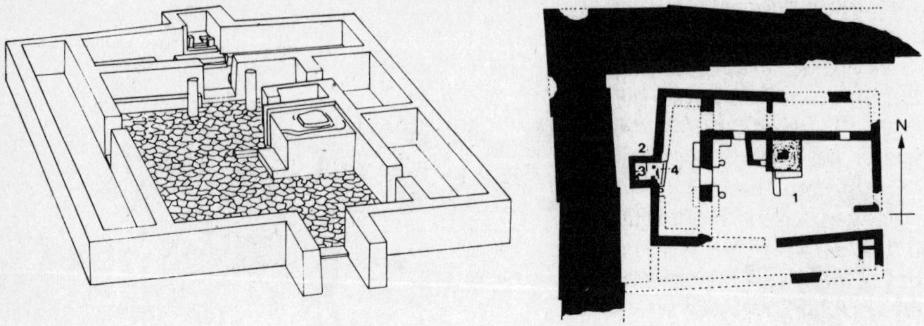

Sanctuary at Arad

supported by rough wooden beams resting on pillars and hollows in the walls. The beams were covered with cane, reeds and straw thatch which was then plastered with clay to waterproof it. Before the rainy season the plaster had to be repaired and rolled with stone rollers. How weather-proof a house was depended on its situation, the building technique used and regular maintenance. The average size of a four-roomed house was between 50 and 75 m^2, comparable to standard subeconomic houses in the RSA (60 m^2).

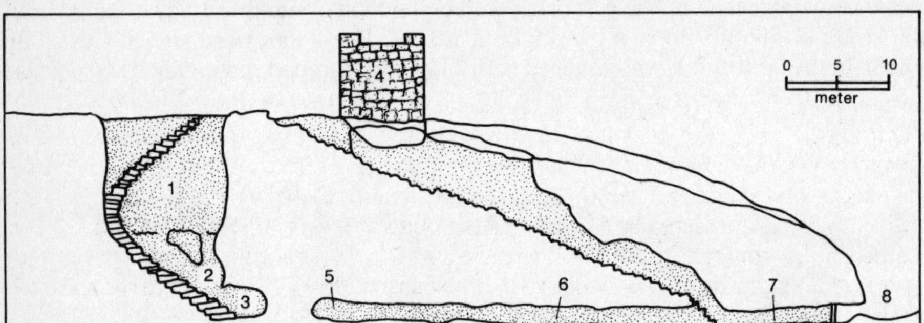

1. Pool
2. Shaft
3. Steps to water level
4. Wall
5. Spring
6. Tunnel
7. Dam (water chamber)
8. Entrance from outside
9. Entrance via tunnel

Schematic representation of the water system of Gibeon

14.52 In addition to four-roomed dwellings there were cluster houses in which an extended family could live. Although the individual units within each complex had fewer and smaller rooms, each had its own fireplace.

14.53 Most private dwellings had a silo to store cereal, wine and fodder and a water cistern. These pear-shaped structures had a capacity ranging from 5 000 to 25 000 litres. Thus each unit was relatively self-sufficient in lean times. A fireplace and oven were essential components. Furnishing was rudimentary. People slept on pelts or on straw mats on the ground. Sanitary facilities were nonexistent. Personal hygiene was probably confined to washing of hands, face and feet.

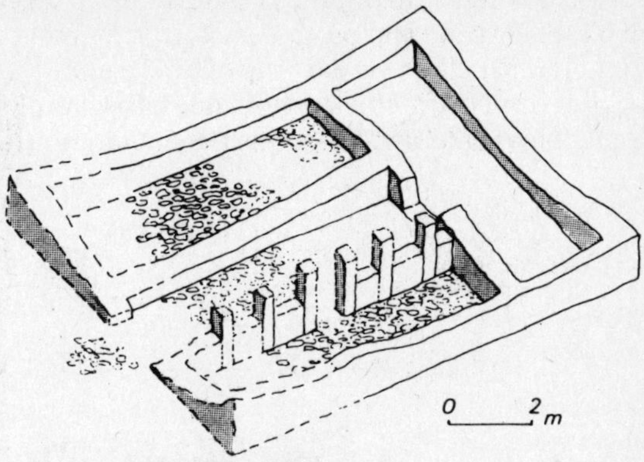

A four-roomed house

The most distinctive feature of every ancient settlement is the large quantities of ceramic shards. Apart from the millstone, the whetstone and weaving weights, virtually all household utensils were earthenware: lamps, jars, canisters, flasks, cooking pots, dishes, basins and the like.

5. Everyday activities of a village community in the central highlands

14.54 Formerly scholars made a rigid distinction between settled farmers (agriculturists) and nomadic pastoralists who were found in various regions of the Holy Land. But this categorisation is always relative: pastoralists cannot exist without cereal and olive oil, any more than agriculturists can manage without animal products (milk, cheese, yogurt, meat and wool). Thus the two groups were necessarily interdependent, as a result of which a fine balance developed between the two ways of life. Agriculturists did not want to be stock farmers, while the pastoralists would not readily have changed places with agriculturists. The eastern desert fringe of the central highlands is excellent stock farming country, while the western part was more suitable for agriculture. Most of the region, however, was only fit for mixed farming.

14.55 The symbiosis of different types of farming is of cardinal importance. The production capacity of fields and terraces depended on regular applications of manure. In early winter (after the grape and olive harvest) sheep and goats were brought to the villages and allowed to graze on the terraces among the olive trees and vines. Thus they manured the soil in the rainy season and trampled the manure and grass shoots into the wet soil. Sheep were even used to crop the new shoots of wheat so that they would bush more. During this time the farmers on the edge of the desert had an opportunity to grow crops of winter wheat in the few places where this was possible. Then, in early spring and summer, the nomadic pastoralists would depart with their stock, back to the desert fringe.

14.56 Agriculture in the central highlands concentrated on the cultivation of grapes and olives for wine and oil, particularly in terraced areas. Wheat was also grown alternately with other cereal crops like sorghum, barley, oats and rye. Vegetables, legumes (especially chick peas) and herbs were planted in kitchen gardens. A fig, pomegranate or almond tree was not uncommon.

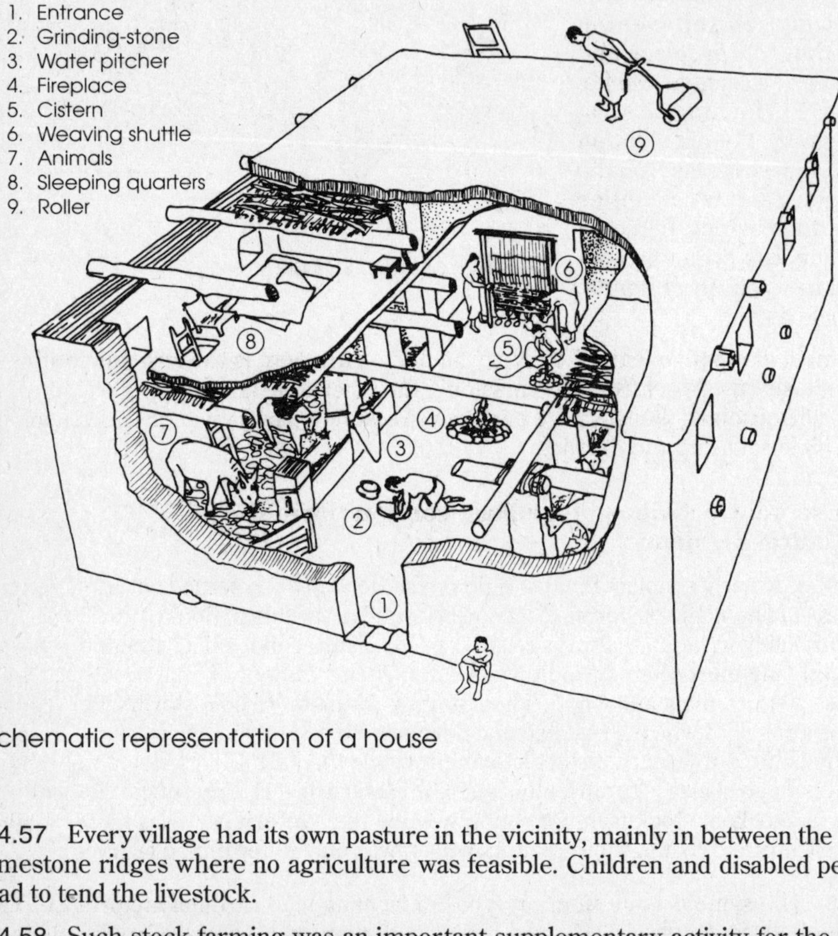

Schematic representation of a house

14.57 Every village had its own pasture in the vicinity, mainly in between the hard limestone ridges where no agriculture was feasible. Children and disabled people had to tend the livestock.

14.58 Such stock farming was an important supplementary activity for the local farming community. Sheep and goats produced milk, which was turned into curds, yogurt, butter and the like. Fifty per cent of the people's diet consisted of dairy products, while wool and hides were the principal by-products and were turned into fabrics, thongs, shields, screens, tents and so forth.

14.59 Meat was eaten only on major occasions. The family flocks and herds were their living "bank" and were bartered only for essential commodities which itinerant merchants offered for sale.

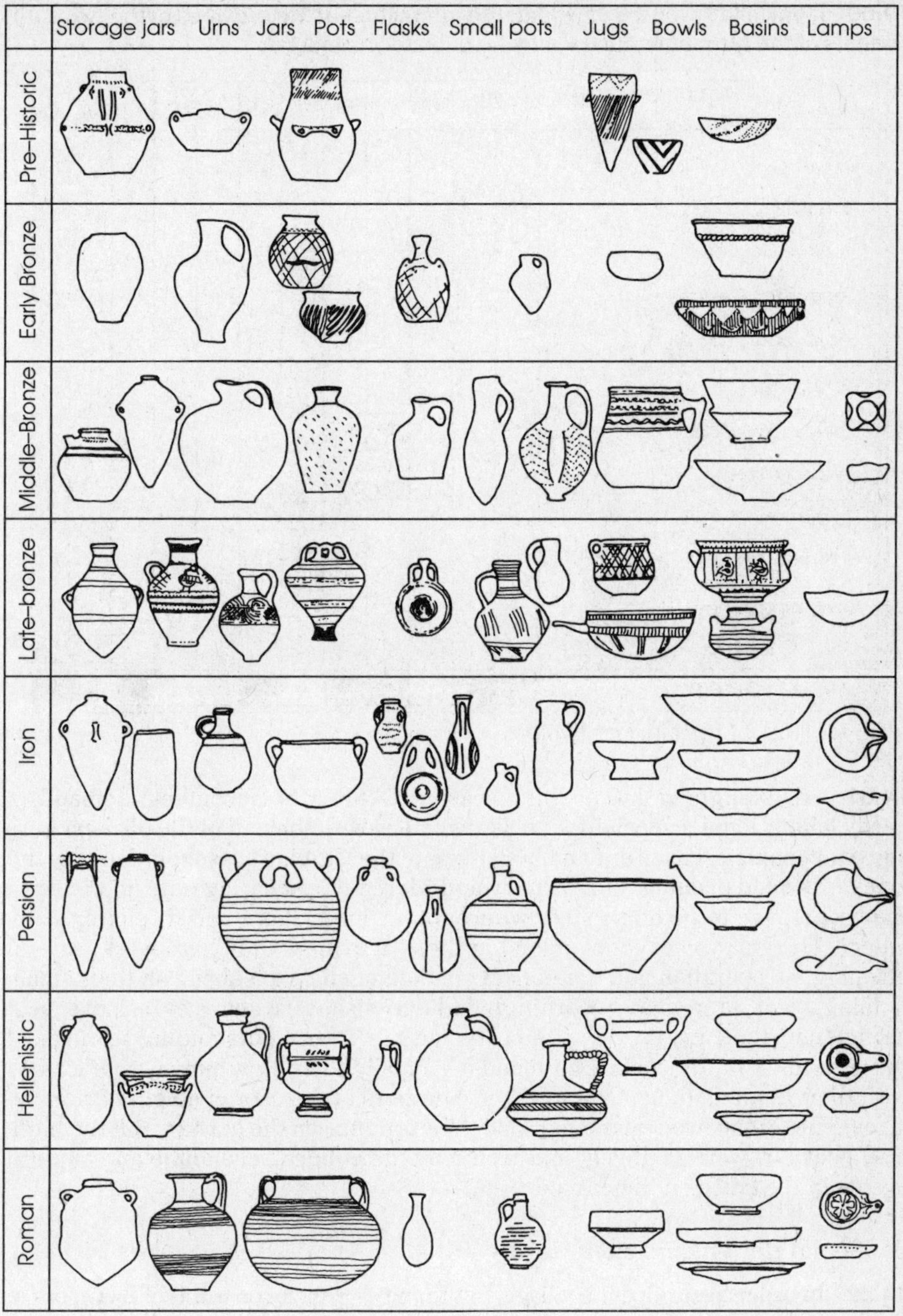

Ceramic ware

14.60 If one allows for the calendar, the interaction of the activities of the two components of the farming industry may be depicted as follows:

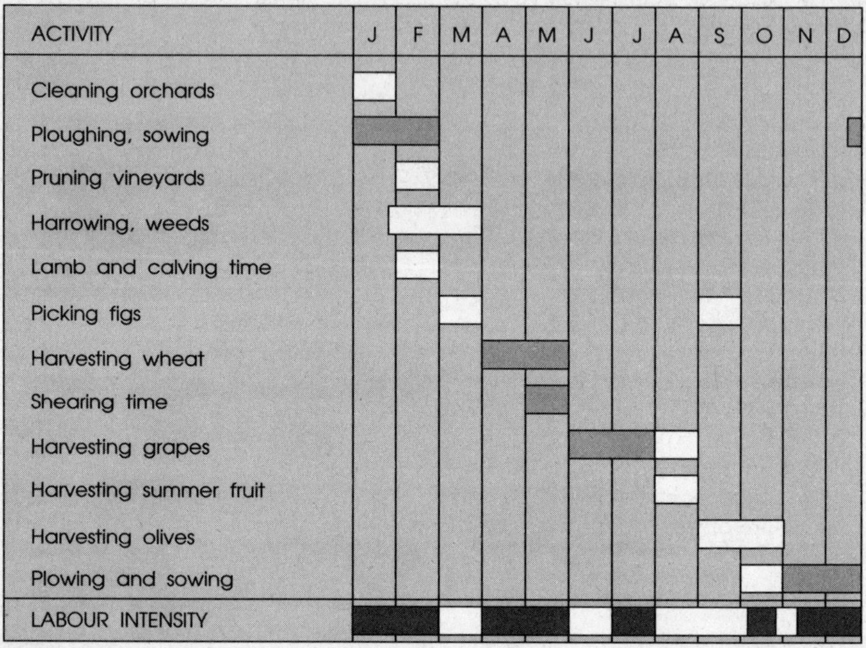

Flow chart of farming activities

14.61 The ploughing and planting season (October to December) demands a heavy labour input, especially since it coincides with the end of the olive-picking and wine-making season and the beginning of the lambing season. In January the vineyards need pruning, in February and March it is shearing time and in April the crops have to be harvested, whereupon wine-making and threshing commence. Obviously everybody joined in these activities. Only hard work, careful planning, co-operation and mutual aid enabled families to subsist on their smallholdings year after year. Accordingly industriousness, a sense of purpose, self-sufficiency, tenacity, loyalty, solidarity and piety were outstanding features of these farmers in the central highlands. Virtually their only human contact was with their immediate family and other members of the clan in neighbouring villages. Those who lived near cities sold their produce on the market. But the highland peasants were relatively unaffected by the political, economic and cultural events in the cities on the coastal plain.

6. Social dimension: community life

14.62 In order to survive the village community – which consisted of members of the same family – had to plan and act collectively under the leadership of the head of the clan. Adequate storage for surplus wheat, oil, wine and wool had to be created by hewing silos in the limestone and sealing and hiding them. Production had to be planned in terms of crop rotation and fallowing. Planning also entailed deciding what had to be planted when and where so that the crop schedule would deploy labour to the best advantage, spread risks, use water resources optimally and prevent soil depletion and erosion by means of crop rotation. Only the locals knew where to plant first (e.g. the higher up the hillside, the colder it was and the longer crops took to ripen) and whether the rains had been adequate to cultivate a southern, and therefore hotter and drier slope. They were familiar with the pattern of the flocks, for instance the fact that stock had to be kept near the village during the lambing season and had to be taken to warmer, low-lying gorges in winter.

14.63 A major consequence of the institution of the monarchy was the rise of a bureaucratic class (palace and national administration) and an official priesthood (cult and temple administration), neither of which produced anything. Their livelihood was secured by taxes and other levies in kind. As the public service (e.g. a standing army) expanded, more and more goods were claimed for palace and temple, which meant that more land was needed for food production. Farmers had to bear the burden of finding more labour to build more terraces, deforest land, hew silos and so on. The age-old fallow period had to be curtailed or eliminated, necessarily impairing soil fertility, and crop rotation was practised less and less because of the greater demand for certain products. This in turn affected stock farming, for there was less pasture near the villages (and further away there was a greater risk of stock theft), so that there was less manure to fertilise the soil. Greater demand also caused greater mobility of goods. And more extensive terracing and intensive cultivation of hillsides forced traffic onto fixed thoroughfares.

14.64 But the most drastic consequence was that surplus production, formerly stored and controlled locally by the village elders, was transferred to the temple, the palace and storage cities where it was controlled by public officials. It was marketed to foreign merchants, in exchange for costly fashionable luxuries (e.g. ivory beds) for public officials. The avarice of the rulers made growing demands on the peasants and ultimately undermined and devastated their community and value system. When risk farming is taxed up to 50 per cent, farmers either rebel, desert the land or lapse into chronic poverty. Another result was that intensive farming was given preference over extensive farming, since wine and oil offered more income per dunam (1 000 m^2) than wheat. Money-lenders – usually Canaanites who cared little about the Mosaic prohibition of usury and the expropriation of inherited land – proliferated and promoted the ownership of larger tracts of land. The results for village communities were disastrous. Urbanites and money-lenders who were hand in glove with officialdom determined what had to be produced. The authority structure, solidarity and stability of the community suffered. Land was overgrazed, erosion and overcultivation led to reduced production, terraces were not maintained and farmers became lessees, tenants and squatters on what had been their own land. This outside interference in an established ecosystem and social order radically changed the lives of all concerned.

C. THE EXPERIENCE OF HIGHLAND FARMERS IN THE COURSE OF HISTORY

14.65 The long history of the Holy Land can be divided into the following periods:

Prehistoric (Stone) Age	before 3200 B.C.
Bronze Age	3200–1200 B.C.
Iron Age	1200–333 B.C.
Hellenistic age	333–64 B.C.
Roman period	64 B.C.–324 A.D.
Byzantine period	324–640
Early Islam period	640–1099
Crusader period	1099–1291
Mammeluke period	1260–1517
Ottoman period	1517–1918
Modern period	1918–

14.66 Of these periods, only the Late Bronze Age (1550–1200 B.C.), Iron Age (1200–333 B.C.) and Hellenistic and Roman ages (333 B.C.–324 A.D.) relate to the biblical people.

14.67 During the Late Bronze Age the Holy Land was very much under the influence (cultural, military, economic and political) of the New Egyptian Empire. The complex history of Israel probably started when Egyptian control over Canaan weakened (finally collapsing in 1150 B.C.) because of internal friction in Egypt and Egyptian inability to prevent the Sea Peoples (who included nations such as the Philistines) from settling on the coast of Palestine. In times of political, military and economic instability people prefer to settle in isolated areas, preferably as families or clans. Premonarchic Israel was in fact characterised by a proliferation of isolated villages in the central highlands, where the people struggled to make the land arable and inhabitable in order to survive. In due course they resolved the water shortage by building cisterns and remedied the dearth of arable land by means of terracing.

14.68 Plundering raids and local conflicts and skirmishes compelled the villages and regions to act collectively. Local charismatic leaders temporarily took charge to deal with such crises. There was hardly any administration or specialisation of labour; the economic system was one of subsistence in which only enough was produced to survive from one year to the next. Soil, water and production capacity had to be exploited and developed maximally. Every family had its own bit of land (its inheritance) comprising four to six dunam (1 000 m^2). Everybody was more or less equally rich or poor and there was no class distinction worth mentioning. The absence of taxation and national service encouraged a subsistence economy. Among the few unifying forces were the mountain villagers' communal labour projects, value system and commitment to certain religious symbols and cultic places where ancient traditions were perpetuated (e.g. the temple at Shiloh where the ark of the covenant was kept).

14.69 In this situation the farmers' toil was richly rewarded in terms of self-sufficiency and independence; however, it also accentuated regional differences and interests. As a result the relatively isolated communities were helpless in the face of any kind of outside aggression – mainly plundering raids by nomadic pastoralists

(Jdg 6) and growing pressure from the Philistine and Canaanite cities on the plains. Attempts to cope with these sporadic attacks were ineffectual because of lack of effective leadership and consolidated power.

14.70 The only solution was a political one. The highland farmers and people of the hill country had to organise politically in order to integrate at national level with the economy, cultus and defence of a larger territory. Their first leader, Saul, was no more than a charismatic military commander who, after a few successful battles, was defeated by the better equipped and better trained Philistine army, especially after he had lost the support of cultic leaders like Samuel and Abiathar. There was no question of any central administration in his time; the Bible mentions only two officials of Saul – Abner in command of the army, and Do-eg in charge of the king's possessions. His "palace" was simply a fortress. But Saul adopted the practice of rewarding his loyal followers with bequests of land (1 Sm 22:7), especially after his power base began to crumble with the rise of his son-in-law David, who had formerly been a soldier under his command. Undoubtedly the wars against the Philistines and the continuing civil war must have affected the life of farmers in the central highlands. From their ranks soldiers had to report, bringing their own rations and arms (cf. 1 Sm 17:17–18). Sometimes they were simply forced to contribute supplies (1 Sm 25:11), even though there are no indications of any formal taxation. But the monarchy paved the way for national unity. And this was David's basis when he extended this unity by contractually binding the territory of the ten tribes (Galilee, Ephraim/Manasseh and Gilead in Transjordania) to him personally and to his successor. Actually David was king of Judah, potentate of Jerusalem and territorial ruler over the ten tribes. His subtle diplomacy in respect of the Phoenicians, Philistines and Aramaeans was aimed at promoting territorial and regional stability. Although he conquered them, he saw to it that they did not lose face. As vassals and partners they could continue fairly independently and could help to develop trade and local markets. To this end he established a relatively extensive administration in Jerusalem (2 Sm 8:15–18; 20:23–26), comprising a standing army and a large cultic and public service.

14.71 While the public service did not produce anything, they controlled and distributed the taxes (in kind), levies and annual tributes which subjects had to contribute. This put growing pressure on farmers to produce a lot more than they and their families needed. Surplus production in silos and the "bank" of livestock of erstwhile village communities were transferred to the palace, the temple and the merchant houses in the cities (which often belonged to foreigners). In this way the control of their surplus production passed into foreign hands. This situation apparently arose only towards the end of David's reign when his empire was torn by civil war (first against Absalom, then against the Benjaminites, etc.). The census of Joab (2 Sm 24) suggests a move to make all his subjects liable to taxation.

14.72 But it was Solomon's sumptuous court (1 Ki 5:1), prodigal officials (1 Ki 4:1–20), ostentatious building programme (1 Ki 6–7) and vast defence system (1 Ki 9:10) which put an intolerable burden on the peasantry. They were taxed not only in terms of *produce*, but also in terms of *service* (i.e. forced labour – 1 Ki 4:6). The forced labour system moreover appears to have discriminated between the people of the northern tribes and those of Judah. Solomon's death in circa 925 B.C. brought a near total collapse of the national economy, the political system and national unity. Attempts at negotiation with the people of the north floundered because of his son's arrogance and insensitivity. War was averted at the last minute, but for most of the ensuing history relations between the two national kingdoms were marked by conflict and tension. Half a century of instability and political consolidation in the northern kingdom (925–875 B.C.) probably did little to restore the former independence of the farmers in the central highlands. The invasion by the Egyptian pharaoh Shishak (c. 921 B.C.) spelled death to numerous cities and markets in the Holy Land. Former allies and trading partners like the Phoenicians and Aramaeans turned their backs on the Israelites. But the economic system of redistribution and control by officialdom had come to stay.

14.73 Once the officials had established their control over the highland villagers, the former at least were assured of a good income. The reverse applied in times of political instability and internal tension. The peasants were no angels and readily joined forces with those who wanted to overthrow the central government or at least curb the power and corruption of the administration. Such reactions arose even in times of economic prosperity such as during Ahab's reign (c. 875–850 B.C.) and that of Jeroboam II (780–750 B.C.).

14.74 These boom periods were the result of favourable international political conditions, when the mighty Assyrian empire passed through periods of decline and internal strife (c. 1075–935 and 812–745 B.C.). In these circumstances, economic cooperation with the Phoenicians of Tyre and Sidon, the Aramaeans of Damascus and the forebears of the Arabs in the south promoted commerce on an unprecedented scale. Israel benefited in two ways: it found lucrative markets for its surplus products (olive oil, wine, wheat, wool, etc.); and its earnings in toll duty soared dramatically as the amount of commercial goods traversing its territory increased. Unfortunately this brought the highland peasants little advantage if any. The people to benefit by the economic revival were again those who had connections at the court and the temple – the agencies who collected, stored and redistributed the produce. The middle man – the merchants – probably profited more than everybody else. They exchanged food products for luxury – mostly useless – imported goods such as ivory carvings, images, beads, beautiful pottery, colourful woven linen, cosmetics, trinkets and the like. These merchants, together with their "friends" at court and in the temple, were only interested in the production of more and more wheat, olive oil, nuts and wool which they could dispose of at great profit. Officials collected part of these products as taxes and forced the peasants into market-related farming. This disrupted the delicate balancing act of ecologically harmonious practices such as crop rotation, fallowing and healthy seasonal interaction between pastoral and agricultural activities, and resulted in further deforestation and cultivation of unsuitable land (which erodes easily). Often market and tax considerations made farmers grow crops about which they knew nothing and for which the soil was unsuitable. If these crops failed they had to procure food on credit to feed their families. This suited the merchants and officials to a tee, for by providing excessive credit in the form of food, seed or even useless trinkets they had the producers in their power. Anything that disrupted production – drought, pests, veld fires, war or whatever – had catastrophic consequences for the impoverished peasant. He had to pawn his children as debt slaves or go and work as a hired hand himself. Before long, he had lost his ancestral land. Thus a large group of landless paupers developed, compelled to work as hired hands for large estate owners who lived a life of dissolute luxury in the cities. The moment the king (the state) failed to uphold the law on land ownership, which permitted a family to reclaim its lost land in the jubilee year, the ancient simple way of life was doomed. An economic system of redistribution made way for a system of interest capitalism which was market-orientated and encouraged extensive land ownership.

14.75 The effect of this was that impoverished peasants who had lost their land took their livestock and retired to the fringe of the desert with their livestock, where they led a type of nomadic existence. In this way they could evade the tax collectors. They were no longer loyal to their rulers and a spirit of rebellion developed that could erupt on the slightest provocation, as in the time of Jehu ben-Nimshi (2 Ki 9–10). The old national hegemony broke down; unofficial religious, sometimes sectarian movements (Nazarites, Rechabites) arose, reviving ancient traditions in terms of which the monarchy and official cult were treated with great suspicion. The symbiosis of city and countryside, the trust between monarch and subjects, the balance between producer and consumer was gone. This, roughly, was the scenario in Amos' day.

14.76 With the rise of the neo-Assyrian (745–626 B.C.) and later the neo-Babylonian empire (696–539 B.C.) the small nation-states in the Syro-Palestinian area were subjected to the worst conceivable form of imperialism. As long as these little states provided tribute, taxes and loyal soldiers for their overlords in Mesopotamia they could still get by. But the pressure increased enormously when Assyrian expansionism began to assert itself ruthlessly over the wealthy Phoenician and Philistine coastal cities, even looking towards Egypt. Attempts at forming anti-Assyrian coalitions failed tragically. Heavy political pressure was put on the respective royal houses during the Syro-Ephraimite war (734–733 B.C.). Politically irrational and ideologically foolish decisions provoked even greater Assyrian pressure, so that the northern kingdom was first divided and eventually, in about 720 B.C., completely destroyed and annexed as an Assyrian province. Such peasants as could still survive in those times were heavily taxed, but the big estate owners paid even more. Exactly the same thing happened in Judah until Jerusalem was finally conquered by the neo-Babylonian king Nebuchadnezzar in 586 B.C.

14.77 Both conquests were accompanied by the deportation of the cream of the population – tradespeople, top officials, priests and the like. Over 80 per cent of the people remained behind. They were mainly the landless poor living on the fringes of the desert. The destruction of the cities entailed the destruction of the commercial and economic infrastructure. It was a long time before the reconstruction process got under way, but eventually families started to repair the old terraces; vineyards were planted; cracks in water cisterns were filled with plaster. A situation reminiscent of the premonarchic era arose once more. To many impoverished peasants the catastrophe of the exile was in fact a great boon. They were back on their ancestral land and could resume their old subsistence economy. Things were to continue like this for the next few centuries under the Persian empire (539–333 B.C.). During this period many ancient traditions were reviewed, laws were collected and past events interpreted. The lack of written records and archaeological remains makes it difficult to know exactly what went on.

14.78 The next era, which was to continue for about a thousand years, started when the conquests of Alexander the Great ushered in the hellenistic era (from 333 B.C.). This continued into the Roman (64 B.C.–324 A.D.) and still later the Byzantine era (324–640). By and large this era was characterised by cultural homogeneity, with the city or *polis* playing a dominant role. Because of commerce and resultant market forces, acting in combination with political control, the life of the peasantry was little different from what it had been under Assyrian and Babylonian rule (Iron Age II). "Attempts were made to introduce Hellenistic-Roman culture, hallmarks of which were temples and gymnasiums, but this influence never really penetrated the central highlands where rural life remained largely unaffected". Constant political resistance movements in the highlands eventually led to rigid control of the inhabitants by the occupying forces. Some were banished and executed. This was when the teaching of a simple Jewish village boy from Nazareth, who cared particularly about the plight of the poor and the powerless, began to catch on in those parts, offering a new and meaningful way of life.

14.79 The physical and cultural situation in which biblical people existed posed a tremendous challenge. Their traditions and legacy show that their lives were by no means idyllic. They had to work hard, plan, co-operate and sometimes struggle under the demands imposed on them. The majority of them were peasants who had once lived in hilltop villages in the central highlands. Their close family ties, shared values and independence were periodically put under severe pressure. From their ranks came kings, prophets, sages, brilliant commanders and religious leaders who were to have a decisive impact on the world events enacted on their doorstep.

15

City and countryside: A sociopolitical perspective on wealth and poverty in ancient Israel

IG GOUS

15.1 All people want to live meaningfully. They want to feel that life is worthwhile. But whether they find life meaningful depends on a number of factors. One of these concerns livelihood and possessions – in other words, wealth and poverty.

15.2 While some people have so much that they can never use all of it, others suffer such deprivation that they actually die of want. This poses a thorny problem that can whip up considerable emotion. There is no agreement about its causes and, more importantly, about the best solution. This is because people's feelings and ideas concerning this issue depend on the angle from which they view it, and on whether they perceive themselves as rich or poor.

15.3 Christians, churches and theologians are also concerned with this problem. Aid programmes launched by churches often feature in the media. Some theologians say that God is on the side of the poor and the enemy of the rich Other Christians espouse a theology of affluence, using the maxim 'Health, Wealth and Prosperity'. It is therefore not inappropriate for believers to ask what the Bible has to say on this score, and biblical scholars should probe the matter to the roots in order to comment responsibly.

15.4 Accordingly this chapter seeks to

- define wealth and poverty, particularly the sociopolitical aspects;
- describe sociopolitical development and conditions in ancient Israel; and
- offer guidelines for a considered modern opinion on this topic.

A. WHAT ARE WEALTH AND POVERTY?

15.5 When answering this question, many people use money as a criterion – those who have lots of money are rich, those who have little money are poor. But what is a lot and what is a little? What is considered poverty in one country is affluence in another. Economists call this phenomenon relative deprivation: people measure wealth and poverty in relation to those with whom they rub shoulders or whom they hear about. Besides, when one speaks of quality of life, while material want is an important consideration, it is by no means the sole one. "Wealthy" people are not necessarily happy, nor are the "poor" by definition wretched and discontented. *Experiencing* oneself as poor matters more than material deprivation. Thus it was found that many impoverished people who belonged to a support group and enjoyed relative freedom of choice in a rural environment felt more positive about life than, for instance, people in urban squatter areas who earned more but were socially uprooted (Möller et al, 1984:19). One therefore has to look for a broader definition of poverty and wealth.

15.6 One way of defining poverty is to take wealth as one's premise and treat poverty as its antipode (Ellis 1984). Wealth has at least two aspects: a material one, which is a matter of possessions, and a sociocultural one, which has to do with circumstances and other intangibles. People are wealthy if they can *channel resources* to satisfy their needs. Important needs are physical and safety needs, security (both present and future), higher needs such as self-actualisation and success, and the ability to arrange one's own circumstances in life. To satisfy these needs one has to control or have access to certain *resources*. Natural resources are raw materials and other items from the environment; human resources concern such things as the right and ability to optimalise one's potential through education; economic resources have to do with the market and marketing; and technological resources are the techniques and appliances people use to perform their daily work more effectively. In order to be affluent people have to have some say over resources and their allocation. To this end they need *power*, exercised by way of persuasion, trust, status and/or political mechanisms.

15.7 If what we have described is affluence or wealth, then poverty is the lack of these things. *Economic* poverty or want is when people lack the resources to increase the wealth of the individual or the group. It entails an absence or dearth of both the resources needed to provide daily commodities, as well as long-term resources such as those needed for the development of human and environmental potential. *Social* poverty arises when there are no supportive structures and networks that permit productive use of opportunities, as when people are removed from their support group. In addition there are restrictive factors that prevent people from exploiting opportunities, such as laws that forbid or inhibit certain activities. *Political* poverty is when the group or the individual does not have the same access to power as other people in that society. By the same token they may not have either the right to appeal or access to some agency to which they can appeal.

15.8 One could find other definitions of wealth and poverty. The one we have given could certainly be expanded and refined, but it suffices to show that wealth and poverty are complex phenomena which cannot be treated simplistically. They have many causes and there are no easy solutions. Thus when scholars turn to the Bible for answers they need to adopt a multidimensional approach

B. A SOCIOPOLITICAL PERSPECTIVE ON WEALTH AND POVERTY IN ANCIENT ISRAEL

15.9 From our definition of wealth and poverty it is evident that people's social and political circumstances play an important but also a complex role in this whole matter. It implies that biblical scholars need to be thoroughly acquainted with sociopolitical conditions in the period in which they specialise, and with scientific discussion in this regard. The introductory chapters have indicated the importance of contextual or background information for the interpretation of texts and sayings. Without it one is inclined to give anachronistic, arbitrary or naive explanations.

15.10 It is difficult, however, to reconstruct the sociopolitical development of ancient Israel. Opinions vary and are often plain confusing. Many theories have been devised but have failed to withstand the test of time and new scientific developments. We shall therefore proceed as follows: first, we comment on how such a study ought to be conducted, and what sources and interpretive models are available; then we discuss the origin of ancient Israel and the factors that led to its emergence as a political entity, always with due regard to the societal implications; finally there is a brief discussion of 1 Kings 21 based on the insight gained.

1. Methodology of the study

15.11 If one wants to research things that happened more than 3 000 years ago, one naturally needs sources, as well as a framework for interpreting these. Since our object of study is the sociopolitical context of ancient Israel the most obvious source is the *Bible*. There is a problem, however, in that most of the biblical texts are of a significantly later date than the events they describe. They were composed or at any rate recorded many years, even centuries after the event. This does not in itself disqualify the Bible as a reliable source. But, as may be gathered from the preceding chapters on exegesis, the Bible was not written for historical purposes: as was customary in those days, the concern was more with the time of the origin or transmission of its texts than with the actual events recounted. Consequently one cannot simply accept the biblical version of history at face value. Its internal consistency has to be considered and it has to be compared with other written sources. *Extrabiblical* sources such as inscriptions and other documents can be extremely useful, but they too are tendentious and have to be used critically. *Archaeological finds* are a valuable supplement to written sources and with new developments in archaeology these are becoming increasingly useful. One problem is that archaeological finds and other artifacts are dumb, so that these have to be interpreted within the same interpretive framework as biblical and extrabiblical texts – see chapter 13 in this regard.

15.12 Models and frameworks are essential lest we unconsciously and unreflectively project our own views onto the Bible. There are any number of interpretive frameworks from different sciences and with differing premises. None of them is sufficiently universal or comprehensive to explain everything. Most of them are geared to clarifying only one facet of reality at a time. One therefore has to choose one's model or framework judiciously. It has to be problem-specific, that is, appropriate to the matter to be researched. It should also not have flagrant weaknesses. Since our concern is with the social and political side of a community we need a model that is sensitive to the social and cultural dimensions of a society very different to our own. To this end sociological and anthropological models would appear appropriate, provided they are applied with the necessary caution and expertise.

2. The origin of Israel

15.13 Most scholars agree that Israel emerged in Palestine round 1200 B.C., that is, in the late Bronze to early Iron Age. The Merneptah column which dates to this period contain the earliest known reference to Israel. The name "Israel" is mentioned between the names "Canaan" and "*Hr*" – the latter being a territory in northern Palestine. This indicates that even at that time there was a group of people in the area who went by the name of Israel. However, opinions differ considerably as to when they became a unified group or nation. Another problematic issue is how they took possession of the land of Canaan. And it is by no means clear by what process and for what reason Israel became a state. Our answers to such questions will significantly influence our manner of describing the social and political structures, and ultimately our conclusions about what should be regarded as the causes of wealth and poverty and the proper solution to the problem.

15.14 According to the Old Testament book of Joshua the nation of Israel originated because Abraham's descendants in Egypt eventually multiplied to the extent that they could be called a nation. Finally they escaped from Pharaoh's oppressive yoke and, after a forty-year sojourn in the Sinai desert, invaded the land of Canaan and forcibly conquered it. In the process they were said to have largely wiped out the indigenous Canaanite population (see e.g. Jos 6:21): "Under the ban they destroyed everything in the city; they put everyone to the sword, men and women, young and old, and also cattle, sheep and asses". Thus, according to Joshua, Canaan was conquered within a relatively short period by a new ethnic group, the Israelites, who established a new culture in that land. By and large William F. Albright and G. Ernest Wright accepted and endorsed this version. In the biblical sciences their theory is known as the *invasion hypothesis.* For a sociopolitical study this implies that the Israelites were a homogeneous ethnic group with a distinctive structure and religion. Originally nomadic pastoralists, they settled after the invasion; that is, they became sedentary and started practising agriculture.

15.15 But this view is no longer generally accepted, partly because the Bible itself suggests a different scenario. Judges 1:27f lists a number of Canaanite cities that were not conquered and whose inhabitants were not exterminated: "Manasseh did not drive out the inhabitants of Beth-shean with its villages, nor of Taanach, Dor, Ibleam, and Megiddo, with the villages of each of them; the Canaanites held their ground in that region". Judges 5 moreover reports the Israelites still at war with the Canaanites, and the very fact that the Israelite victory is acclaimed in such terms indicates that it was a rare and remarkable occasion. One also notes that only the ten northern tribes are mentioned; the southern tribes of Judah and Simeon are not referred to at all.

15.16 Archaeological evidence further contradicts the biblical account of a military invasion by a new ethnic group. Thus the destruction of such cities as Jericho and Ai cannot be attributed to the Israelites; they were probably conquered three centuries before Israel's arrival in Canaan. Some Canaanite cities were indeed destroyed, but it happened over a long period and cannot be ascribed to one group or regarded as a single episode. It was rather the result of a series of victories by various groups (Fritz 1987:90).

15.17 On the strength of these and other considerations, Albrecht Alt and Martin Noth proposed another theory of the origin of Israel, the *infiltration hypothesis.* Like the Albright school, they believed that Israel had originated from nomadic groups who roamed around with their herds in search of pasture. In due course, as a result of contact with the agricultural community, they turned to farming themselves. Thus they settled peaceably in the unoccupied hill country and gradually acquired political control by peaceful means. Faced with the question of how such disparate groups could have been known and have functioned as a political entity before a state was established, Alt and Noth cited the analogy of the amphictyony, a common form of affiliation among Greek and Italian tribes. The cardinal feature of an amphictyony was a central sanctuary which unified the group as a covenanted community. The account of the common assembly in Joshua 24, plus the fact that there were twelve Israelite tribes, convinced Noth that Israel had an amphictyonic system.

15.18 But this hypothesis too, although long regarded as verified in biblical scholarship, is no longer acceptable. Various objections were raised, chiefly the fact that Israel, contrary to Noth's claim, did not have one central sanctuary. Each tribe retained its own sanctuary. Besides, the existence of twelve tribes does not necessarily indicate an amphictyony, since some have been known to have five, six, seven, ten, thirteen, twenty-three and a varying number of members. Thus the main arguments for an *amphictyony hypothesis* were all refuted or at any rate rendered inconclusive.

15.19 In the meantime archaeologists have made finds that cast grave doubt on a key assumption of both the invasion and the infiltration hypotheses. Excavations indicate that there was no major cultural transition round the time of Israel's arrival in Canaan. The material utensils and culture were the same as those of Canaanites of earlier times. The only real change was in the architecture of the new villages that sprang up in the central highlands. Consequently there can be no question of a new ethnic group that exterminated the Canaanites, or that was so influential that it could gradually supersede them. Thus, while it remains possible that nomadic groups might have settled in Canaan, the impact could not have been as great as the foregoing two models would have it.

15.20 Since then a third hypothesis, the *internal revolution hypothesis,* has been proposed. Its main exponents are G. Mendenhall and N. K. Gottwald. Since there is no evidence of a significant influence or invasion from beyond the borders, Israel must have originated in Canaan itself. Mendenhall maintains that the Israelites could not have been seminomads who gradually settled down. Seminomadism is not a phase in an evolutionary process in which groups advance from nomadism via seminomadism to a settled or sedentary existence. On the contrary: seminomadism develops from a sedentary way of life. Besides, nomadic and sedentary groups can coexist peacefully. Mendenhall maintains that the primary opposing groups were the peasants and the urbanites. Israel originated when a discontented peasantry rose against the cities and set up an alternative community, modelled on the ideology of emancipated slaves who had entered the country from Egypt. Gottwald adopted this theory and developed it, with an important difference: whereas Mendenhall ascribed the new group's origin to the ideology of emancipated slaves, Gottwald sees it as the result of a successful revolution against the oppressive city states and the creation of a liberated, egalitarian society. Thus these two scholars consciously apply sociological and anthropological models; they also take a more explicit interest in social and political matters and structures than traditional scholars did.

15.21 According to this hypothesis Israel was an intentionally egalitarian and segmented society. By *intentional* Gottwald means that the groups were not unified on the grounds of a common ancestry, but that they consciously chose to unify. In evidence he cites the fact that these groups were not exogamous (i.e. individuals were supposed to marry within their group) and therefore could not be regarded as traditional tribes. They consisted of non-kindred, and what unified them was a common aversion to city-state society and an egalitarian life-style. By *egalitarian* Gottwald (1979:798, note 635) means that, in contrast to the stratified urban society, everyone had equal right of access to basic resources. These egalitarian groups organised themselves in segmented, decentralised societies. This accounts for the fact that even before a central state was formed they constituted a sufficiently stable community to be perceived as an entity by outsiders. Gottwald cites examples of analogous segmented African societies described in anthropological studies. A *segmented society* is one comprising separate tribes which, like the roots of a tree, hierarchically join a larger root or a trunk. Each is autonomous, but if a common problem or adversary arises, the people of a homestead will join those of a village, which will in turn join the tribe. In such a system equality is the watch-word and one might speak of horizontal division of power. This latter theory of ancient Israel as a segmented society is widely accepted among present-day biblical scholars.

15.22 A person who regards such a social order as ideal would describe the causes of wealth and poverty as follows. Poverty arises when societies stratify and some people obtain more ready access to resources than others. Thus to these biblical scholars the rise of the Israelite state represents a shift from a horizontal to a vertical distribution of power. By this they mean that the wielders of power acquired a monopoly of resources and began to exploit the powerless masses. As a result the cities and the peasantry are antimorphemes, in the sense of irreconcilable opposites. According to these biblical scholars rural society is the ideal because everybody is equal and nobody is exploited. The city, on the other hand, is a place where a small group abuses power to its own advantage, with the result that the majority suffer want and misery.

15.23 But the internal revolution hypothesis also poses problems. Lemche (1985) was profoundly critical of the reconstruction of Israel's origins proposed by Mendenhall, and particularly of Gottwald's, claiming that it was untenable. In his view (Lemche 1985:377–385, 407–410) Gottwald's treatment of his sources is particularly suspect. For one thing, Gottwald did not take proper account of the antiquity of the sources on which he based his reconstruction. The time lapse between the events and the written accounts was so great that a historian cannot use them as primary sources. Lemche (1985:378, note 247) points out that even those sources which are dated in the monarchic period are still three centuries removed from the so-called immigration and four to five centuries from the patriarchal era. Secondly, Lemche finds Gottwald inconsistent when he denies the biblical version of Israel's origin by postulating a revolution, but at the same time accepts the biblical version of the religio-ideological basis that legitimised that revolution. Thus Gottwald does not distinguish between ideology and reality, with the result that he confuses Israel's (eventual) self-perception with its history.

15.24 In addition the revolution hypothesists' description of society fails to satisfy. Their view of Israel as a segmented society is particularly questionable. Rogerson (1986:20–23) points out that, despite certain resemblances between segmented societies and premonarchic Israelite society, there are two fundamental differences. In segmented societies there is no question of primogeniture. This is meant to prevent the accumulation of wealth and power by an individual or a generation. Secondly, such societies show an absence of patriarchal authority and legal power in small groups. Crimes like homicide, fratricide and the murder of a spouse are not taken too seriously and legal action can only be instituted against distant or non-kindred parties. If one compares this with Israelite custom, one finds examples of primogeniture in the patriarchal narratives, such as Esau who had "rights as the first-born" (Gn 25:29–34). The story of Abraham and Isaac in Genesis 22 indicates the power a father had over his son. Homicide was considered a serious crime (Ex 21:12–14), and the account of the Israelite tribes' punishment of the Benjamites in Judges 19–21 indicates that not only distant or non-agnate tribes were punished for offences.

15.25 Gottwald moreover made false assumptions about tribal custom, especially as regards marriage. Tribes are not necessarily exogamous. Although African tribes tend to practise exogamy, Lemche cites studies that indicate that most tribes in the ancient Near East were endogamous (the opposite of exogamous: when a person has to marry someone within his or her group). In this respect, then, Israel conformed to its environment.

15.26 Archaeological evidence likewise conflicts with the revolution hypothesis. The fact that the architecture of the new settlements was similar but differed markedly from that of the Canaanite city states indicates that there were two groups. At the same time the correspondence in material utensils may be attributed to prolonged contact and cultural interchange between these two groups. Thus there were two distinct groups who were in contact with one another.

15.27 In view of this, Lemche's own proposal concerning the origin of Israel, which we could call the ***evolutionary hypothesis,*** seems more acceptable. According to him (Lemche 1985:385–392, 410–416) the nature of the Old Testament sources requires that we should rather rely on archaeological arguments in conjunction with anthropological data. He regards the Old Testament texts on the origin of Israel as a-historical sagas and legends whose possible historical value has to be evaluated with reference to an archaeological reconstruction.

15.28 Lemche (1985:416–435) hypothesises that Israel's origin should be seen as an evolutionary process. In the late thirteenth and subsequent centuries a power vacuum developed, in the sense that for some reason the might of the city states declined. This made it possible for groups that had previously been subjected to the Canaanite city states to establish their own settlements outside the sphere of influence of both the cities and the major powers. Although this evacuation or exodus did not destroy the city states, they were significantly weakened. The dissidents settled in the hilly region in the northern part of central Palestine. Because of their struggle to survive they did not immediately develop into a political entity. Later, when the steep hillsides had been terraced to permit easier cultivation and watertight cisterns lined with limestone had been built, there was time to devote attention to matters such as politics. In their social structure the new settlements adhered to a system centring on kinship and lineage, which culminated in the Israelite tribes. These tribes lived in different villages that were more or less independent or interdependent according to circumstances. Later on, after the institution of the monarchy, closer links were again forged with the Canaanite city state system and tribal ties and kinship featured less prominently (detribalisation). Thus Israel was one of many stateless societies that originated in the Late Bronze and Early Iron Ages and gradually evolved into states. Lemche's interpretation does not exclude the relevance of nomadic elements. This is evident in his attitude towards Alt's hypothesis, his belief that the traditions of Israel were not fabrications even though they were not collected until a much later date, and his insistence that traditions from beyond the borders of Palestine could have had a major influence.

15.29 In favour of Lemche's hypothesis one could point out that he uses both biblical and extrabiblical sources responsibly, readily accommodates archaeological findings and bases his statements on sound first-hand knowledge of anthropological data. Accordingly, we give the following description of the sociopolitical situation prior to the formation of an Israelite state.

3. The sociopolitical structure of Israel

15.30 By the Late Bronze and Early Iron Age there were at least two distinct groups in Palestine – the Israelites and the Canaanites. Although they belonged to the same ethnic group and spoke the same language, there was a basic difference: the one group produced its own food requirements. These were the Israelites, a tribally orientated peasant community. The other group, the Canaanites, were mainly urbanites and inhabitants of city states. Since they did not produce food, they were dependent on the peasants. Unlike the latter, they did not all do the same kind of work but had differentiated occupations – military staff, public servants, merchants, landowners, repairers of implements and the like. Thus they were not antimorphemes (irreconcilable opposites) as Gottwald maintains, but part of a symbiotic or interdependent continuum. The peasants were the basis of society. They provided the agricultural produce without which no city state or empire could exist. Although theirs was largely a subsistence economy, they supplied the urban community with its needs.

15.31 One of the urban groups was the merchant elite. They monopolised the markets and production and taxed the peasants in all sorts of ways. Various relations could have existed between the merchants and the peasants (Lang 1985:84). The first possibly was patronage, in which the lord protected the peasant in return for services rendered. A second possibility was partnership, in which the lord provided the infrastructure. But often the relationship was one of exploitation, with the lord intent solely on maximising profits. Peasants moreover often got into debt. Genesis 47:13–26 relates how, in times of drought or other causes of crop failure, the peasants had to pledge first their livestock, then their land and eventually their very persons to the money-lender or the authorities. Although this example is set in Egypt, it reflects a typical Israelite situation since all the land in Egypt belonged to the pharaoh.

15.32 Thus the city was a stratified, specialised society which to a greater or lesser degree rendered a service to the peasants from whom they obtained essential commodities.

15.33 The life of the peasants was a very different picture. They were often exploited by others. Micah 2:2 tells of a man, his house and his inheritance:

> They covet fields and seize them; and houses, and take them away; they oppress a man and his house, a man and his inheritance.

The *family* was the basic economic unit, and a person was responsible for his own livelihood and that of his family (house). This he got from his land (his inheritance), mainly through agriculture and stock farming. The family was sometimes an extended one comprising about three generations. Such a residential group was self-sufficient and autonomous and it was the primary influence on the daily lives of individuals.

15.34 The concentric circle immediately surrounding the family was the *lineage*. In Israelite society it was the most important group, since this was where one turned for help when in need. One example is Jeremiah's action, as reported in Jeremiah 32, when he had to buy the land of a member of his lineage in order to keep it in the family. Lineages normally trace their descent to a common ancestor.

15.35 The next circle is the *clan* – a group whose members believe that they are related and descended from a common ancestor but are unable to indicate their kinship precisely. The purpose of clan affiliation is that of orientation. Western society usually classifies one according to one's occupation and status or rank in that occupation. In societies where everyone performs the same work (e.g. a peasant community) people are characterised and identified by affiliation.

15.36 The widest circle is the *tribe*. Most tribes have a nuclear group which can usually trace their descent to the founding of the tribe. Aliens are incorporated into this nuclear group, however; some of them may already have adopted the tribal culture, others are in the process of doing so. If people migrate they may join the tribe in whose territory they now live.

15.37 The leadership of tribes is usually transient, being dictated by circumstances. It may, however, be collective – elders or heads of families.

15.38 It is evident that there is a measure of stratification in all societies. According to Lang (1985:48) perfect egalitarianism is wishful thinking. Israel probably consisted of a group of segmented tribes cherishing egalitarian *ideals* without actually being an egalitarian segmented society. Thus there were always rich and poor people, but the impact of the inequality was limited or made tolerable by mutual acceptance of responsibility for one another.

15.39 But Israel did not remain a tribally orientated group. Gradually it developed into a state. This development, as we have seen, is regarded as a betrayal of the egalitarian ideal by some interpreters. Actually it is a predictable, natural response to cultural, demographic and ecological circumstances. Robert Carneiro (Hauer 1986:3–15) cites two causes for the formation of states, namely environmental and social circumscription. The former means that a given area can only accommodate and feed a given number of people. When its capacity is exceeded, conflict and war break out and the first group to organise itself properly gains the upper hand and the power to control resources. Social circumscription, the second cause, refers to population density. If one group becomes numerically superior, it obtains control of resources. The losers have a choice of moving out, submitting or organising. A hierarchical structure is a natural outcome of the formation of a state.

15.40 While the Canaanites and the Israelites were the only groups in Palestine, they were able to coexist. The arrival of the Philistines made a significant difference. These aliens formed a coalition of five city states and, unlike the Canaanites, used infantry rather than war chariots. When they started expanding their territory, they came into conflict with the Israelites. Whereas hilly terrain was inaccessible to chariots and therefore constituted a natural barrier against them, infantry could go wherever the Israelites went. Thus the arrival of the Philistines not only put pressure on the capacity of the environment, but also upset the numerical balance. Israel could not move away and was left with two options. They could either submit, or they could organise and centralise their power. In this way Israel gradually evolved from a tribe to a state.

15.41 Initially statehood had little effect on the daily lives of the Israelites – in fact, the tribal system survived the emergence of the state. It was only later that problematic circumstances developed. As the state system became entrenched it required more and more resources to run its machinery. Consequently it had to resort to practices like those adopted by the Canaanite city states. Markets were monopolised and the state required so much agricultural produce that it launched into production itself. Thus the state, or the king, began to compete with the peasantry, which is the background to the passage on Ahab and Naboth in 1 Kings 21.

15.42 Because of these developments an anti-city attitude developed. It was not so much animosity towards the city as such, neither was it a predilection for a nomadic or any other ideal. It was rather directed against the life-style and ethics that prevailed in the city. Thus it was a matter of divergent world views and ethoses.

15.43 From this discussion the background to the Ahab-Naboth episode becomes clear. Ahab belonged to the Omri dynasty, which seized power by way of a coup d'état. After the death of Zimri one part of the population recognised Omri as their king, while another group anointed Tibni ben-Ginath as their sovereign. Deist (1987:69) maintains that this was probably a case of a division on tribal versus city state lines. Omri, unlike Tibni, is not designated by a clan name (ben-Ginath). He was therefore most likely an alien who had joined Israel as a mercenary and whose principles and conduct differed from those of the tribal people.

15.44 His son Ahab followed him in this respect. The state was geared to surplus production and international trade, to which end it required more and more agricultural land. This resulted in competition with the peasant tribesmen who had the land. The fertile valley of Jezreel was particularly prized. When Ahab wanted to expand his territory, he came into conflict with Naboth, who was probably a traditional leader of the tribal community – he is referred to as Naboth of Jezreel (1 Ki 21:1). Because his land was tribal property he could not sell it even had he wished to. Since the king (actually the queen) was more powerful than he, he could use his power to dispose of Naboth in an underhand way. Hence the point at issue in this passage is political rather than economic poverty. Naboth and his followers did not suffer want because they did not have possessions; they lacked the power to resist the actions of the king. In addition Naboth had no right of appeal. This indicates a situation where the rules and laws were not yet sufficiently evolved to curb or eliminate abuse. In the evolution towards a vertically stratified society, the development of value systems had not kept pace. The real conflict was between two different world views; the cause was political poverty, and the result the arbitrary use of power since the legal system was not yet geared to contend with such a situation.

15.45 Does the solution lie in making the countryside the ideal? It does not appear to be. Deist (1986:203) points out that the patriarchal stories contain frequent references to deceit and fraud within tribal society. The story of Jehu (2 Ki 9–10), about which the sources are remarkably reticent because of Jehu's failure and the resultant poverty (Deist 1987:89), points to the negative features of injudicious idealism. Although Jehu's actions brought greater equality, it was equality in poverty and wretchedness. Thus both groups were at fault. The Omri-ites focused on development at the expense of ethical conduct; their successors tried to reinstate a proper ethical code, but without considering the consequences and the operation of a highly complex society (Deist 1987:98).

15.46 Thus the solution to the problem of wealth and poverty, both in the past and today, is not simply to substitute one ideology for another. A careful analysis of the situation is needed before any statements can be made and before actions can be planned and executed.

16

God, gods and believers: Concepts of God in Israel's religious history

WILLEM BOSHOFF

A. INTRODUCTION

16.1 Religion played an essential role in the lives of the people of the Old Testament. One characteristic of faith – and this applies also to that of Old Testament people – is that it gives meaning to the believers' world. Faith enables them to find meaningful answers to existential questions. In this chapter we shall indicate how believers' perception of God changed in the course of Old Testament history.

16.2 A religio-historical approach to the Old Testament produces startling and exciting results. Such an interpretation of the text acknowledges that it sprang from a faith which, at some point in the past, helped some person to find meaning in life. When we read the expressions of faith of people long ago we identify with them in their situation and thus share in their faith. In such a study it is helpful to remember that contemporaries and co-religionists often differ among themselves on religious matters. There is diversity within every religious community. This internal diversity explains much of the fierce conflict that we read about in the Old Testament, many instances of which may be found in the books of the prophets.

16.3 Chapters four to twelve of this book have sketched the different ways in which the Bible has been interpreted and used over the ages. The methods of, say, the Middle Ages are no longer acceptable. Indeed, we are embarrassed by some of the findings of biblical scholarship in the past. The same thing happened even before the Christian era during the process that gave rise to the Old Testament. Believers in Old Testament times were sometimes embarrassed by the beliefs of earlier ages and they sometimes "edited out" accounts of deviant actions or notions that they found unacceptable.

16.4 Bible readers sometimes take the Old Testament to be a book that was written in one session. In fact it originated over a period of nearly 700 years and the history recorded in its pages extends over an even longer period. In some instances the Old Testament text condenses events that occurred over a protracted span of time into a few verses, as in Exodus 1:1–8 which recounts about 400 years of history.

16.5 History of religion takes account of the fact that the Old Testament originated over a long period and also acknowledges that people in different historical situations had different religious ideas.

16.6 Scholars often ask whether a religious history of the Old Testament can in fact be written. But when one consciously considers the long history of Israel, as well as the process through which the Old Testament originated, religio-historical questions spring to mind almost automatically.

16.7 Such questions are the following:

- Did the people of the Old Testament have an unvarying concept of God?
- Was God always worshipped in the same way? Were there changes as a result of divine revelation, or possibly (also) through contact with people from other cultures, religions and backgrounds?
- Did believers always discover God's will in the same manner?
- What role did changing circumstances play in the way people conceived of God and his work?

16.8 Two things are certain: (1) one can ask historical questions about the religion of the Old Testament; and (2) answers to such questions help us to understand the Old Testament better. Historical questions are ones which ask who did what, where it happened, when it happened, why and how it happened, what it meant and so on.

16.9 In this chapter we deal with various phases in the history of Israel, with the accent on the religious changes that occurred in the course of it.

B. THE PREMONARCHIC PERIOD

1. Features of the religion of the patriarchs

16.10 The patriarchs were Abraham, Isaac and Jacob. Most of our knowledge about their times derives from Genesis 12–50, which deals with Israel's earliest memories, long before anyone had ever thought of it as a cultural and political entity. Possibly these were the recollections of various groups that eventually formed part of the Israelite people. From the nature of the stories one gathers that these people may well have led a semi-nomadic life, sometimes living in settlements and sometimes migrating with their livestock. Many scholars believe that this history was written much later than the events recorded in it and that it is therefore of little value for modern historiography. They emphasise that the history was revised and reinterpreted in the light of subsequent events. Some scholars start their study of Israel's history with David, because they regard all earlier information as too biased to be used for historiographic purposes. There are also too few extra-biblical and archaeological sources to meet the requirements of proper historiography.

16.11 Nonetheless it is worthwhile to note the religio-historical data that one finds in the stories of the patriarchs. When one reads Genesis 12–50, one observes certain religious features that differ considerably from the later Israelite religion. At one time religio-historical scholarship was much interested in these stories and the "God of the fathers" was a major theme of research Although the accent has shifted since then, one can still find interesting information in these accounts. In our discussion of the premonarchic period we shall also take note of other texts (from Psalms and Deuteronomy) which cast light on this period.

16.12 Although certain verses from the history of Jacob's sojourn at Laban's home (Gn 29–31) refer obliquely to the fact that wealth was regarded as a sign of divine blessing, the issue of poverty and wealth is not focal. (For the sake of context it is worth reading these three chapters *in toto*.)

16.13 Genesis 30

> 25 When Rachel had borne Joseph, Jacob said to Laban, "Send me away, that I
> may go to my own home and country ..." 27 But Laban said to him, "If you will
> allow me to say so, I have learned by divination that the Lord blessed me
> because of you ..."

16.14 Genesis 31

> 4 So Jacob sent and called Rachel and Leah into the field where his flock was,
> 5 and said to them: 6 "... You know that I have served your father with all my
> strength, 7 yet your father has cheated me and changed my wages ten times,
> but God did not permit him to harm me ... 9 Thus God has taken away the
> cattle of your father, and given them to me ... 11 Then the angel of God said to
> me in the dream, 'Jacob,' and I said, 'Here I am!' 12 And he said, '... I have
> seen all that Laban is doing to you. 13 I am the God of Bethel, where you
> anointed a pillar and made a vow to me. Now arise, go forth from this land,
> and return to the land of your birth ...'"
> 19 Laban had gone to shear his sheep, and Rachel stole her father's
> household gods ... [Laban said] 29 "It is in my power to do you harm; but
> the God of your father spoke to me last night, saying, 'Take heed that you
> speak to Jacob neither good nor bad.' 30 And now you have gone away
> because you longed greatly for your father's house, but why did you steal
> my gods? ..."
> 42 "If the God of my father, the God of Abraham and the Fear of Isaac, had
> not been on my side, surely now you would have sent me away
> empty-handed. God saw my affliction and the labor of my hands, and
> rebuked you last night" ...
> 53 "The God of Abraham and the God of Nahor, the God of their father, judge
> between us". So Jacob swore by the Fear of his father Isaac.

16.15 In reading the story, one is at once struck by the distinctive way in which it refers to God. The author speaks of God as "the God of my [fore]father[s]", "the God of Abraham", "the God of Nahor" and "the God of their father". Because of these designations, historians of religion have come to refer to the patriarchs' God as "the God of the fathers". In the context of their society, the name suggests an intimate relation between God and his people. There is a special, direct link between God and the clan that worships him. One feature of this relationship is that in patriarchal times there were no intermediaries (e.g. priests) to establish contact between God and people. God speaks directly, sometimes via the "angel of God", to the person he wants to address. He is present among his people wherever they go – he wanders with them, as it were – for he is not tied to any country.

16.16 Genesis 31:13 speaks of God as the "God of Bethel". This designation differs from the "God of the fathers" in that it associates God with a place. Some gods were worshipped at special shrines. In Canaan this happened at several well-known sanctuaries. The use of the title "God of Bethel" reminds the reader (and Jacob) of the events at Bethel recounted in Genesis 28:10–22.

16.17 Shrines like the one at Bethel were identified by means of various objects. Almost invariably there was an altar where sacrifices were offered, as well as cultic objects symbolising certain functions of the gods worshipped at that shrine. The stone that Jacob raised as a memorial and anointed (Gn 28:18) was such a cultic object, typical of shrines from the patriarchal era. The sacred trees regularly mentioned in the patriarchal stories were, like the stones or stone pillars, characteristic of shrines in Canaan. One thinks of the divining oak at Shechem (Gn 12:6), the great oaks at Mamre and Hebron (Gn 13:18; 14:13; 18:1), and the tamarisk at Beersheba (Gn 21:33). Objects such as these stone pillars and sacred tree trunks can be linked to vegetation cults.

16.18 Many of the shrines mentioned in the patriarchal stories feature as prominent cultic places later in the Old Testament. Some scholars maintain that they had originally been Canaanite shrines, but that the Israelites later connected them with events in their patriarchal history in order to sanction them as Israelite shrines.

16.19 Another odd phenomenon in this passage is Laban's household gods, which Rachel stole and took along with her. There is no consensus on their exact function, but their importance may be gauged from Laban's reaction and the very fact that Rachel had stolen them. These idols may have been small amulets worn with a view to fertility, or they may have been part of Laban's household religion. In any event, they are indicative of an essential difference between these people's religion and that of later Israel.

2. A polytheistic world

16.20 In premonarchic times people lived in a world in which many different gods were recognised and worshipped. The first two verses of Psalm 82 make it clear that at one time Israel had believed that there was more than one God:

16.21

> God has taken his place in the divine council,
> in the midst of the gods he holds judgment:
> "How long will you judge unjustly
> and show partiality to the wicked? ..."

16.22 Here God is conceived of as standing up in a gathering of gods, evidently a polytheistic situation. God is depicted as a judge over lesser gods. With regard to our theme of poverty and wealth it is interesting to note that the criterion of divinity that he applies in judging the gods is whether they give justice and rescue the poor:

> Give justice to the weak and the fatherless;
> maintain the right of the afflicted and the destitute.
> Rescue the weak and the needy;
> deliver them from the hand of the wicked (Ps 82:3–4).

16.23 Deuteronomy 32:8–9 affords a further glimpse into the polytheistic past from which Israel's religion developed:

> When the Most High gave to the nations their inheritance,
> when he separated the sons of men,
> he fixed the bounds of the peoples
> according to the number of the sons of God.
> For the Lord's portion is his people,
> Jacob his allotted heritage.

16.24 Elyon, here rendered as "Most High", divides humanity into nations and gives each nation its country. Originally the scene depicted here was one in which each god received a nation and Yahweh's portion was Israel. Such a situation in which the existence of many gods is acknowledged but only one of them is worshipped is called *monolatry*. It differs from the later religion of Israel which recognised the existence of only one God – Yahweh, Israel's God of the covenant. All other gods were downgraded to nondeities. Compare this with what was said in Psalm 82: because they failed to give justice, the gods were condemned to death. Indeed, their very existence is denied – a view that we call *monotheism*.

3. Occupation of the land and the time of the judges

16.25 The period between the sojourn in the wilderness and the first kings is, like the patriarchal period, obscure and a historian's nightmare. Such textual data as we have (Joshua and Judges) describe disconnected events that fail to answer historical questions. Another important consideration regarding these two books is that they did not assume their final form as part of the Deuteronomistic history until relatively late, during the final Deuteronomistic redaction. This was many centuries after the events that they describe.

16.26 Archaeology is not much more helpful, since information from those times are hard to interpret and can hardly be linked to specific events in the days of the occupation of Canaan or the age of the judges. Excavations have actually complicated matters further, for instance by indicating that places like Jericho and Ai were reduced to ruins long before the occupation. We have no extrabiblical sources that cast light on specific events in Palestine at this time. Historians must therefore resort to hypotheses based on the available data.

Features of the God concept

16.27 It is extremely hard to comment on this topic from a religio-historical angle. Achan's theft of objects dedicated to God casts light on a particular aspect of Israel's God concept. It is impossible to say at this late stage whether this was the concept of Achan and his contemporaries or that of a later period projected back onto an earlier time. All we can say is that the episode offers a particular perspective on the God of Israel.

16.28 The events are reported as follows: After the fall of Jericho the army was instructed to destroy everything in the city, except Rahab and her family, as an offering to the Lord (Jos 6:17). But Achan coveted some of the things thus dedicated to God and took them for himself. Joshua 7 tells what followed (only a few verses are quoted here):

16.29 [1] But the people of Israel broke faith in regard to the devoted things; for Achan the son of Carmi, son of Zabdi, son of Zerah, of the tribe of Judah, took some of the devoted things; and the anger of the Lord burned against the people of Israel.
[25] ... And all Israel stoned him with stones; they burned them with fire, and stoned them with stones. [26] And they raised over him a great heap of stones that remains to this day; then the Lord turned from his burning anger. Therefore to this day the name of that place is called, the Valley of Achor.

16.30 Two elements of this God concept are noteworthy. Firstly one observes the holiness of God as demonstrated by the holy war and the accompanying oath of devotion. Secondly, there is the collective guilt of the people because of the offence of an individual.

The holiness of God and the ban

16.31 The practice of ban or a dedicated offering arises from the notion of a holy war which is commanded by Yahweh and in which he secures victory. This implied that everything in the conquered city and all the possessions of its inhabitants belonged to Yahweh and could not be taken as booty by the soldiers. Anyone who took anything from such booty violated the holiness of God, to whom it was devoted.

16.32 This type of war was widespread among the peoples of the ancient Near East. We read that such an oath was taken by king Mesha of Moab, who dedicated the booty to Chemosh, the god of Moab. (We have this information from the Moabite stone, an inscription dating from the ninth century B.C.) The ban may only have applied to the first battle, in recognition of the fact that the entire campaign was dedicated to God. In the case of Jericho it meant that people and animals all had to be killed, the city and everything in it had to be burnt and all metal objects – silver, gold, bronze and iron – had to be deposited in the "treasury of the house of the Lord" (Jos 6:20–24).

16.33 Achan's crime was committed against the background of this blanket dedication to Yahweh of all booty from Jericho. The attraction of the beautiful mantle from Shinar and the small pile of gold and silver had been too strong for him to resist. His greatest offence was not the theft as such, but the fact that he stole things that had been dedicated to Yahweh. Self-enrichment was a secondary crime, as appears from his confession: "Of a truth I have sinned against the Lord God of Israel" (Jos 7:20).

Collective guilt

16.34 But the grave consequences of Achan's crime were not confined to himself. His theft estranged Yahweh from the entire people and led to the failure of a military operation against a relatively easy target, the city of Ai. Hence the propitiation of his guilt had to be a public affair. In a popular assembly Achan is duly indicated by lot as the guilty party. After his confession of guilt and the recovery of the stolen goods, he and his family are publicly executed. The ban is in a sense applied to Achan, in that everything belonging to him is killed or burnt and buried under stones (Jos 7:25).

16.35 The Achan episode can be interpreted in various ways. Some scholars contrast it with the deliverance of Rahab, the prostitute from Jericho. The subsequent incorporation of her and her entire family into Israel contrasts sharply with the expulsion of the family of Achan, a member of the tribe of Judah. The author's message, then, is that lineage does not secure one a place among God's people: actions count for more.

16.36 But there is another interpretation – an aetiological one. According to such a reading the story is designed to explain retrospectively to later readers the existence of a large mound of stones in the Valley of Achor (cf. Jos 7:26).

16.37 Evidently the ban was applied less and less frequently as time went by. Although there are elaborate laws on the ban in Deuteronomy (cf. 13:12–18), it is doubtful if they were ever put into practice. In other instances it would seem that the ban applied only to people, whereas livestock could be taken as booty (cf. e.g. Dt 2:34–35; 3:6–7), and in a few cases young girls were excluded from the ban for certain reasons (Nm 31:14–18; Jdg 21:11).

Other signs of a polytheistic past

16.38 There are plenty of indications in the books of Joshua and Judges that the Israelites were conscious of their polytheistic past. At the prominent shrine of Shechem, when Joshua presents the people with an ultimatum either to serve God or to reject him, his entire argument is based on the fact that their religious history is permeated with worship of other gods.

16.39 Joshua 24:14–15 sums up his case:

> "Now therefore fear the Lord, and serve him in sincerity and in faithfulness; put away the gods which your fathers served beyond the River, and in Egypt, and serve the Lord. And if you be unwilling to serve the Lord, choose this day whom you will serve, whether the gods your fathers served in the region beyond the River, or the gods of the Amorites in whose land you dwell; but as for me and my house, we will serve the Lord".

16.40 Even if this statement about the religion of early Israel was ascribed to Joshua at a much later stage, it is still highly significant, since it would then imply that much later in their history the Israelites were still conscious of their polytheistic past and took account of it in their redaction of these narratives.

The conflict with the vegetation cult

16.41 The history of Israelite religion in Canaan is inextricably tied up with the vegetation cult, usually referred to as the cult of Baal. In chapter 14, which deals with the geography of the Holy Land, we were made to realise the importance of natural phenomena like rain, thunderstorms and dew for human survival. In a society where the activities of the gods were conceived of as real, and where every natural phenomenon was associated with a god, it is obvious that people would try to ensure that the gods of nature were kept happy. A large part of the religious history in the Old Testament deals with the struggle between votaries of this nature religion and the worshippers of Yahweh.

16.42 An early example of the conflict between Yahweh and Baal may be found in the history of the judge Gideon:

16.43

> That night the Lord said to him [Gideon], "Take your father's bull, the second bull seven years old, and pull down the altar of Baal which your father has, and cut down the Asherah [sacred pole] that is beside it; and build an altar to the Lord your God on the top of the stronghold here, with stones laid in due order; then take the second bull, and offer it as a burnt offering with the food of the Asherah which you shall cut down" (Jdg 6:25–26).

16.44 A few elements call for attention. Even though Gideon was of the tribe of Manasseh and his father a prominent member of the community, the latter had a private shrine to Baal, complete with altar and sacred pole. From the townsfolk's reaction one can infer how important this shrine was to them, indicating that the vegetation cult was part of their way of life and that Gideon was the one who acted unconventionally by demolishing the shrine. Possibly the background to these events lies in the history of the birth of the nation of Israel. If a large proportion of the people later known as the Israelites were originally natives of Canaan, as many scholars maintain they were, their religious customs would have reflected the Canaanite vegetation cult. That is what we observe in this bit of history.

C. THE AGE OF THE MONARCHY

1. The united kingdom

16.45 In the chapter on the historical space in which the Old Testament events were enacted it became clear how radically the institution of the monarchy had influenced Israelite history. By the time the monarchy was properly established major religious changes had set in. David and Solomon, who both reigned over the united kingdom, introduced far-reaching changes in the sphere of religion, notably the accommodation of Canaanite and other foreign elements in the worship of Israel. This was necessitated by the centralisation of power over all the inhabitants of the land. David was king not only of Yahweh's worshippers, but also of the Canaanites. Thus the temple which David had longed to build for the Lord (cf. 1 Sm 7), but which was eventually erected by Solomon, was built according to the Canaanite temple architecture of that age.

16.46 The book of Kings describes Solomon as someone who, towards the end of his life, cared more about women than about God (1 Ki:11):

16.47

> 1 Now King Solomon loved many foreign women: the daughter of Pharaoh, and Moabite, Ammonite, Edomite, Sidonian and Hittite women, 2 from the nations concerning which the Lord had said to the people of Israel, "You shall not enter into marriage with them, neither shall they with you, for surely they will turn away your heart after their gods" ... 4 For when Solomon was old his wives turned away his heart after other gods ... 6 So Solomon did what was evil in the sight of the Lord.

16.48 A cardinal feature of this period was the extent to which scope was created for the religion of the other inhabitants of the country. This occurred in two ways: directly or physically, and also spiritually.

Direct "physical" accommodation

16.49 Direct physical accommodation occurred through the erection of shrines of foreign gods and by permitting cultic activities at these, as Solomon appeared to have done (cf. 1 Ki 11:5,7–8). This sort of accommodation occurred to a greater or lesser extent throughout the monarchic period. It was one of the things against which the prophets inveighed.

Indirect spiritual accommodation

16.50 Spiritual accommodation is much harder to demonstrate. It includes the attribution of traits of foreign gods to Yahweh and descriptions of Yahweh's works and nature in terms and concepts normally used to describe other gods. A good example is the description of Yahweh as a king sitting on a throne and living in his temple. He rules from his holy mountain "in the far north" and he is the one "who makes the clouds ... [his] chariot" (cf. Ps 5:3; 48:2–3; 104:3). All these expressions were used in the Canaanite cult. One might say that the Yahweh cult increasingly explored and eventually occupied new territory that had once been foreign to it. The role of Yahweh the martial god of Exodus 15 is extended to include sovereignty over natural phenomena like rain and thunder. This expansion is not limited to the vegetation cult. Yahweh also takes over the role of king of the gods, presiding over their council and ruling over them. Thus Yahweh gradually usurped the territory of other gods until eventually his sphere of influence encompassed the whole of reality.

16.51 Another indication of the extent of spiritual accommodation is the theophoric elements in Israelite names. At this time people's names often referred to a god – the part of the name containing the name of the god or a reference to it being known as a theophoric element. The theophoric element referring to Yahweh is "jeho jo", as in Jehohanan ("Yahweh is merciful") and Jehoiachin ("Yahweh affirms"); or "jah/iah" as in Elijah ("Yahweh is my God"), Hezekiah ("Yahweh strengthens") and Jedidiah ("Yahweh loves him"). The latter is the name that the prophet Nathan gave Solomon at his birth. The name by which he became famous, however, contains – like Absolom – the element "salom", corresponding with the "salem" in Jerusalem. While it may be related to the Hebrew word for peace, it could also be considered a theophoric element indicating a Canaanite presence in David's household. Another example is the name of Saul's son Esh-baal ("man of Baal"), which a later tradition changed to the Ishbosheth ("man of shame") found in 2 Samuel 2:8. The change was introduced at a later stage when, for religious reasons, the name of Baal had become taboo in Israel. Excavated inscriptions from the reign of Jeroboam II (eighth century B.C.) show that only one-third of the still legible names contains a Yahweh theophoric element, all the rest containing a Baal element. This could indicate one of two things about that age: either only one-third of the people worshipped Yahweh, or the name Baal (which could simply mean "lord") was applied uncritically to Yahweh.

2. The northern kingdom (Israel)

16.52 The period immediately after the division of the empire gave rise to circumstances which caused the prophets to take up arms against injustice and exploitation. The position of the king resembled the ideal of a royal representative of God, the real ruler, less and less. In terms of this ideal the king had to be preeminently the upholder of justice and protector of the lowly. The fact that this ideal was not adhered to and especially the way in which this happened relate closely to religious developments at the time. The chapter on the prophetic perspective examines in more detail the prophets' role in pointing out and attacking unjust and reprehensible acts in society.

The Naboth episode

16.53 The story of King Ahab and Naboth fairly illustrates the points made above. The various aspects of the story, such as the underlying legal principles and the sort of society in which it was enacted, are discussed elsewhere in this book.

16.54 1 Kings 21

> [1] Now Naboth the Jezreelite had a vineyard in Jezreel, beside the palace of
> Ahab king of Samaria. [2] And after this Ahab said to Naboth, "Give me your
> vineyard, that I may have it for a vegetable garden, because it is near my
> house; and I will give you a better vineyard for it; or, if it seems good to you, I
> will give you its value in money. [3] But Naboth said to Ahab, "The Lord forbid
> that I should give you the inheritance of my fathers".
> [7] And Jezebel his wife said to him, "Do you now govern Israel? ..."
> [12] ... they proclaimed a fast, and set Naboth on high among the people. [13] And
> the two base fellows came in and sat opposite him; and the base fellows
> brought a charge against Naboth, in the presence of the people, saying,
> "Naboth cursed God and the king".
> [17] Then the word of the Lord came to Elijah the Tishbite, saying, [18] "Arise, go
> down to meet Ahab king of Israel, who is in Samaria; behold, he is in the
> vineyard of Naboth, where he has gone to take possession".

16.55 In the course of the ninth century B.C. the concept of the monarchy underwent a gradual change. In the northern kingdom the changes were particularly dramatic during the Omri dynasty. Many of these changes were in the sphere of practical politics, but they had significant religious undertones. The Naboth episode contains plenty of religio-historical examples to illustrate the point.

16.56 The first thing that strikes one is the way in which Naboth turns down the quite reasonable offer of king Ahab (vv 1–2). He refuses because he shares the view that the land was Yahweh's gift to his people. The belief was that Yahweh had personally measured off the inheritance of each tribe and that no human being might part with this ancestral land. Thus the king present Naboth with an impossible choice, since he cannot accept what is offered. One might ask whether the king did not share Naboth's religion. The story clearly illustrates the difference: Naboth belonged to that part of the population that clung to the traditions of Israel, whereas Ahab apparently did not rate these traditions as highly. It should be remembered that the population consisted of several disparate components. Apart from the Israelites

– and even they did not all think alike – there was a substantial group of Canaanites, who worshipped Baal and did not believe in Yahweh at all. Ahab, being king of all these people, tried to cater for everybody's needs. This brought him into conflict with the traditionalists in his kingdom, as is evident in the constant disputes between him and the prophet Elijah (cf. vv 20–22). Centuries later, when these events were finally recorded, Elijah was still remembered as a true champion of the pure faith in Yahweh as the sole God in existence.

16.57 Marriages for political reasons produced their fair quota of problems (consider Solomon). Ahab's marriage to Jezebel, a princess from Sidon, was no exception (cf. the introduction of Ahab and Jezebel in 1 Ki 16:30–33). Jezebel tested Ahab's political tolerance and it soon turned out that she was a champion of Canaanite rights, and especially of Canaanite religion. Her contempt for the Israelite concept of the monarchy is evident in verse 7, where she snidely asks Ahab, "Do you now govern Israel?" Ahab, on the other hand, still showed some respect for the traditional customs of some Israelites by accepting the fact that Naboth had resisted him. To Jezebel the king had unlimited power over his subjects and his word was law. In her mind there was no question of divine authority over the king's actions.

16.58 Jezebel did not confine herself to promoting certain causes; apparently she meddled in the actual workings of government. The message she sent to the leaders and notables of Jezreel is an instance of this. Some scholars maintain that the knowledge of typically Israelite law that is evident in this passage is too good to be true, and that the story was told thus by later redactors who wanted to exonerate Ahab. Others believe that she merely had competent advisors. Their loyalty was to the government, as was that of the Jezreelite leaders and notables who c-ooperated with Jezebel. Possibly these people were simply more progressive, both politically and economically, than their more traditional fellow Israelites; or they may have had a completely different religious approach Be that as it may, the population that Ahab ruled was clearly complex in structure. The people certainly did not share the same convictions.

16.59 The charge against Naboth – that of cursing God and the king – is significant, testifying as it does to the supreme importance that the community placed on the sacrosanctity of God's name. Whatever the full compass of the charge, in the public opinion it clearly warranted the death penalty. We conclude this from the fact that immediately after the verdict Naboth was executed in the traditional manner (by stoning). Cursing God was a grave offence and this was the basis of Jezebel's conspiracy against Naboth. (The formal legal aspects are treated more fully in the next chapter.)

The prophet Elijah and his message

16.60 A final point of religio-historical importance in the Naboth episode is the position of the prophet Elijah. The story of Naboth is placed in the literary context of the Elijah narrative cycle (1 Ki 17–19, 21; 2 Ki 1–2). Elijah is an enigmatic figure, depicted mainly as a fierce champion of the exclusive and pure worship of Yahweh as God of Israel. In the process he often came into direct conflict with the accommodating king Ahab of Samaria and particularly with Jezebel. Here, at the end of the Naboth episode, it happened yet again. Elijah is instructed by God to go and meet Ahab at the disputed piece of ancestral land and to confront him with the injustice he has perpetrated. Although technically the unjust act had been committed by Jezebel, Ahab has to account for it: God demands that the king, as his representative among his people, should account for the way he governs the country. The prophet acts as Yahweh's mouthpiece and during Ahab's reign Elijah accomplished this task fearlessly and forthrightly.

16.61 Elijah and Ahab personify the two trends in Israelite religious thought at that time. Elijah is an early prophetic exponent of the belief that Yahweh and Yahweh alone may be worshipped in Israel. This view was diametrically opposed to the one that wanted to accommodate elements of the vegetation cult. These divergent views coincide with the diverse groups in society identified in an earlier chapter. In terms of this distinction Elijah speaks on behalf of the more conservative, tribally orientated people who adhered strictly to the law of Moses.

16.62 Elijah's campaign against the Baal cult is clearly illustrated by the episode on Mount Carmel, recorded in 1 Kings 17–18. We cite only a few verses from 1 Kings 18 to see the denouement of the confrontation:

> 18 And he [Elijah] answered, "I have not troubled Israel; but you have, and
> your father's house, because you have forsaken the commandments of the
> Lord and followed the Baals. 19 Now therefore send and gather all Israel to me
> at Mount Carmel, and the four hundred and fifty prophets of Baal and the
> four hundred prophets of Asherah, who eat at Jezebel's table".
> 21 And Elijah came near to all the people and said, "How long will you go
> limping with two different opinions? If the Lord is God, follow him; but if
> Baal, then follow him". And the people did not answer him a word.
> 38 Then the fire of the Lord fell, and consumed the burnt offering, and the
> wood, and the stones, and the dust, and licked up the water that was in the
> trench
> 39 And when all the people saw it, they fell on their faces; and they said, "The
> Lord, he is God; the Lord, he is God".

16.63 Unlike his fellow Israelites who believed that one could worship Yahweh among other gods, Elijah believed that one had to choose either for or against him. The choice Elijah presented to his fellow Israelites was an absolute one: if you choose to worship Yahweh, you worship him only; if not, you reject him totally.

3. The southern kingdom (Judah)

16.64 In the chapter on the historical space in which the Old Testament is enacted it was pointed out that to the people of Judah the Davidic monarchy, the holy city of Jerusalem and the holy land they occupied were their points of reference. After the northern kingdom had toppled before the might of Assyria and in effect vanished from the historical scene, two very important events in the history of religion occurred.

16.65 The first was that some fugitives from the northern kingdom exercised a religious influence on the southern kingdom. It could be regarded as the beginning of the Deuteronomistic movement in Judah. This movement was responsible for the transmission of certain northern ethical and religious ideas to the south which were to have a profound impact on the religion of Judah. The religious reforms instituted by king Josiah in Jerusalem about a hundred years later (cf. 2 Ki 22–23) was probably a later outcome of a movement started in 720 B.C.

16.66 Secondly, the fall of Israel led to a sense of complacency in the southern kingdom. An attitude arose that God had shown his approval of them, at least as far as their religious practice was concerned. Immediately after the division of the empire, king Jeroboam I of Israel had distanced himself religiously from Jerusalem by reactivating the shrines at Dan and Bethel (1 Ki 12:29). This act of Jeroboam's is on record as the classical sin of the northern kingdom and his successors are condemned for it again and again (cf. 1 Ki 15:26 [Nadab]; 15:34 [Baasha]; 16:13 [Baasha and Elah]; 16:19 [Zimri]; 16:23 [Omri]; 16:31 [Ahab]; 22:53 [Ahaziah]; 2 Ki 10:29 [Jehu]; 13:2 [Jehoahaz]; 13:11 [Joas]; 14:24 [Jeroboam II]; 15:9 [Zechariah]; 15:18 [Menahem]; 15:24 [Pekahiah]; 15:28 [Pekah]; 17:2 [Hoshea]).

16.67 A remarkable feature of the smugness of Judah was the way the Judaeans appropriated God for themselves. The presence of the temple in Jerusalem and the knowledge that it belonged to Yahweh gave them all the security they desired. The fate of their co-religionists in the northern kingdom, even the warnings of the prophets, did not have the necessary sobering effect.

16.68 The prophet Jeremiah had the task of persuading the people of Judah to abandon their wicked ways. A few citations from Jeremiah 7 will clarify the sort of problems he had to contend with:

16.69

> 3 "Thus says the Lord of hosts, the God of Israel, amend your ways and your
> doings, and I will let you dwell in this place. 4 Do not trust in these deceptive
> words: 'This is the temple of the Lord, the temple of the Lord, the temple of
> the Lord.' 5 For if you truly amend your ways and your doings, if you truly
> execute justice one with another, 6 if you do not oppress the alien, the
> fatherless or the widow, or shed innocent blood in this place, and if you do
> not go after other gods to your own hurt, 7 then I will let you dwell in this
> place, in the land that I gave of old to your fathers, for ever.
> 20 "Therefore, thus says the Lord God: Behold my anger and my wrath will
> be poured out on this place, upon man and beast, upon the trees of the field
> and the fruit of the ground; it will burn and not be quenched.
> 22 "For in the day that I brought them out of the land of Egypt, I did not speak
> to your fathers or command them concerning burnt offerings and sacrifices.
> 23 But this command I gave them, 'Obey my voice and I will be your God, and
> you shall be my people; and walk in all the ways that I command you, that it
> may be well with you' ..."

16.70 The following are significant elements of the concept of God expressed here: (i) the basic characteristic of a believer's life is being just to other people; (ii) Yahweh is the God of history; (iii) Yahweh's sphere of influence encompasses all creation.

The requirement of justice

16.71 Jeremiah states explicitly that Yahweh had not asked the fathers for sacrifices, but that he had required obedience of them. They had to live as he commanded them to live. Aliens, orphans and widows were preeminently the underprivileged people in society at that time. By identifying injustice with sin, Jeremiah joins forces with earlier prophets of the northern kingdom such as Amos and Hosea. The ethical aspect of religion is stressed as the touchstone of true faith.

Yahweh as the God of history

16.72 The reference to the historical traditions of Israel indicates an essential characteristic of Yahweh: he is the God of history. In the verse we quoted Jeremiah refers to the exodus from Egypt and the history associated with it. But Jeremiah was not the first to accentuate the historical character of Yahweh. In the northern kingdom too the traditions concerning exodus and the sojourn in the wilderness were part of the people's religion – as we may see in the teaching of the prophet Hosea (cf. Hs 11, 12). The Psalter too reflect a belief in Yahweh as the God of history (cf. Ps 78, 105). Yahweh's sovereignty over history has significant implications for his sphere of influence. It implies that he has the power to dictate events – ones that affect nations other than his own as well. He might have decided to enter into a covenant with Israel; but it did not make him manipulable. Judah was secure not because Yahweh's temple stood in its capital city, but because he had decided to align himself with them through their history. But this history had to proceed in the ways of righteousness; if not, he was no longer committed to them by his word.

Yahweh's sphere of influence is all creation: he alone is God

16.73 Jeremiah 7:20 emphasises that all that lives – including animals, trees and fields – comes under Yahweh's wrath. He is in no way restricted to his people, nor is he dependent on them. In other religions there are indications that gods and humans live in a state of reciprocity: the gods provide people with the gifts they need, while the people care for the gods through regular worship and offerings. Yahweh has no such need. Indeed, he can afford to reject the whole sacrificial cult, without any sign of fear that this could affect him (cf. Jr 7:22–23). Apart from requiring his people to live righteously, Yahweh also demands that he alone be served (cf. Jr 7:6). Viewed in conjunction with the fact that Yahweh determines history and rules over all creation, this is clear evidence that Jeremiah had a monotheistic concept of God. This means that the existence of other gods is not recognised at all and any worship of such "gods" was completely pointless.

16.74 The image of Yahweh we get here is one of sovereign power. He is the only God, the God of history, who requires that his faithful be just. If they fail to live up to his expectations he has the power to reject them and drive them from the land he has given their fathers. This, in fact, is what befell Judah during Jeremiah's own lifetime.

D. THE EXILE

1. The fall of Jerusalem

16.75 In 587–586 B.C. Jerusalem was besieged and taken by the Babylonians. It was the culmination of a long period of military threat, political treaties and an internal tug of war between pro-Egyptian and pro-Babylonian Israelites. Zedekiah's insurrection against the Babylonian monarch was ill-timed. Nebuchadnezzar was at the zenith of his power and even a concerted effort by a number of countries and cities would not have shaken him. The consequences for the Judaean capital were dreadful: during the siege the inhabitants of the city starved; after a breach had been made in the wall the king and his soldiers fled from the city but could not escape; the king became a prisoner-of-war; the temple, the palace and the rest of the city were plundered and set alight; the city walls were razed; and the cream of the population was carried off to Babylonia (cf. 2 Ki 24:20–25:21). The Babylonian policy in regard to exiles differed from that of the Assyrians. The Assyrians carried off a substantial portion of the country's population and replaced them with prisoners from other parts of their empire. In this way they sought to combat nationalism and resistance to them. The Babylonians removed only a small percentage of the people physically, but these were the community leaders: priests, rich estate owners and top officials. (Political and military leaders were often killed or tortured either during the war or immediately afterwards.) This strategy meant that large tracts of land were left ownerless. The Babylonian overlords allocated such land to the people who stayed behind so that it could be cultivated and yield crops. To the poor the Babylonian victory offered a way out of their plight and in this way the Babylonians won over many of them.

16.76 The destruction of Jerusalem brought the Judaean monarchy to an end. For many people it also put an end to their faith in Yahweh, their God, who had lived in the temple. Victory by a foreign power and the destruction of the temple meant that Yahweh, their God, had also been defeated. The people's sense of security had rested on the fact that God's temple, and hence God himself, was with them (cf. Jr 7:3–11). In former times they had justified themselves by referring to the destruction of the northern kingdom, inferring from that that Yahweh had rejected the religion of that kingdom and accepted their own. The fall of Jerusalem smashed these illusions.

2. Reactions during the exile

16.77 Two Jewish communities arose at this time: those who remained in Palestine and the exiles in Babylonia. The events in their country had an impact on all believers.

Reaction of those who remained in Palestine

16.78 In Palestine itself there were diverse reactions. Some people's doubts about Yahweh's true character were exacerbated (cf. Zph 1:12); others flatly rejected Yahweh and turned to foreign cults, a trend that had been apparent even before the exile (cf. Ezk 8:10–18); yet others opted for a syncretist faith, worshipping Yahweh as one of many gods. In such a situation the Judaean religion differed little from that of the Canaanites and other neighbouring peoples. Others, however, remained faithful to Yahweh. They saw the catastrophe as his judgment which the prophets had proclaimed. They asked themselves when the punishment would end and when Yahweh would once again take pity on his people (cf. Ps 74:9–10; 102:14). In the devastated city the ruins of the temple were apparently still recognised and used as a shrine; it was also the place where rituals of lamentation and penitence were practised.

Reaction of the exiles in Babylonia

16.79 In Babylonia too Yahwism was under severe pressure. One of the implications of the exile was that it was not permitted to bring offerings to Yahweh in an unclean, foreign land. A further complication was that Marduk, the Babylonian national god, had proved to many Jews that he was stronger than Yahweh. Some of them began to worship Marduk, or to worship both Marduk and Yahweh (cf. Ezk 14:1–11). Some, however, remained faithful to Yahweh. Eventually the Babylonian Jews came to play a leading role in the development of Judaism as a whole, possibly because of some very important changes in their religious practice. Most significant of these was probably that of worshipping in synagogues, which essentially replaced the temple-centred sacrificial cult of traditional Yahwism in Jerusalem. In the synagogues scholars of the law emerged as a new group of leaders. Worship was on the sabbath, giving new meaning to this day. Sabbath observance became an essential new religious rule. Other elements that either developed or were given new emphasis during the exile were circumcision, fasting and elaborate dietary and purity regulations. During the exile and subsequently religious rules and historical recollections were also recorded once and for all (e.g. the Deuteronomistic history and the redaction of the Pentateuch).

16.80 The religious implications of the exile were clearly not homogeneous. There were many ideas and the people were scattered far and wide. Some exiles were content with their new circumstances, others could not wait to return to Jerusalem. Innumerable new influences profoundly changed their religious practice.

E. AFTER THE EXILE

16.81 Eventually the exile came to an end. By 539 B.C. the Persian king Cyrus had defeated the Babylonian forces of Nabonidus. As king of Babylonia Cyrus automatically obtained control of Syria and Palestine as well. This ushered in a new era. Cyrus' style of government permitted subject nations greater autonomy, both political and religious, than they had enjoyed under Babylonian rule. The writings of the anonymous prophet Deutero-Isaiah ("second Isaiah", author of Is 40–55) reflect something of the spirit that arose as a result of Cyrus' policy (cf. Is 41:1–7; 45:1–7). The prophet expected Cyrus to release the Jews from exile and allow them to return to Jerusalem to rebuild the temple.

16.82 The new Persian reign opened up immediate possibilities for the exiles. The first group returned to Jerusalem in 538 B.C., some fifty years after the fall of that city. The foundations of a new temple were laid under the direction of Sheshbazzar, but the venture fizzled out. Eighteen years later, in 520 B.C., a fresh start was made under the governor Zerubbabel and the high priest Joshua. The prophetic basis for the new project was provided by Haggai and Zechariah. Haggai was critical of the returned exiles who took good care of themselves while the temple of Yahweh lay in ruins.

16.83 Haggai 1

> [2] "Thus says the Lord of hosts: This people say the time has not yet come to
> rebuild the house of the Lord". [3] Then the word of the Lord came by Haggai
> the prophet, [4] "Is it a time for you yourselves to dwell in your paneled houses, while this house lies in ruins? ...
> [7] "Thus says the Lord of hosts: Consider how you have fared. [8] Go up to the
> hills and bring wood and build the house, that I may take pleasure in it and
> that I may appear in my glory, says the Lord. [9] You have looked for much, and, lo, it came to little; and when you brought it home, I blew it away. Why? says the Lord of hosts. Because of my house that lies in ruins, while you busy yourselves each with his own house".

16.84 By 515 B.C. the new temple had been completed and was inaugurated with a paschal celebration. Then followed several decades about which we know very little. The veil is lifted towards the middle of the fifth century with the appearance of Ezra and Nehemiah. There is considerable uncertainty about the exact relationship, chronologically and otherwise, between these two prominent figures. Details about this problem may be found in histories on that time. In all events, the books of Ezra and Nehemiah show that by 450 B.C. there was a need for strong political and especially religious leadership.

16.85 While we cannot solve the historical problems concerning that period, we can take a look at Nehemiah 5, which tells of some of Nehemiah's radical reforms. This particular chapter is about helping the poor and the exploited. Nehemiah's general aim was to establish external and internal order. External order was created by repairing the walls of Jerusalem (Neh 2), resettling people in the city (Neh 11:1–2) and proclaiming a general rescinding of debt (Neh 5). Internal order was created by giving the Levites their rightful share (Neh 12:44–47; 13:10–13), enforcing rest on the sabbath (Neh 13:15–22) and instituting measures to prevent marriages between Jews and non-Jews (Neh 13:23–29). Although Nehemiah was a political administrator, his reforms were clearly based on both religious conviction and sound administrative principles. Such was his influence that one cannot underestimate his role in the emergence of Judaism as a religion.

16.86 Nehemiah 5

> [1] Now there arose a great outcry of the people and of their wives against the
> Jewish brethren. [2] For there were those who said, "With our sons and our
> daughters, we are many; let us get grain, that we may eat and keep alive".
> [3] There were also those who said, "We are mortgaging our fields, our
> vineyards and our houses to get grain because of the famine". [4] And there
> were those who said, "We have borrowed money for the king's tax upon our
> fields and our vineyards. [5] Now our flesh is as the flesh of our brethren, our
> children are as their children; yet we are forcing our sons and our daughters to be slaves, and some of our daughters have already been enslaved; but it is not in our power to help it, for other men have our fields and our vineyards".

> [6] I was very angry when I heard their outcry and these words. [7] I took council with myself, and I brought charges against the nobles and the officials. I said to them, "You are exacting interest, each from his brother". And I held a great assembly against them, [8] and said to them, "We, as far as we are able, have bought back our Jewish brethren who have been sold to the nations; but you even sell your brethren that they may be sold to us!" They were silent, and could not find a word to say. [9] So I said, "The thing that you are doing is not good. Ought you not to walk in the fear of our God to prevent the taunts of the nations our enemies? [10] Moreover I and my brethren and my servants are lending them money and grain. Let us leave off this interest. [11] Return to them this very day their fields, their vineyards, their olive orchards, and their houses, and the hundredth of money, grain, wine, and oil which you have been exacting of them". [12] Then they said, "We will restore these and require nothing from them. We will do as you say".

16.87 Thus economic inequality existed again quite soon after the exile. Unlike his predecessors, Nehemiah appeared to have been concerned about the lot of the poor. But his reaction was not just humanitarian and sympathetic; it had a religious basis. Nehemiah bases his criticism of the leading citizens on the fact that they should "walk in the fear of our God". In studying postexilic times one should always consider the complexity of the population as far as religious belief was concerned. Although Nehemiah's audience consisted of Jews, the chances are that they differed sharply on religious issues. As their leader, he moreover had to win his subjects over to his side. The vast majority were poor, almost destitute people – not returned exiles, but those who had remained in Palestine and had been given vacant land to cultivate. Those who stayed behind had sometimes despised the exiles (who were from the upper class) and considered their deportation to have been their just reward. In their turn some of the exiles, especially those who cherished the ideal of a return to Palestine, despised the ones who had remained. The decline of the cultus and the wretched conditions prevailing in Judah made the returned exiles look at those who had remained with contempt.

16.88 The religious overtones of the disunity are hard to reconstruct, but it would seem that both in Babylonia and among the returned exiles, and among the ones who had stayed behind, there were still people who took their religion seriously. In both communities there were those who had not yielded to the attractions of a syncretist religion, nor rejected Yahweh as their God.

16.89 At any rate, Nehemiah's appeal is based on the common aspects of their faith. He invokes the authority of the laws that prohibit Israelites from charging their fellow Jews interest, thus plunging them into debt so that they have to sell their land or sell themselves into slavery to get out of debt.

16.90 This argument of Nehemiah's, and some of his other reform measures (especially those aimed at establishing internal order) display a feature of the cult that developed during this period: a growing emphasis on the law as criterion of God's will. This emphasis on the law had emerged in the synagogal worship in Babylonia, where the application of the law in a changed situation was a major religious exercise. The enhanced status of the "lawyers" relates directly to this development. Although the temple was rebuilt, the cultus was never restored to what it had been before the fall of Jerusalem. This may be attributed to the fact that many Jews no longer lived in Palestine and had no intention of returning there; they had to practise their religion far away from the temple.

16.91 Finally we should comment on the changed concept of Yahweh himself. The exile had posed the problem of where Yahweh is located. Before the exile the temple had been his holy house and Jerusalem the holy city. As the notion grew that Yahweh could only be worshipped in Jerusalem, other places were declared unclean and it became a sin to worship him anywhere else. These ideas about Yahweh had to be reconsidered, otherwise it would mean that the exiles had been totally separated from him and could not worship him. Some of them in fact believed that Yahweh's influence was confined to Jerusalem, and they renounced him. But eventually Yahweh's territory, formerly confined to Israel (cf. Dt 32), was extended to include other nations (cf. Ps 99:1, "The Lord reigns; let the peoples tremble!"). In the end his realm encompassed the whole earth, the whole of creation and everything in it (cf. Ps 19:2–7; 104; Job 38–39).

F. SUMMARY

16.92 The religion of Israel changed greatly over the ages. Ideas arising from this religion were gradually adapted to changing circumstances. People in different ages and differing situations respond variously to the questions posed by their societies.

16.93 The few citations from the rich variety of Old Testament texts, read with religio-historical questions in mind, have opened new perspectives on the faith of the people and of individuals. Readers of the Old Testament should be aware not only of the different kinds of biblical texts, but also of the diversity of religious ideas found in the Bible.

16.94 The Old Testament does not have a uniform conception of wealth and poverty. Sometimes wealth is presented as evidence of God's blessing; sometimes it is a wedge driven in between people and God; alienating people from God's requirements and expectations.

D

perspectives on the phenomenon of wealth and poverty

17

"Such a thing is not done in Israel". The judicial system of ancient Israel

HENDRIK BOSMAN

A. INTRODUCTION

17.1 The title of this chapter, which cites a saying by Tamar, assumes a certain consensus in Israel on how an Israelite should behave (2 Sm 13:12). This consensus on what was accepted as proper conduct in Israelite society can be researched in their judicial system.

17.2 To understand what wealth and poverty were about in Old Testament times one also has to look at the development of the judicial system in Ancient Israel. While there are various ways of interpreting legal texts, we shall adopt a sociojudicial approach In so doing we are not denigrating the value of a literary-historical or a narrative approach, or of an approach based on comparative law, jurisprudence or structural anthropology. In certain circumstances each of these can contribute greatly to an understanding of the judicial system of ancient Israel.

17.3 A sociojudicial approach assumes that the judicial system in a given society is shaped so that the judiciary can function as an acceptable intermediary between disputing parties and the law. In effect it means that the appointment of a judge, the procedure followed in court and the sentence that is eventually passed will be acceptable to that society. Consequently the Israelite legal system has to be assessed in conjunction with the sociological context of ancient Israel. As a result some overlapping with the chapter on the social development of Israel is unavoidable.

17.4 Certain features of the ancient Israelite judicial system have to be borne in mind when studying it. These features also illustrate in what way that system differs from its modern equivalent.

17.5 Firstly, one should remember that Israelite law had divergent origins. Some of the early stipulations derived from family law, others originated from the legal proceedings conducted at the city gates and from temple worship.

17.6 Secondly, it must be remembered that Israelite law had religious and political functions in addition to its juridical function. Thus legal rules were used to ensure privileges for the royal house of David and the temple in Jerusalem.

17.7 Thirdly, every set of laws has a distinctive focus. No single set of laws claims to give a ruling on all possible disputes.

17.8 The first section of this chapter deals with the development of the judicial system of ancient Israel from before the monarchy up to the exile. Then there is a brief exposition of the various collections of legal texts with special reference to laws pertaining to wealth and poverty. The final section focuses more specifically on the Naboth episode against the background of the Israelite judicial system.

B. DEVELOPMENT OF THE JUDICIAL SYSTEM OF ANCIENT ISRAEL

1. The judicial system before the period of the monarchy

17.9 The premonarchic period in Israel may be subdivided into a seminomadic or pastoral period and an age of gradual urbanisation.

Pastoral period

17.10 Not all Israelites were agriculturists and urbanites from the outset. From the tales of the patriarchs (Abraham, Isaac and Jacob) it is evident that some of the forebears of Israel were pastoralists who migrated in search of pasture. During this period the judicial system was typical of a pastoral or seminomadic society.

17.11 Genesis 16 recounts the dispute between Sarai (later Sarah), the barren wife of Abram (later Abraham), and Hagar, Sarai's pregnant maidservant. In verse 5 Sarai calls on Abram to redress the wrong done to her:

> "May the wrong done to me be upon you! I gave my maid to your embrace, and when she saw that she had conceived, she looked on me with contempt. May the Lord judge between you and me!"

17.12 Abram does not enquire any further but forthwith pronounces judgment in verse 6 by telling Sarai: "Behold, your maid is in your power; do to her as you please".

17.13 The lawsuit in Genesis 16 may strike a modern reader as unjust towards Hagar. But the story should be seen against the background of that society and the judicial system of a pastoral age. In such an age the extended family (which could include up to three or four generations) and the clan (comprising several extended families) were the principal social units and the heads of such families and clans were the chief juridical officers.

17.14 Thus Abram, as head of his house (*paterfamilias*), is called upon to do justice to Sarai and, on the strength of his authority as head of the family, without any trial, he pronounces judgment in favour of his wife. The judgment is made with no regard to Hagar since, being a slave, she has no legal persona and her owner could deal with her "property" without consulting anyone.

17.15 Other familiar instances of heads of families acting in a judicial capacity are Laban who, after the theft of his household gods, tells Jacob, "It is in my power to do you harm" (Gn 31:29); and Judah, who summarily sentences his pregnant, widowed daughter-in-law Tamar: "Bring her out and let her be burned" (Gn 38:24).

17.16 Two of the most ancient features of Israelite law – the principles of a life for a life, retribution and of corporate accountability – also date to the pastoral era. In Genesis 4:23, 24 Lamech invokes the principle of retribution when he tells his wives:

> "I have slain a man for wounding me,
> a young man for striking me.
> If Cain is avenged sevenfold,
> truly Lamech seventy-seven-fold".

17.17 The description of the second inscription of the ten commandments contains a statement by God which illustrates the principle of corporate accountability. Here the Lord is said to "[visit] the iniquity of the fathers upon the children and the children's children, to the third and the fourth generation" (Ex 34:7). This pronouncement refers to the extended family comprising three to four generations. The assumption is that the sin of an individual redounds on the entire family as a corporate entity.

17.18 Another instance of corporate accountability may be found in Joshua 7, where the entire people is punished by defeat at the hands of the inhabitants of Ai because Achan had appropriated some of the articles consecrated to the Lord during the conquest of Jericho. Here Joshua, in his capacity as leader of all the people, acts as judge; the elders of the various tribes do not play any demonstrable role.

17.19 When Achan is shown to be guilty by casting the lot, he and his entire family are stoned to death by the people. The conviction of Achan by Joshua as leader of the people, and the people's participation in the execution of the sentence, suggest a type of judicial system extending beyond the family and the clan.

17.20 One should be careful not to see the development of the Israelite judicial system too simplistically in evolutionary terms. In such a view it may be assumed that before Israel became a nation-state the family was an extended one comprising three to four generations, and that when the people became urbanised families declined in size. Recent research has established the existence of small (nuclear) family units in the earliest stages of Israel's social development.

17.21 The story of Dinah in Genesis 34 presupposes the existence of small family units, and Genesis 42 mentions the families of Joseph's brothers independently of their father's house. This raises problems for the dating of legal texts since the assumption of smaller families in a text does not necessarily indicate a later period.

17.22 Researchers of Israel's juridical history (e.g. Gerstenberger, 1965) often characterise the judicial system prior to the establishment of the state as "clan law". This designation does not acknowledge the importance of the family (extended or nuclear) as the basic social institution. By and large it seems more likely that early Israel had a system of family law. Thus the book of Judges uses the word "house" eight times and only one of these refers to the clan or house as an exclusively Israelite institution.

Early period of urbanisation

17.23 In the time of the judges there was growing urbanisation. During this transitional phase governmental and judicial powers gradually became centralised, although this trend was inhibited by the hilly landscape of Palestine which was conducive to the functioning of semi-independent family, clan and tribal authorities.

17.24 Judges 19 to 21 records the gruesome story of the rape of a Levite's concubine and the subsequent action by the tribes of Israel. According to Judges 20:2 "the chiefs of all the people, of all the tribes of Israel" assembled. First the Levite was asked to testify to what the people of Gibeah had done to his concubine (Jdg 20:4–5). Then "all the people" decided unanimously that the "base fellows" of Gibeah should be handed over by the tribe of Benjamin so that the criminals may be punished (Jdg 20:8–10). When the tribe of Benjamin refused to surrender the guilty parties, a full-scale war was waged in order to execute sentence on the inhabitants of Gibeah (Jdg 20:13–48). Although this story underwent subsequent redaction, it probably still reflects something of the centralisation of Israel's judicial system prior to the establishment of a state.

17.25 During this period, however, justice was administered mainly by the family and clan elders at the gates of the city or town. In the crowded cities and towns of ancient Israel the gate was the only unbuilt-up area where the inhabitants could gather for trade, recreation and the administration of justice.

17.26 A good example of the procedure of the juridical elders at the city gates is to be found in the book of Ruth. There we have a detailed description of how Boaz had to obtain permission from the elders to act as next of kin on Naomi's behalf in redeeming her late husband's land:

> And Boaz went up to the gate and sat down there ... And he took ten men of the elders of the city, and said, "Sit down here"; so they sat down (Ruth 4:1–2).
> Now this was the custom in former times in Israel concerning redeeming and exchanging: to confirm a transaction, the one drew off his sandal and gave it to the other, and this was the manner of attesting in Israel. So when the next of kin said to Boaz, "Buy it for yourself," he drew off his sandal. Then Boaz said to the elders and all the people, "You are witnesses this day ..." (Ruth 4:7–9).
> Then all the people who were at the gate, and the elders, said, "We are witnesses ..." (Ruth 4:11).

2. The judicial system under the monarchy

17.27 When the monarchy was instituted the judicial system did not change much at first. In the description of Jonathan's trial in 1 Samuel 14, Saul calls the "leaders" of the people: "Come hither ... and know and see how this sin has arisen today" (1 Sm 14:38). Saul was probably acting in his capacity as king and military commander when he instituted legal process by calling the "leaders" together.

17.28 It is evident, however, that at that stage the king's juridical powers were by no means unlimited, for the men refused to accept Saul's death sentence on Jonathan (Sm 1 14:44–45). The same restriction of royal juridical power is evident in the trial of the priests of Nob, when the king's officials refused to execute Saul's death sentence on the priests (1 Sm 22:17).

17.29 During the reigns of David and Solomon the king's juridical power became more extensive, particularly in cases where the monarchy was in jeopardy. Political assassins and rioters were frequently condemned to death by the king, such as the Amalekite who killed Saul (2 Sm 1) and the murderers of Ishboseth (2 Sm 4); Shimei, who had cursed David, was executed by Solomon for breaking an oath (1 Ki 2).

17.30 As was customary in the ancient Near East, the king of Israel was personally involved in maintaining law and justice and in ensuring that all members of the population had equal access to the process of law. The prophet Nathan's parable about the rich and the poor man (2 Sm 12:1–6), the behaviour of the wise woman of Tekoa (2 Sm 14) and Solomon's settlement of the dispute between the two mothers (1 Ki 3:16–28) all suggest that the populace had direct access to the king as judicial officer. This surmise is strengthened by Absalom's crafty action when he waylaid Israelites who were going to the king with a lawsuit at the city gates and won them over before they got to the king (2 Sm 15:1–5).

17.31 The Naboth episode (1 Ki 21), where Jezebel instituted legal process in Ahab's name, and the account of the woman who had recourse to the king in Samaria because of cannibalism (2 Ki 6:24–31) both show that after the division of the kingdom of Israel the ruler of the northern kingdom remained in charge of the administration of law and justice.

17.32 During the period of the monarchy there were, in addition to the king, judges to see to the administration of justice at the local level. Numerous oracles by the prophets against corrupt judges affirm their existence, such as the prophet Micah's reference to judges who require bribes (Mi 7:3).

17.33 Notwithstanding the gloomy picture painted by the prophets, the Deuteronomic laws give us some idea of what the juridical ideal was. This legislation was not finalised until a fairly late stage of the monarchy (more about this below) and it affords valuable information about the legal system in the last century before the exile (seventh century B.C.):

> "You shall appoint judges and officers in all your towns which the Lord your God gives you, according to your tribes; and they shall judge the people with righteous judgment. You shall not pervert justice; you shall not show partiality; and you shall not take a bribe, for a bribe blinds the eyes of the wise and subverts the cause of the righteous. Justice, and only justice, you shall follow ... (Dt 16:18–20).

17.34 Besides the ordinary lawsuits heard by local judges, Deuteronomic law also provided for extraordinary cases. These were heard by the Levitical priests and a judge, without any reference to the king:

> "If any case arises [concerning homicide or a court decision] ... which is too difficult for you, then you shall arise and go up to the place which the Lord your God will choose, and coming to the Levitical priests, and to the judge who is in office in those days, you shall consult them, and they shall declare to you the decision. Then you shall do according to ... all that they direct you (Dt 17:8–10).

17.35 Deuteronomic law emphasises the need to have at least two witnesses in a court case: "A single witness shall not prevail against a man for any crime or for any wrong in connection with any offense that he has committed; only on the evidence of two witnesses, or three witnesses, shall a charge be sustained" (Dt 19:15).

17.36 To illustrate how a lawsuit had to be conducted according to Deuteronomic law, let us consider the case of someone who was unfaithful to the Lord (this same law will be referred to again when we deal with the Naboth episode):

> "If a malicious witness rises against any man to accuse him of wrongdoing, then both parties to the dispute shall appear before the Lord, before the priests and the judges who are in office in those days; the judges shall inquire diligently, and if the witness is a false witness and has accused his brother falsely, then you shall do to him as he had meant to do to his brother; so you shall purge the evil from the midst of you. And the rest shall hear, and fear, and shall never again commit any such evil among you. Your eye shall not pity; it shall be life for life, eye for eye, tooth for tooth, hand for hand, foot for foot (Dt 20:16–21).

17.37 The Deuteronomic view of the process of law, then, is that punishment is a deterrent to similar offences being committed in the future. It is also noteworthy that the legal rule of "an eye for an eye and a tooth for a tooth" (known as *ius taliones*) sought to circumscribe the extent of retribution. Although the *ius taliones* may strike modern readers as inhumane, it was in fact a way of restricting retribution to only an eye for an eye. Thus there had to be a correlation between the magnitude of the offence and the severity of the punishment.

3. Justice during and after the exile

17.38 After the end of the Babylonian exile round 530 B.C. the Judaic exiles returned to their own county as subjects of the Persian king. Judah became a province of the mighty Persian empire. This period was characterised by the absence of a Jewish king and the heightened prominence of the priesthood. The status of the priests was further enhanced by the rebuilding of the temple in Jerusalem and the decline of prophetism.

17.39 It should be noted that in the new Persian province the temple was not simply a cultic or religious centre, but also served as the financial and administrative headquarters.

17.40 After the exile a clear distinction was made between royal and religious law. The Persian king Artaxerxes gave the priest Ezra full jurisdiction, maintaining the distinction between imperial and religious law:

> "And you, Ezra, according to the wisdom of your God which is in your hand, appoint magistrates and judges who may judge all the people in the province Beyond the River, all such as know the laws of your God; and those who do not know them, you shall teach Whoever will not obey the law of your God and the law of the king, let judgment be strictly executed upon him, whether for death or for banishment or for confiscation of his goods or for imprisonment" (Ezr 7:25–26).

17.41 The Chronicler, author of 1 and 2 Chronicles, wrote the history of Israel in the perspective of the exilic situation. Thus he provided information not only about the kings, but also, indirectly, about the period of the exile. His description of

Jehoshaphat's juridical rulings (2 Chr 19:4–11) permits certain inferences about the judiciary after the exile.

17.42 Firstly, a clear distinction was made between religious and secular laws. In 2 Chronicles 19:8 there is a distinction between "judgment for the Lord" and "disputed cases" (between inhabitants of the city). The distinction is not only between royal (secular) law and religious law, but also between the people responsible for its administration: "And behold, Amariah the chief priest is over you in all matters of the Lord; and Zebadiah the son of Ishmael, the governor of the house of Judah, in all the king's matters; and the Levites will serve you as officers" (2 Chr 19:11).

17.43 Secondly, it is significant that the priests should have the main say as regards religious law, whereas the king does not have ultimate responsibility even for royal law. Thirdly, the Levites did not seem to play a direct role as judges in the administration of justice, but they did serve as court officials.

17.44 Fourthly, justice is administered "not for man but for the Lord" (2 Chr 19:6) and judges are enjoined to perform their task "in the fear of the Lord" (2 Chr 19:9). The description of Jehoshaphat's juridical rules concludes with a reference to the Lord as the final guarantor of the maintenance of law and justice: "Deal courageously, and may the Lord be with the upright!" (be on the side of the righteous) (2 Chr 19:11).

17.45 There are strong indications that, roughly at the same time as the return from exile, legal reforms were instituted in the Persian empire; as a result of which a distinction was made between universally valid royal edicts and local law. Among the returned exiles this crystallised in a separate secular/royal code as opposed to local Jewish law which was predominantly religious.

17.46 The emphasis on the law in postexilic times is often seen as retrogressive and an attenuation of Jewish religious life. However, this is a gross generalisation. After all, the postexilic period is characterised by the centrality of the "law" as "instruction" (*Torah*) both in public worship and personal devotions:

> The law of the Lord is perfect, reviving the soul;
> the testimony of the Lord is sure, making wise the simple;
> the precepts of the Lord are right, rejoicing the heart;
> the commandment of the Lord is pure, enlightening the eyes (Ps 19:7–8).

17.47 By way of summary the development of the Israelite judicial system can be depicted schematically as follows:

PERIOD	**CONTEXT**	**FUNCTIONARIES**
Prior to establishment of state (before 1000 B.C.)	Family	Father as *paterfamilias*
Age of monarchy (1000–587 B.C.)	City gates Royal court Local cultic place	Elders King Levites
Postexilic age (after 539 B.C.)	Temple	Priests

C. MAJOR LAW COLLECTIONS IN THE OLD TESTAMENT

17.48 Although the influence of the law is discernible in certain passages throughout the Old Testament, the three main law collections afford an illuminating perspective on the three stages in the development of the law that we discussed above. For the sake of continuity with our overall theme of poverty and wealth in the Old Testament, the discussion of each code will indicate how it deals with poverty and wealth.

17.49 Before we turn to the major law collections in the Old Testament, we should first note their fragmentary character. None of them can be regarded as a complete collection that seeks to cater for every possible legal problem. Old Testament legal texts were collated mainly for theological reasons and may be seen as expressive of God's will in certain socioeconomic circumstances and as subject to certain ethical and theological considerations.

1. The Book of the Covenant

17.50 Exodus 20:2–17 is considered to be the earliest collection of legal texts in the Old Testament. According to a later narrative passage it was known as the "book of the covenant"; Moses had received these commandments and ordinances from the Lord, whereupon he read them to the people of Israel (Ex 24:1–7).

17.51 The substance of this collection often suggests an agriculturally based economy, implying that it could only have been finally codified after the settlement in Palestine. Despite this later redaction, there is a core of commandments dating to the period before the monarchy. The injunction to "give" or sacrifice "the first-born of your sons" to the Lord (Ex 22:29) is a macabre relic of an ancient custom.

17.52 Even a cursory glance through the Book of the Covenant indicates unmistakably that the commandments were phrased in different ways.

17.53 First there are those laws which are phrased conditionally or casuistically. This style of legal phraseology usually starts with "when" or "if" in the protasis which defines the legal case. The final part of the law, the apodosis, prescribes the penalty for the offence.

17.54 The law governing theft illustrates how the conditional introductory description of the legal case is followed by the prescribed penalty:

> "If a man steals an ox or a sheep, and kills it or sells it (protasis), he shall pay five oxen for an ox, and four sheep for a sheep (apodosis) ... If the stolen beast is found alive in his possession, whether it is an ox or an ass or a sheep (protasis), he shall pay double" (apodosis) (Ex 22:1,4).

17.55 Secondly, certain commandments are formulated unconditionally or apodictically. In this formulation there is a succinct reference to the legal case, concluding with the punishment incurred by the offence. Thus the precept relating to homicide simply states: "Whoever strikes a man so that he dies shall be put to death" (Ex 21:12). Such a legal formulation does not provide for special circumstances or possible exceptions; it stipulates categorically what has to be observed in any situation.

17.56 In the first half of this century scholars like Albrecht Alt supposed that the apodictic laws were the distinctively Israelite. More recently excavations in the Near East have proven these scholars wrong, since this legal style occurred more widely than they had suspected.

17.57 The Book of the Covenant ends with cultic laws which form a theological framework within which these laws eventually came to be interpreted. They start with the altar laws (Ex 20:22–26) and conclude with laws governing the sabbath, feasts and sacrifice (Ex 23:10–19). Even if it were true that most of the casuistic laws in the Book of the Covenant correspond with customary law in the ancient Near East, especially that of the Canaanite peoples, the theological framework nonetheless implies that they are closely associated with the Israelites' relationship to the Lord.

17.58 A broad outline of the rest of the Book of the Covenant is as follows:

Exodus 21:2–11	Rules governing slaves
21:2–11	Capital crimes
21:12–17	Various forms of assault and injury
22:1–15	Precepts governing property
22:16–31	Precepts about damage to people
23:1–9	Precepts governing false witness and love for one's neighbour

17.59 The Book of the Covenant shows concern for the lot of the poor, widows, orphans and aliens. In this respect it is in harmony with Canaanite texts and Egyptian wisdom literature that display a similar concern.

17.60 Equal justice for the poor is a basic tenet of the law in the Book of the Covenant: "You shall not pervert the justice due to the poor in his suit" (Ex 23:6).

17.61 The poor receive special consideration in special stipulations regarding the sabbath year to ensure that they may still have access to food:

> "For six years you shall sow your land and gather in its yield; but the seventh year you shall let it rest and lie fallow, that the poor of your people may eat; and what they leave the wild beasts may eat" (Ex 23:10–11).

17.62 The poor are further accommodated by prohibiting the charging of interest on loans to a compatriot and by sympathetic treatment when clothes are pawned. One observes that poor people who have been wronged are assured that the Lord will hear them because of his own compassion:

> "If you lend money to any of my people with you who is poor, you shall not be to him as a creditor, and you shall not exact interest from him. If ever you take your neighbor's garment in pledge, you shall restore it to him before the sun goes down; for that is his only covering, it is his mantle for his body; in what else shall he sleep? And if he cries to me, I will hear, for I am compassionate" (Ex 22:25–26).

17.63 Besides the stipulation to protect the rights of the poor, the Book of the Covenant also warns against privileging the poor: "... nor shall you be partial to a poor man in his suit" (Ex 23:3).

17.64 The protection of widows and orphans was prompted by the fact that neither category had a legal persona and were therefore in danger of being excluded from the legal process. This made them an easy prey to exploitation if no protective measures were instituted:

> "You shall not afflict any widow or orphan. If you afflict them, and they cry out to me, I will surely hear their cry; and my wrath will burn, and I will kill you with the sword, and your wives shall become widows and your children fatherless" (Ex 22:22–24).

17.65 The "strangers", who also needed protection because of lack of a legal persona, were most probably members of the original Canaanite population who had lost their land and thus became "strangers" in their own country. In this regard there is an interesting reference to the oppression that Israel had suffered in Egypt as a motive not to treat these "strangers" in the same way: "You shall not wrong a stranger or oppress him, for you were strangers in the land of Egypt" (Ex 22:21).

2. The Deuteronomic law collection

17.66 The name "Deuteronomy" derives from the Septuagint's inaccurate Greek translation which rendered the "copy of this law" in Deuteronomy 17:18 as "a second law". Nevertheless, the title of the book is appropriate in the sense that, if one compares it with the earlier Book of the Covenant, the Deuteronomic laws are to some extent a repetition.

17.67 The very first verse describes the book as the "words of Moses", spoken when he addressed the people before they entered the promised land (Dt 1:1). The Deuteronomic laws are part of a great speech or sermon and are marked by many repetitive phrases and expressions used for rhetorical reasons.

17.68 As in the Book of the Covenant, the laws of Deuteronomy cannot be isolated from the narrative and theological context in which they are placed. Some of the main theological themes in Moses' "sermon" that are reflected in the laws are the following:

17.69 The Lord is the only true God: "Hear, O Israel: The Lord our God is one Lord" (Dt 6:4).

17.70 The people should love God unreservedly: "... and you shall love the Lord your God with all your heart, and with all your soul, and with all your might" (Dt 6:5).

17.71 Israel is a people chosen by grace: "It was not because you were more in number than any other people that the Lord set his love upon you and chose you, for you were the fewest of all peoples" (Dt 7:7).

17.72 The Lord must be worshipped at one sanctuary, in Jerusalem: "But you shall seek the place which the Lord your God will choose out of all your tribes to put his name and make his habitation there" (Dt 12:5).

17.73 The law collection in the book of Deuteronomy comprises chapters 12 to 26, which are placed in a double framework. This framework is evident in the succession of introductory and concluding sections:

Deuteronomy 1–4:	First introduction with historical references
5–11	Second introduction on essence of first commandment
12–26	Laws
27–28	Ratification of covenant with blessing and curse
29–30	Admonitory closing speech by Moses
31–34	Conclusion of Pentateuch (first five books)

17.74 The following broad themes may be discerned in the laws:

Deuteronomy 12–16:17	Laws on cultic unity and purity
16:18	Rules for dignitaries, e.g. judges, kings
16:19–25	Laws governing social relations, e.g. asylum, war
16:26	Firstfruits of the harvest and tithes

17.75 Socioeconomically, the Deuteronomic laws are best interpreted against the background of the monarchy. With the rise of the monarchy massive building projects (e.g. the temple in Jerusalem), an expanding bureaucracy and the maintenance of a large military force put a heavy financial burden on the population of Israel and Judah. The results of these economic circumstances were that peasants lost their land, extensive land ownership was encouraged and a sharper division between rich and poor emerged.

17.76 Ever since the nineteenth century scholars have based their interpretation of the cultic laws of Deuteronomy on the correspondence between Josiah's late seventh century religious reforms (640–609 B.C.) and the law collection. According to 2 Kings 22:8 the high priest found a lawbook in the temple while it was being repaired, and this book led to a series of religious reforms by Josiah.

17.77 These reforms coincided with Josiah's attempts at achieving greater political independence from the Assyrian overlords. A similar coincidence of religious reform (to counteract all pagan practices) and political emancipation (from Assyria) had occurred earlier in the reign of Hezekiah (715–687 B.C.). One surmises, then, that a reform-minded group had been present in Judah over a fairly long period and that Deuteronomy represented a broad outline of their principles.

17.78 The Josiahan reforms and the Deuteronomic laws reaffirm the sovereignty of the Lord and reject any form of pagan idolatry. The Deuteronomic lawbook goes beyond the establishment of a purified cult in its striving for a more just society generally. The laws about wealth and poverty are indicative of such a striving.

17.79 The laws have a combination of utopian and realistic undertones. On the one hand they are simplistic and utopian:

> "But there will be no poor among you (for the Lord will bless you in the land which the Lord your God gives you for an inheritance to possess), if only you will obey the voice of the Lord your God, being careful to do all this commandment which I command you this day" (Dt 15:4–5).

17.80 On the other hand there is a sober, realistic view of poverty: "For the poor will never cease out of the land; therefore I command you, You shall open wide your hand to your brother, to the needy and to the poor, in the land" (Dt 15:11).

17.81 The Deuteronomic law book is far more radical in its precepts concerning the poor than the Book of the Covenant. Thus it recommends that all debts be written off at the end of every seventh year: "every creditor shall release what he has lent to his neighbor" (Dt 15:2). Similar measures are introduced to alleviate the burden of the poor:

17.82 The prohibition of exacting interest from fellow Israelites (Dt 23:19–20)

17.83 The injunction to return the poor person's pledge before sundown (Dt 24:12–13)

17.84 Emancipation of Israelite slaves after seven years (Dt 15:12)

17.85 Prohibition of tightfistedness and exhortation to lend to the poor (Dt 15:7–8)

17.86 An attempt is made to restore the rights of the impoverished peasants, expressed in the prohibition of moving one's neighbour's landmark. This prohibition is justified as follows: "In the inheritance which you will hold in the land that the Lord your God gives you to possess, you shall not remove your neighbor's landmark, which the men of old have set" (Dt 19:14).

17.87 In the framework surrounding the Deuteronomic laws relations to strangers are defined far more positively than in the Book of the Covenant. Whereas the latter merely prohibits oppression, Deuteronomy positively insists that the Lord's example of love for these strangers should be emulated: "He ... loves the sojourner, giving him food and clothing. Love the sojourner therefore; for you were sojourners in the land of Egypt" (Dt 10:18–19).

17.88 Safeguarding of property in general is given such priority in Deuteronomy that it even extends to birds' nests! (Dt 22:6–7) This emphasis on respect for property is closely linked to the view of the people as a large family of brothers and sisters. Although the prosperity of the rich was regarded as a blessing from the Lord, there is consistent concern with charity to the poor. As brothers and sisters of one family, all Israelites had to share the land and its bounty, to which end landownership was essential. The Deuteronomic laws did not assign the poor special status, but alleviation of their plight was regarded as part of obedience to the law and, fundamentally, as observance of the Lord's will.

3. The Holiness Code

17.89 The most recent collection of legal texts is that in Leviticus 17 to 26. These are known as the Holiness Code, since the theme of the collection is spelled out in the pronouncement: "You shall be holy; for I the Lord your God am holy" (Lv 19:2).

17.90 The Holiness Code treats the following themes:

Leviticus 17	Sole place of sacrifice and prohibition of eating blood
18	Sexual relations
19–20	Theological and ethical commandments
21–22	Rules governing priests and sacrifices
23:1–24:9	Religious feasts
24:10–23	Criminal cases (e.g. murder and slander)
25	Sabbath year

17.91 After the exile the reconstructed temple in Jerusalem became the centre of Jewish society. The priests adapted the existing laws of Israel to preserve the people from any form of impurity which would disqualify them from cultic participation. In the Holiness Code the rules governing purity are related to the general exhortation to holiness.

17.92 There are numerous examples of how the Holiness Code amplifies the prescribed attitude towards the poor:

17.93 Certain legal principles now apply to Israelites and aliens (Lv 24:22).

17.94 The prohibition of charging interest now applies to Israelite, sojourner and stranger (Lv 25:35–36).

17.95 Israelites who are obliged to have themselves sold into slavery may not perform menial work (Lv 25:39).

17.96 The institution of the jubilee year was designed to enable Israelites or Jews who had had to sell their land to recover it in that year so as to restore the family estate. Even though the jubilee year was never put into effect, it remained a major ideal to be pursued (Lv 25:10). According to priestly law economic determinants were not the main ones in business transactions. The ideal was always that every Israelite or Jew be entitled to personal freedom, to which end landownership was essential – not only for men, but for dependants such as women and children as well.

17.97 The jubilee year and the prohibition of the enslavement of Israelites are both based on the Lord's proprietorship: the Lord owns all land (Lv 25:23) and Israelites are the Lord's servants (Lv 25:42).

D. NABOTH AND HIS VINEYARD (1 KINGS 21)

17.98 By way of supplementing the various other perspectives the events involving Naboth, Ahab and Jezebel can be viewed from a legal angle. A legal perspective moreover casts new light on the contrast between rich and poor which underlies the description of the events associated with Naboth's vineyard.

17.99 From the very *first verse* the main characters, Naboth and Ahab, are contrasted with one another with reference to their adjacent properties. Although the two are neighbours, the one is a farmer and the other a king; the one owns a vineyard (the most basic land owned by an Israelite) and the other a palace; the one is a local Jezreelite and the other comes from Samaria. This makes the contrast between basic landownership (relative poverty) and wealth highly significant for our understanding of the rest of the story.

17.100 The *first scene* in *verses 2 to 4* is enacted between Ahab and Naboth. It starts in *verse 2* with Ahab's perfectly reasonable offer to exchange Naboth's vineyard for a better one or to purchase it. Despite the apparent fairness of Ahab's offer one observes that he wants to convert the vineyard into a herb or vegetable garden and that he is prepared to pay generously for it.

17.101 Naboth's response in *verse 3* amounts to a categorical, almost rude refusal of Ahab's fair offer. The refusal is justified by citing the inalienability of ancestral land. Although this does not involve any law in the modern sense of the word, one could regard it as a sort of legal principle.

17.102 This principle is summed up in the stipulations concerning the land of Zelophchad's daughters In Numbers 36: "The inheritance of the people of Israel shall not be transferred from one tribe to another; for every one of the people of Israel shall cleave to the inheritance of the tribe of his fathers ... so that every one of the people of Israel may possess the inheritance of his fathers" (Nm 36:7–8).

17.103 The later priestly laws on the institution of the sabbath and jubilee years prohibit the permanent sale of land because the land belongs to the Lord (Lv 25:23). Religious justification of legal principles governing land transactions was typical of Israel, in contrast to the more secular approach of neighbouring peoples.

17.104 *Verse 4* tells how Ahab goes home, depressed and angry, and takes to his bed, sulking because he had not got his way. Still, there is no indication at this stage that Ahab is going to take any further action to obtain the vineyard. Illuminatingly, the motive for Naboth's refusal is repeated and we get the impression that Ahab accepts the rejection of his offer.

17.105 The *second scene*, between Ahab and Jezebel, in *verses 5 to 7* has Jezebel take the initiative in establishing the reason for Ahab's gloom (*v 5*). Ahab's response in *verse 6* is a repetition of his reasonable offer to Naboth and Naboth's categorical rejection of it. However, Ahab's repetition of Naboth's motive for refusing does not refer to "the inheritance of my fathers" but merely to "my vineyard". The distinction between "vineyard" and "inheritance of my fathers" is very pertinent to the interpretation of the story. It is not a matter of the contrast between rich and poor only, but also of that between two different perceptions of landownership.

17.106 A further contrast is made in *verse 7* where Jezebel assumes that, as king, Ahab can dispose over Naboth's land despite the latter's refusal to sell it. Jezebel's exclamation, "Do you now govern Israel?" presupposes a type of monarchy that permits royal intervention in matters of landownership. It could be that Jezebel, being a Phoenician princess, had a more autocratic conception of the monarchy and that this conception is being contrasted with the Israelite view of the king as someone with limited powers. Jezebel's comment at the end of the scene, "I will give you the vineyard of Naboth the Jezreelite", remains unexplained till later in the story.

17.107 The *third scene* in *verses 8 to 10* shows Jezebel, with no attempt to conceal her plans, persuading the leaders of Naboth's city by letter to stone Naboth to death on a false accusation. Having written the letters in Ahab's name, Jezebel seals them with the king's seal, which had more or less the same validatory value as a modern signature (*v 8*). She addressed the letters to "the elders and the nobles" of the city; the "leaders" probably refers to the elders or heads of families who often acted in a juridical capacity. The word translated as "nobles" occurs again in Jeremiah (39:6), where their role largely corresponds with the stipulation in Deuteronomy 16:18 that "judges and officers" had to be appointed in every city.

17.108 *Verse 9* divulges the contents of the letters: the leaders are instructed to proclaim a fast. According to 2 Chronicles 20:3 and Jonah 3:5 the king was empowered to proclaim a fast, in both cases as a result of a national disaster. This leads one to surmise that the great drought could have been adduced as a reason for the fast. Naboth is put at the head of the assembly, which gives him the place of honour from where he could well have acted as a venerable judge. This eminent position makes the charge of blasphemy that was to be laid all the more damning.

17.109 *Verse 10* stipulates explicitly that there had to be two witnesses, since Israelite law required two witnesses before a person could be convicted (Dt 19:15). The charge was that Naboth had cursed both God and the king. According to Leviticus 24:10–16 blasphemy was a capital offence; cursing the king amounted to blasphemy as well since the king represented God (Ex 22:28). Stoning was the punishment for blasphemy (Lv 24:10–16) and was usually executed outside the city in order not to incur impurity (Lv 24:14; Nm 15:36).

17.110 The *fourth scene* in *verses 11 to 14* describes the response of the elders and nobles to Jezebel's request. As stories tend to do, the scene repeats the events requested by Jezebel in her letter, indicating that everything proceeded according to plan. The minute correspondence between what Jezebel had schemed and what the elders did could also have a juridical motive. The repetition could suggest that the actual responsibility for the abuse of the law lay with those who had planned it rather than with the ones who executed the plan. Jezebel and Ahab were guilty, not the city fathers.

17.111 In the *fifth scene* in *verses 15 to 16* Jezebel and Ahab are once more the main actors. In the face of explicit laws governing the conduct of a king in Deuteronomy 17:14–20, the king exceeds his powers. It should be noted that both verses stress the fact that Ahab was free to take possession of the vineyard (*v 15*) and that he then proceeded to do just that (*v 16*). The repeated reference to "take possession" probably signifies that the king confiscated the land and unlawfully appropriated it.

E. CONCLUSION

17.112 The question is: how do we benefit by a juridical interpretation of 1 Kings 21?

17.113 The story of Naboth reflects cognizance of the principal law collections in the Old Testament.

17.114 Naboth's attachment to his ancestral land concurs with the view in antiquity that the land of a family or clan is inalienable (cf. the Priestly laws, Nm 36:7–9).

17.115 The false charge that Naboth had blasphemed against God and the king is a contravention of the laws governing blasphemy in the Book of the Covenant (Ex 22:27).

17.116 The requirement that at least two witnesses had to give evidence against Naboth accords with Deuteronomic law (Dt 19:15).

17.117 The practice of stoning outside the city walls is in keeping with the Holiness laws (Lv 24:13–23).

17.118 It appears that a legal interpretation of the story of Naboth makes it possible to identify the decline and decay of Israelite administration of justice as a major theme of the narrative. This decline is dramatically illustrated by the "legal murder" (i.e. murder within the law) of Naboth on the strength of false charges and the manipulation of the elders – the judicial body – by the king and queen. The autocratic action and flagrant abuse of power by Ahab, at the insistence of his Phoenician queen, when he "took possession" of an Israelite's ancestral land indicates a non-Israelite conception of the monarchy, of which the author of the Naboth story is critical.

17.119 There are interesting parallels between the legal circumstances in the Naboth incident and those in South Africa at the end of the twentieth century.

17.120 It is clear that the dispute over landownership in South Africa will be highly topical for some time to come. Readers should judge for themselves whether there are Naboths in South Africa who seek to obtain or retain a claim to ancestral lands. In the same breath one might ask whether there arc Jezebels and Ahabs who claim a prerogative to intervene autocratically in matters affecting the property of their subjects. Such intervention may be aimed at redistribution of wealth, or at the redressing of past wrongs.

17.121 The relationship between Roman-Dutch and indigenous law is far from being resolved satisfactorily. Sociopolitical changes in South Africa are bound to influence the judicial system and the basic social contract prevailing in this society.

17.122 Readers will furthermore have to ask themselves if the abuse of power by decision makers in this country has not assumed alarming proportions already.

17.123 The exorbitant costs of legal procedure in South Africa often makes it impossible for impoverished wronged parties to defend their interests in court. Affluent people can afford better legal representation, which gives them an immediate unfair advantage over less well-to-do litigants.

17.124 Although there is no uniform or consistent legal perspective on wealth and poverty in the Old Testament, it nonetheless deals with important issues which remain relevant for twentieth century South Africa. While the Old Testament is not a textbook for modern judicial or economic systems, it is an important source of reference for the ethical decisions that Christians have to take every day.

18

Prophets and profiteers: Prophetic perspectives on wealth and poverty

WILLIE VAN HEERDEN

A. INTRODUCTION

18.1 A historical-critical interpretation of the Naboth story enables us to see that 1 Kings 21 views these events from different perspectives. From verse 17 onwards we are looking through the eyes of a prophet, a perspective not found in the first sixteen verses. Verses 17 to 21a give one a fair idea of what a prophetic perspective is about:

> Then the word of the Lord came to Elijah the Tishbite, saying, "Arise, go down to meet Ahab king of Israel, who is in Samaria; behold, he is in the vineyard of Naboth, where he has gone to take possession". And you shall say to him, 'Thus says the Lord: "Have you killed and also taken possession?'" And you shall say to him, 'Thus says the Lord: "In the place where dogs licked up the blood of Naboth shall the dogs lick your own blood'".

Ahab said to Elijah, "Have you found me, O my enemy?" He answered, "I have found you, because you have sold yourself to do what is evil in the sight of the Lord. Behold I will bring evil upon you; I will utterly sweep you away ..."

18.2 The following points are noteworthy:

- The *Lord* enters into the picture far more than in the first sixteen verses.
- The king is the *ruler of Israel*, the head of the *community.*
- Verse 18 refers to a *specific king* who ruled at a *specific time.*
- The prophet, speaking for the Lord, refers to specific *offences* of the king and the *punishment* that awaits him.
- This oracle appears *outside* the texts that we know as the *books of the prophets.*

18.3 These points highlight some important features of the prophetic perspectives. After looking into these a bit more closely we shall return to the Naboth story. After that we shall let a few prophets speak for themselves.

B. CHARACTERISTICS OF LITERATURE THAT OFFERS A PROPHETIC PERSPECTIVE

1. The prophets direct their minds towards God's will for the community

18.4 One could say that the prophets went through life with their *eyes and ears open*. Their eyes were wide open to the social problems of their day; at the same time their ears were attuned to hearing God's will for the community. For this reason politics and religion were inseparable to the prophets. The king – the one who had to watch over the community – was himself subject to God's law. Royal abuses and exploitation of ordinary Israelites were seen by the prophets as an offence against the Lord.

18.5 The words "justice" and "righteousness" abound in biblical passages with a prophetic perspective. To the prophets these words do not merely relate to a nice way in which people ought to treat one another; they are focal to God's will and actions: "And I will make justice the line, and righteousness the plummet" (Is 28:17).

18.6 Bringing all manner of offerings will not set matters right with God while injustice continues to rage unabated. Jeremiah 7 states explicitly that God does not ask for offerings, but for obedience. Someone who oppresses and exploits other people does not fear the Lord (Ml 3:5). By the same token people today refer to the church's "prophetic calling" as its duty to speak out boldly on justice and righteousness in the economic and political spheres and in regard to human rights.

18.7 The prophets were not primarily interested in abstract philosophical issues, nor in definitions and intricate arguments. They speak about the *lot of simple people* – widows, orphans, aliens. They also speak about the daily conduct of the rich, public officials and heads of state. The prophets felt intensely about injustice and their oracles were their way of expressing their agonised struggle over it. Consequently they use strong, often shocking language.

18.8 People in those societies attached great importance to wisdom, power and wealth. Consequently a king who possessed all these attributes could rely on their adulation, even if he was an oppressor of the underprivileged. In the eyes of the prophets this was wrong:

> Thus says the Lord: "Let not the wise man glory in his wisdom, let not the mighty man glory in his might, let not the rich man glory in his riches; but let him who glories glory in this, that he understands and knows me, that I am the Lord who practice kindness, justice and righteousness in the earth; for in these things I delight, says the Lord" (Jr 9:23–24).

18.9 There is a popular notion that prophets are primarily people who predict what will happen in the future. From what we have said so far it is clear that they were mainly intent on declaring God's will for the *here and now*. Predictions of the future merely help to clarify what is happening in the present.

18.10 At this stage it may seem as if the prophets were merely gripers and prophets of doom. This is not so. Prophets are found in all religions and are preeminently *intermediaries* between a religious community and a supernatural being or power. This implies that not all prophets were peripheral figures in society. In Israel, moreover, prophets did not always sing the same tune. Some were so much part of the establishment that they consciously tried to justify it. Others could voice their social criticism from a key position in society. Still others were probably peripheral figures without much influence or power. We might expect that the problems associated with wealth and poverty would have occupied these last two groups in particular.

18.11 The fact that the prophets occupied various positions in society casts doubt on certain *popular conceptions* about them. Some people say that it was the hallmark of all prophets to be social reformers. Others try and understand the prophets in the light of their criticism of urban culture. These people claim that the prophets advocated an agrarian life style similar to that which had prevailed before the time of the monarchy with its taxes and officials. Yet others believe that the prophetic voice related directly to the corruption of the traditional legal system. We are also told that the prophets should be understood against the background of the Canaanite and, later, the Babylonian customs that gradually infiltrated the Israelite way of life. All these explanations – which rightly accentuate the prophets' social involvement – contain an element of truth. But they do not allow for the diversity found among the prophets themselves.

2. In which parts of the Bible do we find prophetic perspectives on wealth and poverty?

18.12 As we have gathered from the Naboth episode, prophetic perspectives are also found *outside the books that were named after prophets*. Most of our information about prophets derives from the Deuteronomic history (especially Samuel and Kings) and the collection of books bearing the names of prophets (Isaiah, Jeremiah, Ezekiel and the twelve minor prophets). In the rabbinic tradition the books of which the Deuteronomic history forms a part (Dt to 2 Ki, excluding Ruth) are known as the Early Prophets, and the books named after prophets are known as the Later Prophets. This acknowledges that the two sets of biblical books have certain perspectives in common. In the Pentateuch (the first five books of the Bible) there are occasional references to prophets, including the story and oracles of Balaam in Numbers 22–24.

18.13 It is noteworthy that the prophets we encounter in the Bible ministered mainly in times of *crisis*. One such crisis was just before the Assyrians topped the northern kingdom in 721 B.C. Three prophets ministered in the northern kingdom at that time – Amos, Hosea and Jonah (about whom we read in 2 Ki 14:25). At the same time two prophets, Isaiah and Micah, were active in the southern kingdom. A hundred years later these very Assyrians were conquered by the Babylonians, who immediately started putting pressure on Judah. In this period a number of prophets came to the fore – Jeremiah, Nahum and Zephaniah. A few decades later, in 586 B.C., the Babylonians conquered Judah. This was when Ezekiel acted as prophet. This period also forms the background to the book of Daniel. Less than a century later the Babylonians succumbed to the Persians. The Persians permitted the Jewish exiles to return to Jerusalem. In this period of radical change prophets such as Haggai, Zechariah, and later Malachi were active.

18.14 It was mainly the prophets who ministered before the fall of the northern kingdom (eighth century B.C.) who spoke out on social issues relating to poverty and wealth. Amos, Hosea, Isaiah and Micah were the main figures. The prophets of the seventh and sixth centuries B.C. (i.e. before and after the fall of the southern kingdom) also had occasion to address themselves to the problem of poverty, as we read in Jeremiah, Zephaniah and Ezekiel. Isaiah 58 is an interesting passage if one wants to know what the prophets thought about wealth and poverty after the fall of Judah.

3. The prophets' oracles were directed to the people and circumstances of a specific time

18.15 Just as the prophet Elijah was instructed in 1 Kings 21:18 to speak specifically to king Ahab, so the other biblical prophets all addressed a *particular person* or *group of persons*. Thus Amos addresses the notables (Am 3:9–10; 4:1–3; 6:1–8), the wealthy people in the cities (Am 5:11f.) and business people (Am 8:4–8). Hosea mentions the politically influential (Hs 7:3–7; 8:4a) and the merchants (Hs 12:8–10). Isaiah directs himself against the elite, public officials, the king, the judges (Is 1:10–17, 21–28; 5:23; 10:1–4) and against the rich and the large estate owners (Is 1:29–31; 5:8–10). Micah mentions the large estate owners (Mi 2:1–3; 3:9–12) and the leaders and administrators (Mi 3:1–4; 3:9–12). Jeremiah refers to community leaders and the affluent (Jr 5:26–29; 6:13–15; 34:8–22). In addition he mentions the kings Jehoiakim and Zedekiah by name (Jr 22:13–19; 34:8–22). Ezekiel is thinking of the shepherds of Israel, hence the king and other leaders (Ezk 34). Only on rare occasions do the prophets address the nation as a whole (Am 2:6–16; Hs 4:1–3; Is 1:10–17; Jr 7:1–15).

18.16 Virtually all these targets of the prophets' attention were involved with problems associated with poverty and wealth. This will become clear when we examine some of the prophetic oracles more closely.

18.17 If the prophets addressed specific people about their offences, it follows that we have to understand these social problems against the socio-historical background of each prophet's time. In recent years scholars have greatly broadened their knowledge of the lot of ordinary people in ancient societies. Until fairly recently these scholars, notably archaeologists, were more interested in the lives of eminent people such as kings. But nowadays there is a trend to research the life style of the ordinary folk as well, and this trend may be helpful if we want to understand the problems that the prophets were concerned about.

18.18 As mentioned before, the prophets of the eighth century were particularly concerned about the social problems relating to poverty and wealth. This is understandable if we consider the society in which they lived. In the *eighth century B.C.* there were certain changes in the existing social structure which greatly affected the lives of ordinary citizens. Originally society had been organised into village communities whose inhabitants were to a large extent interdependent. Society was well structured for co-operation and mutual aid. In such a close-knit, interdependent community a change in one segment would be likely to influence the others, and in the eighth century such changes began to happen on a large scale. The transition was made from a subsistence to a manufacturing and commercial economy. Although these changes had actually been triggered by the institution of the monarchy, there were additional factors that made the disruption assume crisis proportions.

18.19 One of these was rapid population growth. This led to greater occupational differentiation, which meant that matters of common interest had to be co-ordinated on an ever broader basis. This gave rise to a bureaucratic system. For many of the unemployed, the landless, the destitute of this time, the public service, army and priesthood offered a way out. As a result control over cardinal community affairs was taken away from the village elders of families and became the responsibility and privilege of officialdom.

18.20 This had various results: the tribal structure began to crumble; a powerful middle class of officials arose, standing between the king and the populace; and the Canaanite element of the population was integrated into the process of bureaucratisation. The farming industry was hard hit. Land rights were at issue and the flow of farm produce came under the control of officials in the form of taxes, various types of interest, tithes and mandatory tribute.

18.21 Against this background it is easier to understand what the prophets meant when they spoke about the favouring of influential people in the law courts, unfair taxes, exploitive business practices and lack of security which were associated with such phenomena as debt slavery and confiscation of property.

18.22 Prophets who ministered in *different times* and hence different historical circumstances do not always focus so sharply on the problems relating to wealth and poverty. Besides, the term "the poor" meant something quite different to Zephaniah than it did to the other prophets. The author(s) of the second part of Isaiah assign yet a third meaning to this term. Such differences in meaning and emphasis will be dealt with more fully later on.

4. The form of the prophetic oracles

18.23 In the few verses from the Naboth episode which we cited at the beginning it was remarkable that the prophet Elijah *prefaces* three of his sayings with "Thus says the Lord ..." The first is followed by an indication of the offences of which Ahab is *accused* after the introductory formula. The second is followed by a pronouncement of the *punishment* he was to receive. In the third instance we are told about both the charge and the punishment. The prophets often cast their oracles in fixed forms. In addition to the introductory formula, accusation and pronouncement of punishment mentioned above, one can distinguish between warnings, threats, calls to repentance, admonitions and oracles of woe.

18.24 When prophets are expressing social criticism, accusations and pronouncements of punishment feature most prominently, leading scholars to the following conclusions:

- To the prophets there is a definite connection between social misdeeds and misfortune that will befall people.
- The prophets do not really expect people to mend their ways, even though they know that this would be the right thing to do.
- The prophets are not primarily social reformers, otherwise injunctions to different behaviour would have been their first concern.
- Since punishment is always inflicted by God, one concludes that the prophets see

a close connection between people's conduct towards one another and their relationship to God.

5. Restrictions on our knowledge about the prophets

18.25 So far we have only lifted the curtain veiling the complex phenomenon of Old Testament prophetism ever so slightly. On the one hand there is a great deal more to be said about the prophets and prophetism; certain problem areas have not been mentioned at all. On the other hand what we have already seen is *not as simple* as it may seem.

18.26 It should be evident that the *societies of those days* were very different to modern ones. And, despite a great deal of study and considerable gains in knowledge about those societies in recent times, we still know relatively little about them. Consequently one hesitates to say that one understands the prophets of those days properly. Then we must remember that the prophets themselves came from different periods. Between Amos and Malachi a whole three hundred years elapsed. Even prophets who were contemporaries were not always in the same boat. Thus Hosea and Isaiah were both eighth century prophets, but the former operated in the northern kingdom and the latter in the south.

18.27 Because poverty is an acute problem in modern societies as well we may too easily read the prophets as if they were speaking about problems that *we* are aware of. This is not necessarily the case.

18.28 But this is not all that complicates an understanding of the prophets. The actual prophetic books display clear signs of *compilation* and *later redaction* and *insertions* by people who wanted to make these books relevant to their own times. The chapter on historical criticism concentrated on these matters. Did you observe the reference a few paragraphs earlier to the author(s) of the second part of Isaiah which deals with the time when the people of Judah were in exile? You will also hear about Trito-Isaiah who was responsible for the third part of this text, and of the so-called Deuteronomic redactor(s) whose touch is discernible throughout the prophetic books.

18.29 As though the issue was not complicated enough already, there is uncertainty about *exactly who and what a prophet was*. Some scholars question whether the Israelites themselves always knew who were prophets and who were not. This is evident in the way the concept of a prophet is used in 1 Samuel 9–10. Throughout the Old Testament there is a strange tension between a positive and a condemnatory attitude towards prophets. Some prophets are even derided as deceivers and people with a "lying spirit" (1 Ki 22:13–23). There is also a tendency in some parts of the Old Testament to call any very important person a prophet (Gn 20:7; Dt 34:10–12).

18.30 In this chapter you are invited to examine social problems like wealth and poverty through the eyes of a prophet. So far we have attempted to do two things:

- We have tried to broaden your insight into what lies ahead by sketching the background to the literature that adopts a prophetic perspective.
- We have tried to indicate some pitfalls in the interpretation of prophets.

18.31 After this digression we return to the Naboth episode.

C. ELIJAH AND THE STORY OF NABOTH

18.32 There is no consensus about *which parts* of 1 Kings 21 were written from a prophetic perspective. In the chapter on historical criticism we learnt that scholars such as Fohrer and Gray ascribe the entire chapter to authors from the prophetic movement. They hold that the prominence given to Jezebel in this chapter indicates that this is a prophetic version of the historical events, since it reflects the hatred felt for her in prophetic circles. We know that Jezebel herself was a Canaanite. The prophets were already opposed to the policy introduced by Omri (Ahab's father) to synthesise the Israelite and Canaanite traditions – or at any rate to recognise the latter alongside the former.

18.33 Other scholars, such as Manfred Oeming, maintain that only the passage from verse 17 onwards was written from a prophetic perspective. He points out a number of differences between the first sixteen verses and the remainder of the chapter, including the following:

- The first sixteen verses focus on *Jezebel;* from verse 17 onwards we are dealing with Ahab.
- The first part of the chapter continually refers to Naboth as coming from *Jezreel.* Since we are told that his vineyard adjoins Ahab's palace, one may assume that this refers to Ahab's palace in Jezreel. But from verse 17 onwards this topographical reference disappears. In fact, verse 18 says that Ahab rules in *Samaria*, where he had another palace, as king of Israel. Oeming suggests that this indicates the presence of two different traditions about the same event.
- It is also striking that the first sixteen verses contain hardly any reference to *the Lord*, in sharp contrast to the ensuing passage. Here God, through the words of the prophet, is present, demanding obedient living and punishing those who spurn his will.
- The prophet *Elijah* does not feature in the first part of the chapter, whereas verse 17 opens with the Lord's instruction to him to go and speak to Ahab.

18.34 The last two differences in particular convince Oeming that the two parts of the chapter were written *from different perspectives*. He assigns to verses 1 to 16 a wisdom perspective, about which you learn more in the next chapter. The ensuing passage, he says, indicates a prophetic perspective. The two passages follow like a question and an answer. After reading the first sixteen verses one wonders: but where is God? As you proceed you get the answer: he is present in the way he declares and executes his will.

18.35 From verse 21 onwards there are a number of *insertions*, which were pointed out in the chapter on historical criticism. Some of these may in fact be attributable to the marked differences we have noted here. Verse 23 may have been added because Jezebel – who should have been the real target of the Lord's anger – is nowhere on the scene when punishment is meted out from verse 17 onwards. The other insertions may be attributed to the discrepancy between what the story says will happen and what actually happens. In actual fact Ahab did not die; so verses 27 to 29 recount how Ahab repented and that this was why the punishment would befall his descendants.

18.36 So far we have merely presented the case for 1 Kings 21 (or part of it) being written from a prophetic perspective. Now we must ask to *which prophetic tradition* Elijah belonged and why he was so dissatisfied with the policy and actions of members of the royal house. Elijah's attitude towards Ahab was typical of the aversion that the Yahwist prophetic movement felt towards those who tolerated worship of multiple gods. Ahab is never accused of ceasing to worship Yahweh. His offence is that he permitted the God of the Canaanites to be worshipped alongside Yahweh. It is a question of serving two lords. It encroaches on the honour due to Yahweh and amounts to idolatry.

18.37 Some scholars, including Gottwald, maintain that neither *Ahab* nor *Jezebel* propagated a country-wide introduction of the Canaanite cult. It was purely because Jezebel herself was a Canaanite that she was allowed to worship her Canaanite God – probably Baal Melqart or Baal Shemahim. Seen thus, the antagonism that Ahab and Jezebel evinced towards the Yahwist prophets was not so much because they wanted the Canaanite faith to triumph; it might rather have related to the politics of the day and the resultant economic policy. Ahab had settled for a policy of national reconciliation, the implications of which angered the prophets.

18.38 The religious conflict with the prophets was only one of Ahab's problems. He had to contend with difficult political and *economic issues* as well. His country was situated on the main connecting routes, including trade and military routes, which made it vulnerable. He therefore launched major building projects to secure his capital city. Because of a shortage of skilled artisans and labourers he imported Phoenician workers. These imports had to be paid for in kind. Consequently his country had to produce more food than the population needed. At the same time a fairly large bureaucracy was established.

18.39 One can see at once the *implications* these developments had for the peasants. The state needed more land for its expanding agricultural projects. At the same time they were under pressure to produce more. They now had to feed mouths other than those of their own families by way of tribute, taxes and interest. In the process many peasants were driven from their land. It was standard practice in Israel that debtors' land could become state property through confiscation.

18.40 This is where the Yahwist prophets entered into it. One of their powerful traditions was that the land belonged to the Lord, who had given it to the Solomonite patriarchs. For this reason the land was inalienably the property of the Israelite families occupying it. That explains why it was such an abomination in Elijah's eyes when Ahab took possession of Naboth's land and that it was wrong "in the eyes of the Lord".

18.41 The Yahwist notion that the land belonged inalienably to the Israelite clans had another significant implication. Every time a new generation inherited land, it was subdivided. This meant that eventually they had to subsist on minuscule plots of land. In Ahab's time the government was putting pressure on them to produce more, which put a severe strain on the peasants. They had to accomplish this on what had become non-viable agricultural units.

18.42 Thus there was frustration on both sides. On the one hand the Yahwists felt that Ahab's government did not take some of their religious traditions seriously. Added to this was the pressure caused by Ahab's economic measures. On the other hand the government was frustrated because Yahwist traditions obstructed their carefully co-ordinated economic projects by refusing to part with their land on any terms. Consider how flatly Naboth rejects Ahab's offer to buy his land in verse 3.

18.43 It is noteworthy that Elijah does *not* accuse Ahab of contravening *the law*. After all, Jezebel had taken the greatest care to ensure that Ahab stayed on the right side of the law in the way Naboth was eliminated. There was a legal "hearing" with the requisite witnesses who were to accuse Naboth; the death penalty was also in accordance with the official reasons for its imposition. Naboth was even stoned in the "proper" place, outside the city.

18.44 It makes one question the value of such a legal system. How can injustice flourish in the name of the law? This was a theme that was to arouse many prophets in the years that followed – especially when they were fighting the cause of the poor.

D. THE PROPHETS BEFORE THE FALL OF THE NORTHERN KINGDOM

18.45 The eighth century prophets dealt at great length with social problems, of which wealth and poverty were part. These prophets will be central to this discussion. Although they identify much the same problems, they occasionally differ on the nature of the punishment to come and the grounds for the judgments they pronounce. Later, when we come to the seventh century prophets, we will find that they sometimes differed from the eighth century prophets and from one another in their views of the poor.

1. Amos

18.46 By the *middle of the eighth century BC,* Amos, a stock trader from Tekoa in Judah, was a prophet in the northern kingdom. It was a time of reasonable prosperity and political stability, but also of grave social abuses. The poor were the prime victims of these. Earlier in this chapter we showed that texts with a prophetic perspective are more readily understood against the background of contemporary social conditions. We also gave a thumbnail sketch of social conditions in the eighth century. Against that background the oracles of Amos (and other eighth century prophets) become more meaningful.

18.47 The book of Amos gives some indication of *what happened to many poor people* once they fell victim to exploitation. Initially price increases forced the poor to borrow money and pledge their possessions (Am 2:8). This soon led to a situation where the poor were working for someone else on what had been their own land, simply to meet their commitments to their creditors (Am 5:11). Eventually some of the poor were sold into debt slavery (Am 2:6; 8:6). People who were enslaved for nonpayment of debt were often sold to foreigners. Such people could rightly claim to have lost everything. Amos could not tolerate the idea that Israelites could forfeit their position in society in this way, particularly not if one considered the practices that had led to their plight.

18.48 The *people with economic power* were the ones that were most insensitive to the lot of the poor. Amos 6:1, 4–7 describes the attitude of those who were living in luxury:

> "Woe to those who are at ease in Zion, and to those who feel secure on the mountain of Samaria, the notable men of the first of the nations, to whom the house of Israel come! ... Woe to those who lie upon beds of ivory, and stretch themselves upon their couches, and eat lambs from the flock, and calves from the midst of the stall; who sing idle songs to the sound of the harp, and like David invent for themselves instruments of music; who drink wine in bowls, and anoint themselves with the finest oils, but are not grieved over the ruin of Joseph! Therefore they shall now be the first of those to go into exile, and the revelry of those who stretch themselves shall pass away".

18.49 These rich people enjoy the peasants' produce but give no thought to the people on whom they are in fact dependent. Amos 4:1–3 opens on much the same note:

> "Hear this word, you cows of Bashan, who are in the mountain of Samaria, who oppress the poor, who crush the needy, who say to their husbands, 'Bring, that we may drink!' The Lord God has sworn by his holiness that, behold, the days are coming upon you, when they shall take you away with hooks, even the last of you with fish-hooks. And you shall go out through the breaches, every one straight before her; and you shall be cast forth into Harmon", says the Lord.

18.50 In these verses we observe that Amos – as elsewhere in his book – stresses the link between the people and the *land*. The people will be driven like cattle from the land that nourishes them.

18.51 The book of Amos identifies certain areas in which the injustice of the rulers towards the people is most evident. Amos 5:10–12 reads:

> Therefore because you trample upon the poor and take from him exactions of wheat, you have built houses of hewn stone, but you shall not dwell in them; you have planted pleasant vineyards, but you shall not drink their wine. For I know how many are your transgressions, and how great are your sins – you who afflict the righteous, who take a bribe, and turn aside the needy in the gate.

18.52 The reference to turning away "the needy in the gate" at the end of verse 12 indicates the city gates where lawsuits were traditionally conducted in the presence of all free male adult Israelites. These cases were often concerned with problems about inheritance, but even cases that entailed a death penalty were sometimes heard. These assemblies also had to allocate the taxes and forced labour imposed by the state. The poor who had lost their freedom because of debt also lost their right to be present at these meetings. This created scope for all manner of abuses which meant that they no longer received just treatment.

18.53 Some scholars maintain that the decision-making and executive power of these assemblies at the city gates was violated by the establishment of a central government. The people at the city gates simply had to rubberstamp what the government had decided. Government decisions would obviously be in the interests of the treasury and the public officials. In any event, the poor were the ones to suffer because of all the violations of truth, extortion and bribery.

18.54 The punishment for this offence (v 11) was that the people will no longer enjoy the blessings of the land. Their houses were a sign of their ties with the land and wine was a product of it.

18.55 Secondly, there were unjust *business dealings:. Amos 8:5–8 reads:*

> [You say], "When will the new moon be over, that we may sell grain? And the sabbath, that we may offer wheat for sale, that we may make the ephah small and the shekel great, and deal deceitfully with false balances, that we may buy the poor for silver and the needy for a pair of sandals, and sell the refuse of the wheat?" The Lord has sworn by the pride of Jacob: "Sure I will never forget any of their deeds. Shall not the land tremble on this account, and every one mourn who dwells in it, and all of it rise like the Nile, and be tossed about and sink again, like the Nile of Egypt?"

18.56 The prophet condemns the contempt people showed for religious feast days in their greed to make more money. In addition, the poor buyers had to take what they could get, even though the commodities were less and of poorer quality than what they had paid for. Again the consequences of the merchants' actions relate to the land on which they are dependent.

18.57 Thirdly the prophet maintains that the people's religious *celebrations* were abhorrent while injustice was rife among them. Amos 5:21–24 reads:

> "I hate, I despise your feasts, and I take no delight in your solemn assemblies. Even though you offer me your burnt offerings and cereal offerings, I will not accept them, and the peace offerings of your fatted beasts I will not look upon. Take away from me the noise of your songs; to the melody of your harps I will not listen. But let justice roll down like waters, and righteousness like an ever flowing stream".

18.58 Joining in festive religious activities for the sake of appearances is wrong. The punishment for this (v 27) would be exile. The Lord is not to be simply "celebrated"; he wants to guide the people towards greater justice and righteousness. This theme features prominently in the literature that adopts a prophetic perspective.

18.59 To demonstrate the extent of the injustice, Amos cites (in the fourth place) the *physical exploitation* of defenceless people. Amos 2:7 reads: "they ... trample the head of the poor into the dust of the earth ... a man and his father go in to the same maiden, so that my holy name is profaned".

18.60 In typical prophetic fashion Amos regards such acts as a violation of the Lord's honour. By now it is evident that the prophet is not referring merely to the indigent when he speaks of the poor. What makes people poor is their defencelessness in the face of (the brutality of) the rulers. Thus the poor are the suffering ones

– the ones in danger of extermination, whose chances of a meaningful existence are in jeopardy.

18.61 Amos had certain *grounds* for his criticism. Basically it was a matter of the tradition of Israel's relationship to the Lord who had chosen them and given them the land to live on. This relationship, which was founded on justice and righteousness, determined all other relationships. Thus justice and righteousness had to impart a special character to the social legislation, especially those laws that governed interpersonal relations. Hence justice and righteousness were concerned with the relations between God, people and the land.

2. Hosea

18.62 Like Amos, Hosea prophesied in the northern kingdom before the fall of Samaria in 721 B.C. In his book wealth and poverty as a component of the social problematics of his day are somewhat overshadowed by cultic abuses and idolatry.

18.63 Nonetheless the specific social problems that Amos outlined and depicted so vividly are apparent in Hosea's book. Thus we read (Hs 13:5–6, 9–11):

> It was I who knew you in the wilderness, in the land of drought; but when they had fed to the full, they were filled, and their heart was lifted up; therefore they forgot me ... I will destroy you, O Israel; who can help you? Where now is your king, to save you; where are all your princes, to defend you – those of whom you said, "Give me a king and princes?" I have given you kings in my anger, and I have taken them away in my wrath.

18.64 In these verses the prophet is speaking about people who live in luxury. But with affluence came arrogance, and arrogant people push the thought of the Lord out of their minds. The prophet deplores this. The affluent in those days were certainly the king and his officials, and Hosea mentions them explicitly. When the Lord decides to destroy Israel they will be unable to avert it.

18.65 In Hosea 8:14 the Lord says that he will destroy the things that people have erected with their riches – again because they have forgotten him:

> For Israel has forgotten his Maker, and built palaces; and Judah has multiplied fortified cities; but I will send a fire upon his cities, and it shall devour his strongholds.

18.66 In Amos we were told repeatedly that the Israelites will be driven from their land because of the injustices they had perpetrated. This theme is also found in Hosea, albeit in slightly different form. He sees the exile as a return to the wilderness – where the people were before they came to Canaan and became rich, forgot the Lord and began to worship idols. He refers to Assyria, Egypt (the place from which they had emigrated) and wilderness as places they would go to (cf. Hs 2:13–14; 9:3). He sees the times ahead as a period of purification, so that they may once more occupy the land honourably. Thus we read in Hosea 2:1–15:

> "Therefore, behold, I will allure her, and bring her into the wilderness, and speak tenderly to her. And there I will give her vineyards, and make the

Valley of Achor a door of hope. And there she shall answer as in the days of her youth, as at the time when she came out of the land of Egypt".

18.67 Occasionally Hosea mentions the specific offences in the society of his day that led to unjust treatment of the poor. He compares the whole nation with a crooked merchant:

> A trader, in whose hands are false balances, he loves to oppress. Ephraim has said, "Ah, but I am rich, I have gained wealth for myself"; but all his riches can never offset the guilt he has incurred. I am the Lord your God from the land of Egypt; I will again make you dwell in tents, as in the days of the appointed feast.. If there is iniquity in Gilead they shall surely come to nought; if in Gilgal they sacrifice bulls, their altars shall be like stone heaps on the furrows of the field (Hosea 12:7–9).

18.68 Riches and the offering of sacrifices cannot safeguard them against the Lord's punishment for their exploitation and self-satisfaction. In fact, this punishment has already befallen Gilead. This touches on a theme which occurs elsewhere in the prophetic literature as well – offerings are not as important as good relations with other people and with the Lord. Hosea 6:6 says in this regard: "For I desire steadfast love and not sacrifice".

18.69 When the Lord speaks to the people in Hosea 14:8, it becomes clear how people ought to regard their possessions: "O Ephraim, what have I to do with idols? It is I who answer and look after you. I am like an evergreen cypress, from me comes your fruit".

18.70 The Lord wants to care for his people, but that implies that they have to keep away from idols and not become complacent about their possessions as if they owed these things to their own efforts (cf. 12:8). This one verse at the end of the book in a sense summarises Hosea's contribution to the prophetic perspective on wealth and poverty.

3. Isaiah

18.71 The book of Isaiah comprises three parts. The first 39 chapters deal mainly with the time of Isaiah (740–690 B.C.) when Judah and Israel were in danger of Assyrian conquest. Isaiah prophesied in the southern kingdom, where he probably had a long ministry. His earlier oracles are very similar to those that Amos pronounced in the northern kingdom. They deal mainly with the doings of his own people. His later oracles focus more on international relations. One would therefore expect his oracles on wealth and poverty to date to the earlier period.

18.72 One difference between Isaiah and Amos lies in their descriptions of the punishment to be visited on the people. To Amos it was exile, but to the early Isaiah it was the collapse of the internal political dispensation.

18.73 One of the most moving passages in Isaiah is the vineyard song in chapter 5, which reaches a climax in verse 7:

> For the vineyard of the Lord of hosts is the house of Israel, and the men of

Judah are his pleasant planting; and he looked for justice, but behold, bloodshed; for righteousness, but behold, a cry!

18.74 Justice and righteousness are a common theme in Isaiah. If one reads the entire vineyard song (5:1–7), one observes that justice and righteousness are a *response* to what the Lord has already done for his people. In Isaiah 1:17 justice and righteousness are mentioned in the same breath as "doing good", which consists in counteracting oppression and caring for widows and orphans. They require *action*. When justice and righteousness are neglected, God will himself act as judge on behalf of the poor (Is 3:13–15).

18.75 Isaiah mentions a number of ways in which the poor are oppressed. The rich grab all the houses and land for themselves, so that the poor in the end have no place of their own (Is 5:8). The laws made by the mighty cause the people to suffer: the poor are deprived of their rights, widows are exploited and orphans are victimised (10:1–2). There are even instances of robbery and murder (Is 3:14–15).

18.76 Isaiah 3:16–23 vividly describes the wealth and pride of those who perpetrate injustice:

> The Lord said: Because the daughters of Zion are haughty and walk with outstretched necks, glancing wantonly with their eyes, mincing along as they go, tinkling with their feet; the Lord will strike with a scab the heads of the daughters of Zion, and the Lord will lay bare their secret parts. In that day the Lord will take away the finery of the anklets, the headbands and the crescents; the pendants, the bracelets, and the scarfs; the headdresses, the armlets, the sashes, the perfume boxes, and the amulets; the signet rings and nose rings; the festal robes, the mantles, the cloaks, and the handbags; the garments of gauze, the linen garments, the turbans, and the veils.

18.77 About the *future* Isaiah says that the punishment that must be expected will not consist solely in wrath and vengeance (Is 1:24). It will also be a time of purification:

> I will turn my hand against you and will smelt away your dross as with lye and remove all your alloy. And I will restore your judges as at the first, and your counselors as at the beginning. Afterwards you shall be called the city of righteousness, the faithful city (Is 1:25–26).

18.78 According to this passage it is the leaders and the rulers that will be purified; and the distinctive feature of the city will be the righteousness and faithfulness of its people.

18.79 Isaiah also foretells that a light will appear to the people who walked in darkness. It has to do with a "son" who will bring peace and prosperity for ever. He will establish the kingdom of David for ever and maintain it through justice and righteousness (Is 9:1–6).

18.80 In this future age the poor will occupy a certain position. In contrast to the oppressors, they will have food to eat and will live in safety (14:30). They will find refuge, it is specified, in Zion (14.32). They will be glad and rejoice in the Lord (29:19). The Lord will be their refuge and their fortress.

18.81 As in the case of certain other prophets, Isaiah *bases* his judgments on the close connection between people's actions and the fate they may expect. When one casts justice and righteousness aside one is indeed arrogant towards the Lord, the source of both these. He will bring the proud to a fall (Is 2:6–18).

4. Micah

18.82 The book of Micah consists of two parts. The first five chapters are directed to the southern kingdom, while the last two are probably aimed at the northern kingdom. Scholars assume that there were two different prophets who were both called Micah, hence the one associated with the final two chapters is known as Deutero-Micah. Both parts of the book offer perspectives on wealth and poverty.

18.83 In 2:1–2, 6–9 *Micah* outlines the circumstances that cause injustice to the poor:

> Woe to those who devise wickedness and work evil upon their beds! When the morning dawns they perform it, because it is in the power of their hand. They covet fields and seize them; and houses, and take them away; they oppress a man and his house, a man and his inheritance ... "Do not preach" – thus they preach – "one should not preach of such things; disgrace will not overtake us". Should this be said, O house of Jacob? Is the Spirit of the Lord impatient? Are these his doings? Do not my words do good to him who walks uprightly? But you rise against my people as an enemy; you strip the robe from the peaceful, from those who pass by trustingly with no thought of war. The women of my people you drive out from their pleasant houses; from their young children you take away my glory for ever.

18.84 These verses describe people whose power has enabled them to put into effect everything that enters their minds. Because of their self-assurance they refuse to believe that God will oppose them, even though they usurp people's property unlawfully and deprive them of their clothes and their dwellings. These houses were, after all, given to them as their inalienable property (Mi 2:9). The actions of the rulers are an insult to God, and the punishment is derision and loss of the land (Mi 2:4–5).

18.85 Micah 3:1–4 is addressed to the rulers who are guilty of brutality. The language in which the prophet's accusation is couched suggests a merry banquet. The ease with which they perpetrate injustice is reminiscent of people slaughtering an animal for the table, carving it up and devouring it. Their punishment is that when they call to God, he will not answer.

18.86 In Micah 3:1–4 the offenders are prophets who are guilty of taking bribes. If people do not line the prophets' pockets, the latter declare war on them. Their punishment will be an endless night in which they see no vision that they can transmit (Mi 3:6). They too will mourn because God does not answer them (Mi 3:7).

18.87 In Micah 3:9–12 the prophet condemns the judges, priests and prophets. The judges look on while people (in performing forced labour) are maltreated to death. They also take bribes in return for their judgments. The same applies to the priests and prophets who make favourable predictions provided the price is to their liking. This is false piety, and the punishment is again the destruction of the land. It is noteworthy that in this instance Micah does not once mention the name of the Lord. This is in deliberate contrast with the prophets and priests who continually say, "The Lord is in the midst of us". Micah is contrasting their conduct with his own. He himself has the Spirit of the Lord, a sense of justice and the courage to tell Judah where they are transgressing (Mi 3:8).

18.88 Micah sees no *future* for the people of Judah. They face total destruction (Mi 2:4; 3:12). In only one instance does he relate this destruction to the exile (Mi 1:16). The destruction will occur while God remains deaf to the people's entreaties (Mi 3:4, 7).

5. Deutero-Micah

18.89 Deutero-Micah's judgments on the northern kingdom return us to the situation in which Amos and Hosea operated. People steal. They measure with false measuring rods, a misleading measure, unreliable scales and deceitful weights (Mi 6:9–11). It is the rich who perpetrate violence and deceive the poor (Mi 6:12). As a result the wealthy will no longer get what they expect (Mi 6:13–15). Their destruction is due to their acquiescence in the laws of Omri and Ahab. (Earlier in this chapter you learned about the changes these kings introduced.)

18.90 Deutero-Micah also rebukes the ruler and judges for taking bribes. The elite talk about nothing except what they desire to possess. In the process they are ready to distort everything (Mi 7:3). The result is social disintegration. The confusion will be so great that one will not be able to trust even one's nearest and dearest (Mi 7:5–6).

E. THE PROPHETS BEFORE THE FALL OF THE SOUTHERN KINGDOM

18.91 By the time Jeremiah, Zephaniah and Habakkuk prophesied the northern kingdom had fallen. The Assyrians who had brought about its fall had themselves been conquered by the Babylonians, also called the Chaldeans. This nation had become a real threat to Judah. Yet in the midst of this danger there were people who with false equanimity persisted in living a life of injustice.

1. Jeremiah

18.92 Jeremiah spoke about the poor in several different contexts. Firstly, he – like most of the prophets – referred to them in his *oracles of judgment* (Jr 2:34; 5:4, 28; 22:16f.). In all these instances certain people (kings, officials, priests, prophets and the wicked rich) deserve to be punished, partly because they have wronged the poor. In Jeremiah 5:26–30 the prophet refers to these great, rich, self-indulgent people's offences (fraud, wickedness and perversion of justice) in a way that is reminiscent of the oracles of Amos and the early Isaiah on this subject.

18.93 A second context in which Jeremiah speaks of the poor is when, in one of his confessions, he sees *himself* as one of them. In this passage he *appeals* to the people to praise the Lord, since the Lord rescues the poor (like Jeremiah himself) from the clutches of the rich (Jr 20:13). Actually Jeremiah was a man of means who employed a secretary, a land owner and a priest to boot. Hence "poor" has a different meaning here and contrasts with "evil".

18.94 The third context in which Jeremiah speaks of the poor is that of the *fall of Jerusalem*. The vineyards and fields were given to the poor to cultivate (Jr 39:10; 52:16). They were entrusted to governor Gedaliah's care (Jr 40:7) and some of the very poorest people were also carried off (Jr 52:15).

18.95 Fourthly, *the poor themselves are accused*. In 5:4 (in the course of 5:1–6) Jeremiah says that at first he had thought that the poor act foolishly because they are ignorant of the Lord's will; but he found that they – like the great (5:5) – were rebelling against God. This could be a pun, since the Hebrew words for "the poor" and "the great" are very similar. Some scholars believe that the author had deliberately chosen these words in order to suggest that people with similar names tend to behave similarly as well.

18.96 The fifth and final context in which Jeremiah refers to the poor is when he *judges a king* (Jr 22:13f.). King Jehoiakim's actions are unacceptable because he is intent on enriching himself at the expense of others – in contrast to his father, king Josiah, who had fought the cause of the weak and the poor.

18.97 In Jeremiah ownership of the "land" is a major theme. He personifies the land by comparing it to its inhabitants. Like the land, the people are Yahweh's inheritance (Jr 12:7–13). Yahweh has brought the people to a fertile land (Jr 2:7), but their own lives have not borne the fruit that God had expected of them. Consequently they will be driven from the land (Jr 4:5f.; 6:1f.), although there is some hint that they may return (Jr 32:15). Through this theme of the land this prophet too establishes a close link between the people's relationship with Yahweh and the loss of a country of their own.

2. Zephaniah

18.98 The book of Zephaniah contains two sections in which the poor feature. In Zephaniah 3:12 the prophet speaks thus about the poor:

> For I will leave in the midst of you a people humble and lowly. They shall seek refuge in the name of the Lord.

18.99 Here the concept of poverty (rendered as "humble" and "lowly") does not refer to a specific socioeconomic stratum of society, but to a specific *attitude* towards the Lord. The humble and lowly in 3:12 contrast sharply with the "proudly exultant" in the previous verse. Zephaniah, like his contemporary Jeremiah, places the emphasis slightly different from that of the other prophets.

18.100 In Zephaniah 2:3 the prophet enjoins the poor to seek to discover the Lord's will, and to strive for righteousness and humility. If they do this they may escape the punishment of the Lord. So far Jeremiah and Zephaniah have been the only of the prophets where we have found that the poor refers to people with a particular *attitude to life*. This trend is only discernible in the books of prophets who prophesied shortly before and after the exile.

18.101 The people whom Zephaniah accuses are once again the priests (Zph 1:4–5;

3:4), public officials (Zph 1:8; 3:3), the self-satisfied (Zph 1:12) and the merchants (Zph 1:11). The judgment is linked with the coming of the day of the Lord (Zph 1:7, 14–16).

3. Habakkuk

18.102 Habakkuk's depiction of injustice assumes the form not of an oracle of judgment, but of a lament (Hab 1:2f.). To him the suffering ones, among whom he includes himself (Hab 1:2–4) and the poor (Hab 3:14), are exposed to oppression both from within and from outside. His own society is guilty of injustice, oppression, strife, contention and perversion of the law (Hab 1:2–4). On top of that they live under threat from the Chaldeans. The latter are a nation of greedy and haughty people who became rich on goods that were not their own (Hab 2:5–9). In this way they built themselves a "nest on high" (Hab 2:9) to secure themselves against calamity. But in this way they in fact forfeit their lives (Hab 2:10).

18.103 The punishment that awaits his own nation is that the Lord will summon the Chaldeans to do to Judah as they have already done to many other peoples: to conquer what is not theirs (Hab 1:5f.). Ultimately God's judgment will come on the Chaldeans as well – they will suffer the same fate as their victims (Hab 2:7–10, 15–17).

F. THE PROPHETS DURING AND AFTER THE EXILE

1. Ezekiel

18.104 Ezekiel believes that the exile was well-deserved. Before the exile the Judaeans lived a life of injustice. As many of the prophets have pointed out, part of this injustice was self-enrichment at the expense of the poor. Ezekiel 22 describes this in detail. The words he addresses to the rulers, officials and citizens (Ezk 22:25, 27, 29) puts the problems of the poor in clear perspective:

> Her princes in the midst of her are like a roaring lion tearing the prey; they have devoured human lives; they have taken treasure and precious things; they have made many widows in the midst of her ... Her princes in the midst of her are like wolves tearing the prey, shedding blood, destroying lives to get dishonest gain ... The people of the land have practiced extortion and committed robbery; they have oppressed the poor and needy, and have extorted from the sojourner without redress.

18.105 The exiles have a proverb that went: "The fathers have eaten sour grapes, and the children's teeth are set on edge" (Ezk 18:2). This proverb refers to cause and effect. The fathers have committed injustice and the children bear the punishment for it. But this will change. In the remainder of chapter 18 Ezekiel comments on this proverb that in future every person's lot will depend on his own actions. Those who sin will die. The one who lives according to God's will survives. If one has a son who

> oppresses the poor and the needy, commits robbery, does not restore the pledge, lifts up his eyes to the idols, commits abomination, lends at interest, and takes increase; shall he then live? (Ezk 18:12–13)

18.106 The people's actions have earned them the exile. Since everyone is judged by his actions, it is also an earnest call to repentance (Ezk 18:25–32).

18.107 The people's transgressions are compared to those of Sodom, which was totally destroyed (Ezk 16:46–50). Sodom's sin was that its inhabitants "had pride, surfeit of food, and prosperous ease, but did not aid the poor and needy. They were haughty and did abominable things before me" (Ezk 16:49–50).

18.108 The Judaean people had done the same or much worse (Ezk 16:51).

18.109 From chapter 40 onwards there are a number of precepts, arising from a vision that Ezekiel had during the exile. According to some biblical exegetes the final section of the book contains the so-called school of Ezekiel's programme for the restoration of the land after the exile. The precepts tell the returned exiles how to arrange their lives. The future rulers are given clear guidelines on how they ought to act. In Ezekiel 45:9–12 the prophet warns them against the very kind of conduct that led to their fall. It is virtually a summary of the words of earlier prophets:

> ... Put away violence and oppression, and execute justice and righteousness; cease your evictions of my people, says the Lord God. You shall have just balances, a just ephah, and a just bath. [This is followed by details concerning the standard, consistent measures that should be used for both fluids and solids.]

18.110 In Ezekiel 46:16–18 the Yahwist tradition concerning the inalienability of ancestral land enters into the picture. On exactly the same grounds as Naboth had refused to sell his land to king Ahab, Ezekiel pleads that the future ruler should not take the people's land away from them: "[a man] shall give his sons their inheritance out of his own property, so that none of my people shall be dispossessed of his property" (Ezk 46:18).

2. Daniel

18.111 The book of Daniel contains one statement about the poor (the needy). It takes the form of an appeal to king Nebuchadnezzar of Babylonia to abandon his sin and unrighteousness, to do what is right and to be charitable towards the poor (Dn 4:27). This is one of three postexilic appeals to take care of the poor (cf. also Zch 7:10; Is 58:7). The remarkable thing about this verse is that the accent is not so much on the need of the poor but on the conduct of their patron. Mercy to the poor will entail continued prosperity.

3. Zechariah

18.112 The book of Zechariah provides another summary of the oracles of earlier prophets (Zch 7:7–10), which forms part of a "history sermon":

> "... were not these the words which the Lord proclaimed by the former prophets?" And the word of the Lord came to Zechariah, saying, "Thus says the Lord of hosts, Render true judgments, show kindness and mercy each to his brother, do not oppress the widow, the fatherless, the sojourner, or the poor; and let none of you devise evil against his brother in your heart".

18.113 Thus, to Zechariah, the familiar theme of justice and righteousness, practically applied in the treatment of widows and orphans, is the crux of the message of earlier prophets (Zch 7:9).

18.114 As in the books of some of the other prophets (e.g. Isaiah, cf. 9:7), Zechariah refers to a future king. In this case he will be like one of the poor – humble, riding on an ass (Zch 9:9).

4. Malachi

18.115 Malachi prophesied in the fifth century B.C., after the temple had been rebuilt. Although he was more concerned about problems in the areas of liturgy, married life and future expectations, he mentions the people's attitude towards the poor in Malachi 3:5. Malachi maintains that the Lord will send a messenger before him, after which he will suddenly come to his temple as judge (Ml 3:1). He will then judge such sins as underpaying hired hands, injustice towards widows and orphans and thrusting aside aliens. Those who are guilty of these things do not fear the Lord.

G. SUMMARY

18.116 Although wealth and poverty affect individuals, they are to a large extent associated with broad *social factors*. The prophets' minds were primarily directed to discovering God's will in regard to certain social problems. Consequently they sometimes focused directly on the problems of wealth and poverty.

18.117 This perspective on wealth and poverty as social problems implied that the prophets associated the causes of such problems with influential people in society and with transgressions that had great social impact. In particular they isolated kings, public officials, priests, prophets and merchants as people who commit injustices in this area. They were responsible for

- causing poverty, and/or
- exploiting those who were already poor.

18.118 According to some prophets, poverty was *caused* mainly by the effects of national socioeconomic policies. This led to the enrichment of a powerful emerging class of bureaucrats and the impoverishment of ordinary citizens, especially peasants. An influential group emerged which had a decisive say in such spheres as the judiciary and commerce. Poor people had nobody to fight their cause. Price increases, the introduction of taxes, interest, mandatory tribute and the confiscation of land were all results of this policy.

18.119 *Exploitation* of impoverished, defenceless people assumed various forms. The prophets described it as contempt for justice and righteousness. In concrete terms it mean injustice especially towards widows, orphans and aliens by way of perversion of the law, business abuses, theft or confiscation of the property of the poor and personal or bodily harm done to the defenceless. Sometimes it culminated in robbery or even murder.

18.120 The prophets frequently pronounced a particular *punishment* for such offences. Before the fall of the northern and southern kingdoms the penalty was often exile from their country. Some prophets (e.g. Micah) saw deportation as the complete destruction of God's people; others thought it would be a time of purification (Isaiah, Jeremiah as well as Hosea, who thought it would be a return to the wilderness situation). In the early part of his career Isaiah predicted the collapse of the existing political dispensation without the intervention of a foreign nation. The theme of the land features prominently in several prophets' writings.

18.121 In other instances the punishment for injustice towards the poor was that the perpetrators would share the fate of the oppressed (Micah); that they would forfeit the produce of their own land (Amos); that God would destroy everything they had established with their wealth (Hosea); and that a time of total confusion awaited them (Deutero-Micah).

18.122 The *grounds* for punishment are to be found in the interrelationship between God, other people and the land. Somebody who treats a person unjustly offends God and forfeits all right to the land God has given him.

18.123 The prophets speak of the rich and the poor in various *contexts*. The prophets of the eighth century B.C. (before the fall of the northern kingdom) mention them almost exclusively in a context of *condemnation* of rich people who treat the poor unjustly. Isaiah places the poor in a *future perspective*: a king will come who will take care of the poor (cf. also Zechariah). They will find a refuge in Zion, where they will have food to eat and a safe abode.

18.124 From the seventh century B.C. onwards prophets speak of the rich and the poor in a variety of contexts. Apart from judgments, they make *appeals* for certain kinds of conduct. People should be humble like the poor (Zephaniah). They must praise the Lord because he delivers the poor (Jeremiah). Their actions – including their treatment of the poor – determine how the Lord will judge them. Consequently they must repent (Ezekiel). Even king Nebuchadnezzar is exhorted to be charitable towards the poor (Daniel).

18.125 Jeremiah occasionally *accuses* the *poor* of rebellion against God. People's attitude towards the poor, according to the prophets, is a *measure* of their acceptability (Jeremiah and Daniel). Habakkuk composed a *lament* on the oppression of the poor, while Zechariah in his *history sermon* recounts what the early prophets had said about the rich and the poor.

18.126 Not all the prophets sang the same tune. Some of the biblical prophets in fact condemned the popular prophets, and differ among themselves in their emphases. They have, however, one thing in common: their eyes are wide open to social injustice and their ears are attuned to hearing God's will. It follows that they would have been sensitive to the problems associated with wealth and poverty, and that God's honour and people's relationships with God were at stake when it came to the conduct of the rich towards the poor.

18.127 Social problems associated with wealth and poverty are focal in our day, both internationally and more specifically in Southern Africa. If we take the prophetic cause seriously we must have an eye for these problems and an ear for what we ought to do in these circumstances. At the same time we must allow for the fact that we, like the prophets of old, view the problem of poverty from different angles and in terms of different (personal) circumstances. That makes it more complex, but no less urgent, that we adopt a stance in regard to poverty.

19

"The poor will always be with you". Wealth and poverty in a wisdom perspective

IZAK SPANGENBERG

A. INTRODUCTION

19.1 When people who are conversant with the history of Israel read the books of Proverbs, Job and Ecclesiastes, they soon discover that these books differ considerably from the rest of the Old Testament. These books do not mention the promise to the patriarchs, the deliverance from Egypt, the covenant concluded at Sinai, the conquest of the land of Canaan, the election of king David or the rest of Israelite history. They are literary products with quite a different slant on the world and on God. This slant is known as a wisdom perspective.

19.2 Modern Old Testament scholars agree that the wisdom perspective is not confined to the books of Proverbs, Job and Ecclesiastes, but that it is discernible in other Old Testament books as well. Thus one observes it in certain psalms (cf. Ps 1; 32; 34; 37; 49; 73; 112; 127; 128) and in narrative literature (the Joseph story, Gn 37–50; the Esther narrative, Est 1–10).

B. THE WISDOM PERSPECTIVE

19.3 In order to understand and identify this perspective we need to define the word "wisdom". As understood by the wisdom teachers of those days, wisdom meant something like "common sense". A dictionary definition of common sense is: "a person's natural ability to make good judgements and to behave in a practical and sensible way" *(Essential English Dictionary)*. The wisdom teachers were intent on gaining a sound, practical grasp of reality based on *insight* and *understanding*, and to live accordingly (i.e. to make good judgements). They also chose to communicate their insight and understanding to others – hence the wisdom perspective in these texts.

19.4 The insight these teachers arrived at was that there is a certain order underlying reality. If people are in harmony with this order (i.e. live their lives according to it), all goes well with them; if they go against it, things go badly. One could also say that they described typical courses of action and the consequences of these. What they were saying was that this or that action usually (*not always, nor inevitably*) had this or that consequence:

> He who guards his mouth preserves his life; he who opens wide his lips comes to ruin (Pr 13:3).

He who tills his land will have plenty of bread, but he who follows worthless pursuits will have plenty of poverty (Pr 28:19).

19.5 To experience happiness, success and prosperity, one has to do the right thing at the appointed time:

To make an apt answer is a joy to a man, and a word in season, how good it is! (Pr 15:23).
The sluggard does not plow in the autumn; he will seek at harvest and have nothing (Pr 20:4).
He who sings songs to a heavy heart is like one who takes off a garment on a cold day, and like vinegar on a wound (Pr 25:20).

19.6 This is the background against which we should understand the following apparently contradictory counsel:

Answer not a fool according to his folly, lest you be like him yourself. Answer a fool according to his folly lest he be wise in his own eyes (Pr 26:4–5).

19.7 Those who are mindful of the time and the situation will know which counsel to follow. Doing the right thing at the right time will secure them happiness and prosperity.

19.8 The wisdom teachers usually expressed their insight in the form of aphorisms (pithy sayings) and in this way actually created order. They realised that people do not simply have a medley of experiences, but that the medley can be organised. When people organise the world around them by describing it and when they discover regularities and articulate these, they are practising wisdom. As a result the wisdom teachers set great store by a talent for apt description and articulation. They also respected people who had the ability to persuade others verbally, or who argued calmly when tempers flared:

The tongue of the wise dispenses knowledge, but the mouths of fools pour out folly (Pr 15:2).
He who keeps his mouth and his tongue keeps himself out of trouble (Pr 21:23).

19.9 The wisdom teachers moreover insisted that people should submit to authority. Throughout their writings they enjoin their pupils to obey, respect and submit to their fathers and mothers, their teachers and their superiors. These injunctions to obedience and submissiveness accord with the teachers' emphasis on order. If the social order is maintained intact, everyone is happy and prosperous:

He who heeds instruction is on the path to life, but he who rejects reproof goes astray (Pr 10:17).
Listen to advice and accept instruction, that you may gain wisdom for the future (Pr 19:20).
Hearken to your father who begot you, and do not despise your mother when she is old (Pr 23:22).
My son, fear the Lord and the king, and do not disobey either of them (Pr 24:21).

19.10 All the proverbs quoted above refer to everyday life. Indeed, scholars used to believe that Israelite wisdom was originally secular and only acquired a religious character once some of the proverbs had been reformulated and reinterpreted in terms of Israelite faith. This view has now been abandoned, for scholars have come to realise that the order discovered by the wisdom teachers was a divine order, created and sustained by God. One could say that God is the guarantor of the order. After all, it is he who ensures that good deeds (ones that conform to the order) are rewarded and wicked deeds (ones that contravene the order) are punished:

> He who is kind to the poor lends to the Lord, and he will repay him for his deed (Pr 19:17).

Do not rob the poor, because he is poor, or crush the afflicted at the gate; for the Lord will plead their cause and despoil of life those who despoil them (Pr 22:22–23).

19.11 In summary we could say that a wisdom perspective refers to the recognition of order in nature and society. Also that it is important not just to recognise this order, but to express it in aphorisms and to live accordingly. People who live wisely reap the rewards of happiness, prosperity, success and long life.

C. PERIODS AND PHASES OF DEVELOPMENT IN THE HISTORY OF ISRAELITE WISDOM

19.12 We can distinguish three major periods in the history of Israelite wisdom: the *premonarchic,* the *monarchic* and the *postexilic* periods. We should briefly dwell on each of these periods, for the context of wisdom (the place and community where it originated and was applied) differed in each one.

19.13 In addition to these historical periods, one can distinguish three phases of development in the wisdom tradition. At first wisdom was *flexible*: a proverb would state that a certain act *usually* (but not necessarily) had a certain outcome. These aphorisms were not intended to be eternally valid sayings; their applicability was relative to time and circumstances. Consider, for instance, the two "conflicting" wisdom precepts cited in the previous section. Later on a certain *rigidity* set in, insofar as that the proverbs were considered to be eternally valid rules. This rigidity in turn provoked a *protest reaction*. It should be noted that the historical periods and the phases of development do not coincide exactly. We cannot say that wisdom in the premonarchic period was flexible, that it became rigid during the monarchy and that it evoked a postexilic protest reaction. Often the three developmental phases existed side by side.

1. The premonarchic period

19.14 We are not altogether sure what Israelite society was like before the institution of the monarchy. The view that there were a number of nomadic tribes that eventually settled and occupied some of the Canaanite cities is no longer widely supported. Some scholars believe that the forebears of the Israelites were simply peasants – not nomads at all – who rebelled against the oppression of the rulers of the Canaanite city states. In any event there must have been some kind of social system before the institution of the monarchy. Most probably it was a clan system, and within these clans informal instruction was given to the young. The elders and sages of the clan instructed young people in such matters as social and sexual conduct, agricultural and stock farming problems and so on. The head of the clan saw to it that the moral code and traditions of the clan were observed. His word was law to all members of the clan (cf. Jr 35:6–7). Some of the aphorisms in the book of Proverbs that deal with daily life, relations with neighbours and care of livestock (cf. Pr 15:1, 17; 17:17; 19:15; 20:20; 22:13; 25:17; 26:13–14; 27:10b, 23) probably derive from the informal instruction given in the clan.

19.15 One could classify this kind of wisdom as *experiential wisdom*. Wisdom (insight and understanding) was acquired in the school of life. Often people had to learn the do's and don'ts the hard way; parents then taught this to their children and sages instructed the youth. This wisdom was probably transmitted in the form of simple proverbs (short, pithy aphorisms expressing existential truths).

2. The monarchic period

The period of the united kingdom

19.16 After the institution of the monarchy a new kind of wisdom emerged in Israelite society – that of the *court*. This wisdom may be said to have originated because of the requirements of the monarchy. The administration of the empire required qualified officials trained in the skills of writing and rhetoric – officials who knew how to consort with their king and their colleagues. The officials were not the only ones who were schooled in court wisdom; the princes too had to be versed in it (cf. Pr 16:10, 12; 25:4–5; 29:4, 14). Clan education was not adequate in these circles. It is understandable, therefore, that during this period there was extensive borrowing from the wisdom of neighbouring peoples, particularly that of Egypt.

19.17 Egyptian wisdom literature was directed entirely to the ruler and his officials and was taught exclusively at court schools. During the reigns of David and Solomon such court schools were probably established in Jerusalem for the instruction of princes and prospective officials. When one studies Egyptian wisdom one finds that here too the idea of order is focal. Egyptian wisdom teachers held that the deity had instituted a particular order in creation and society. Those who conformed to that order, so they taught, experienced prosperity and happiness, while those who contravened it experienced misery and adversity. This idea was not foreign to the Israelites, who were conversant with the notion of order as it functioned in clan wisdom. After the introduction of court wisdom this notion was merely communicated more consciously. Henceforth the idea of a connection between actions and their consequences would feature more prominently. Good deeds, it was believed, had good consequences and evil deeds had bad consequences. *He who angers the king forfeits his life* (Pr 20:2b). *He who behaves presumptuously in the king's presence will be humbled* (Pr 25:6—7). *A king who is just to the socially underprivileged will have a long reign* (Pr 29:14).

19.18 Court wisdom did not supersede or replace the wisdom of the clan. The teachers responsible for instruction at Israelite court schools undoubtedly drew on

Israelite clan wisdom. In my view this explains the paucity of royal proverbs and precepts for officials in the book of Proverbs.

19.19 Although it is unlikely that Proverbs 10:1–22:16 was written down in this period, individual proverbs in this collection may have been recorded. It is difficult to determine whether Solomon had a hand in the creation of these proverbs. Some scholars maintain that one cannot attach too much value to the statements about Solomon's wisdom and his involvement in the creation of proverbs (cf. 1 Ki 4:29–34; 10:1–10, 23–24). These statements, they maintain, are based on popular tradition. These scholars maintain that Israelite wisdom literature was composed during the reign of king Hezekiah (700 B.C.), a golden age of culture and literature. In my opinion they are far too sceptical. There must surely be some reason why Solomon rather than Hezekiah was traditionally acclaimed as the wise king par excellence. In addition Solomon's reign was characterised by great openness to foreign cultural influence, especially that of Egypt (cf. 1 Ki 3:1; 7:7–8; 10:28–29). Solomon certainly did not compose all the proverbs found in the two Solomonic collections (Pr 10:1–22; 25–29). But it is more than likely that he stimulated the practice of wisdom at his court, whether by composing proverbs of his own or by cultivating contact with Egypt.

19.20 During this period a text was produced which could serve as illustrative material for future officials and rulers. This was the Joseph novelette (Gn 37–50). Gerhard von Rad was the first Old Testament scholar who pointed out the parallels between the Joseph narrative and early wisdom and classified it as a didactic wisdom narrative. The story demonstrates how wise conduct leads to good fortune and happiness and thus propagates the ideals which the teachers at court schools inculcated in their pupils. It is unlikely that this story originated in any place other than the royal court of Jerusalem.

The period of the divided kingdom

19.21 After the division of the kingdom – or rather, after the abrogation of the agreement between the people of the north and those of the south (1 Ki 12:1–6) the two kingdoms that arose went their respective ways.

The southern kingdom

19.22 In the southern kingdom court wisdom became increasingly important. This is evident in the action of king Hezekiah who saw to it that the traditional wisdom material was recorded (cf. Pr 25:1). Proverbs 25–29 were probably written during his reign, as were Proverbs 22:17–24:34. Part of this latter collection (Pr 22:17–23:11) is associated with the Egyptian book of wisdom, "The wisdom of Amen-em-opet", dated between 1000 and 600 B.C.

19.23 The prominence of court wisdom in the southern kingdom is also evident in the preaching of the prophet Isaiah, which displays a definite wisdom influence. Some scholars even maintain that this was because he had been a courtier before he became a prophet. I think that the wisdom influence could also be attributed to Isaiah's awareness of his audience and the importance of the wisdom teachers at court. As in the case of Amos (cf. 19.27), the form and content of Isaiah's preaching was influenced by his audience.

19.24 During this period wisdom underwent a systematic change. Initially both clan and court wisdom had been flexible. The teachers were aware of their inability to prescribe categorically the way to act in a given situation, as there were far too many unknown variables (cf. Pr 21:30–31). In any case, how can one dictate to people who are engaged in interaction with one another? At most one can provide guidelines (cf. Pr 26:4–5). But as time went by wisdom began to classify people as either wise or foolish (righteous and wicked), so that the consequences of their actions and attitudes acquired a certain predictability. A progressive *rigidity* set in. To my mind this process was promoted by the fall of the northern kingdom (722 B.C.), which substantiated the claim that evil deeds lead to a fall. The notion of a connection between actions and their consequences now developed into a *doctrine of retribution.*

19.25 The important role played by the doctrine of retribution is evident in the book of Deuteronomy. The expansion of this book during the reign of king Josiah (640–609 B.C.) underscored this doctrine. Further proof of its prominence was a proverb dating to this time: "The fathers have eaten sour grapes, and the children's teeth are set on edge" (cf. Jr 31:29; Ezk 18:2).

19.26 The fall of the southern kingdom (586 B.C.) further strengthened the influence of the doctrine of retribution. The idea arose that the mere fact that people suffer adversity was evidence that they had committed wicked deeds (sins). If you are wretched you must have sinned, for God requites one's actions.

The northern kingdom

19.27 We know little about the wisdom of the northern kingdom. It probably did not disappear entirely from the scene, although it may have been hampered by the continual coups. But the fact that Amos's preaching shows signs of wisdom influences indicates that wisdom did survive in the north. Hans Walter Wolff attributes the wisdom influence in Amos's preaching to the fact that he came from Tekoa where (according to him) wisdom was practised (cf. 2 Sm 14:1–2). I am more inclined to think that it had to do with the audience to which he preached. To convey his message Amos used the forms and themes of wisdom which continued to feature in the northern kingdom. Further possible evidence of the survival of wisdom in the northern kingdom is the book of Deuteronomy. If it is true that the nucleus of this book originated among the rural Levites in the northern kingdom, it would explain to some extent the wisdom influences that Moshe Weinfeld identified in it.

3. The postexilic period

19.28 The exile had an enormous impact on wisdom. It not only promoted the tendency to rigidity, but also disrupted the practice of wisdom. Court wisdom disappeared from the scene when the king and his officials were carried off: the setting in which wisdom had been taught and transmitted disappeared overnight. But in the course of the exile the social life of the exiles underwent considerable change and after a while one finds writers and scribes playing an increasingly prominent role. These people devoted themselves to preserving and studying traditional literature, and so these early scribes became the new patrons of wisdom. One result was that many Old Testament texts acquired wisdom overtones. Consider in this regard the book of

Hosea (Hs 14:10) and the introductory psalm of the Psalter (Ps 1). We could call the wisdom of this period *school wisdom*, for the early scribes probably established schools where they studied and taught the traditional literature.

The Persian era

19.29 The wisdom of this era differs in character from that before and during the exile. Shortly before and during the exile wisdom had become very rigid. People were flatly categorised as wise or foolish, as righteous or wicked. The idea that actions are linked to their consequences made way for a doctrine of retribution. In postexilic times one finds people wrestling with this doctrine. This is evident not only in the book of Job, but also in some of the wisdom psalms dating to this period (cf. Ps 37; 49; 73). But the way in which they wrestled with the doctrine of retribution and the way the struggle was resolved differ from one text to another.

19.30 But the wisdom of this period cannot simply be classified as *protest wisdom*, for other texts written at this time extolled the excellence of wisdom (cf. Pr 1–9; Job 28). These texts differ from earlier wisdom literature in that they were long poems rather than aphoristic proverbs. In some passages wisdom is personified and often displays traits of a mythological figure (cf. Pr 1:20–33; 8:1–36; 9:1–18).

19.31 Thus the wisdom of the Persian era displays a certain diversity. There is one element which reacts to the crisis in which wisdom had landed as a result of a rigid notion of retribution; a second element in a sense ignores the crisis and sidesteps the problems associated with the rigid doctrine of retribution. It is in these circles that the wisdom psalms extolling the law were written (Ps 1; 19b; 119). In postexilic times the law and wisdom became increasingly interrelated – understandably, since the scribes and writers were patrons of both wisdom and the law. The law, too, now became a guideline for happy, successful living.

19.32 An interesting text dating to this period and displaying a distinct wisdom influence is the Esther novelette. This story does not fall in either of the two categories mentioned above, but stands in a class of its own, showing us how wisdom material may be used to convey a message. The novelette also proves that it is not possible to reduce the wisdom of a given period to a single common denominator.

The Hellenistic era

19.33 The same diversity that we discerned in the wisdom of the Persian period is noticeable in the hellenistic era. Protest wisdom reaches its acme in the book of Ecclesiastes. In this book the doctrine of retribution is swept aside with one great gesture and vehemently declared non-existent (cf. Ec 8:10–15; 9:1–10). Another component continues the trend to identify the law with wisdom and, hardly batting an eyelash, reintroduces the question of retribution. Thus Jesus son of Sira declares: "All wisdom is the fear of the Lord and includes the fulfilling of the law" (Sir 19:20). Those who obey the law and fear God – that is, act wisely – will receive good rewards: "Consider the past generations and see: was anyone who trusted the Lord ever disappointed? Was anyone who stood firm in the fear of him ever abandoned?" (Sir 2:10; cf. also 1:13; 27:26; 33:1).

D. WEALTH AND POVERTY IN A WISDOM PERSPECTIVE

19.34 Against the background depicted above we can now consider how the wisdom teachers and their pupils regarded wealth and poverty. I shall use the same historical periods as a basis for the discussion of these perspectives.

1. The premonarchic period

19.35 As we have learned elsewhere (ch 15), the phenomenon of poverty was virtually non-existent during this period, for the clans functioned as integrated units. Their individual members lived together in such close relationship that no one member was permitted to suffer want while others lived a life of plenty. Consequently proverbs dating to this period make no mention of poverty. Consider the following ones:

> A son who gathers in summer is prudent, but a son who sleeps in harvest brings shame (Pr 10:5).
> He who tills his land will have plenty of bread, but he who follows worthless pursuits has no sense (Pr 12:11).
> The sluggard does not plow in the autumn; he will seek at harvest and have nothing (Pr 20:4).

19.36 Although sloth was condemned as a vice, it was not said to lead to poverty. In proverbs from later ages one does, however, find this notion (cf. Pr 12:11 with Pr 28:19, which will be discussed in 19.46). Parents taught their children virtue and warned them against vice (as parents have always done). Those who took these teachings to heart usually experienced happiness and good fortune, while those who disregarded them often lived to regret it.

2. The monarchic period

THE PERIOD OF THE UNITED KINGDOM

19.37 During this period the solidarity that had characterised the clan gradually crumbled. People followed diverse occupations and some joined the public service. The economy, once geared to subsistence, now hinged on manufacturing and commerce. Solomon's reign in particular saw great social change. The Joseph novelette (probably written in this period) gives us some idea of what was happening in Israelite society. In Genesis 47:13–26 we read about arrangements Joseph made during a famine. Once the buyers (probably peasants) had exhausted their money, they had to pay for food first with their livestock, then with their land, finally becoming slaves to the king. Since this description does not tally with what we know about the Egyptian economic system, it more probably depicts the growing dependence of Israelite peasants on the wealthy townsfolk. By providing credit to peasants, wealthy town-dwellers (mainly merchants) gradually acquired the former's land and in the end the peasants became their serfs. Proverbs 22:7 also indicates something of this nature: "The rich rules over the poor, and the borrower is the slave of the lender".

19.38 Although there is no mention of a famine during the reigns of David and Solomon, the fact that one of the punishments that David could choose (2 Sm 24:13) was a seven-year famine and that the Joseph novelette speaks of a famine seems to me to indicate that the country was subject to frequent droughts and famines. It was preeminently during such times that peasants had to forfeit their independence. Proverbs 11:26 refers to exploitive practices during famines: "The people curse him who holds back grain but a blessing is on the head of him who sells it".

19.39 There are always those who in times of want exploit the needy, for instance by hoarding wheat and then selling it at exorbitant prices. Although the wisdom teachers were not in favour of such practices, they did little to prevent it except to express their disapproval in proverbs.

THE PERIOD OF THE DIVIDED KINGDOM

The southern kingdom

19.40 During this period the process of forfeiture continued. Land barons began to feature more prominently, jeopardising the livelihood not only of the peasantry, but also of widows and orphans. The following proverbs should be read against this background:

> Do not remove an ancient landmark or enter the fields of the fatherless; for their Redeemer is strong; he will plead their cause against you (Pr 22:10–11).
> The Lord tears down the house of the proud, but maintains the widow's boundaries (Pr 15:25).

19.41 This concern was not confined to exploited widows and orphans, but extended to all the poor. Consider the following proverbs:

> He who is kind to the poor lends to the Lord, and he will repay him for his deed (Pr 19:17).
> Do not rob the poor, because he is poor, or crush the afflicted at the gate; for the Lord will plead their cause and despoil of life those who despoil them (Pr 22:22–23).

19.42 But the wisdom teachers' concern for the poor had a very different motive from that of the prophets. I mentioned earlier that these teachers believed a certain order underlie nature and society. Their concern related to their desire to maintain the social order, in which rich and poor had to co-exist. The following proverbs express this view:

> The rich and the poor meet together; the Lord is the maker of them all (Pr 22:2).
> The poor man and the oppressor meet together; the Lord gives light to the eyes of both (Pr 29:13).

19.43 A society without poor people was no more conceivable to them than one consisting only of rich people. Thus one of the aims of their teaching was maintenance of the status quo in which rich and poor live side by side, rather than social reform.

19.44 The king's duty was to maintain the integrity of the social order. If he failed to do so and the order crumbled, it ultimately affected his own well-being. Among other things he had to ensure justice for the poor, the widows and the orphans:

> If a king judges the poor with equity his throne will be established for ever (Pr 29:14).

19.45 This proverb does not require the king to launch social reform programmes to alter the lot of the poor. All he has to do is to ensure just treatment and not to tolerate injustice (cf. also the precepts of king Lemuel's mother in Pr 31:1–9).

19.46 The causes of poverty identified by wisdom teachers during this period include laziness and the pursuit of pleasure:

> A slack hand causes poverty, but the hand of the diligent makes rich (Pr 10:4).
> He who tills his land will have plenty of bread, but he who follows worthless pursuits has no sense (Pr 12:11).
> He who loves pleasure will be a poor man; he who loves wine and oil will not be rich (Pr 21:17).

19.47 Here too we observe the notion that actions are linked to their consequences. The one who works diligently (good deed) will be rich (good result), but those who shirk work (bad deed) will become impoverished (bad result). One gathers from this that the wisdom teachers had a positive attitude towards wealth. Poverty is not commended or glorified anywhere in the wisdom literature (in diametrical contrast to the poverty ideal of the mendicant monks of the Middle Ages). The explanation for their positive attitude towards wealth and their denigration of poverty surely lies in the fact that both teachers and pupils were from the monied class. Being rich, they knew that wealth was a key to life and its opportunities. They also knew poverty to be wretched and painful, depriving one of many possibilities. Consider this one adage which indicates their awareness of the depressing, isolating effect of poverty: "The poor is disliked even by his neighbor, but the rich has many friends" (Pr 14:20).

19.48 Although the wisdom teachers judged wealth positively and often regarded it as a reward for good deeds (cf. Pr 22:4), they were conscious of the hazards it entailed. They knew that wealth could blind one and cause one to lose one's sense of values. Consequently we also find that they denigrate wealth:

> A good name is to be chosen rather than great riches, and favor is better than silver or gold (Pr 22:1).
> Better is a poor man who walks in his integrity than a rich man who is perverse in his ways (Pr 28:6).

19.49 It also mattered to them how one came by one's money. Those who exploit others in order to get rich (bad deed) will meet with calamity some time and lose their wealth (bad result) (Pr 28:8). Those who chase wealth as if it were the greatest good in life (bad deed) will not prosper (bad result) (Pr 23:4–5).

19.50 Interestingly, the wisdom teachers do not refer to the exodus experience when they appeal to people to take pity on the poor, the widows and the orphans. Instead they point out that God, as their Creator, will act on their behalf. In this one sees once more how the wisdom teachers thought in terms of an order (in creation):

> He who oppresses a poor man insults his Maker, but he who is kind to the needy honors him (Pr 14:31).

He who mocks the poor insults his Maker; he who is glad at calamity will not go unpunished (Pr 17:5).

19.51 Thus the existence of poverty was attributed to a few causes (laziness, chasing pleasure, sometimes exploitation of other people). But no reform programme was ever launched to combat poverty. The wisdom teachers simply accept that society must have its quota of poor people: they are part and parcel of it. Not reform but maintenance of the status quo was the purport of their teaching.

19.52 But as time went by their wisdom became rigid (cf. 19.24), a rigidity reflected in certain proverbs about poverty and wealth which probably date from this period:

No ill befalls the righteous, but the wicked are filled with trouble (Pr 12:21).
Misfortune pursues sinners, but prosperity rewards the righteous (Pr 13:21).
The righteous has enough to satisfy his appetite, but the belly of the wicked suffers want (Pr 13:25).
The crown of the wise is their wisdom, but folly is the garland of fools (Pr 14:24).

19.53 These proverbs no longer accentuate the connection between act and consequence, but indicate that certain types of people have a certain kind of experience. And according to this rigid wisdom there are only two types of people: the righteous (wise) and the wicked (fools). Eventually wisdom became so inflexible that it was assumed that a person who is happy and prosperous was righteous, and that anyone suffering calamity and tragedy must be wicked.

The northern kingdom

19.54 The same social changes that occurred in the south happened in the northern kingdom as well. Here too wealthy land barons played an increasingly prominent role. Although court wisdom was hampered by constant coups, it probably did not die out altogether. Thus Amos's preaching shows signs of wisdom influences (cf. 19.27). Before we examine these influences we should first turn to the story of Naboth's vineyard (1 Ki 21).

19.55 Manfred Oeming believes that verses 1–16 of this story originated in wisdom circles. He adduces the following evidence: (1) These verses make no mention of God. (2) The issue of *power* features prominently and is viewed from a sceptical angle. He cites the following proverbs in this regard:

For the word of the king is supreme, and who may say to him, "What are you doing?" (Ec 8:4)
A king's wrath is a messenger of death (Pr 16:14a).
And I found more bitter than death the woman whose heart is snares and nets, and whose hands are fetters (Ec 7:26).
Moreover I saw under the sun that in the place of justice, even there was wickedness, and in the place of righteousness, even there was wickedness (Ec 3:16).

19.56 I think that Oeming is mistaken in speaking of a wisdom perspective. In the first place it is a misconception to assume that wherever God is not mentioned we are dealing with a wisdom perspective. Such a perspective does not exclude God, but allows for him. In addition the theme of virtually every Old Testament story can be illustrated by means of proverbs. It is not sufficient reason in itself to infer a wisdom influence. To illustrate the "wisdom character" of the first sixteen verses, Oeming moreover cites proverbs (three of the four from Ecclesiastes) that derive from a totally different age and situation than that of the story.

19.57 This passage does not reflect a wisdom perspective, neither is it contrasting rich and poor. It underscores the abuse of power by a king. We do find aphorisms in the book of Proverbs that warn against the anger of a king:

> A king's wrath is like the growling of a lion, but his favour is like dew upon the grass (Pr 19:12).
> The dread wrath of a king is like the growling of a lion; he who provokes him to anger forfeits his life (Pr 20:2).

19.58 But even these proverbs are not sufficient reason to identify a wisdom perspective. The wisdom teachers were preparing their pupils (who often became royal officials) for service at court. Thus they would have to know how to soothe the king's rage (cf. Pr 16:14). But Naboth was not a court official; neither was he acting foolishly in refusing to sell or barter his ancestral land to Ahab. The law was on his side, for the land the king wanted to procure was inalienable. The king's request was unreasonable and his abuse of power is evidence of his folly. One could say that he was acting against the order of things, but the author of the story does not judge the king's conduct in such a perspective. To my mind he was merely emphasising that Ahab, under the influence of his wife Jezebel (a Phoenician by birth), disregarded Israelite customary law.

19.59 In contrast to the Naboth story, the book of Amos does show influence of wisdom and we can conclude that wisdom continued to play a role in the northern kingdom. Thus Amos uses literary genres that are found mainly in wisdom literature, such as his use of graded numerical proverbs (cf. Am 1:3, 6,13; 2:1, 4, 6 with Pr 30:15–16, 18–19, 21–23, 29–31). He also makes use of didactic questions, the content of which is derived from everyday life and which illustrate the connection between cause and effect (cf. Am 3:3–6). Amos is moreover fond of antitheses like good and evil, love and hate, life and death (cf. Am 5:4, 14–15), and of references to justice and righteousness (Am 5:24) – all contrasts and topics encountered in wisdom literature as well (cf. Pr 11:19; 12:28). Significant for our theme are his sayings about the poor and the needy and his condemnation of questionable business practices:

> ... they sell the righteous for silver, and the needy for a pair of shoes – they that trample the head of the poor into the dust of the earth, and turn aside the way of the afflicted (Am 2:6–7).
> They hate him who reproves in the gate, and they abhor him who speaks the truth. Therefore because you trample upon the poor and take from him exactions of wheat, you have built houses of hewn stone, but you shall not dwell in them; you have planted pleasant vineyards, but you shall not drink their wine (Am 5:10–11).
> [You say], "When will the new moon be over, that we may sell grain? And the sabbath, that we may offer wheat for sale, that we may make the ephah small and the shekel great, and deal deceitfully with false balances ..." (Am 8:5).

19.60 His pronouncements about the poor and the helpless and about questionable business practices show a startling correspondence to certain proverbs. Consider only the following three:

> A false balance is an abomination to the Lord, but a just weight is his delight (Pr 11:1).
> Diverse weights are an abomination to the Lord, and false scales are not good (Pr 20:23).
> Do not rob the poor, because he is poor, or crush the afflicted at the gate (Pr 22:22).

19.61 These parallels are no coincidence. In all probability they derive from Amos's familiarity with wisdom literature, as well as the book of Deuteronomy (cf. Dt 25:13–16 with the first two proverbs above). Thus we could say that in its concern for the poor and defenceless and its rejection of shady business practices, the wisdom of the northern kingdom corresponds with that of the south. But here, as in the south, the wisdom teachers were not social reformers. Neither did they, as the prophets did, subject the exploitive rich to relentless criticism.

3. The postexilic period

19.62 I mentioned earlier that during this period wisdom became extremely rigid and that this provoked a protest reaction (cf. 19.28). The Old Testament texts include two exponents of this reaction. The first (Job) was probably written in the Persian era, and the other (Ecclesiastes) in the Hellenistic era. The two texts contain a number of sayings on wealth and poverty that demonstrate clearly how differently these issues were regarded by wisdom teachers in different historical periods. The wisdom psalms probably also date from this period. One of them, Psalm 49, contains sayings about wealth and poverty that are pertinent to our subject. And we must not forget to look briefly at the important deutero-canonical text, "The wisdom of Joshua ben-Sira", also written in the Hellenistic era.

The Persian era

19.63 When one reads the arguments of Job's friends one soon discovers that they shared the rigid concept of wisdom. Their discourses constantly make the point that the righteous experience good fortune and happiness, while the wicked experience disaster and misery. In their view it is the wicked who oppress and exploit the poor. But these wicked people will not go scot free:

> For he [the wicked man] has crushed and abandoned the poor, he has seized a house which he did not build. Because his greed knows no rest, he will not save anything in which he delights ... In the fulness of his sufficiency he will be in straits; all the force of misery will come upon him. To fill his belly to the full God will send his fierce anger into him, and rain it upon him as his food (Job 20:19–20, 22–23).

19.64 Their arguments repeatedly lead them to classify Job, because of his suffering and misfortune, as a wicked person and to charge him with oppression and exploitation of the poor:

> For you have exacted pledges of your brothers for nothing, and stripped the naked of their clothing. You have given no water to the weary to drink, and you have withheld bread from the hungry. The man with power possessed the land, and the favored man dwelt in it. You have sent widows away empty, and the arms of the fatherless were crushed. Therefore snares are round about you, and sudden terror overwhelms you (Job 22:6–10).

19.65 Job defends himself against their accusations by pointing out that the facts are different from what his friends imagine. The wicked prosper and are happy; they do not experience unhappiness and calamity. In his view there is no such thing as just retribution. Indeed, God is not concerned about injustice:

> Why do the wicked live, reach old age, and grow mighty in power? Their children are established in their presence, and their offspring before their eyes. Their houses are safe from fear, and no rod of God is upon them (Job 21:7–9).
>
> Men remove landmarks; they seize flocks and pasture them. They drive away the ass of the fatherless; they take the widow's ox for a pledge. They thrust the poor off the road; the poor of the earth all hide themselves. Behold, like wild asses in the desert they go forth to their toil, seeking prey in the wilderness as food for their children ... From out of the city the dying groan, and the soul of the wounded cries for help; yet God pays no attention to their prayer (Job 24:2–5, 12).

19.66 Job insists that his wretchedness cannot be attributed to his wickedness, for which he is receiving his deserts. There is no such thing as just deserts, for God does not consider himself bound by the doctrine of retribution. If he had, he – Job – would still have been living the good life, for he had always been concerned about widows and orphans:

> I was eyes to the blind, and feet to the lame. I was a father to the poor, and I searched out the cause of him whom I did not know. I broke the fangs of the unrighteous, and made him drop his prey from his teeth. Then I thought, "I shall die in my nest, and I shall multiply my days as the sand, my roots spread out to the waters, with the dew all night on my branches" (Job 29:15–19).

19.67 Job's declaration of innocence (Job 29–31) largely reflects what the prophets expected of the affluent. They (like Job) had to care for the poor, the widows and the orphans and see to it that they were justly treated. The prophets were scathing about their contemporaries because these turned a blind eye to injustice and oppression (cf. ch 18).

19.68 Job had acted correctly, yet had failed to experience the good life that the wisdom teachers had promised. His experience was that one cannot rely on good deeds having good results. The author of this book is trying to teach his readers that God's power is unbounded and that one cannot predict his actions. God is not bound by human systems. We have to care for the poor, the widows and orphans – not because it is to our benefit, but because we are human and should have compassion with other human beings. Being human means being compassionate or, as someone once put it in Latin, "*compatior, ergo sum*" (I suffer with others, therefore I am).

19.69 Another text from this period that has something to say about wealth and poverty is Psalm 49. This psalm was probably edited at a later stage by a redactor who was sceptical about the wisdom tradition. The redaction is apparent in the introductory verses of the psalm as we know it today (vv 2–5) and a few other verses that refer to wise men and fools (cf. vv 11, 21). The original poem was about death and the fate that awaited human beings beyond the grave (cf. vv 8, 12, 17, 18, 20). The original poem clearly shared the traditional notion of death and life thereafter: no one can escape death and one cannot take one's possessions with one. Consequently there is no reason for the poor to envy the rich:

> Be not afraid when one becomes rich, when the glory of his house increases. For when he dies he will carry nothing away; his glory will not go down after him (Ps 49:16–17).

19.70 The redactor of the psalm equated the wise with the rich This should not surprise us, for we have already seen that the wisdom teachers were among the socially advantaged and presented wealth as a reward for wise conduct (cf. 19.47). The redactor (probably a poor person conversant with wisdom teachings) found solace in the thought that rich sages, like poor fools, have to die and leave their possessions behind:

> Yea, he shall see that even the wise die, the fool and the stupid alike must perish and leave their wealth to others. Their graves are their homes for ever, their dwelling places to all generations, though they named lands their own (Ps 49:10–11).

19.71 Personally he hopes that God will ransom him from death (v 16). Here we have the beginnings of the hope of life after death, a hope that was to culminate in the belief in the resurrection of the dead. This idea of a resurrection and retribution after death was later offered as comfort to those who had to endure injustice and suffering this side of the grave. It seems to me that we also see here the beginnings of the trend to regard the poor as the truly pious people of God.

The Hellenistic era

19.72 Although the book of Ecclesiastes, like Proverbs, contains a number of aphorisms, the two texts differ considerably. The book of Ecclesiastes is no longer just a loose concatenation of short, pithy sayings such as that found in older collections in the book of Proverbs (cf. Pr 10–22:16; 25–29). Instead it has extensive prose sections incorporating a few proverbs, although parts of the book are pure poetry and others contain a series of proverbs (cf. Ec 1:2–11; 3:1–9; 7:1–9; 11:7–12:8). When reading these proverbs one gets the feeling that they might just as well have appeared in the book of Proverbs because their form and content are identical with the ones found there. Compare the following few proverbs:

> The wise man has his eyes in his head, but the fool walks in darkness (Ec 2:14).
>
> The way of a fool is right in his own eyes, but a wise man listens to advice (Pr 12:15).

The fool folds his hands, and eats his own flesh (Ec 4:5).
"A little sleep, a little slumber, a little folding of the hands to rest,"
and poverty will come upon you like a robber, and want like an armed man (Pr 24:33–34).
Wisdom gives strength to the wise man more than ten rulers that are in a city (Ec 7:19).
A wise man scales the city of the mighty and brings down the stronghold in which they trust (Pr 21:22).

19.73 If one reads the proverbs quoted above in the context in which they appear in Ecclesiastes, one observes that the author (the Preacher) is usually sceptical about the ideas they contain. He appears to be arguing with older colleagues, and that he was critical of the tradition in which he had been educated: as a rule life was not the way they had taught him. An interesting feature of the book is that the Preacher often raises an issue by quoting a proverb expressing a traditional piece of wisdom and then responds to it. One should be alert to this when reading this book and not regard everything it says as the Preacher's own words.

19.74 In his book he is arguing with older wisdom teachers about their view that wealth is the reward of hard work and that it offers people security. Consider the following two excerpts from a section of the book which deals with the worthlessness of wealth (Ec 5:9–6:9):

Sweet is the sleep of a laborer, whether he eats little or much; but the surfeit of the rich will not let him sleep. There is a grievous evil which I have seen under the sun: riches were kept by their owner to his hurt, and those riches were lost in a bad venture; and he is father of a son, but he has nothing in his hand. As he came from his mother's womb he shall go again, naked as he came, and he shall take nothing for his toil, which he may carry away in his hand. This also is a grievous evil: just as he came, so shall he go; and what gain has he that he toiled for the wind (Ec 5:12–16).
There is an evil which I have seen under the sun, and it lies heavy upon men: a man to whom God gives wealth, possessions, and honor, so that he lacks nothing of all he desires, yet God does not give him power to enjoy them, but a stranger enjoys them; this is vanity; it is a sore affliction (Ec 6:1–2).

19.75 According to the Preacher wealth is not a reward but a gift from God, to be disposed of as he pleases. Just because you have received wealth does not mean that you will enjoy it. God may arrange it so that you lose everything you have gathered. Besides, you cannot even take it with you into the grave (cf. Ps 49:18). In any case, there are too many unknowns in life (death, fate and God) to assign a positive value to wealth. Pursuing riches is pointless and possessing wealth is risky. A superficial reading of the passages quoted above could easily mislead one into thinking that the Preacher was simply pointing out the dangers of materialism and commending contentment. His statements may be mistakenly put on a par with passages such as Luke 12:13–21 and 1 Timothy 6:3–10. However, his intention is not to show that greed and materialism can impair one's faith in God; he is arguing against older wisdom teachers that human beings are helpless in the face of God's superior power. God disposes over life and happiness, hence over wealth and poverty, and he dispenses these as he sees fit. If you own riches you must realise that God can cause you to lose them in an instant. On the other hand, if you are rich, use your wealth to enjoy life to the full:

> Let your garments be always white; let not oil be lacking on your head. Enjoy life with the wife whom you love, all the days of your vain life which he has given you under the sun (Ec 9:8–9).

19.76 Someone has pointed out quite rightly that only a person who has the means to enjoy life could offer this sort of advice. The Preacher undoubtedly belonged to the elite. To argue with older wisdom teachers and to philosophise about the meaning of life was a luxury that ordinary folk who lived from hand to mouth could not afford. Like his older colleagues, the Preacher was not intent on reforming the society in which he lived. But he did observe anomalies in society that he could not explain and resign himself to on the basis of earlier wisdom. His advice in the face of such anomalies is to accept placidly what comes one's way:

> Consider the work of God; who can make straight what he has made crooked? In the day of prosperity be joyful, and in the day of adversity consider; God has made the one as well as the other, so that man may not find out anything that will be after him (Ec 7:13–14).

19.77 The society in which the Preacher lived must indeed have been full of anomalies. The type of polemical protest literature to which this book belongs is not written in times of peace and placidity, but in periods of unrest and tension. The book was probably written at a time when Hellenism swept across the ancient Near East and when the Jews were once more living under foreign overlords. Most scholars date it between 250 and 200 B.C., when Palestine was under Ptolemaic rule. Scholars believe that the Ptolemies adopted a moderate policy towards the Jews and did not try to hellenise them at all costs. Yet the scepticism evident in this book indicates that the changes taking place in society and the influence of the new culture did leave an imprint on the minds of some Jews.

19.78 From this discussion it is evident that we cannot put the Preacher's statements about wealth and poverty on a par with those of the earlier wisdom teachers. He could no longer assure people that if they worked hard they would become rich (cf. Pr 10:4). In other words, good deeds did not necessarily have good results. This is because he no longer saw God as the Guarantor of order. God does not act according to a set pattern; he is arbitrary. The only advice he can offer the rich in such a situation is to enjoy the wealth that befalls them. Comfort for the poor and the oppressed he had none (cf. Ec 4:1–3; 5:7–8). Reading between the lines, he appears to tell them to accept their lot without demur.

19.79 The wisdom of Jesus son of Sirach (Ecclesiasticus), which also dates from this period (180 B.C.), represents a complete antipode to Ecclesiastes. It is in line with the wisdom encountered in the book of Proverbs, so that it is not surprising that its pronouncements on wealth and poverty concur with those in that book. Like the older wisdom teachers, the author of this piece of wisdom literature condemns sloth and the pursuit of pleasure, pointing out that these lead to poverty. Consider this proverb: "Squandering and drunkeness will leave you with nothing in your purse" (Sir 18:33).

19.80 To him poverty was perfectly normal and a society without it inconceivable (cf. Sir 11:14; 33:14–15). The last thing he wanted was to be a beggar (Sir 40:28–29). Being poor meant that one was at the tender mercies of the rich:

> "What has a wolf in common with a lamb, or a sinner with someone who fears God? What peace can there be between hyena and dog, what peace between rich and poor? As lions prey on the wild asses of the desert, so the rich live off the poor" (Sir 13:17–19).

19.81 Wealth is rated highly and the rich are advised to enjoy the good things in life (Sir 14:11–12, 16–17). But he also denigrates wealth: it is better to be poor and in good health, he says, than rich but sickly (Sir 30:14–16). He was not blind to the fact that the rich often exploited the poor, and he exhorts people to take pity on the indigent (Sir 4:4–5; 29:8–9). The imagery he uses to describe exploitation makes one suspect that the rich in his society treated the poor very harshly (cf. Sir 13:17–19, quoted above).

19.82 In other ways the book differs from Proverbs, for instance by referring to the history of Israel. Sometimes it also seems as if the author joins forces with the prophetic tradition in his condemnation of exploitation and unjust treatment of the poor:

> "A sacrifice from ill-gotten gains is tainted, and the gifts of the wicked win no approval. The Most High has no pleasure in the offerings of the godless, nor do countless sacrifices win his forgiveness. To offer a sacrifice from the possessions of the poor is like killing a son before his father's eyes. Bread is life to the destitute, and to deprive them of it is murder. To rob your neighbour of his livelihood is to kill him, and he who defrauds a worker of his wages sheds blood" (Sir 34:18–22).

E. SUMMARY

19.83 It should be clear by now that the teachers of wisdom did not have only one perspective on wealth and poverty throughout the centuries of Israel's history. It would be an oversimplification to say that they all ascribed poverty as people's own doing. The earlier wisdom teachers did in fact present poverty as the result of foolish behaviour and wealth as the result of wise conduct. In their teaching poverty is usually presented as a deterrent to encourage people to be wise. Although they were aware of injustice and exploitation and therefore concerned about the lot of the poor and of widows and orphans, their motivation was different from that of the prophets. Their admonitions, counsel and precepts were not primarily aimed at radically changing the lot of the poor. They were more concerned to preserve the existing social order. Thus one of the aims of their teaching was maintenance of the status quo in which rich and poor live side by side, rather than social reform. One way of preserving the order was to keep the underdogs and the poor happy – hence the appeals to take care of the poor. Because of the rigidity that set in in the wisdom tradition, people began to adopt oversimplified positions and to assume that the righteous and the wise will prosper and be happy while the wicked and the foolish will experience disaster and misery. The author of Job and the authors of Psalm 49 and Ecclesiastes are reacting against this oversimplification.

19.84 What the development of the wisdom tradition teaches us is that we should not adopt oversimplified positions on wealth and poverty. There is no single cause for the fact that some people are rich while others live in poverty. To combat poverty requires a thorough study of the society in which it occurs, since there are usually several reasons for it. In addition poverty cannot be combated by only one or two isolated agencies. In modern society the fight against poverty requires a team effort. On the other hand we should be realistic and face the fact that poverty can never be wiped out completely. The poor, so a wisdom teacher (Jesus Christ) told us once, will always be with us. Not that we can use this saying to soothe our conscience when we observe people in need, for the same wisdom teacher also said that when we see someone in need and do something about it, we are doing it to him. By the same token, if we pass by unconcerned, we are passing him by unconcerned.

e

conclusion

20

Biblical studies, wealth and poverty in South Africa: Retrospect and prospect

FERDINAND DEIST

A. AIM OF THIS BOOK

20.1 This book is meant to start a dialogue on the problem of wealth and poverty in South Africa from a religious – more specifically a Christian – angle. In the first chapter we provided some comparative statistics to give an impression of the enormous disparity between the First and the Third Worlds, and between rich and poor within South Africa.

20.2 This is the framework in which biblical scholars and other believers in this country should work at a *meaningful* interpretation of their lives, since a key function of faith is to enable people to find meaning in their lives.

B. THE INFLUENCE OF ONE'S PERSPECTIVE ON BIBLICAL EXEGESIS

20.3 To Christians the *Bible* is a source of possible interpretations of life. But to interpret the Bible correctly for specific situations one must be conscious of the influence of one's own perspective on both life and the Bible.

20.4 The discussion of the early and the medieval church's views of wealth and poverty showed how strongly exegetes' *environment* and *experience* can influence their exposition of the Bible. The Pseudo-Clementines (10.31) and Chrysostom (10.27) were opposed to all forms of private ownership and regarded proponents of it as "children of Cain". Consequently their sermons focused on biblical texts that condemned large proprietors. The early church, which comprised mainly poor people, largely shared these sentiments.

20.5 The *situation* changed as more and more wealthy and eminent people joined the church That was why Clement of Alexandria (ch 11), himself a learned and affluent man, drastically changed the early church's disapproving attitude towards wealth and considered "poverty" to be a *spiritual* quality rather than an economic category. Hugh of Fleury (ch 9), a dyed in the wool conservative and supporter of the status quo, was concerned that the king should take good care of the *church* Hence he held that while a good king should show concern for the poor, this was not his primary task.

20.6 In his treatment of the problem of poverty in South Africa, Mosala (ch 4) employs a completely different *exegetical method* from both the Pseudo-Clementines and Chrysostom (these two use a typological and Mosala a materialistic method); yet he arrives at virtually the same conclusion as the two Antiochans. The reason for this is that all three of them study the Bible *from the perspective of poor/oppressed people.* There is a similar parallel between the "prosperity interpretation" outlined by Domeris (ch 5) and the approach of monastic theology expounded by Hugh of Fleury (ch 9).

C. PERSPECTIVE AND METHOD

1. "Perspective" can dominate method

20.7 In view of what was said above one could say that biblical exegetes' biographies (which shape their perspective) play an important role in their interpretation of the Bible. It even seems as if exegetes' biographies and sentiments override the significance of their exegetical *method.* For example: although methodologically typology and allegory are closely related, Chrysostom (ch 10) and Clement of Alexandria (ch 11) arrive at opposite conclusions about the Bible's message concerning wealth and poverty. In the discussion of the historical-grammatical method of exegesis (ch 8), Scheffler continually observes that Keil tends to "spiritualise" certain concepts in order to steer away from what the text itself is about – possibly because in Keil's perspective certain other issues were more important than poverty. Similarly, whereas Mosala (4.9) believes the Naboth episode to be the prime example of the biblical perspective on wealth and poverty, our discussion of the historical-critical exegesis of the same story (ch 7) shows that Gray does not deal with the problem of wealth and poverty at all, but merely unravels the history of the text. In our own synopsis of the result of his historical critique we pointed out, however, that the "additions" to the text indicate that later readers found it difficult to accept that the oppressor Ahab had escaped punishment, and that *that* was why they wrestled with the text. We gave a certain interpretation of Gray's basic text. Thus Loader's comment on immanent exegesis (6.26) applies to all exegetical methods: "And just as a map cannot take the place of an actual journey across a landscape, nor determine the traveller's *impression* of the scene, so an exegetical map can never replace the readers' further discovery of the text or their *impressions* of it".

2. Applying a method is not in itself exegesis

20.8 All exegetical methods are means whereby exegetes clear a path through the forest of the biblical text, and therefore do not constitute the actual "journey". These methods help us to "crack" the text we are studying or to break it up into smaller, more manageable units. They also help us to scrutinise that text attentively and to make us aware of all sorts of details and connecting lines. But no exegetical method can expound a biblical text. Biblical interpretation – that is, understanding what is written in the Bible – is something that happens *inside the mind of the exegete.* That is why the exegete's perspective on the problem and on the Bible is of such cardinal importance and why we must be careful that our perspectives do not totally silence the text's own voice – as often happened in the application of allegory, typology and the search for the "deeper" meaning of the Bible.

3. Is method a matter of taste?

20.9 The last, somewhat pejorative comment on three exegetical methods indicates that not all methods are equally suitable for interpreting the Bible. The fact that the exegete's perspective plays an important role in interpretation does not mean that exegetical *methods* are all much the same. As biblical scholars we are concerned to know what the *Bible* says. Consequently an exegetical method that disciplines us to wrestle with the *actual text* is better than methods that simply latch on to odd expressions or isolated words in the biblical text. Allegory, typology and "spiritual" exegesis have a way of latching on to biblical words and expressions without proper regard to their *context*. The function of an exegetical method is in fact to submit our own perspectives and biases to the discipline of the biblical text and to criticise them. If we are really *looking for* meaning in life and if we really want to know what the *Bible* has to say about it in our situation, we must be ready to let the Bible *change* our own perspective. Stringent application of a sound exegetical method can help us to thus discipline our own perspectives.

4. What is "good exegesis"?

20.10 What, then, is a "good" exegetical method? A number of methods were discussed in this book, and in each case we listed the advantages and disadvantages. Thus we can say that there is no method that can be regarded as the *only correct* one. New methods emerge as people arrive at fresh insight into the workings of literature – for the Bible is, after all, *literature* (inter alia). When the Renaissance brought the insight that *the historical circumstances* in which a text originated have to be taken into account when interpreting it, the historical-grammatical method arose. When the insight dawned that the biblical texts were not always written in a single session but often originated over a protracted period, the historical-critical method was developed to help us read each passage *in its own historical context*. When the insight came that *interrelationship* is an important indicator of the meaning of a text, the immanent methods developed.

20.11 But this does not mean that each new method invalidates and replaces all the earlier ones. Where the historical-grammatical method pays close attention to linguistic details in a text, structural analysis extends this by paying even more minute attention to its linguistic structure. And where the historical-grammatical method is alert to the importance of the historical context of a text, the historical-critical method elaborates by making an even finer distinction between portions of the text that derive from different periods. Thus we can use several methods in expounding the Bible – and the more adept one becomes in applying the various methods, the easier it becomes to use several of them *simultaneously*. The stricter we are in our methodic dealings with biblical texts, the more stringent the discipline that the text can exercise on our own wishes, interests and perspectives. One point is vitally important in exegesis, and that is to pay special attention to the fact that the biblical texts themselves were also written from different perspectives and that our own perspective on a problem should not disregard those perspectives or simply harmonise them.

D. PERSPECTIVES AND COMMUNITIES IN THE BIBLICAL TEXT

1. Many viewpoints can be "biblically" substantiated

20.12 The Bible sometimes – one might say usually – offers several possible interpretations of the same problem. Merely comparing the wisdom and the prophetic perspectives on wealth and poverty reveals a difference: whereas the wisdom teachers eventually came to the conclusion that poverty was God's punishment for laziness and an unreflecting life, most prophets regard the main cause of poverty to be the oppressive way in which the rich treat the poor. And whereas some wisdom teachers believed poverty to be God's punishment for laziness, other saw it simply as one's allotted "fate", for which one is not to blame but about which one can do little. In due course the situation changed, so that the expression "the poor" no longer necessarily referred to *economic* poverty but to "the helpless" and eventually simply to "the humble". Scheffler's exposition of New Testament views on wealth and poverty indicates that a similar diversity existed in that period. Nowhere is this more evident than in Matthew's and Luke's versions of the beatitudes:

> Blessed are the poor in spirit ... (Mt 5:3)
> Blessed are you poor ... (Lk 6:20)

20.13 From this brief summary it is evident that Chrysostom's and Mosala's denigratory views of wealth and property, no less than the positive evaluation of wealth by Clement of Alexandria and the "prosperity" interpretation (discussed by Domeris), are all represented in the Bible itself. Mosala could invoke the Mosaic tradition (to which the prophets also belonged) and the prosperity reading could invoke the wisdom tradition.

20.14 Whether prosperity readers are aware of this problem is not clear. They would probably be inclined, like Clement of Alexandria, to spiritualise texts that conflict with their reading. Mosala, whereas he is aware of this diversity in the Bible, makes a particular *choice*. Certain trends in the Bible, he maintains, do not function in a *liberating* manner for people living in poverty (e.g. the monarchic tradition of *power*). Such "non-functional" trends, he maintains, should be criticised and rejected.

2. Should one choose whatever suits one?

20.15 Many people will be shocked at the notion that a Christian may choose to "reject" certain parts of the Bible. One must ask, however, whether an impermissible spiritualisation of biblical passages that conflict with one's own interests or views is not in effect as much of a "rejection". To spiritualise a tradition like Moses' (as reflected in the laws and the prophets) or to apply it only partially (e.g. in the form of tithing) is to invalidate a large part of it.

20.16 Possibly the best solution is not to make a *choice* between biblical trends – either by rejecting certain parts outright or by removing the sting from certain parts by spiritualising them – but to throw *all* viewpoints open for debate and to conduct the discussion in the midst of the diversity. The will of God cannot be revealed by exegesis; it has to be found in the *community of believers*. What we have are certain texts that inform us about the perception of the problem of wealth and poverty. These perceptions were formed *in specific societies* and made possible by faith in God. What we are stuck with is a problem of wealth and poverty in *our own particular society*. There is *no* bridge between those societies and ours; the community of believers has to *build* one in dialogue with the Bible. That is to say, we must *look for* God's will for our situation.

3. God's will must be looked for

20.17 The Bible offers us religious perspectives that arose in different societies in biblical times – societies which differed quite dramatically from one era to the next. The societies of the northern and southern kingdoms differed. So did the structures of premonarchic and monarchic society. The social structures of pre-exilic Judah differed from those of the postexilic Jewish communities. And after the exile some believers aligned themselves as precursors of a new (political) Davidic empire. Others organised themselves purely as a "congregation". Yet others waited all but passively for God to initiate something altogether new.

20.18 In each of these societies there were poor people, God's will was sought and God revealed his will. We should therefore note the *way* in which God made himself and his will known.

20.19 The cardinal symbol of the Christian gospel is that God became *human*. God did not dictate his will once and for all like a thunderbolt from heaven, but made it known by *joining in human history*. God was at work *among* his people and *by means of* them – whether in the patriarchal structures of premonarchic times, in the monarchic structures of that era or in the hierocracy of the postexilic epoch God made himself known *in* history. The texts we have tell us how God's will was embodied time and again, always *in a different way*. Our task now, by analogy with the biblical example and in reliance on God's Spirit, is to look for God's will and the way in which God seeks to become as it were incarnate in our society.

E. WEALTH AND POVERTY IN SOUTH AFRICA

1. The Naboth episode and the South African situation

20.20 Many of the themes and circumstances reflected in the Naboth narrative are manifestly relevant to South Africa. We mention a few.

20.21 There are *two perceptions of land ownership*: Naboth sees land as an inalienable gift from God; to Ahab it is a commercial article that can change hands. The same perspectives exist in South Africa. There are exponents of capitalism who see property merely as a *means* to an end, and there are those with a socialist orientation who regard the communal ownership of property as an essential element of human life. There are people (both black and white) who regard the land as a divine "inheritance"; and there are people to whom it is not important.

20.22 There are *two types of community*: a community organised according to traditional tribal structure (like that of Naboth and his people) and a state structure in which the central authority of government was vested. In South Africa we have a variety of social structures, ranging from traditional tribal structures among black rural citizens to the loose – sometimes anarchistic – structures in squatters' camps and communities organised according to the values of liberal democracy. Each of these has its own value system and religious convictions.

20.23 There are *two kinds of economy*: the subsistence economy of the Israelite peasants and the profit economy of Ahab. In South Africa we have a variety of economic systems: ranging from subsistence economy in some sectors, through informal economic and semisocialistic structures to the ideals of capitalism and socialism.

20.24 There are *two kinds of law*: that of the tribal system and that of a fairly totalitarian state. In South Africa there are legal systems in operation that range from traditional law, to the law of "people's courts" in some black communities and the township law of the comtsotsis, to the courts where Roman-Dutch law is applied.

20.25 There are *two views of religion*: the one (Elijah's side) exclusive, the other (Ahab's side) inclusive. South Africa is not only a religiously heterogeneous country, but a country in which Christianity itself comprises a diversity of ecclesiastic traditions, each with its own idea of what constitutes "true" religion. The chapters by Mosala and Domeris are expressive of two traditions within this diversity.

20.26 There are *two views of culture*: to Naboth culture is basically exclusive and conservative, to be preserved unchanged from one generation to the next – hence his refusal to have his ancestral land alienated; Ahab regards culture as something that can change through assimilation and exposure to other cultures (like that of Phoenicia). In South Africa people's approaches to culture range from the conservative to the liberal extreme.

20.27 There are *two perceptions of righteousness*: Naboth sees righteousness as the right to possess property, Ahab as the right to alienate land at a fair price. In South Africa there are people who oppose with might and main the idea that the state has the *right* to alienate private property (with or without compensation), and others who feel that the state is *in duty bound* to expropriate the "rich" and give their property to the "poor".

20.28 There are *two situations before the law*: Jezebel is in a position to manipulate the law, Naboth in a position where he cannot defend himself. In South Africa legal procedure has become so expensive that virtually only the affluent still have access to the courts; the poor – even though they may have justice on their side – do not have the instruments to ensure that justice be done.

20.29 We could go on identifying *themes* in the Naboth story that are significant for our society as well. But having done so, and with reference to these themes, we will have to

- analyse our own *situation* carefully in order to discover the exact differences in perspective that exist (e.g. as regards ownership and property, the right to alienate property, the state's role in the economy and the right to ownership);

- introduce the *entire* Bible (Old and New Testaments) into our discussion of these themes;
- voluntarily expose our own perspectives on our community and on the biblical message to discussion within the community of believers, and not simply make a prior choice of our own.

2. The Old Testament, wealth, poverty and South Africa

20.30 Because the matter is more complex than it appears and because we as believers must *look for* God's will, we cannot attempt to give a final answer in this book. What we can say on the strength of our study of the various perspectives in the *Old Testament* is that, where wealth and poverty are concerned, the Old Testament insists on more than mere (liberal) sympathy; it requires compassion. That is to say, the Old Testament requires that we must stand *with* the poor in their need and not simply dispense alms from above, and that the poor must be able to *rely* on it that the wealthy will not exploit and oppress them, but will physically help to deliver them from their poverty. South Africa, which has its own history in this regard, undoubtedly needs such an approach

20.31 The Old Testament acknowledges different causes of poverty. Some people are poor because they have been impoverished by the rich; others because it simply "happened" through unavoidable circumstances (like drought). Others are poor because they won't exert themselves and work systematically. And if we look at the history of Israel in Ahab's day we observe that poverty and the oppression of the poor also stemmed from the fact that the legal system of Israel could not keep abreast of economic and political change in the country. One could probably advance all these reasons for poverty in South Africa as well. But the Old Testament is not content with merely looking into the *causes* of poverty. Neither does it discriminate between the poor on the basis of the *causes* of their poverty. When the prophets or the wisdom teachers or the legislators speak about "the poor" they are referring to a single group of people.

20.32 The Old Testament allows for the fact that there will always be rich and poor – as there will probably be in South Africa too. But the biblical authors are not fatalistic about poverty. The perpetual distinction between rich and poor in fact *activated* the sages, the prophets and the legislators to encourage people to *do* something about the situation. A purely fatalistic attitude that "the poor will always be with us" makes economically wealthy people *spiritually* poor, so that they neglect their responsibilities towards the poor, which God counts as their sin.

20.33 The Old Testament shows that throughout the biblical history God was on the side of the poor and the wronged in a special way – a fact that was long denied by (particularly some) white churches in South Africa: he did so in the exodus events, in the preaching of the prophets, in the laws of Israel. Some of the wisdom teachers even said that anyone who gave to the poor was lending to *the Lord*. In Jesus of Nazareth God assumed the form of a *poor carpenter and a servant*, saying that the cardinal religious questions are not dogmatic but practical ones: whether the poor and the wretched and the prisoner are *safe* and *secure* with us.

20.34 Thus *the fact* that the Bible insists that religious people have a special responsibility towards the poor and towards their human dignity is indisputable. Consequently any political system that does not explicitly extend protection to the poor will stand condemned from a religious perspective. *How* the responsibility of affluent believers towards the poor is embodied both politically and economically outside their private lives – how the security, safety and freedom of the poor are to be embodied constitutionally and otherwise – is for us to work out.

3. The Old Testament, poverty, wealth and meaning in life

20.35 The provisional religious perspective on the South African problem of wealth and poverty which we have inferred from our study of the Old Testament indicates that the rich will not find meaning in life by collecting riches and perpetrating injustice. On the contrary, such values *destroy* meaning in the lives of the rich and that of the entire society. The rich will find meaning in life through such things as *compassion and kindness towards the poor*, because the meaning of their lives will be enriched by representing God among the poor.

20.36 Our provisional religious perspective moreover indicates that the meaning of poor people's lives may be enriched by the knowledge that they are not abandoned to a fate of perpetual poverty and exploitation, but are taken into a *caring community* which guarantees the rights, freedom and opportunities to improve themselves by raising their standard of living. Thus the meaning in the lives of the poor may be enriched by the fact that *God*, in the form of the rich, is *on their side* and not against them. The meaning of their lives may be enriched by a realistic *hope* that their labour is not in vain but that it will be blessed.

20.37 The biblical narrative also tells us, however, that the poor who become affluent through divine concern should not forget *God* and should not neglect to represent *God* among the poor. When the Israelites, who had once been slaves, went to live in Palestine they lost this religious perspective, which brought their society and their country to a fall. Only *caring* people and a *caring* community will have long life in the land God has given them.

20.38 The question that the Bible leaves us to ponder is whether we really *believe* all this and therefore want to become caring people.

Bibliography

CHAPTER 1

Boesak, A 1984. Poverty: the moral challenge. Get up and walk, in *Second Carnegie inquiry into poverty and development in Southern Africa*, vol 32. Cape Town: (Carnegie conference paper No 308).

Budlender, G B 1984. Lawyers and poverty: Beyond "access to justice", in *Second Carnegie inquiry into poverty and development in Southern Africa*, vol 10. Cape Town: (Carnegie conference paper No 91).

Chisholm, L 1984. Redefining skills: South African education in the 1980s, in *Second Carnegie inquiry into poverty and development in Southern Africa*, vol 10. Cape Town: (Carnegie conference paper No 96).

Economist, The 1987. *The world in figures.* Boston: Hall.

Ellis, G F R 1984. The dimensions of poverty, in *Second Carnegie inquiry into poverty and development in Southern Africa*, vol 1. Cape Town: (Carnegie conference paper No 4).

Fabian, J 1983. *Time and the other: how anthropology makes its object.* New York: Colombia University Press.

Fanon, F 1982. *The wretched of the earth.* Harmondsworth: Penguin.

Gentle, R 1984. Crime and poverty, in *Second Carnegie inquiry into poverty and development in Southern Africa*, vol 10. Cape Town: (Carnegie conference paper No 93).

Hewatt, G et al 1984. An exploratory study of the overcrowding and health issues at Old Crossroads, in *Second Carnegie inquiry into poverty and development in Southern Africa*, vol 32. Cape Town: (Carnegie conference paper No 14).

Hugo, P 1984. Afrikaans farmers in the Transvaal: a quality-of-life profile, in *Second Carnegie inquiry into poverty and development in Southern Africa*, vol 29. Cape Town: (Carnegie conference paper No 287).

Huntley, B, Siegfried, R & Sunter, C 1989. *South African environments into the 21st century.* Cape Town: Tafelberg.

Le Roux, P 1984. Poor whites, in *Second Carnegie inquiry into poverty and development in Southern Africa*, vol 32. Cape Town: (Carnegie conference paper No 248).

Moller, V, Schlemmer, L & Strijdom, H G 1984. Poverty and quality of life among Blacks in South Africa, in *Second Carnegie inquiry into poverty and development in Southern Africa*, vol 1. Cape Town: (Carnegie conference paper No 6).

Ntoane, C N & Mokoetle, K E 1984. Major problems as perceived by the community, in *Second Carnegie inquiry into poverty and development in Southern Africa*, vol 1. Cape Town: (Carnegie conference paper No 2).

Roodt, M & Lawrence, M 1984. The effect of socio-economic locality on student aspirations in three Bophutatswana schools, in *Second Carnegie inquiry into poverty and development in Southern Africa*, vol 10. Cape Town: (Carnegie conference paper No 99).

Vorster, W S (ed) 1987. *Are we killing God's earth? Ecology and theology.* Pretoria: UNISA.

CHAPTER 2

Geertz, C 1973. Religion as a cultural system, in *The interpretation of cultures. Selected essays*. New York: Basic Books.

Gous, I G P 1988. Die herkoms van Klaagliedere. DTh-thesis, Universiteit van Suid-Afrika, Pretoria.

CHAPTER 3

Burden, J J & Deist, F E 1981. *An ABC of biblical exegesis*. Pretoria: Van Schaik.

Deist, F E & Vorster, W S (eds) 1986. *Words from afar.* Cape Town: Tafelberg.

CHAPTER 4

Cabral, A 1980. *Unity and Struggle*. London: Heinemann.

Clevenot, M 1985. *Materialist Approaches to the Bible*. Maryknol: Orbis.
Gramsci, A 1971. *Prison Notebooks*. London: Lawrence and Wishart.
Gottwald, N K 1983. *The Bible and Liberation*. Maryknoll: Orbis.
Gottwald, N K 1980. *The Tribes of Yahweh*. London: SCM.
Marx, K 1976. *Capital* (vol 1). Harmondsworth: Penguin Books.
Marx, K & Engels, P 1957. *On Religion*. Moscow: Progress.
Macpherson, C B 1962. *The Political Theory of Possessive Individualism*. Oxford: Oxford University Press.
Maimela, S 1987. *Proclaim Freedom To My People*. Johannesburg: Skotsville.
Meeks, M D 1989. *God the Economist*. Minneapolis: Fortress.
Mofokeng, T 1983. *The Crucified Among the Crossbearers*. Kampen: Kok.
Mosala, I 1989. *Biblical Hermeneutics and Black Theology in South Africa*. Grand Rapids: Eerdmans.
Schottroff, W & Stegemann, W 1984. *God of the Lowly*. Maryknoll: Orbis.

CHAPTER 5

De Vaux, R 1973. *Ancient Israel: Its life and institutions.* Paperback. London: Darton, Longman & Todd.
Hollenbach, P 1987. Defining rich and poor using social sciences, in Richards, K H (ed) *Society of biblical literature 1987 seminar papers*. Atlanta: Scholars Press.
Malina, B J 1981. *The New Testament world: Insights from cultural anthropology*. Atlanta: John Knox.
Myers, A C 1979. s v 'Bless'. *The International Standard Bible Encyclopedia*. Rev ed.
Nuernberger, K 1990. *The scourge of unemployment in South Africa*. Pietermaritzburg: Encounter.
Scharbert, J 1977. s v 'Brk'. *ThDOT*. Rev ed.
Vos, C J 1988. s v 'Riches; Wealth'. *The international standard Bible encyclopedia*. Rev ed.

CHAPTER 6

Bronner, L 1968. *The stories of Elijah and Elisha as polemics against Baal worship*. Leiden: Brill.
Cohen, M A 1975. In all fairness to Ahab: A socio-political consideration of the Ahab-Elijah controversy. *Eretz Israel* 12, 87-94.
Gray, J 1970. *I & II Kings: A commentary.* 2nd ed. London: SCM.
Jones, G H 1984. *1 & 2 Kings.* Grand Rapids: Eerdmans. (NCB).
Loader, J A 1986. De structuuranalytische methoden, in Van der Woude, A S (ed), *Inleiding tot de studie van het Oude Testament*, 128-142. Kampen: Kok.
Long, B O 1984. *1 Kings.* Grand Rapids: Eerdmans. (FOTL).
Würthwein, E 1984. *Die Bücher der Könige: 1. Kön. 17 — 2 Kön. 25.* Göttingen: Vandenhoeck & Ruprecht. (ATD 11/2).

CHAPTER 7

Deist, F E 1978. *Mosaic of Moses: Pentateuch research since the Reformation*. Pretoria: D R Booksellers.
Gray, J 1964. *I & II Kings. A Commentary*. London: SCM. (OTL).

CHAPTER 8

Alexander, D & Alexander, P (eds) 1973. *The lion handbook to the Bible: a full-colour guide to all the books of the Bible.* Herts: Lion Publishing.
Barr, J 1973. *The Bible in the modern world.* London: SCM.
Bright, J 1967. *The authority of the Old Testament.* Grand Rapids: Baker.
Burden, J J & Deist, F E 1984. Inleiding: historiese oorsig van verskillende eksegetiese metodes, in Burden, J J et al, *Bybelkunde (Honneurs): enigste gids vir HBS408-6: (Bybeluitleg)*, 1-26. Pretoria: UNISA.
Deist, F E & Burden, J J 1981. *An ABC of biblical exegesis.* Pretoria: Van Schaik.
Gray, J 1970. *I & II Kings: a commentary.* 2nd.ed. London: SCM.
Keil, C F [1876] 1988. *Die Bücher der Könige.* 2. Aufl. Giessen: Brunnen Verlag.
Kelsey, D 1975. *The uses of Scripture in recent theology.* Philadelphia: Fortress.

Schreiner, J 1971. Zur Geschichte der altestamentliche Exegese: Epochen, Ziele, Wege, in Schreiner, J (Hrsg), *Einführung in die Methoden der biblischen Exegese*, 1-17. Würzburg: Echter.
Unger, M F 1954. *Archaeology and the Old Testament.* Grand Rapids: Zondervan.
Verhoef, P A 1973. *Metodiek van die eksegese.* Pretoria: N.G. Kerk-Uitgewers.
Würthwein, E 1984. *Die Bücher der Köninge: 1. Kön. 17–2. Kön. 25.* Göttingen: Vandenhoeck & Ruprecht. (ATD 11/2).

CHAPTER 9

Boockmann, H 1988. *Das Mittelalter. Ein Lesebuch aus Texten und Zeugnissen des 6. bis 16. Jahrhunderts.* München: Beck.
Daly, L J 1965. *Benedictine monasticism. Its formation and development through the 12th century.* New York: Sheed and Ward.
Gaybba, B P 1988. *Aspects of the mediaeval history of theology, 12th to 14th centuries.* Pretoria: University of South Africa.
Giddens, A 1984. *The constitution of society. Outline of the theory of structuration.* Cambridge: Polity Press.
Härdelin, A 1987. Monastische Theologie – eine "praktische" Theologie vor der Scholastik. *Zeitschrift für katholische Theologie* 109(4)400–415.
Landman, C 1987. *Skrifhantering in die "Tractatus de regia potestate et sacerdotali dignitate" van Hugo Floriacensis.* Ongepubliseerde D.Th.-proefskrif, Universiteit van Suid-Afrika.
Leclercq, J 1974. *The love of learning and the desire for God. A study of monastic culture.* London: SPCK.
Monumenta Germaniae Historica. Libelli de lite imperatorum et pontificum saeculis XI. et XII. conscripti. Tomus II. Hannoverae: Impensis Bibliopolii Hahniani.

CHAPTER 10

Barr, J 1966. *Old and new in interpretation: a study of the two Testaments.* London: SCM.
Blenkinsopp, J 1967. sv Type and antitype. *New Catholic encyclopedia.* Vol. 14.
Charity, A C 1987. *Events and their afterlife: the dialectics of Christian typology in the Bible and Dante.* First paperback edition. Cambridge: University Press.
Darbyshire, J R 1921. sv Typology. *Encyclopedia of religion and ethics.* Vol. 12.
Deist, F E & Burden, J J 1980. *'n ABC van Bybeluitleg.* Pretoria: Van Schaik.
Downey, G 1961. A history of Antioch in Syria: *From Seleucus to the Arab conquest.* Princeton: Princeton University Press.
Hengel, M 1974. *Property and riches in the early Church: aspects of a social history of early Christianity,* tr by J Bowden. Philadelphia: Fortress.
Laurence, J D 1984. *'Priest' as type of Christ: the leader of the eucharist in salvation history according to Cyprian of Carthage.* New York: Lang.
M'Clintock, J & Strong, J 1970. sv Type. *Encylopedia of Biblical, theological and ecclesiastical literature.* Vol 10.
Rogerson, J 1988. The Old Testament, in Rogerson, J, Rowland, C & Lindars, B 1988, 3–149.
Rogerson, J, Rowland, C & Lindars, B 1988. *The history of Christian theology:* Volume 2: *The study and use of the Bible.* Grand Rapids: Eerdmans.
Sundkler, B 1962. *The Christian ministry in Africa.* Liverpool: Birchall.
Verhoef, P A 1954. Tipologie en die Ou Testament. *Gereformeerde Vaandel* 22, 13–20.
Von Rad, G 1979. Typological interpretation of the Old Testament, in Westermann, C 1979, 17–39.
Westermann, C (ed) 1979. *Essays on Old Testament hermeneutics.* Atlanta: Knox.

CHAPTER 11

Adam, A 1965. *Lehrbuch der Dogmengeschichte*, vol 1. Gütersloh: Gerd Mohn.
Altaner, B 1951. *Patrologie.* Freiburg: Herder.
Bakhuizen van den Brink, J N 1965. *Handboek der kerkgeschiedenis*, vol 1. Den Haag: Bert Bakker.
Baus, K 1980. *From the apostolic community to Constantine.* London: Burns & Oates.
Berkhof, H 1955. *Geschiedenis der kerk.* Nijkerk: Callenbach

Butterworth, G W 1960. *Clement of Alexandria*. Harvard: University Press.
De Jong, O J 1980. *Geschiedenis der kerk*. Nijkerk: Callenbach
De Knijff, H W 1980. *Sleutel en slot*. Kampen: Kok.
Duvenhage, S sj. *Die dekor van die Nuwe Testament*. Pretoria: Interkerklike Uitgewerstrust.
Frend, W H C 1982. *The early church from the beginnings to 461*. London: SCM.
Frend, W H C 1984. *The rise of Christianity*. London: Darton, Longman & Todd.
Heussi, K 1960. *Kompendium der Kirchengeschichte*. Tübingen: JCB Mohr.
Lietzmann, H 1967. *A history of the early church*, vol 2. London: Butterworth Press.
Pelikan, J 1971. *The emergence of the Catholic tradition*, vol 1. Chicago: University of Chicago Press.
Reicke B & Rost L 1969. *Bijbels-historisch woordenboek*, vol 1. Utrecht: Het Spectrum.
Von Campenhausen, H 1963. *The fathers of the Greek church* London: Adam & Charles Black.
Von Harnack, A 1964. *Lehrbuch der Dogmengeschichte*, vol 1. Darmstadt: Wissenschaftliche Buchgesellschaft.
Willoughby, H R 1962. s v 'Alexandria'. *The interpreter's dictionary of the Bible*.
Wood, S P 1954. *Clement of Alexandria: Christ the educator*. Washington: Catholic University.

CHAPTER 12

Bammel, E 1959. s v *ptochos ktl. ThDNT.*
Barret, C K 1970. The interpretation of the Old Testament in the New, in Ackroyd, P R & Evans, C F (eds), *The Cambridge history of the Bible*. Cambridge: University Press.
Bright, J 1975. *The authority of the Old Testament*. Grand Rapids: Michigan.
Deist, F 1990. *A concise dictionary of theological and related terms*. 2nd ed. Pretoria: Van Schaik.
Hengel, M 1974. *Property and riches in the early Church* Philadelphia: Fortress.
Hoppe, L J 1987. *Being poor: A biblical study*. Wilmington: Michael Glazier. (Good News Studies 20).
Lindijer, C H 1981. *De armen en de rijken bij Lukas*. Amsterdam: Stichting Lutherse Uitgeverij.
Pilgrim, W E 1981. *Good news to the poor: Wealth and poverty in Luke-Acts*. Minneapolis: Augsburg.
Scheffler, E H 1983. Die verhouding tussen die Ou en Nuwe Testament. *ThEv* 16/1, 38-52.
Scheffler, E H 1988. On suffering in Luke's Gospel, in Breytenbach, C (red/ed), *Church in context: early Christianity in social context: Kerk en konteks: die vroeë Christendom in sosiale verband*. Pretoria: N G Kerkboekhandel.
Scheffler, E H 1988. *Suffering in Luke's Gospel*. DD thesis, University of Pretoria.
Seccombe, D P 1983. *Possessions and the poor in Luke-Acts*. Linz: A Fuchs.
Van Tilborg, S 1988. An interpretation from the ideology of the text. *Neotestamentica* 22, 205-215.

CHAPTER 13

Anderson, B A 1988. *The living world of the Old Testament*. 4th ed. Essex: Longman.
Craigie, P C 1986. *The Old Testament: Its background, growth, and content*. Nashville: Abingdon.
Deist, F E (red) 1982. *Die Bybel leef*. Pretoria: Van Schaik.
Deist, F E & Du Plessis, I J 1982. *God and his kingdom*. Pretoria: Van Schaik.
Deist, F E & Vorster, W S (eds) 1986. *Words from afar*. Cape Town: Tafelberg. (The literature of the Old Testament 1).
Deist, F E & Le Roux, J H 1987. *Revolution and reinterpretation: Chapters from the history of Israel*. Cape Town: Tafelberg. (The literature of the Old Testament 4).
Hermann, S 1981. *A history of Israel in Old Testament times*. London: SCM.

CHAPTER 14

Aharoni, Y 1979. *The land of the Bible: A historical geography*. Philadelphia: Westminster Press.
Aharoni, Y & Avi-Yonah, M 1979. *Bybelse Atlas*. ('n Afrikaanse uitgawe van *The MacMillan Bible Atlas*. Afrikaanse verwerking deur A H van Zyl). Durban: Butterworths.
Cansdale, G S 1980. s v 'Animals'. *The illustrated Bible dictionary*.
Callaway, J A 1983. A visit with Ahilud: A revealing look at village life when Israel first settled the Promised Land. *BAR* 9, 42-53.
Callaway, J A 1984. Village Subsistence at Ai and Raddana in Iron Age I, in Thompson 1984:51-67

Coote, R B & Whitelam, K W 1987. *The emergence of early Israel in historical perspective.* Sheffield: Almond Press.
De Geus, C H J 1984. *De Israëlitische stad.* Kampen: Kok.
Donner, H 1976. *Einführung in die biblische Landes- und Altertumskunde.* Darmstadt: Wissenschaftliche Buchgesellschaft.
Edelstein, G & Gibson, S 1982. Ancient Jerusalem's rural food basket: The "new" archaeology looks for an urban center's agricultural base. *BAR* 8, 46-54.
Finkelstein, I 1988. *The archaeology of the Israelite settlement.* Jerusalem: Israel Exploration Society.
Frick, F 1977. *The city in ancient Israel.* Missoula: Scholars Press.
Heyns, M 1989. Amos – Kampvegter vir vryheid en reg: 'n Sosiaal-historiese studie. D Litt et Phil-proefskrif, Universiteit van Suid-Afrika, Pretoria.
Hopkins, D C 1985. *The highlands of Canaan: Agricultural life in the Early Iron Age.* Sheffield: Almond Press.
Hopkins, D C 1987. Life on the Land: The subsistence struggles of early Israel. *BA* 50, 178-191.
Kempinski, A et al 1981. Excavations at Tel Masos: 1972, 1974, 1975. *Eretz-Israel* 15, 154-180.
Malherbe, W 1990. Die gesin in oud-Israel. M Th-verhandeling, Universiteit van Stellenbosch
McClellan, Th L 1984. Town planning at tell en-Nasbeh. *ZDPV* 100, 53-69.
Millard, A R 1980. s v 'Potter, Pottery'. *The illustrated Bible dictionary.*
Miller, J M & Hayes, J H 1986. *A history of ancient Israel and Judah.* Philadelphia: Westminster Press.
Olivier, H 1988. A Land flowing with milk and honey: Some observations on the modes of existence in ancient Israel. *NGTT* 29, 1-13.
Shiloh, Y 1987. The casemate wall, the four room house, and early planning in the Israelite city. *BASOR* 268, 3-15.
Stager, L E 1985. The archaeology of the family in ancient Israel. *BASOR* 260, 1-35.
Stager, L E 1989. The song of Deborah: Why some tribes answered the call and others did not. *BAR* 15, 50-64.
Thompson, H O (ed) 1984. *The answers lie below: Essays in honor of Lawrence Edmund Toombs.* New York: University Press of America.
Van Nieuwenhuize, C A O 1962. The Near East village: A profile. *MEJ* 16, 295-308.
Weippert, H 1988. *Palästina in vorhellenistischer Zeit.* München: C H Beck.
Zohary, M 1982. *Plants of the Bible.* Tel-Aviv: Sadan Publishing House.

CHAPTER 15

Deist F E 1986. Texts with a legal perspective, in Deist, F E & Vorster, W S (eds) 1986:186-212.
Deist, F E & Vorster, W S 1986. *Words from afar.* Cape Town: Tafelberg. (The literature of the Old Testament 1).
Ellis, G F R 1984. The dimensions of poverty. Carnegie conference paper No 4. *Second Carnegie inquiry into poverty and development in Southern Africa.*
Fritz, V 1987. Conquest or settlement? The early Iron Age in Palestine. *BA* 50, 84-100.
Gottwald, N K 1979. *The tribes of Yahweh.* London: SCM.
Hauer, C 1986. From Alt to anthropology: the rise of the Israelite state. *JSOT* 36, 3-15.
Lang, B 1982. The social organization of peasant poverty in biblical Israel. *JSOT* 24, 47-63.
Lemche, N P 1985. *Early Israel. Anthropological and historical studies on the Israelite society before the monarchy.* Leiden: Brill. (VTS 37).
Möller, V, Schlemmer, L, Strijdom, H G and colleagues at the HSRC 1984. Poverty and quality of life among blacks in South Africa. Carnegie conference paper No 6. *Second Carnegie inquiry into poverty and development in Southern Africa.*
Rogerson, J W 1986. Was early Israel a segmentary society? *JSOT* 36, 17-26.

CHAPTER 16

Albright, W F 1957. *From the stone age to Christianity* 2 ed. New York: Doubleday Anchor Books.
Blenkinsopp, J 1986. Yahweh and other deities: conflict and accommodation in the religion of Israel. *Interpretation* 40, 354–366.
Bosman, H L & Loader, J A (reds) 1987. *Vertellers van die Ou Testament.* Kaapstad: Tafelberg.
Cross, F M 1973. *Canaanite myth and Hebrew epic.* Cambridge: Harvard.

Deist, F & Le Roux J H 1987. *Rewolusie en Reïnterpretasie.* Kaapstad: Tafelberg.
De Vaux, R 1973. *Ancient Israel. Its life and institutions.* London: Darton, Longman & Todd.
Fensham, F C & Pienaar, D N 1982. *Geskiedenis van ou Israel.* Pretoria: Academica.
Fohrer, G 1972. *History of Israelite religion.* London: SPCK.
Garbini, G 1987. *History and ideology in ancient Israel.* London: SCM.
Ringgren, H 1966. *Israelite religion.* London: SPCK.
Rowley, H H 1967. *Worship in ancient Israel.* London: SPCK.
Schmidt, W H 1982. *Alttestamentlicher Glaube in seiner Geschichte* 4. überarbeitete Aufl. Neukirchen-Vluyn: Neukirchener.
Schmidt, W H 1986. The problem of the "centre" of the Old Testament in the perspective of the relationship between history of religions and theology. Old Testament Essays: 4, 46–64.
Smith, M 1971, 1987. *Palestinian parties and politics that shaped the Old Testament.* London: SCM.
Soggin, J A 1984. *A history of Israel.* London: SCM.
Van Zyl, A H et al 1977. *Israel en sy bure.* Durban: Butterworths.
Von Rad, G 1975. *Old Testament theology.* 2 vols. London: SCM.

CHAPTER 17

Alt, A 1953. Die Ursprünge des israelitischen Rechts, in *Kleine Schriften zur Geschichte des Volkes Israel* I, 278-332. München: Beck.
Andersen, F 1966. The socio-juridical background of the Naboth incident. *JBL* 85, 46-57.
Barton, J 1978. Natural law and poetic justice in the Old Testament. *JThS* 30, 1-14.
Beattie, D R G 1974. The book of Ruth as evidence for Israelite legal practice. *VT* 24, 251-267.
Bigger, S F 1979. The family laws of Leviticus 18 in their setting. *JBL* 98, 187-203.
Blenkinsopp, J 1983. *Wisdom and law in the Old Testament.* Oxford: Oxford University Press.
Boecker, H J 1976. *Recht und Gesetz im Alten Testament und im Alten Orient.* Neukirchen: Neukirchener Verlag.
Brongers, H A 1975. Rijkdom en armoede in Israel. *NThT* 29, 20-35.
Carmichael, C M 1974. *The laws of Deuteronomy.* Ithaca: Cornell.
Cholewinski, A 1976. *Heiligkeitsgesetz und Deuteronomium.* Rome: Biblical Institute. (AnBib 66).
Daube, D 1961. Direct und indirect causation in biblical law. *VT* 11, 246-269.
Daube, D 1969. *Studies in biblical law.* New York: Ktav.
De Vaux, R 1961. *Ancient Israel: its life and institutions.* New York: McGraw Hill.
Diamond, A S 1957. An eye for an eye. *Iraq* 19, 151-155.
Falk, Z W 1964. *Hebrew law in biblical times.* Jerusalem: Wahrmann.
Gerstenberger, E 1965. *Wesen und Herkunft des apodiktischen Rechts.* Neukirchen: Neukirchener Verlag. (WMANT 20).
Gnuse, R 1985. *You shall not steal: Community and property in the biblical tradition.* Maryknoll: Orbis.
Jackson, B s 1973. Reflections on biblical criminal law. *JSS* 24, 25-63.
Kaufmann, S A 1979. The structure of Deuteronomic law. *Maarav* 1, 105-158.
Killian, R 1963. Apodiktisches und kasuistisches Recht im Licht ägyptischer Analogien. *BZ* 7, 185-202.
Liedke, G 1971. *Gestalt und Bezeichnung alttestamentlicher Rechtssätze.* Neukirchen: Neukirchener Verlag. (WMANT 39).
Macholz, G C 1972. Die Stellung des Königs in der israelitischen Gerichtsverfassung. *ZAW* 84, 157-182.
Malchow, B V 1986. Social justice in the Israelite codes. *Word & World* 3, 299-306.
McKay, J W 1971. Exodus 23:1-3, 6-8 a decalogue for the administration of justice in the city gate. *VT* 21, 311-325.
Mendenhall, G 1954. Law and covenant in Israel and the ancient Near East. *BA* 17, 49-76.
Merendino, R P 1969. *Das deuteronomische Gesetz.* Bonn: Hanstein. (BBB 31).
Niehr, H 1987. *Rechtssprechung in Israel.* Stuttgart: KBV. (SBS 130).
Noth, M 1966. *The laws in the Pentateuch and other essays.* Edinburgh: Clark.
Patrick, D 1985. *Old Testament law.* Atlanta: John Knox.
Paul, S M 1970. Studies in the book of the covenant in the light of cuneiform and biblical law. *VTS* 18, 112-124.
Phillips, A 1970. *Ancient Israel's criminal laws.* Oxford: Blackwell.
Phillips, A 1973. Some aspects of family law in pre-exilic Israel. *VT* 23, 349-361.

Richter, W 1966. *Recht und Ethos*. München: Kösel. (STANT 15).
Rofé, A 1988. The vinyard of Naboth, *VT* 38, 89-104.
Schottroff, W 1977. Zum alttestamentlichen Recht. *VuF* 22, 1-29.
Thiel, W 1969. Erwägungen zum Alter des Heiligkeitsgesetzes. *ZAW* 81, 40-73.
Wagner, V 1972. *Rechtssätze in gebundener Sprache und Rechtssatzreihen im israelitischen Recht*. Berlin: De Gruyter. (BZAW 127).
Weinfeld, M 1972. *Deuteronomy and the deuteronomic school*. Oxford: Clarendon.
Westbrook, R 1985. Biblical and cuneiform law codes. *RB* 92, 247-264.
Wilson, R R 1983. Israel's judicial system in the pre-exilic period. *JQR* 74, 229-248.

CHAPTER 18

Blenkinsopp, J 1969. *The men who spoke out: The prophets*. London: Darton, Longman & Todd.
Fohrer, G 1974. *Die Propheten des Alten Testaments. Band I, Die Propheten des 8. Jahrhunderts*. Gütersloh: Gerd Mohn.
Gottwald, N K 1964. *All the kingdoms of the earth. Israelite prophecy and international relations in the ancient Near East*. London: Harper & Row.
Heyns, M 1989. Amos – kampvegter vir vryheid en reg: 'n Sosiaal-historiese studie. D Litt et Phil-thesis, Universiteit van Suid-Afrika, Pretoria.
Kaiser, O 1969. Gerechtigkeit und Heil bei den israelitischen Propheten und griechischen Denkern des 8.-6. Jahrhunderts. *Neue Zeitschrift für Systematische Theologie und Religionsphilosophie* 11, 312-328.
Koch, K 1982a. *The Prophets. Vol. I, The Assyrian Period*. Philadelphia: Fortress.
Koch, K 1982b. *The Prophets. Vol II, The Babylonian and Persian Periods*. Philadelphia: Fortress.
Limburg, J 1977. *The prophets and the powerless*. Atlanta: John Knox.
Lohfink, N 1985. Zephaniah and the church of the poor. *ThD* 32, 113-118.
Oeming, M 1986. Naboth, der Jesreeliter: Untersuchungen zu den theologischen Motiven der Überlieferungsgeschichte von 1 Reg 21. *ZAW* 98, 363-382.
Pleins, J D 1986. Biblical ethics and the poor: the language and structures of poverty in the writings of the Hebrew prophets. Ph D thesis, The University of Michigan.
Swanepoel, F (red) 1990. *Nuwe lig op Ou-Testamentiese profete (met besondere aandag aan Amos)*. Pretoria: C B Powell-Bybelsentrum, Universiteit van Suid-Afrika.
Vawter, B 1961. *The conscience of Israel. Pre-exilic prophets and prophecy*. New York: Sheed & Ward.
Von Rad, G 1968. *The message of the prophets*. London: SCM.
Wanke, G 1972. Zu Grundlagen und Absicht prophetischer Sozialkritik. *KuD* 18, 2-17.
Wilson, R R 1980. *Prophecy and society in ancient Israel*. Philadelphia: Fortress.
Wolff, H W 1986. *Die Stunde des Amos. Prophetie und Protest*. München: Kaiser.

CHAPTER 19

Brongers, H A 1975. Rijkdom en armoede in Israel. *NThT* 29, 20-35.
Coggins, R J 1987. The Old Testament and the poor. *ET* 99, 11-14.
Crenshaw, J L 1985. Education in ancient Israel. *JBL* 104, 601-615.
Deist, F E (red) 1982. *Die Bybel leef*. Pretoria: Van Schaik.
Fensham, F C 1962. Widow, orphan and the poor in ancient Near Eastern legal and wisdom literature. *JNES* 21, 129-139.
Gese, H 1984. Wisdom literature in the Persian period, in Davies, W D & Finkelstein, L (eds), *The Cambridge history of Judaism (Volume one: Introduction; the Persian period)*, 189-218. Cambridge: Cambridge University Press.
Gillingham, S 1988. The poor in the Psalms. *ET* 100, 15-19.
Gordis, R 1943/44. The social background of wisdom literature. *HUCA* 18, 77-118.
Gowan, D E 1987. Wealth and poverty in the Old Testament: The case of the widow, the orphan, and the sojourner. *Intp* 61, 341-353.
Hobbs, T R 1989. Reflections on 'the poor' and the Old Testament. *ET* 100, 291-294.
Hoppe, L J 1987. *Being poor: A biblical study*. Wilmington: Michael Glazier. (Good News Studies 20).
Lang, B 1985. The social organisation of peasant poverty in biblical Israel, in Lang, B (ed),

Anthropological approaches to the Old Testament, 83-99. Philadelphia: Fortress. (Issues in religion and theology, 8).
Loader, J A 1982a. Egipte as agtergrond by die Ou Testament, in Deist 1982:37-52.
Loader, J A 1982b. Politiek, ekonomie en kultuur in die tyd van Salomo, in Deist 1982:88-96.
Loader, J A 1986. Texts with a wisdom perspective, in Deist, F E & Vorster, W S (eds), *Words from afar*, 103-122. Cape Town: Tafelberg. (The literature of the Old Testament 1).
Loader, J A 1989. Inleiding tot die Spreuke van Salomo, in Van Zyl, A H (red), *Verklarende Bybel*, 684-692. Kaapstad: Lux Verbi.
Lohfink, N F 1987. *Option for the poor: The basic principle of Liberation Theology in the light of the Bible.* Berkeley: Bibal.
Malchow, B V 1982. Social justice in the wisdom literature. *BTB* 12, 120-124.
McPolin, J 1989. Psalms as prayers of the Poor, in Cathcart, K J & Healey, J F (eds), *Back to the sources: Biblical and Near Eastern studies in honour of Dermot Ryan.* Dublin: Glendale.
Murphy, R E 1983. *Wisdom literature and Psalms.* Nashville: Abingdon. (Interpreting biblical texts.)
Oeming, M 1986. Naboth, der Jesreeliter: Untersuchungen zu den theologischen Motiven der Überlieferungsgeschichte von 1 Reg 21. *ZAW* 98, 363-382.
Olivier, J P J 1975. Schools and wisdom literature. *JNSL* 4, 49-60.
Olivier, J P J 1982a. Israel en Juda as selfstandige kleinstate in die internasionale politieke arena: die Omriede (878-845 vC), in Deist 1982:130-139.
Olivier, J P J 1982b. Israel en Juda as selfstandige kleinstate in die internasionale politieke arena (850-750 vC), in Deist 1982:140-153.
Olivier, J P J 1982c. Israel en Juda onder vreemde heerskappy (745-586 vC), in Deist 1982:154-173.
Pleins, J D 1987. Poverty in the social world of the wise. *JSOT* 37, 61-78.
Porteous, N W 1976. The care of the poor in the Old Testament, in Porteous, N W, *Living the mystery: Collected essays*, 143-155. Oxford: Blackwell.
Von Rad, G 1953. Josephgeschichte und ältere Chokma. *VTS* 1, 293-301.
Wanke, G 1984. Prophecy and psalms in the Persian period, in Davies, W D & Finkelstein, L (eds), *The Cambridge history of Judaism (Volume one: Introduction; the Persian period)*, 162-188. Cambridge: Cambridge University Press.
Weinfeld, M 1972. *Deuteronomy and the Deuteronomic school.* Oxford: Clarendon.
Weir, E 1988. The poor as powerless: A response to R J Coggins. *ET* 100, 13-15.
Whybray, R N 1989a. Poverty, wealth, and point of view in Proverbs. *ET* 100, 332-336.
Whybray, R N 1989b. The social world of the wisdom writers, in Clements, R E (ed), *The world of ancient Israel: Sociological, anthopological and political perspectives*, 227-250. Cambridge: Cambridge University Press.
Williams, J G 1981. *Those who ponder proverbs: Aphoristic thinking and biblical literature.* Sheffield: Almond.
Wittenberg, G H 1986. The lexical context of the terminology for 'poor' in the book of Proverbs. *Scriptura* (Special issue) 2, 40-85.
Wittenberg, G H 1987. The situational context of statements concerning poverty and wealth in the book of Proverbs. *Scriptura* 21, 1-23.
Wolff, H W 1973. *Amos the prophet: The man and his background.* Philadelphia: Fortress.

Addendum A

Lists of abbreviations

Gn = Genesis
Ex = Exodus
Lv = Leviticus
Dt = Deuteronomy
Jos = Joshua
Jdg = Judges
Ruth = Ruth
1 Sm = 1 Samuel
2 Sm = 2 Samuel
1Kn = 1 Kings
2Kn = 2 Kings
1 Chr = 1 Chronicles
2 Chr = 2 Chronicles
Ezr = Ezra
Neh = Nehemiah
Es = Esther
Job = Job
Ps = Psalms
Pr = Proverbs
Ec = Ecclesiastes
Can = Canticles (Song of Songs)
Is = Isaiah
Jr = Jeremiah
Lm = Lamentations
Ezk = Ezekiel
Dn = Daniel
Hs = Hosea
Jl = Joel
Am = Amos
Ob = Obadiah
Jnh = Jonah
Mi = Micah
Nah = Nahum
Hab = Habakkuk
Zph = Zephaniah
Hg = Haggai
Zch = Zechariah
Ml = Malachi
Mt = Matthew
Mk = Mark
Lk = Luke
Jn = John
Ac = Acts
Rm = Romans
1 Cor = 1 Corinthians
2 Cor = 2 Corinthians
Gl = Galatians
Eph = Ephesians
Phlp = Philippians
Col = Colossians
1 Th = 1 Thessalonians
2 Th = 2 Thessalonians
1 Tm = 1 Timothy
2 Tm = 2 Timothy

Tt = Titus

Phlm = Philemon

Heb = Hebrews

Ja = James

1 Pt = 1 Peter

2 Pt = 2 Peter

1 Jn = 1 John

2 Jn = 2 John

3 Jn = 3 John

Jude = Jude

Rv = Revelations

Sir = The wisdom of Jesus son of Sirach

NIV New International Version

REB Revised English Bible

RSV Revised Standard Version